TI
TATTOOI
OF TRIBAL EN

Other titles from Bennett & Bloom/Desert Hearts:

Tattooed Mountain Women and Spoon Boxes of Daghestan:
Magic Medicine Symbols in Silk, Stone, Wood and Flesh
By Robert Chenciner, Gabib Ismailov & Magomedkhan Magomedkhanov

Women in Islam: An Anthology from the Qur'an and Hadiths
Translated and edited by Nicholas Awde

Racism in Russia
Edited by Nicholas Awde & Fred James Hill

In the Shadow of Aliyev: Travels in Azerbaijan
By Jason Thomson

The Azerbaijanis: People, Culture and History
Edited by Nicholas Awde & Fred James Hill

The Armenians: People, Culture and History
Edited by Nicholas Awde

The Georgians: People, Culture and History
Edited by Nicholas Awde

Georgia: A Short History
Edited by Nicholas Awde

Witness through Troubled Times: A History of the Orthodox Church of Georgia,
1811 to the Present
Edited by Tamara Grdzelidze, Martin George, Lukas Vischer

Georgians in the Holy Land
Edited by Tamila Mgaloblishvili

The Wellspring of Georgian Historiography:
The Early Medieval Historical Chronicle 'The Conversion of Kartli'
and 'The Life of St. Nino'
Translated with introduction, commentary and indices
by Constantine B. Lerner

The Mediterranean Legacy in Early Celtic Christianity:
A Journey from Armenia to Ireland
By Jacob G. Ghazarian

The Pre-History of the Armenians, Volume 1
Gabriel Soultanian

The Pre-History of the Armenians, Volume 2 :
The Proto-Armenian Hieroglyphic Inscriptions of Aram
Gabriel Soultanian

The History of Bishop Sebeos: Redefining an Ancient Armenian History
Gabriel Soultanian

Afghanistan: The Taliban Years
S. Iftikhar Murshed

Arabic-English/English-Arabic Dictionary
N. Awde & K. Smith

Arabic for Today: Beginner's Course
John Mace

Arabic Verbs: For Revision and Practice
John Mace

Basic Arabic Workbook: For Revision and Practice
John Mace

Intermediate Arabic Workbook: For Revision and Practice
John Mace

The Vibrators: 21 Years of Punk Mania
Ian M. Carnochan (a.k.a. "Knox")

Mellotron: The Machine and the Musicians that Revolutionised Rock
Nick Awde

Pashto Dictionary *(forthcoming)*

The Afghans: People, Culture and History *(forthcoming)*

The Iraqis: People, Culture and History *(forthcoming)*

The Cubans: People, Culture and History *(forthcoming)*

The Nigerians: People, Culture and History *(forthcoming)*

THE TATTOOING ARTS OF TRIBAL WOMEN

Lars Krutak

BENNETT & BLOOM / DESERT ♥ HEARTS

First published
in 2007 by
**BENNETT & BLOOM/
DESERT♥HEARTS**
www.bennettandbloom.com
www.deserthearts.com
PO Box 2131
London W1A 5SU
England

Typeset and designed by Desert♥Hearts

Printed and bound by
Newton Printing, London, England

British Library Cataloguing in Publication Data
A catalogue record for this book is available from the British Library

ISBN 1-898948-75-5 • 978-1-898948-75-9 (paperback)
ISBN 1-898948-74-7 • 978-1-898948-74-2 (hardback)

For Paul Krutak
&
In memory of my mother
Jerri Krutak (1934-2005)

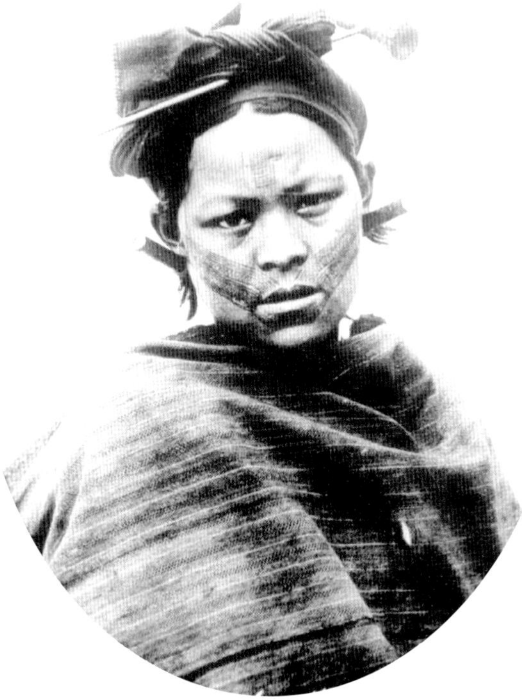

Atayal woman, ca. 1920.
Postcard from the collection
of the author.

Contents

Preface and Acknowledgments

Exactly ten years ago today, I was an anthropology graduate student at the University of Alaska, Fairbanks. On a crisp fall morning, a small aircraft carried me from Nome across the Bering Sea to St. Lawrence Island, Alaska (Sivuqaq). Landing on a gravel airstrip, I exited the plane to begin my first research project focusing on indigenous tattooing practices and the women who created them.

Since then, the 2,000-year-old custom of Yupik tattooing on St. Lawrence Island has died along with its final two practitioners (2005). And in 1998, the last living Ainu woman in Japan with traditional tattooing passed away, and so too did an indelible custom that some scholars believe was 10,000 years old.

Sadly throughout the indigenous world today, tribal tattooing practices and the gatekeepers of knowledge associated with them are largely on the decline. And for this reason, I have crisscrossed the globe to document this rapidly vanishing art form; one that, until recently, has traveled on living bodies for millennia.

Of course, this book would have been impossible without the support and tutelage of numerous indigenous elders and historians I have worked with over the last decade. In fact, many of these individuals encouraged me to explore more deeply the complex symbolism of indigenous tattooing practices before it began to disappear from view. To these elders and their families, I extend my appreciation and deepest gratitude.

Several archivists, librarians, professors, writers, editors, artists, anthropologists, translators, publishers, institutions, and academic mentors also offered invaluable support or inspiration during the completion of this research in the form of photographs, written documents and publications, archaeological collections, field contacts, permissions, personal communications, and simple suggestions. In this context, I would like to single out Dr. Molly C. Lee, Dr. Edmund Carpenter and the Rock Foundation, Dr. Igor Krupnik, Dr. Peter Schweitzer, Dr. Lydia Black, Dr. William Merrill, Dr. Marvin Allison, Dr. John T. J. Ho, Dr. Gen Suwa, Dr.

Calogero Santoro, Chris Koonooka (Petuwaq), Wilson Aqumigalnguq, Jr. (Ayuqliq), Tim Sczawinski, Mark Planisek, Simon and Eddie David, Vince Hemingson, Thomas Lockhart, Michael "Travelin' Mick" Laukien, Elle Festin and the Tatak Ng Apat Alon Tribe, Ikin Salvador, Steve Gilbert, Bob Baxter, Dirk-Boris Rödel, Neil Dalleywater, Keone Nunes, Don McClelland, National Anthropological Archives, University of Alaska Fairbanks Archives, John Wesley Powell Library of Anthropology at the National Museum of Natural History, Sarawak Museum Archives, National Museum of Ethnology (Rijksmuseum voor Volkenkunde), Blackwell Publishing, University Museum of the University of Tokyo, American Museum of Natural History Library, Peabody Museum of Archaeology and Ethnology, University of Oklahoma Press, and the Native Village Councils of Gambell and Savoonga, Alaska.

Moreover, documenting the history and significance of indigenous women's tattooing would have been quite difficult without financial support provided by the University of Alaska Museum Otto Geist Fund, and the Whatcom Museum of History and Art Jacobs Research Fund. I would also like to give special recognition to *Skin and Ink Magazine*, *Skin Deep Magazine*, *TätowierMagazin*, and *The Vanishing Tattoo* for publishing my tattoo research over the years.

I would also like to applaud Nick Awde and the crew at Bennett & Bloom and Desert Hearts for supporting the production of this publication—since most publishers nowadays are rarely interested in the theoretical underpinnings and roots of tattooing itself. Countless others also helped me during the course of writing and editing this book, and you know who you are.

I started this project as a single man, and now find myself married to the love of my life. Heidi has always been unwavering in her support and enthusiasm for this project and I thank her for accompanying me on several trips to far off places.

Finally, I dedicate this book to my father Paul Krutak and to my mother Jerri Krutak whom I miss deeply. Both encouraged me to pursue my interests wherever they might take me.

Lars Krutak
Washington, D.C., 2007

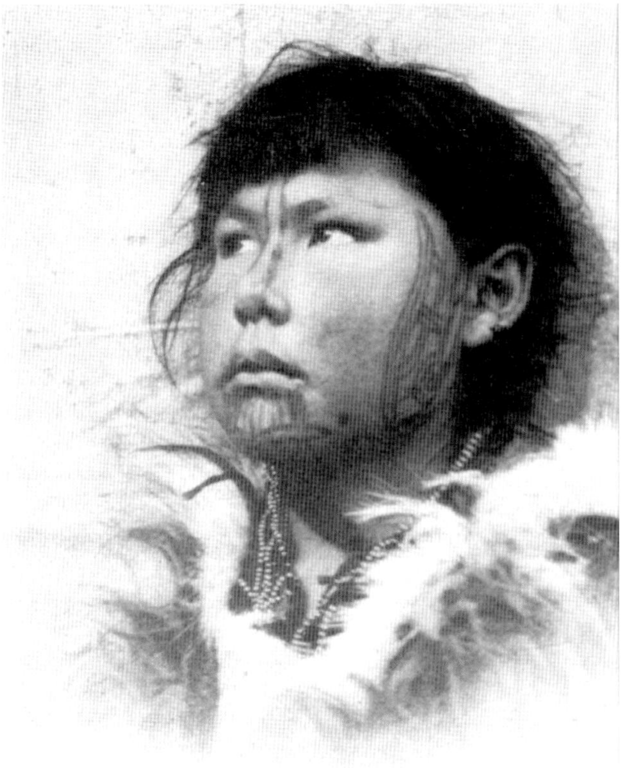

Siberian Yupik woman of the Arctic. After Cantwell (1902:210).

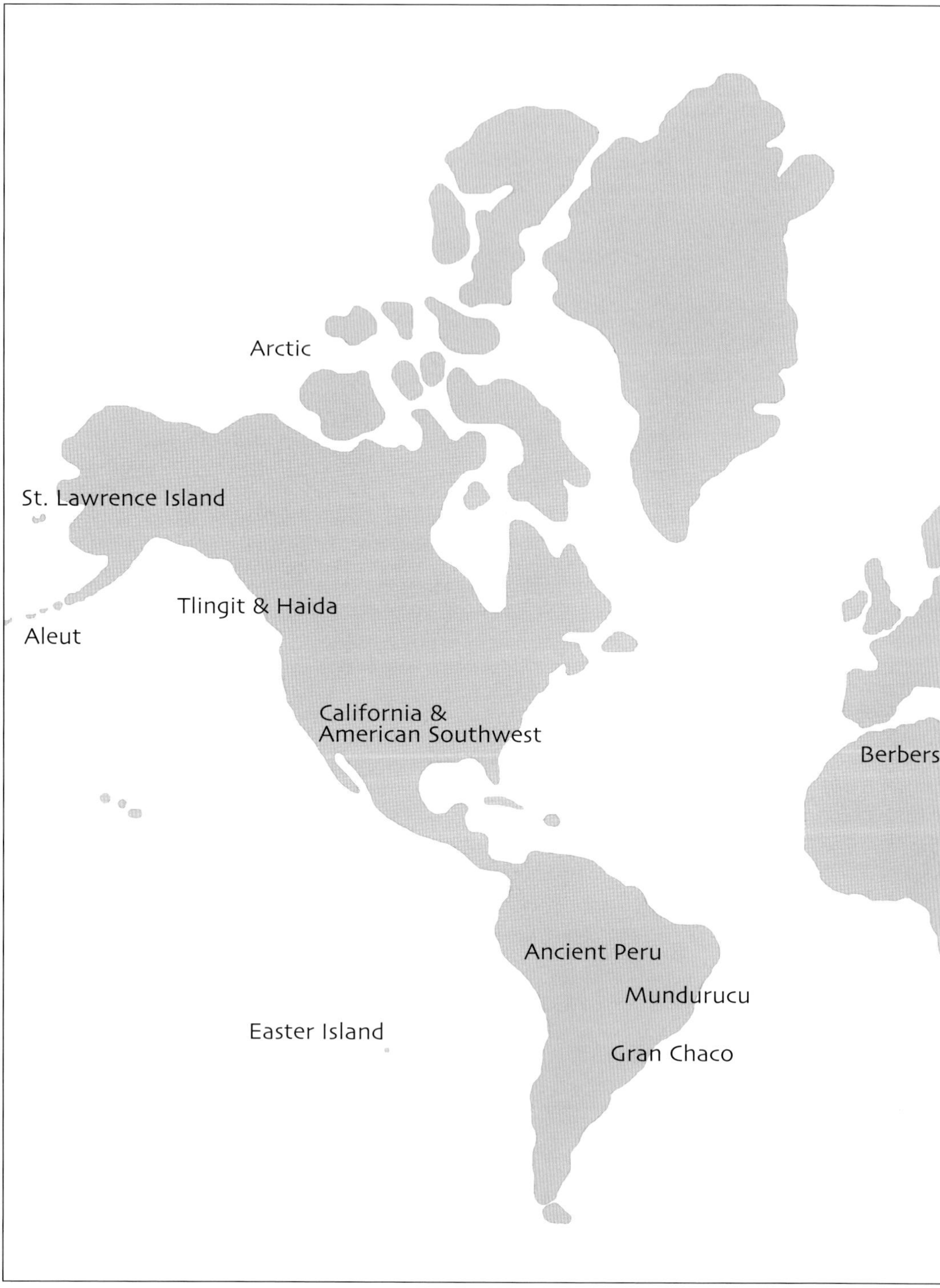
Arctic
St. Lawrence Island
Tlingit & Haida
Aleut
California &
American Southwest
Berbers
Ancient Peru
Mundurucu
Easter Island
Gran Chaco

Tattooing Peoples and Areas

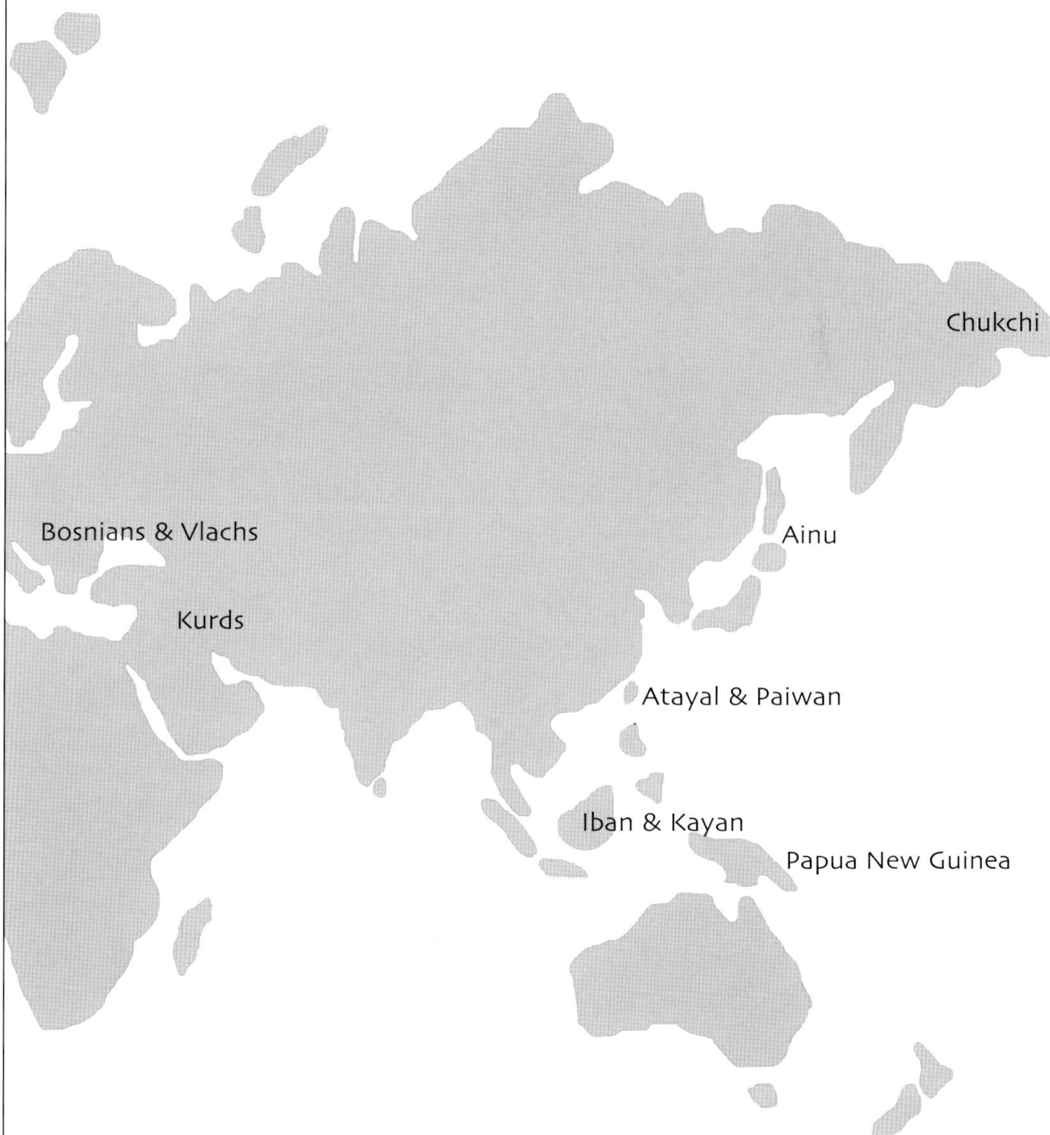

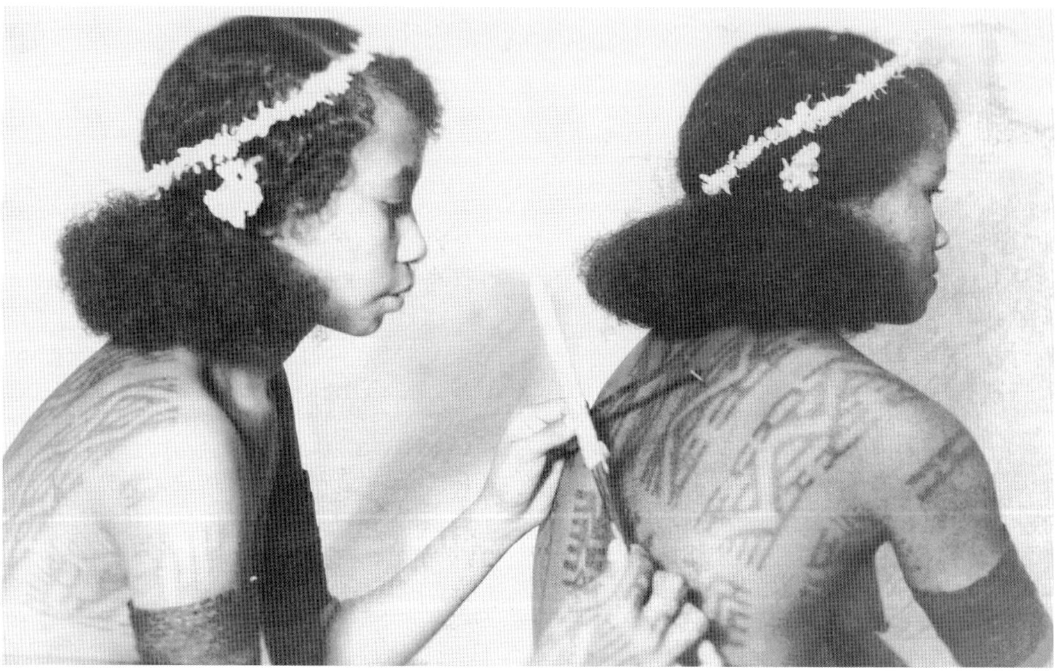

Hand-tapping in Papua New Guinea, ca. 1940.
Postcard from the collection of the author.

Introduction

> Fashions aside, tribal arts offer a valuable—perhaps the only—means of penetrating certain areas of ancient art, hitherto *terra incognita*. Schematic art of prehistoric times will remain a subject of futile speculation as long as it is *not* placed on a comparative basis with modern tribal designs. The basis for this approach is simple: art begets art; if you seek the springs of traditional art, be prepared to dig deep.
>
> —Edmund Carpenter, *Patterns That Connect*[1]

For thousands of years the tattoo arts of indigenous women have been important vehicles for expressing, reinforcing, and camouflaging the psychological dimensions of life, love, health, illness, and death. Artistic creation involved the use of natural materials—wood, bone, and various pigments—in which supernatural power resided. And as the tattooist transformed them into tattoo instruments, motifs and designs, she initiated a spiritual relationship with non-human entities; entities that sometimes became tutelary spirits until death. Her ultimate creation, the tattooed body, was a vessel imprinted by successive generations of indigenous belief that at once embodied personal, social, ecological, and metaphysical values through a wide array of visual symbolism. Thus, as a cultural practice deeply rooted within the memory of ancestral and everyday life, tattooing defined local perceptions of existence.

Among indigenous cultures, women were not only praised for their skill in tattooing, but also for their roles in religious ceremonies or in maintaining the household. Moreover, a woman's role in the hunt was pivotal. Through the creation of spiritually-charged clothing, to the use of magical incantations, or by feeding sacred household hunting amulets, women fulfilled a central position. With thread and needle in hand, women indirectly participated in hunting by reconciling humans and animals through the garments they created. From the moment an animal was taken to the time it was skinned, tanned, and sewn into a piece of clothing, the qualities and characteristics ascribed to it in life were preserved and passed on to the wearer. In fact, in many circumpolar cultures, seamstresses and embroiderers enabled their husbands in becoming successful hunters, for animals were pleased and attracted by precisely stitched, immaculate, and beautiful clothing.

In headhunting cultures, like the Iban of Borneo, women were revered for their skills in textile weaving. Textile work, which commonly depicted the feats of headhunting husbands, was considered a hazardous spiritual undertaking complimentary to men's warfare. Among the Iban textile work was the "warpath of the women,"[2] a highly elaborate prestige system based on the weaver's ability to execute complex and spiritually-significant designs often in association with ancestral spirits who imparted valuable wisdom, knowledge, and protection over the course of creating a new textile.

Apart from their role as the guardians of tattooing, sewing, and weaving traditions, however, women actively participated in more esoteric shamanistic activities. Atayal "priestesses" in Taiwan kindled sacred fires during their agricultural rites to attract the spirits of the ancestors. This helped induce fertility in the millet fields.[3] In Borneo, Kayan shamans, usually women, made supernatural flights into the spirit world to retrieve the "wandering" souls of sick patients. If the body of the client was not restored with its soul intact, it was believed that the victim would soon die.[4] Among the Paiwan of Taiwan and the Yupiget of St. Lawrence Island, Alaska, female shamans also worked via supernatural channels to cure their patients of "soul-loss."[5] Sometimes proper treatments included the application of medicinal tattoos at particular points on the body or tattoo foils to disguise the identity of the sufferer from disease bearing spirits. In such cases, Paiwan and Yupiget shamans were proactive in rearticulating the surfaces of their patient's bodies by multiplying its inscriptions and reinscribing its parts. But the perceived efficacy of these treatments was not only confined to the technical or performative aspects of the tattoo application itself; rather the shaman's power arose from helper and ancestral spirits who communicated their magical and curative powers through her.

Nevertheless, not all tattooists were shamans: although many worked under the guidance and protection of one or more spiritual helpers. However tattoo artists were like shamans in that they employed methods of spiritual and physical medicine to "cure" their patients of sometimes malevolent spirits that infested the landscape. Indelible treatments often included remedies for rheumatism, goiter, and heart palpitations;[6] each of which were believed to have been brought upon humankind by evil forces. As noted, the tattooist also had the power to prevent soul possession. While ordinary healers had knowledge and control of traditional medicines, charms and spells, and malevolent spirits, only shamans and tattooists had the power to control human souls. Therefore, the tattoo artist was an active participant in a particular socio-religious order where body, ritual, and tattoo were linked to indigenous cosmology and nature: a place where moral duties to the deities, to the ancestors, to the spirits of the animals and to the land itself were inextricably bound in an integrated system of belief.

To a considerable extent, it is from this religious core that indigenous life and tattooing evolved, and where indigenous people placed themselves and their world in religious and socio-moral terms. However, if an individual trespassed against the customary laws, accepted codes of conduct, manners and conventions set forth by these traditions, they risked disturbing the balance of life and harmony in the universe.

In this sense, the profession of tattoo artist was particularly dangerous. A woman's epidermic talents, made possible through ritual acts of bloodletting and spiritual tutelage, not only affected individuals but entire communities. Thus, it was very important for the tattooist to strictly follow the traditional laws that prescribed her profession. In Borneo, for example, a Kayan girl could not be tattooed during rice seeding time or when a corpse lay in the longhouse, because it was disrespectful to let blood during these occasions for fear of disturbing the ritual harmony of the household.[7] Moreover, Kayan girls could not be tattooed at the onset of their menses and were instead tattooed only on the ninth day after a new moon,[8] since by then their menstrual blood had "cooled" and was no longer appealing to marauding spirits. Among the Gran Chaco tribes of South America, however, girls were tattooed precisely at the onset of the new moon and menses. Although their flowing menstrual blood left them temporarily exposed to evil spirits—the blood luring evil near—the tattoo and magical pigments were believed to work as a kind of trap, and once made manifest on the skin they subsequently offered "permanent" purification against spiritual contagions in the future, more or less "hardening" women—and the community—against evil forever.[9] Arab girls in Iraq also feared encounters with evil spirits (*jnoun*) during menstruation. But they accepted the inherent risks and tattooed at this time to induce pregnancy, since it was believed that a woman's flowing blood enhanced the power of this type of fertility tattoo.

Sometimes a female *mullah* read verses from the Qur'an to bring about a positive result.[10]

Regardless of the cultural conditions set forth in these brief examples, it is obvious that the process of tattooing, from beginning to end, was an experience for women that transcended time and space. Tattoo knowledge and practice was traditional; it was handed down over successive generations and was a time-tested and time-honored method to affect change. Among many cultures, tattoo motifs traveled between generations of individuals, and because each new tattoo was a composite of elements drawn from other tattoos, they brought together in one place simultaneous reference to the past, present, and future. Thus, whenever the tattoo ritual was enacted by females throughout the indigenous world, the release of endorphins and blood was considered to be a powerful *moment* cognate with the recurring cycles of re-birth, transformation, and accomplishment;[11] because as the needle began to hit or stitch the skin, the girl became a woman—like all of those before and of those still to come. And through this act of repetition, tattooing reproduced social action; for it animated ideas and feelings of life and death within the fabric of indigenous culture.[12]

For me, the knowledge embodied in learning from that which gave rise to tattoos is as fascinating as it is ancient. Tattoo was a component of a complex and often unrecognized system essential to the reproduction of indigenous cultures. And although only a handful of recent publications have focused on tribal tattoos and their global distribution, not one focuses on the importance of indigenous women tattoo artists and the work they performed for their clients. This may be attributed to the paucity of information on tattooing practices and ultimately to the virtual disappearance of the art form in the modern world.

Nevertheless, tattooing was a system of ceremonial and ritual action: the modification of the flesh as a means of exciting and influencing the thoughts and agency of others—both human and spiritual—that controlled destiny and the surrounding world. Indigenous tattoo transformed the body into a microcosm of the indigenous universe, creating a ritual space that concretely replicated and provided a means from which to actively intervene in the cosmos itself.

A comment on the "tribal"

Before jumping headlong into the text, it is important to note here that we must be aware of the complexities of using particular words to describe

Native peoples. The terms "Indian," "indigenous," "tribal," or even "autochthonous" are English language definitions used in ethnology to designate "non-Western" peoples on the basis of purely geographical but never political character.[13] These designations have crept into the literature because a trader, a missionary, a government agent, or an anthropologist found the term or terms definitive and useful. However, monikers such as "tribal" are designations that are not complimentary when applied to a particular group by outsiders because they embody notions of alienation, perhaps even unsophistication, in contrast to Western society.[14] Of course, there are more appropriate self-designations that are used by indigenous peoples to describe themselves. For example, Inuit ("person," "people") replaces "Eskimo" in many regions of Arctic Canada whereas Yupik ("real, genuine person") replaces "Inuit" in many regions of Arctic Alaska.[15] In Japan, the term Ainu ("people," "human") replaces "aboriginal,"[16] and in Borneo Iban ("person") replaces the Western and colonial formulation "Sea-Dayak."[17] Obviously, these surviving self-designations are neither alienating nor judgmental; rather they are inclusive and describe one's position in a community today as well as before contact with missionaries or anthropologists.

From the standpoint of tattoo art history and contemporary culture, however, "tribal" is thought of as a major trope in identifying both non-Western peoples and the subaltern exotic within the West.[18] From Cuba to Kosovo, places where I have interviewed tattoo artists,[19] "tribal" is a self-designation of its own for a kind of tattoo movement, even a lifestyle, embedded in popular culture and rituals of personal transformation. And because it is so widely used and identifiable in contemporary tattoo culture, I have chosen to use "tribal" in my title; although it is quite tricky to suggest that some of the peoples in this text were or continue to be "tribal," especially in the cases of state-based societies in Peru or the Middle East. Therefore, in no sense am I attempting to denigrate or demean anyone by using the term "tribal," nor I am attempting to "rank" particular societies on the basis of some kind of socio-cultural system of development. Rather, I use "tribal" in an attempt to reach a wider audience.

For those students interested in pursuing the subject, "the concepts of 'tribe' and 'tribal' have since become, within certain circles, a metaphor for the modern tattoo community, incorporating as it does notions of both community as well as the ideology of modern primitivism."[20] The tribal style of tattooing was spearheaded by Leo Zulueta and Don Ed Hardy in the 1970s who borrowed heavily from the tattoo cultures of Oceania.[21] Zulueta, a Hawaiian of Filipino descent, who now works in Ann Arbor, Michigan, has explained: "I think people are looking for more of a roots, or spiritual [connection] . . . Here in the West we live in such a cultural wasteland such that people tend to gravitate towards things from the past."[22] Zulueta, working under the tutelage of Hardy, sees the tribal movement as a vehicle through which to admire and praise the tattoo cultures of the past. Don Ed Hardy believes "the tribal style was good because it liberated [Western] tattooing from being totally content-oriented. There's even a weird sort of snobbery among people who get black pattern tattooing. Some of them take the attitude that their tattoos are somehow more refined or pure because they are not pictures of something and they don't tell a story [per se]."[23] Of course, and from an aesthetic, objective, and practical standpoint, tribal tattooing, characterized by its bold black silhouettes, wears on human skin longer than more colorful, fine-lined work, "especially in skin that gets much exposure to the sun and elements."[24] And perhaps it was this aesthetic aspect that captured the attention of many photographers long ago.

The colonial gaze

In this book our picture of ordinary indigenous life is somewhat blurred by the fact that we glimpse it through arrested time, that is via the medium of the photograph. Photographs have the ability to appropriate and decontextualize time and space not to mention indigenous people who were portrayed in the late 19th and early 20th centuries as "exotic" objects within the gaze of the camera.[25] Photographs also denaturalize their subject matter, and through processes of enclosure, capture, and dissemination (e.g. *cartes de visite* and postcards) they symbolically gain power over their "subjects" by transforming them into "objects" that can be displayed, traded, or even destroyed.

Many of the photographers working in the Victorian era endorsed a particular political perspective whereby anthropological "understanding" was an aid to more efficient colonial administration of "primitive" peoples living in colonized territories. Oftentimes they, and government officials alike, used staged photographs of indigenous peoples as propaganda and ethical justification for European control. Indigenous peoples were not merely Victorian Age curiosities to be "collected" and displayed at the local museum, World's Fair, or Exposition Universalle in Paris, but also manifestations of how low "uncivilized" people had fallen on the evolutionary ladder.[26] Photographic representations of exotic and naked "savages" posed in natural settings, heightened by the inclusion of piercings and strange figures incised into the skin like tattoos, were part of the stereotypical "display-kit" that comprised Euro-Western views of indigenous bodies and persons as living "artifacts" to be collected and later curated by the colonial regime. As such, anthropological investigations of this era were skewed toward efficient administration of particular "races" rather than elucidating coherent cultural systems, and few Americans or Europeans were motivated to examine indigenous people in attempts to explain why they looked the way they did, or why they practiced customs as they did. Instead, they reconstructed their origins and evolutions to heighten the aura of exoticism and threatening otherness.[27]

Although it can be argued that the photography of this period worked as a "literally colonizing process of inscription"[28] whereby the tattooed bodies of indigenous peoples were read by Western audiences as "evidence of a savage inferior state," I choose instead to address more positively the value of historical photographs through highlighting the articulation between them, memory, and tattoo (art) history. Therefore, I analyze these images systematically in order to extract new anthropological data from them. The task of this book, then, is not that of defining what makes certain types of photography controversial or even stereotypical, although I acknowledge that many of the images here perhaps carry such tags while others fetishize female bodies as objects of colonial male desire. Instead, I offer to take these representations literally as texts, to disclose long-forgotten details of largely vanished customs, esoteric meanings, etc. in order to establish new ways of seeing the messages and stories encoded in indigenous tattooing practices. As lasting images of the past that remain behind for the future, these photographs and illustrations relay important information; they record real, functioning communities, which only then were beginning to be pervaded by the destructive influence of Western civilization. Moreover, many of the anthropologists, ethnographers, government agents, and photographers featured in this book were fully aware that they were collecting unique testimony of the disappearing world, and that they were observing its fateful encounter with the aggressively advancing civilization of Euro-Western culture. Sometimes, the documentarian's personal encounters with indigenous peoples fostered intense feelings of camaraderie.

In this light, I think we should remain somewhat indebted to these researchers for leaving behind such vast visual, textual, and historical materials for our use in the present—no matter how exploitative their personal and social inclinations for "collecting" people, texts, and material objects may have been in the past. Nowadays, it is hard for us to imagine the difficulty that an explorer or ethnologist had to overcome one-hundred years ago in the bush. Cameras were bulky and cumbersome, glass plates were heavy and fragile, supplies were expensive, transportation unreliable, weather unpredictable, and then there was the constant threat of disease, at least in tropical areas (typhoid, malaria, dysentery, etc.). Let us not forget that field photographers had to carry chemicals, because exposed negatives had to be developed on the spot, in water sometimes full of microorganisms, in heat and damp which not only eroded the plate's sensitive emulsions but also damaged the wood of the camera.[29] Another danger was termites, which ate anything and everything, including the bellows of the camera. In the Arctic, photographers faced other hazards and concerns: frigid temperatures, floating darkrooms, polar bears, pack ice, scurvy, starvation, and flash powder that had the capacity to "take the roof off the cabin [of the ship]" if not fixed correctly.[30]

Because it is true that travelers, explorers, ethnographers, anthropologists, and photographers have not always been accurate in their portrayals of indigenous peoples (e.g. staging, manipulating, and modifying texts, images and other materials to fit preconceived notions of "primitive" humanity or to fill their pocketbooks!), the quality of "good" vs. "bad" science lies in the eye of the beholder; and what may seem as a "good" text to one reader may seem "bad" to another, whereas a photograph that may be a stereotypical "ethnographic" representation to one viewer may be deemed a portrait of a grandmother to an indigenous person.[31]

The tattooing arts of tribal women

With that said, *The Tattooing Arts of Tribal Women* is a preliminary and encyclopedic exploration of the indelible traditions of indigenous women that exposes a previously undocumented world of *permanent* body art knowledge. Drawing from the early accounts of explorers, ethnologists, anthropologists, and my own publications and field research, this book focuses on the skin as a "locality" or place-in-the-world that is embodied by indigenous experience, or those processes of consciousness, memory, and bodily rhythms molded by living in a particular cultural world since birth.[32] Furthermore, it serves to explore how the environment interactively shaped conceptions of individual and social personhood and how feelings of inclusion, belonging, and connectedness to particular places in the indigenous landscape generated tattooing practices themselves. Finally, it looks at tattooing as a type of action-centered technology that enmeshed tattooists, clients, spirits, ancestors and deities in relations and intentionalities in manifest and powerful ways.[33] Tattooing animated and enabled individuals to change the world they lived in by influencing the forces that generated and controlled it, because the skin—the body's integument—was worn as a garment of power. A garment that did not simply serve to remind that the indigenous lineage was an artifact of the past, but a living thing, something that extended into the present and onwards into the future.

Although *The Tattooing Arts of Tribal Women* examines a vast majority of the aboriginal world, focusing largely on cultures where women worked as tattooists, it excludes many other regions like the Indian Subcontinent and most of Polynesia where recorded information on tattooing practices has either been analyzed[34] or is waiting to be synthesized in its proper context. I admit that I have been extremely selective in this volume because the emphasis is more on establishing points of connection and affinity rather than exploring the distinctive cultures in each case presented. Perhaps I may even be accused of using some sources uncritically, while some of the concepts and terminology might be considered inappropriate by professional anthropologists. Nevertheless, I believe that over the course of reading this book it will become obvious that many questions about the history and symbolism of tribal tattoo arts remain unanswered. My purpose is to call attention to these problems, to sharpen our focus, in the hope that other readers will contribute to a broadening of the basis upon which more definite conclusions may eventually be built.

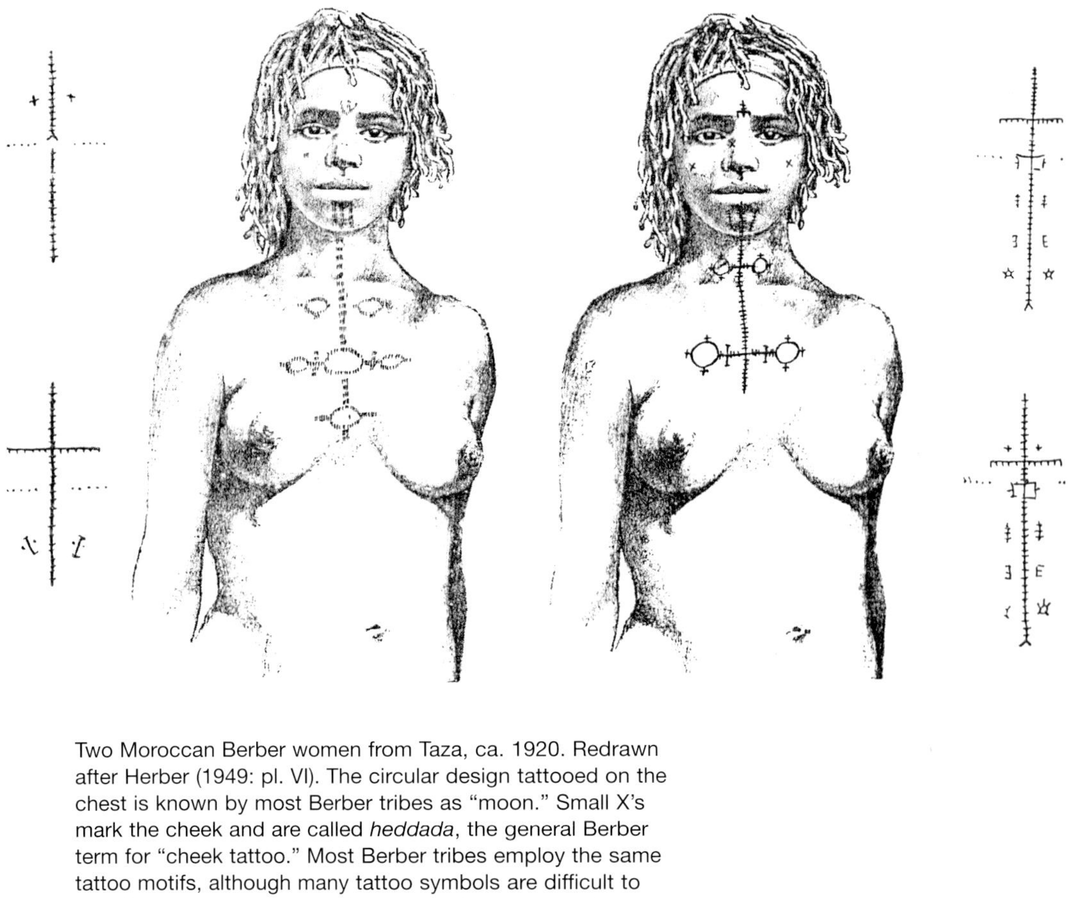

Two Moroccan Berber women from Taza, ca. 1920. Redrawn after Herber (1949: pl. VI). The circular design tattooed on the chest is known by most Berber tribes as "moon." Small X's mark the cheek and are called *heddada*, the general Berber term for "cheek tattoo." Most Berber tribes employ the same tattoo motifs, although many tattoo symbols are difficult to classify by name because tribes interpret each symbol differently. For example, the stepped design continuing from breast to chin (right) can be "millipede," "that which has wings," "horses chimera," or "stick," whereas tattoo between the eyes can be variously classified as "comb," "claw," or "chicken's foot" (Searight 1984).

North Africa, Iraq, and the Balkans

Despite allusions to its prohibition in the Qur'an, tattooing has survived for centuries in the Islamic societies of North Africa. According to the opinion of Moroccan lawyers interviewed in the 1920s, tattoo was strictly "forbidden" and was accursed in the holy book, since the seat of the tattoo caused injury; the pigment, impregnated with blood, remained under the wounds thus rendering the body imperfect in the eyes of Allah.[1] Furthermore, the tattoo was an obstacle preventing water from penetrating the skin during the ritual ablutions of purification: one of the five fundamental precepts of Islam.

However, Moroccan women considered certain tattoos as legitimate.[2] The Hadiths, the religious collection of sayings of the Prophet Muhammad that constitute a major source of guidance for Muslims after the Qur'an, claims that *ghemaza* (tattoo between the eyebrows) and *siyâla* (tattoo on the chin) are traditional. For example, it is known that tattoo existed in Arabia at the time of the Prophet Muhammad: "All women were tattooed and Lalla Fatima Zahra, the daughter of Muhammad, very probably wore the *siyâla*, which is attributed to her Moroccan belief."[3] Even women living today sometimes say, "Fatima gave this [*siyâla*] to us," or "*Tasnida D-Lalla Fatima Zahra*," this tattoo is "dedicated to Lady Fatima Zahra."[4]

Of course, many traditional forms of tattoo in North Africa can be associated with the indigenous Berber peoples. Living in Morocco, Algeria, Libya, Tunisia, and Egypt, the Berbers are Muslims who follow a specialized branch of that religion, but one that retains elements of atavistic animism: a belief that supernatural energy (*baraka*) resides in all things.[5] Berber tattoo designs hold the sacred energy of *baraka* which can be used to deal with the darker forces of life, to cure illnesses and to protect oneself against spirits called *jnoun* (singular: *jinn*).[6] Oftentimes Berber tattoos were placed near body orifices (eyes, mouth, nose, navel, vagina) or surfaces believed to be vulnerable to the machinations of evil.[7] For example, tattoos usually marked the feet to protect women from *jnoun* who attempted to enter the body through the earth. Other designs on the ankles, hands, and face were believed to protect individuals from the evil eye. Thus, it is not surprising that many Berber tattoos carry the tag of *jedwel* or "talisman."[8]

Generally speaking the Berber term for tattoo is *oucham* ("to mark").[9] Tattoos were traditional or *l-qayda* ("custom") and some motifs were rooted in the ancient Berber alphabet known as Tifinagh, a figurative alphabet derived from tools used in agriculture, sea products, and constellations. It is no longer written but continues to be used by some hill tribes today. Upon examining the list of extant letters, more than a dozen Berber tattoo motifs are common to the alphabet and these symbols generally appear on the chins of Berber women as *siyâla*.[10]

But not all Berber tattoos were literal in this sense. In the early 20th century, the Rif Berber women of Morocco, among others, practiced tattooing as a prerequisite for marriage.[11] When a girl was certain that she was to be married and when all arrangements for her wedding had been made, her family called in an old woman of the same *awar*, or sociological family, who was expert in the indelible art.[12] If no such woman was available, one was called in from outside and if the tattooist was related to the client no fee was paid.

Next, the old tattooist began preparing her liquid tattoo pigment of lampblack and juice squeezed from the leaves of broad (fava) beans. According to Berber scholar Pierre Bourdieu, broad beans (*ajedjig*) embodied multiple referents for the Kabyle of Algeria.[13] First, dried broad beans were male symbols akin to human bones.[14] Second, "being a desiccated seed which, after burial in the damp womb of nature, [it] swells and comes up again, more numerous, in spring,"[15] the broad bean also symbolized the refuge of the soul awaiting resurrection.

After the broad bean pigment was thoroughly mixed, the tattooist began breaking up the usual monotony of her preparatory routine with outbursts of conversation and advice for her tattoo client. Whether or not she came from within or outside the girl's *awar* was not important, for the tattooist spread the local gossip, newsworthy events, and her own personal views on men and the institutions of marriage which she had gained throughout her lifetime working with other women.[16] These intimate conversations gathered experiences, thoughts, and memories to generate a given view of the world, one which engendered commitment to existing institutional

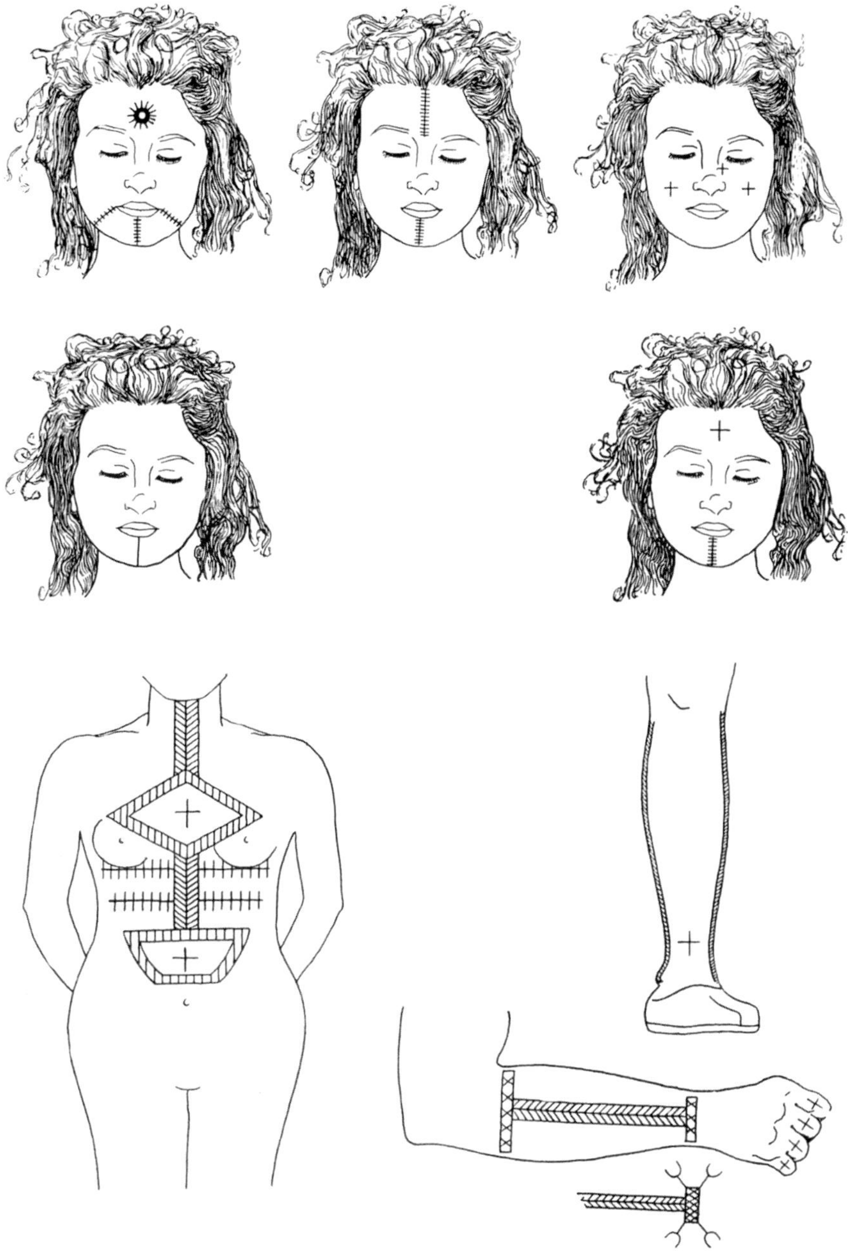

Women's tattoos of the Rif Berber of Morocco, ca. 1930. Redrawn after Coon (1931: fig. 29). When the facial tattoos of Rif Berber women consisted of cross-patterns on the chin, the body was also tattooed extending down to the throat to the abdomen in one continuous design (Coon 1931: 88).

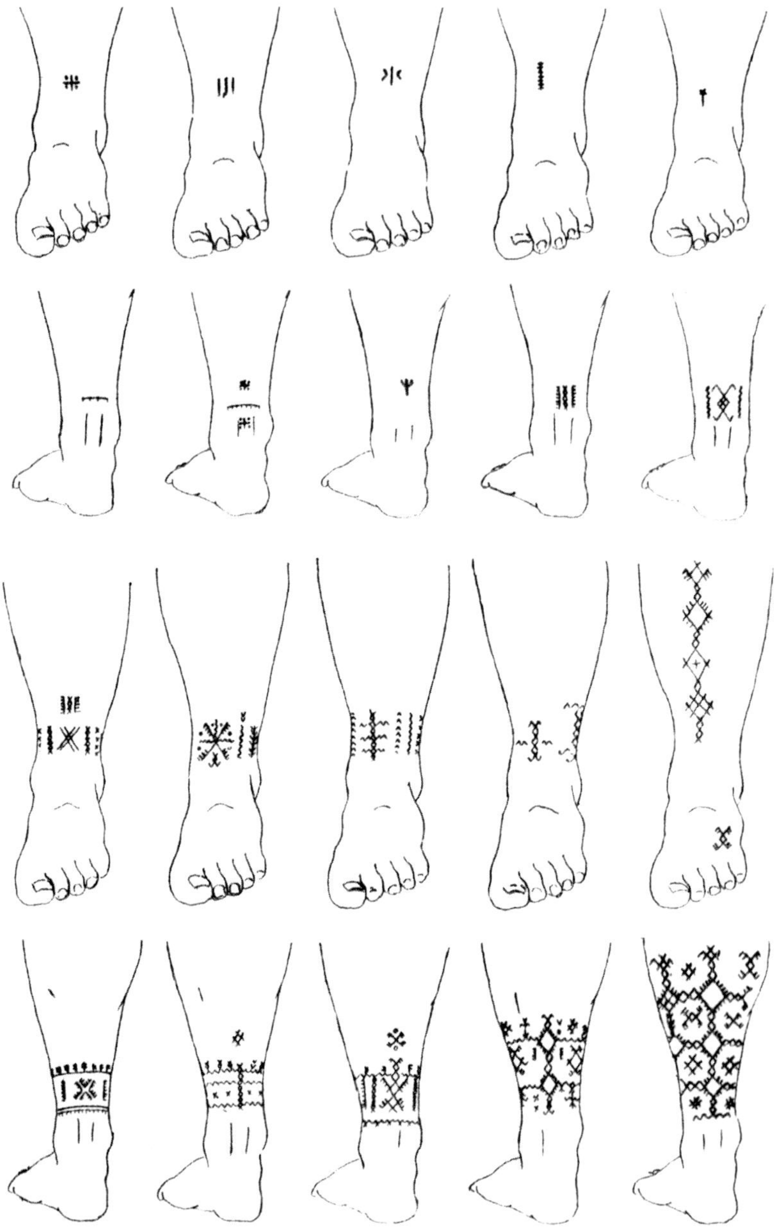

Berber women's leg tattoo (*ahdjdjdam eddarr*) from Morocco, ca. 1920. Redrawn after Herber (1923: 95). One elder woman said that a woman without tattoo marks on the left heel would have no children. Berber women also tattooed themselves in order to ward off malign influences which might threaten their children (Herber 1923: 92-93).

structures of marriage that soon would shape the new identity of the client. However, before the girl moved outside the familiar confines of her family's *awar* to that of her husband's, her position or place in the world at that moment seemed to be separated in time and space from normal everyday existence. Ultimately, this transition to a new life would be filled with discovery, but more importantly it would be marked by transformation; since after the tattooing the girl would become a woman, a sexual being who was accorded a new status that had the potential to bring her greater social recognition and fulfillment via the sanctity of motherhood.[17] Berber women, as the center of the family's sacred identity and guardians of the family's honor and reputation, were situated within a socio-moral universe that affirmed their importance in everyday society. They were responsible for all magical practices intended to safeguard life (e.g. rites against the evil eye), and those designed to maintain the life of their children for which they were responsible—as well as the generative powers of which they are the bearers.[18]

Among the Kabyle, women, as mothers and guardians of the family, were obliged to perform "all the tasks concerned with protecting things that grow and shoot [up], that are green and tender. It [was] a women's duty to watch over the growth of the young [children] and young animals."[19] But they were also seen as a social danger being susceptible to the advances of evil spirits (*jnoun*) who could steal the life of their children as easily as that of their husbands. According to Islamic tradition, Moroccan women were especially susceptible to the malevolence brought by *jnoun* who infested the landscape:

> whole tribes of *jnoun* are waiting to be inflamed by the smell of [menstrual] blood, they become irritated by scalding water in the household and that in the *hammam* or bathing house; they are made jealous by the sight of a pretty baby; *Et Tabi'a*, "The Pursuer" and Queen of the *jnoun* hangs around to make women abort; Lalla Kandicha [an evil spirit] is waiting to bewitch her husband.[20]

But *jnoun* did have their weaknesses and were susceptible to the *baraka* that was embodied in specific types of tattoos, pricked upon the skin of women in differing patterns. Legey wrote that tattooing "combated a woman's evil fate" and was part of a complex of anti-sterility rites to induce pregnancy.[21] Michaux-Bellaire and Salmon stated that in north Morocco if a child died

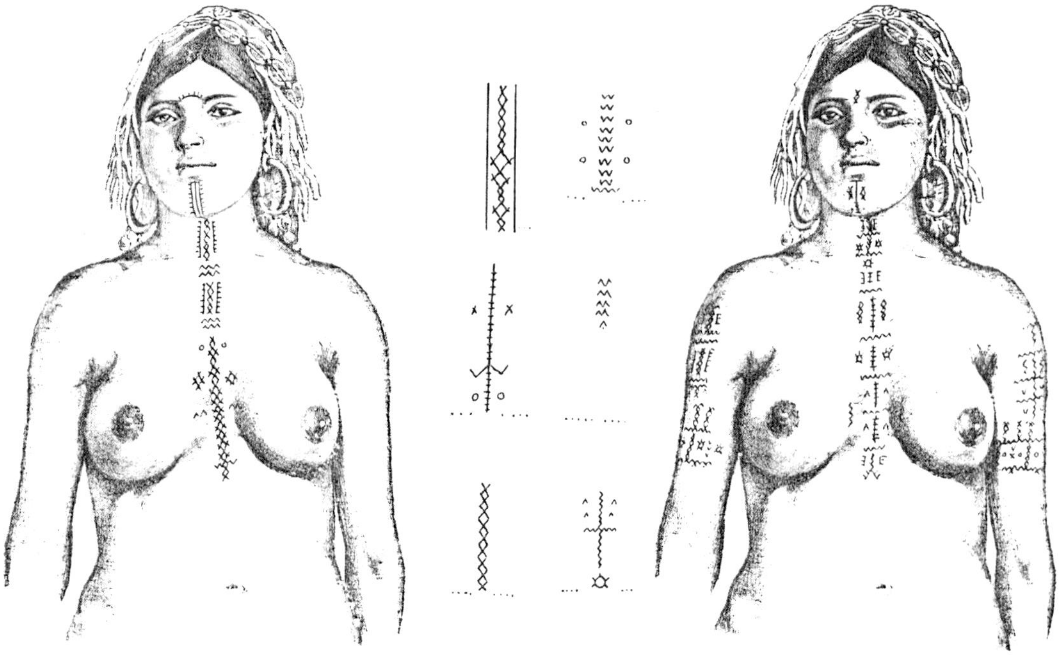

Two Chaouian Berbers from Algeria, ca. 1916. Redrawn after Herber (1949: pl. V). Some of the tattoo motifs used are "star," "sun," "iron fetters," "5 and lines," and "palm tree." Another design, "mouth of the stomach" is thought to maintain fertility and possibly protect the navel from *jnoun* (Searight 1984). Berber women also tattooed the *usham la-hmel*, or "pregnancy" tattoo on their backs (Herber 1923, 1946, 1949).

in the family, subsequent youths were tattooed with two little lines on the side of the nose called *l-'ayyasha* ("that which gives life").[22] Herber[23] and Westermarck[24] also discussed the protective power of *l-'ayyasha* and Blackman[25] alludes to it in her study of tattooed *fellahin* villagers and farmers in Egypt. Searight, discussing the account of an American woman in Morocco in the 1960s, attributed that elements of the tattoo's *baraka* were embodied in the tattooist's spittle:

> She was staying with an Arab woman in Meknes who was heavily pregnant. The expected day of birth passed, and nothing happened. A few weeks later she returned to the house to find a stranger on her knees beside her friend, scraping black off the bottom of a pot; she spat on it, rubbed the back of the ankle of the pregnant woman and tattooed a cross with a needle 'to drive away the evil that was preventing her from giving birth.'[26]

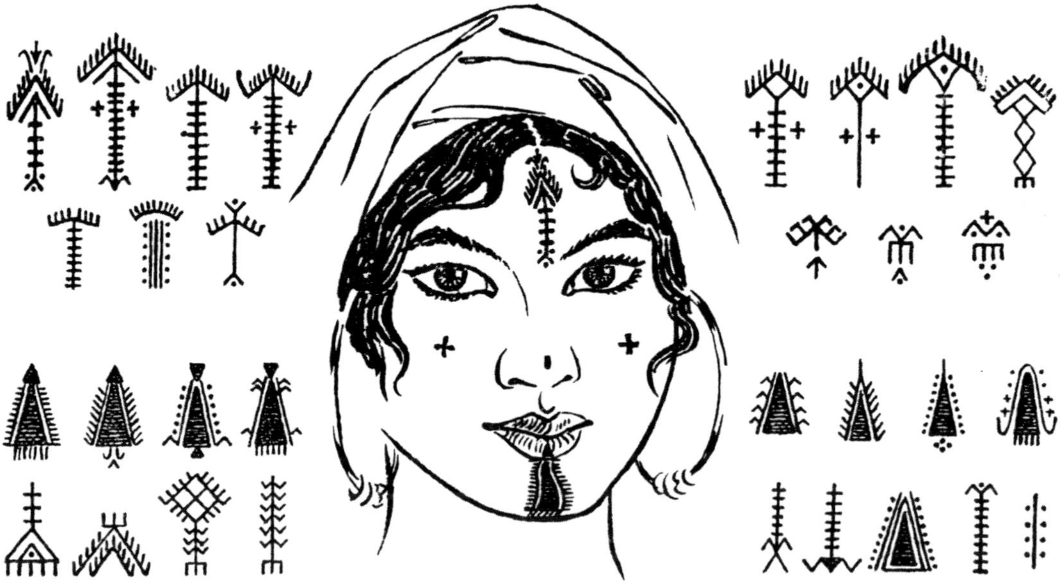

Tunisian Berber facial tattoos, ca. 1920. Redrawn after Gobert (1924: 61). "Palm tree" motifs (*nahla*), often in the form of chin markings (*siyâla*), were thought to induce fertility. The origin of the symbol is identified with the ancient Carthaginian goddess Tanit (Bertholon and Chantre 1913; Carton 1909: 18).

In another reference, Searight witnessed a female tattooist working in Rabat who spat on the tattoo "because her spittle had *baraka* and the tattoo would not get infected."[27]

It has been widely documented that *jnoun* disliked sharp objects, and Westermarck noted that iron daggers, swords and needles were often used at weddings as safeguards against *jnoun*.[28] Iron objects such as these, and others including ploughshares, sickles, and carding combs, were believed to dispel malevolent entities because of their symbolic association with the blacksmith, the master of fire. Iron tools made or associated with fire, iron objects which were used to cut and sever (especially the throats of sacrificial animals, and of men), to pierce and tattoo, to burn, bleed and circumcise, were all products of the work of the blacksmith and used in virilization and prophylactic rites intended to ward off disease and illness associated with *jnoun*.[29] Thus, the Kabyle rites of circumcision and tree pruning, like tattooing and ritual bleeding, operated on the level of purification in which the iron instruments used to carry out these rituals, each forged from fire, had a beneficent function. Similarly during the Kabyle summer solstice (*insla*), purifying fires were lit in the house, among the flocks of sheep, in the orchards, by the beehives, on the threshing floor, and among other places, to cleanse, sterilize, and prepare the community for the coming of summer: a time regarded as unpropitious for any act of procreation, and hence for weddings, but a propitious period when purificatory tattooing, scarification, piercing and bleeding are performed on men and animals.[30]

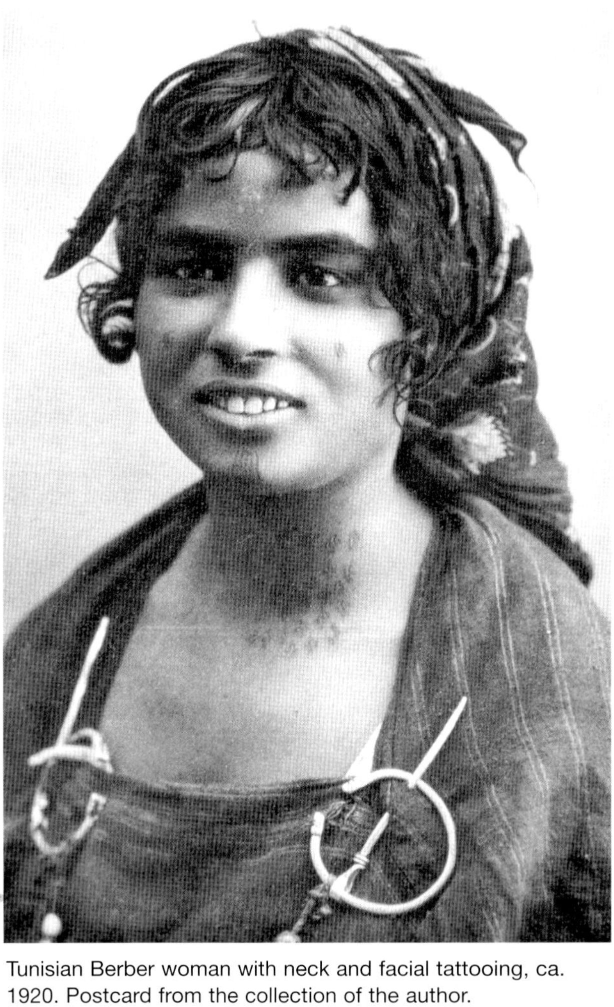

Tunisian Berber woman with neck and facial tattooing, ca. 1920. Postcard from the collection of the author.

Within the complex of tattoo designs, the role of particular motifs—like crosses—or especially others with pointy or finger-like protuberances, were magical and believed to have the power to pierce the evil eye.[31] Westermarck recorded that Berber women in many regions of Morocco wore small crosses on their faces and the tips of their noses.[32] He also noted "a man whose nose was thus decorated with a cross. [He] told me that the tattooing had been done in his infancy because his two elder brothers had died shortly after birth, and that was one of the methods prevalent in his tribe of preserving the life of a child if the previous children had died; but the same charm may in similar circumstances be tattooed underneath the lip instead [or on the] forefinger of the right hand."[33] Westermarck, however, believed that such cruciform elements had a deeper meaning, one related to the idea that the symbol seems "to disperse the evil energy emanating from the eye to all [four] quarters of the wind in order to prevent it from injuring the person or object looked at,"[34] a belief common to indigenous peoples from North Africa to the Punjab of India. Of course, the cross as a tattoo symbol predates the era of Christianity and can be seen not only as a form of body adornment among ancient Libyans represented on Egyptian monuments, but also on the five-thousand year old skin of the Iceman mummy whose tattoos were likely therapeutic.[35]

In North Africa, the human hand, called *khamsa*—a symbol of human creative activity, power and dominance—also had magical properties believed to defend individuals from the evil eye and *jnoun* alike.[36] Representing the protective hand of Fatima, daughter of the Prophet Muhammad, *khamsa* takes many forms, especially in tattoo or jewelry, and can be depicted in realistic or abstract fashion with its fingers open, spread, or joined. Oftentimes it is painted on the backs of trucks or seen dangling from rear-view mirrors in cars, not to mention being painted on the gates of houses.[37] In Tunisia, various abstract renderings of horns or fingerlike projections were tattooed on the backs of hands to "double" their protective potential.[38]

Berber tattooists and their motifs

Although there are hundreds of Berber tribes living throughout northern Africa today, tattoo techniques were largely uniform in the past, as were the choice of pigments (e.g. lampblack). However, the natural products chosen to heal the tattoo wounds were diverse and varied: ashes of watermelon rinds, saffron, henna, crushed belladonna, cabbage leaves, barley, ivy, spittle, and mint among other things.[39] Sometimes these substances enhanced the color of the tattoos, sometimes not, or they contained *baraka* which added curative power.

Nevertheless, nearly all Berber tattooists were women, praised for their knowledge of healing substances and their skill in epidermic artistry. In the High Atlas of Morocco, excerpts from the late 1920s Berber poem *Chants de la Tessaout* reveal that the tattooist Lalla Taouchamt, "The Madame Tattooer," was divinely blessed, demonstrating that tattooists were locally recognized and often remembered by their community histories:

Afakem! Afakem! "Madame the Tattooer!"
In verity, you are incomparable
With both the big and little needle!
You know how to use the pot-black and the ivy so well
That the blue of your tattoos remains for ever
And your designs are unrivaled in the region.
It is well-known, they wrangle over your talent,
All the girls and the women of our villages.
No man gets married without asking you
If it is really your needle which has pricked . . .
Prick and pat, our beloved tattooer!

May God give you his blessing!
May God overwhelm you with his favours![40]

Generally speaking, Berber tattoo designs were passed from mother to daughter. Those that were perceived to have medicinal qualities, like the fertility inducing palm tree (*nahla*) whose origins are grounded in prophylactic magic, were especially reproduced over successive generations.

In the Aurès region of Algeria, the Chaouian Berbers tattooed small diamond-shaped lozenges between a child's eyes to keep the evil eye at bay and even a tattooed wheel was believed to cure cancer.[41] Lozenges of this sort were believed to reflect the evil back towards the person who cast it and were also embroidered on saddle cloth in the Atlas region of Morocco or were tattooed on the arms or forehead of

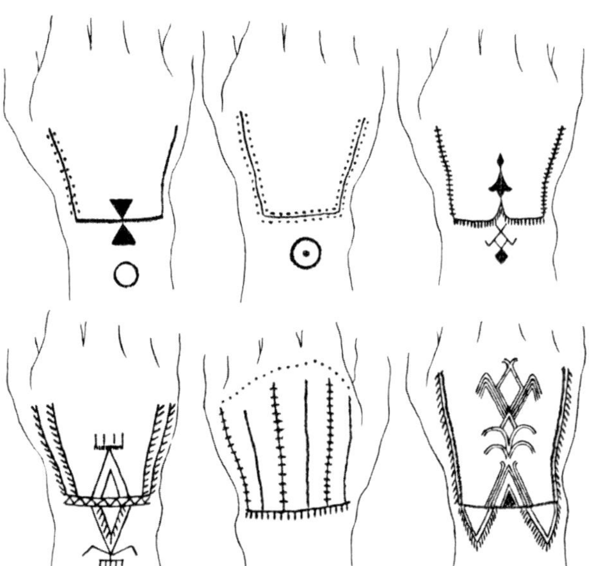

Protective hand tattoos from Tunisia, ca. 1920. Redrawn after Gobert (1924: 75).

women.[42] They also appear in Berber, Turkish, Kazakh, and Bosnian rugs, arranged in rows along the borders. In other cases, a carding comb was tattooed on weavers to make them more efficient.[43] Among the Kabyle, similar comb designs were tattooed on weavers since they were, as previously noted, considered to be purificatory fire symbols.

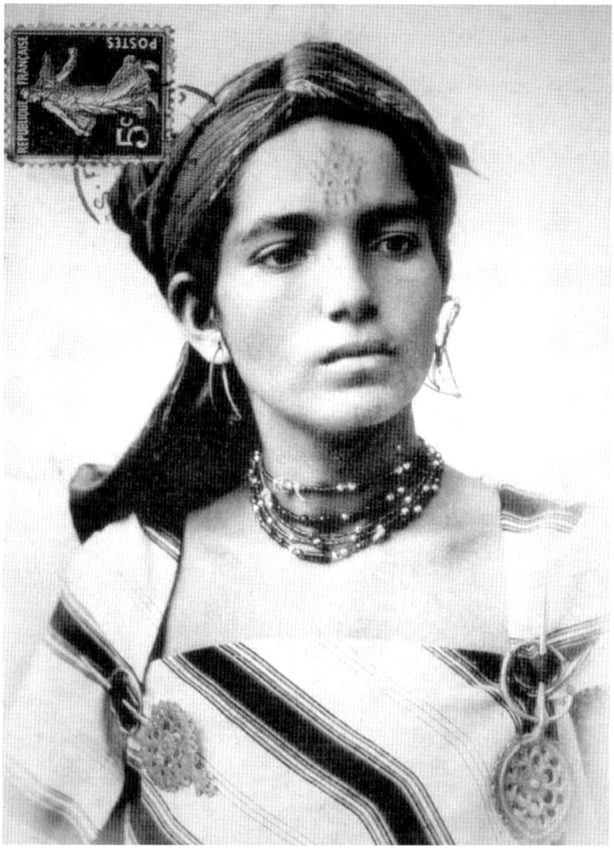

Berber woman from Algeria with facial tattooing, ca. 1920. The forehead design is a composite motif perhaps associated with magic that was believed to repel the evil eye (see Westermarck 1926, I: 465-468). Postcard from the collection of the author.

For the Kabyle and other Berber peoples, weaving wool was the female activity *par excellence*. There are other indications that weaving was practically identified with procreation, since *thanslith*, the triangular motif with which weaving starts is a fertility symbol.[44] But the loom and the area surrounding it in the house were also believed to be powerful apotropaic spaces. Bourdieu explained that:

> . . . by her work on the wool, woman produces the beneficent protection of weaving, whose whiteness symbolizes happiness . . . The loom, the [primary] instrument of female activity, raised facing the east like a man and like a plough, is at the same time the east of an internal space and has a male value as a symbol of protection. [T]he hearth, the navel of the house (which is identified with the belly of the mother), where the embers smolder in a secret, hidden, female fire, is the domain of the woman of the house, who is invested with

total authority in all matters concerning cooking and the management of the food stores. However, in all rites in which they play a part, the fireplace and the stones surrounding it derive their magical power, whether to give protection from the evil eye or from illness, or to bring fine weather, from the fact that they belong to the order of fire . . . and the heat of the sun.[45]

Nevertheless the loom, a seemingly benign object, was also considered to be a dangerous object which, like the crossroads or the blacksmith, could bring sterility and other misfortune:

> The dangerous character of the loom, which combines within itself the two forms of male violence, crossing and cutting, is reinforced by the properties attached to some of its parts, such as *ilni* (the strings separating the threads of the warp), an ambivalent object, evoking cutting and tying, which is used in rites of malign magic as well as in prophylactic magic. Without telling him, a woman measures her husband with string, ties seven knots in it, takes a piece of one of his old garments, wraps the string in it with a bouquet of *asa foetida*, often used in expulsion rites, and buries everything in the grave of a stranger or at the boundary between two fields. To measure is to make a double, a substitute for the thing measured and so gain power over it (the reed with which a corpse is measured is always buried at the bottom of the grave to prevent women from making magic use of it). This measuring—that is, cutting—operation, performed with an object associated with cutting and dryness, is also applied to a cow to prevent theft of the milk or to a child in the rites to protect against the evil eye.[46]

Arab tattooing

While the Berbers have retained a distinct culture and language over the centuries, Arabs and Berbers share many beliefs, including belief in the evil eye, *jnoun*, and the therapeutic power of tattooing. In Iraq, Arabs placed tattoos over a region of pain to cure rheumatism, wounds, bruises, or sprains.[47] More complex and beautiful designs were applied to Arab women for purposes of ornamentation and as enhancements to physical beauty. Arab proverbs praise the beautifully tattooed woman: "*foulana tabagha khir men mra kamla*," meaning, "the limb of such a person was worth more than an entire woman."[48]

Of course, other forms of more "magical" tattooing existed, each of which combined to create potent love charms; to guard children against death; and more importantly, to induce pregnancy in women.

The most substantial record of women's tattooing in Iraq was compiled by Dr. Winnifred Smeaton, a physical anthropologist and fluent Arabic speaker, in the 1930s. Working as a member of the Field Museum Anthropological Expedition to the Near East under the guidance of the anthropologist Henry Field, she secured detailed information on tattooing from Iraqi tattooists and numerous women who were patients at hospitals across the country. Due to the scope and importance of this work, I will briefly paraphrase the most important aspects of her article entitled "Tattooing Among the Arabs of Iraq," which appeared in volume 39 of the *American Anthropologist* for 1937. Many comparable details to tattooing practices in northern Africa are mentioned:

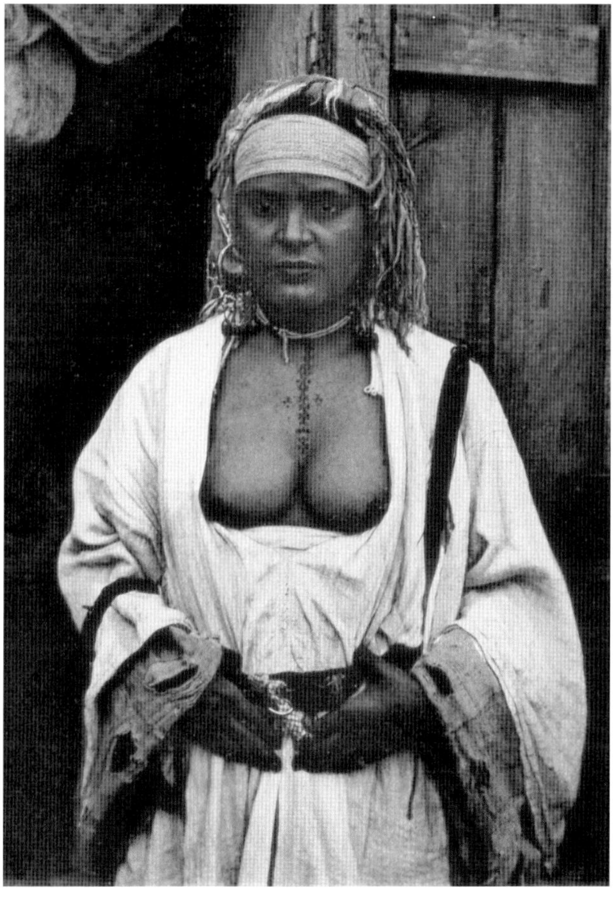

Moroccan Berber woman with chest tattooing, ca. 1920. Postcard from the collection of the author.

> Women, mostly professionals, do nearly all tattooing among the Arabs of Iraq. It is not a hereditary profession, but any woman who has the skill and inclination can become a *daggagah* or tattooer. There are various methods of making the pigment for tattooing, which is known as *kohl* or *basmah*, but the principle is the same, for the chief ingredient is always carbon in the form of lampblack. The word *kohl* usually refers to the powdered antimony that is put around the eyes, but it is also used to mean lampblack, which is used by the poor in the same way as the antimony. Burning either the ordinary kerosene of lamps, tallow

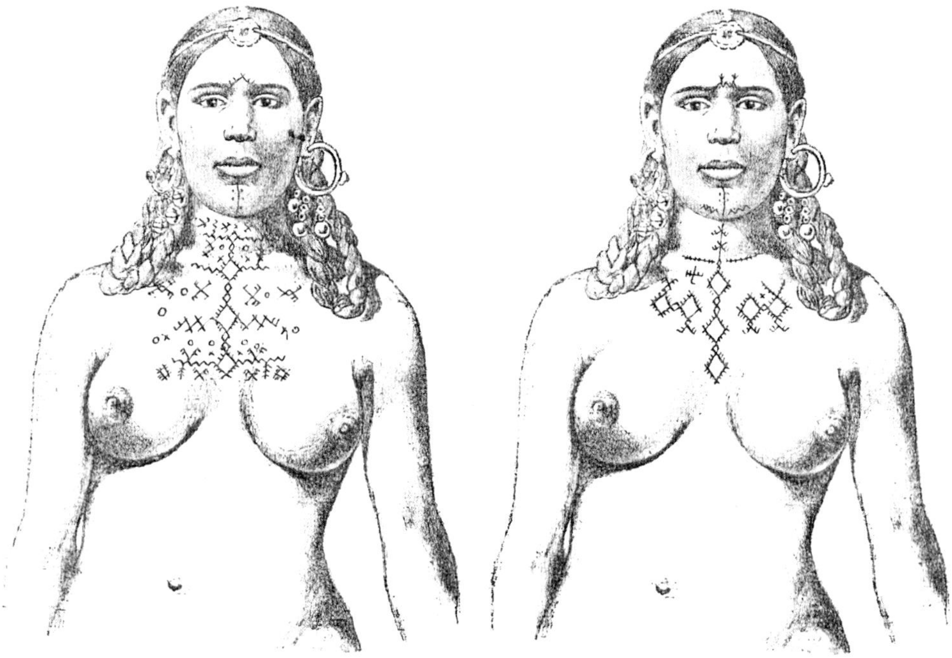

Two Beraber Berbers from Morocco, ca. 1920. Redrawn after Herber (1949: pl. IV). Motifs seen here include "serpent's bone" (chin) and "stars" (breast); "chains," "mirrors," swastikas (chest); and linked lozenges. Three linked lozenges form the *'aqreb* or scorpion motif.

or a piece of cloth dipped in *dihn*, the mutton fat used for cooking, precipitates the carbon. Sometimes indigo is added, or bile from the gall-bladder of an ox, which sets the dye, but the commonest method is to gather the soot precipitated on the bottom of a dish held over the lamp, and make a paste. Many people hold that the soot must be moistened with *halib umm al-bint*, the milk of a woman nursing a daughter, which has magic properties. The use of human milk was noted in several places, always the milk of a woman nursing a girl, as the milk for a girl is supposed to be specially soothing and cooling.

In all cases the instruments used are ordinary sewing needles of varying number according to their size and the technique of the operator. Usually they are of good size, but smaller than a darning needle, from two to four bound together for at least half their length. First the design, which in most cases depends on the taste and skill of the operator, is drawn on the skin with the needles dipped in the dye, and then pricked through. The tattooed surface may or may not bleed; whether it does or not is not important, except

> that some women said that it is better to perform the operation in the morning because it bleeds a lot if it is done at noon.
>
> One woman had three large dots irregularly placed on the lower abdomen, as well as a design around the navel. The dots in particular were to insure her having children, but she said she had already had one child when the tattooing was applied. This was done on the third day of menstruation. A midwife also mentioned this type of tattooing to insure child bearing. According to her, the tattooing may be a single dot or a small design consisting of three to five dots, applied below the navel, or on the back just above the buttocks. It must be done on the second or third day of menstruation.
>
> The efficacy of a third type of magical tattooing, which is a form of sympathetic magic, is aided by having someone read the Koran while the tattooing is being applied. Women practice this secretly. A woman in Baghdad had three dots tattooed in a triangle on the palm of her right hand to insure her keeping her husband's love. A similar design on the left hand would mean that the woman no longer wanted her husband's devotion. A midwife had a circle of five dots on the palm of her right hand. She said that she was her husband's second wife, and when he took a third, she decided that something must be done to ward off any possible conjuring on the part of the new wife. So one Friday noon, the most effective time, she had her right palm tattooed while a woman mullah read the Koran. The potency of the tattooing could not be doubted, for the result was that her husband divorced both his other wives and kept her![49]

Qur'anic reading sessions for women, led by female *mullahs*, are ceremonial occasions termed *krayas*. In Iraqi Shi'a villages, these readings or recitations

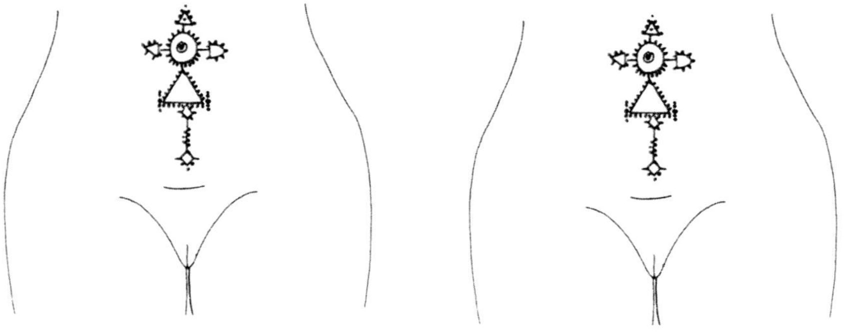

Women's body tattooing from Iraq, ca.1930. Redrawn after Field (1958: Fig. 36).

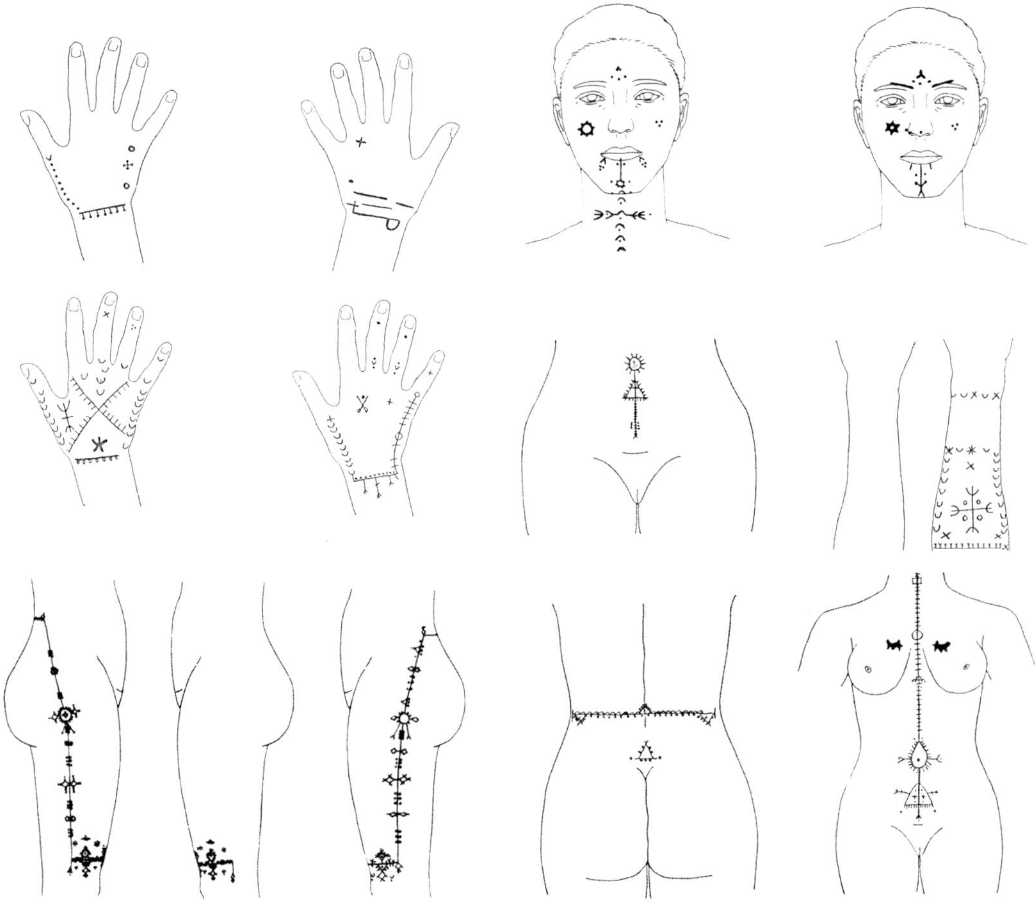

Women's body tattooing from Iraq, ca. 1930. Redrawn after Smeaton (1937: Figs. 1, 2) and Field (1958: Figs. 26, 36). Winnifred Smeaton (1937: 61), who studied the tattooing of women in Iraq, noted that one of her informants, a midwife, said that "the cross, or as she called it, the four-sided, is the best, that is, the strongest design."

of Qur'anic text, often in the form of chant, or poetry, are based on time-honored Islamic traditions of oral performance that focus on narratives of ethnic origin.[50] The *mullah*, working in tandem with the tattooist, moved in and out of a sacred history and space with her words to effectively convert the confines of the tattoo client's home into a sacred sanctuary. Seen from this way, the tattoo ritual thus generated a rhythmic interweaving of patterns of worldly and heavenly life, linking women as the guardians of family traditions to the realm of the sacred.[51] This highly personal landscape, activated by the divinely ordained words of the Qur'an and by the *baraka* laden tattooist and her potent tattoo pigments, created not only a physical and social space that was experienced collectively, but one that became more sacred with each repetitive instance. Therefore, just like any Muslim turns any worldly place into an individual sacred space by performing the five prescribed daily prayers to Mecca,[52] the *mullah* and tattooist performed similar repetitive signifying acts. By using their speech and actions, they created their own sacred space from which their client's tattoos took their meaning.

Kurdish tattooing

Henry Field expanded on Smeaton's studies of Iraqi Arab tattoo to include other ethnic groups that inhabited the region, like the Kurds of northern Iraq, as well as indigenous populations living in southwestern Asia.[53] Of considerable interest are his ethnographic notes focused upon the Kurds who live today north of Baghdad and in parts of Syria, the Caucasus, and Iran.

The history of the Kurdish people is as complex as it is ancient. By the middle of the 2nd millennium B.C., the culture and society of Kurdistan appear to have been unified under the Hurrians, a people who spoke a language belonging to the Caucasian family distantly related to modern Georgian and Laz.[54] The fundamental legacy of the ancient Hurrians to the contemporary culture of the Kurds is manifest elementally in their religion, mythology, martial arts, genetics, and tattoos.[55] But other religions left their mark on the tattoo traditions of the Yezidi Kurds, including the Aryans who extinguished the last Hurrian states in the Zagros-Taurus mountain regions by 850 B.C.

Today, the Yezidi Kurds comprise less than five percent of the entire Kurdish population,[56] but their tattooing traditions remain, as do many of their religious ceremonies like the Jam. Held at the sacred shrine in modern Lalish, Iraq, Jam coincides with the great Aryan festival of Mithrakan which celebrated the act of world creation by the sun god Mithras. The earliest

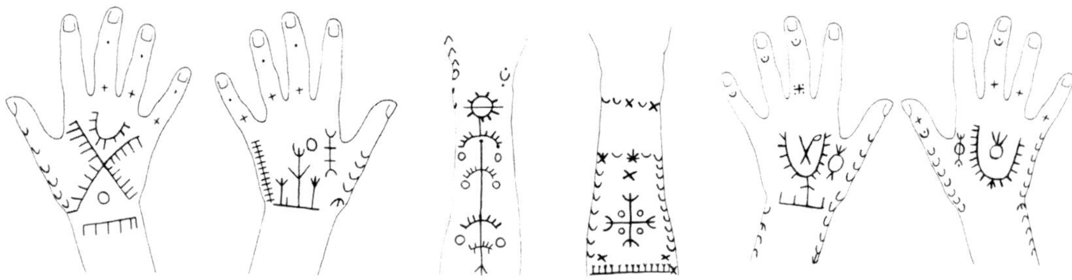

Kurdish women's tattoo designs from Iraq, ca. 1930. Redrawn after Field (1958: Figs. 4, 12).

known reference to Mithras dates to the 14th century B.C. and according to clay tablets excavated on the Anatolian plateau, he was worshipped for over two-thousand years.[57] The Roman Emperor Commodus (180-192 A.D.) even brought "the cult of light" to his empire and afterwards Roman emperors more and more identified themselves with the Unconquered Sun, took the title of "Invictus" and wore a crown with sun rays.[58]

According to Izady, Kurdish men and women still wear tattoos (*kutra'i* in Kurdish) associated with Mithras. Some of the motifs are found adorning the outer walls of the Yezidi shrine at Lalish:

> The symbol combining a dog, a serpent hole, and the sun disc used by Yezidi women is a fascinating reminder of this combination in ancient Mithraic religious sculptures (the sun god Mithras killing the bull of heaven, from whose blood springs a serpent and a dog, the symbols of balancing forces of good and evil).[59]

Field remarked that the Yezidis tattooed most frequently a comb design, called *misht* or *meshed*, and a rayed circle or disc with a varying number of rays and sometimes a circular branded scar called *kawi* in the center.[60] Westermark illustrates a related tattoo motif in Morocco which was called *meshta*, "comb," very similar to the etymology of the Kurdish word *misht*, that resembles the carding comb tattoos of the Kabyle and Chaouian Berbers of Algeria.[61] Cola Alberich reported that rayed crosses tattooed in Morocco were "expressions of the solar cult."[62] Thus, it seems that comb tattoos in Iraq were perhaps in some way related to solar motifs, because we know that iron carding combs and tattoos were used as fire symbols in North Africa.

As such, we see in the dominant motifs of Kurdish tattooing the value of a type of "holy formula" that Izady says "cannot be altered without losing its power. These markings are of considerable antiquity, and are 'living' examples of many ancient motifs preserved in this way."[63] In this vein, rayed semicircles enclosing a star and two dots were said by some Yezidi women to ward off the evil eye, while other tattoos were therapeutic used to cure rheumatism and headaches because of their perceived healing properties.[64] It should be noted that tribal peoples in Iran also practiced these forms of medicinal tattooing.[65]

Yet other authorities have argued that because the sun brought forth the new growth of plants, coinciding in a sense with animals giving birth to their young each spring, the heliolatrous significance of the tattooed cross, as a solar symbol, connoted procreation and ultimately served as a fertility mark;[66] whereas the swastika, present in tattoo traditions of the Kurds, Berbers and indigenous groups in India, metamorphosed into a related form (via spirals, concentric circles, and rosettes). However, the sun ideograph may have also represented deified fire symbolizing properties of purification.

Balkan tattooing

Interestingly the same tattoo motifs occur in varying degrees among several indigenous peoples in the Balkan countries of Albania, Bosnia, and Greece. Edith Durham, who traveled extensively in the region in the early 20th century, noted that "among the Moslems of North Albania tattooing is common . . . [they] were marked with a triangle—which forms a star and is the substitute for the rayed sun."[67] It is likely that these tattoos had some sort of prophylactic significance, but none was recorded by Durham because she "could only observe and make secret notes."[68] She did, however, see many of the tattoo designs painted on Muslim houses of the region, similar to cultural practices in northern Africa.

Durham, arguably one of the most important British writers on the

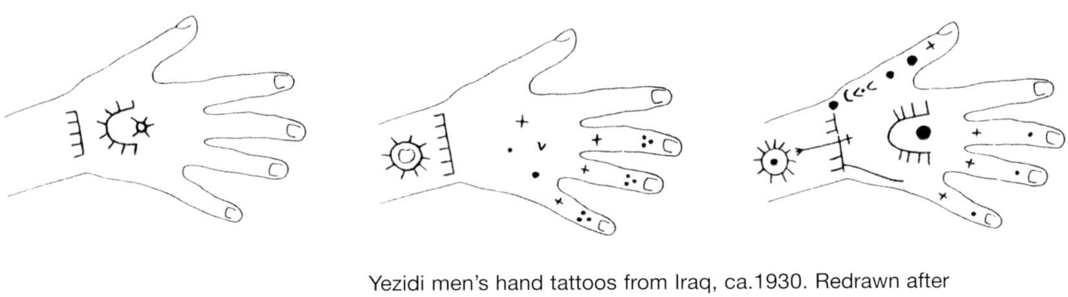

Yezidi men's hand tattoos from Iraq, ca.1930. Redrawn after Field (1958: Fig. 13).

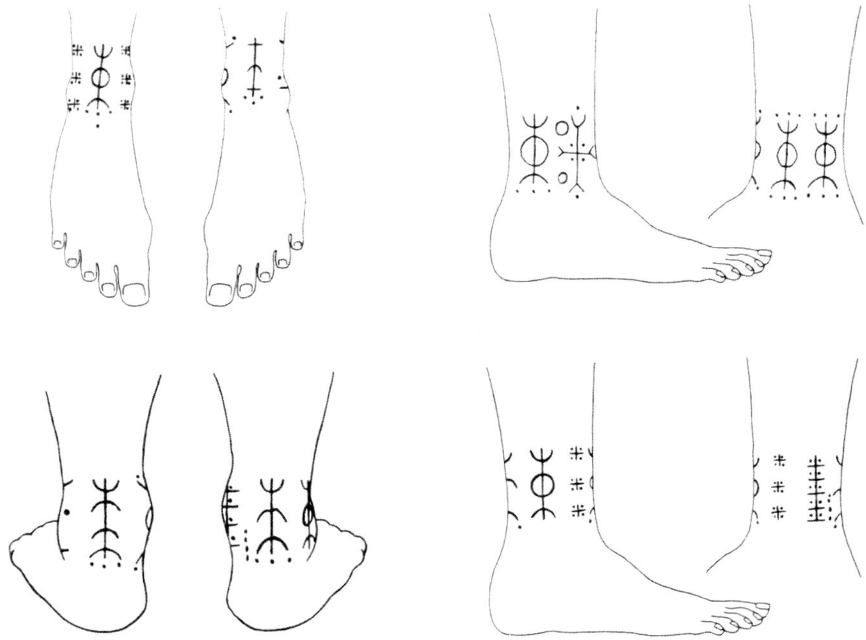

Yezidi women's ankle tattoos from Iraq, ca. 1930. Redrawn after Field (1958: Fig. 16).

culture of Albania, documented the existence of many tattooed Albanian Catholics, most of whom had migrated to the area from Bosnia to evade the Turks in the 15th century: "the bulk of these Catholic . . . tribes-folk, both men and women, are tattooed on the back of the hand, the forearm, or the breast with a cross; but never a plain cross. It has a crescent above and below it; or the arms terminate in small circles; or some in circles and some in crescents; or the cross is in the 'sun-wheel' form."[69] Durham stated that "most people said they did it because they were Catholics. One man remarked it was to ensure you a Christian burial, if you died abroad."[70] When Durham asked what the meaning of the circle and crescent represented, she was told, "*Dielli*—the sun, and *Hana*—the moon. The cross was to show you were Christian." A local priest offered, "They have a number of curious pagan beliefs which they will not tell me. I have found that they believe in two powers—Light and Darkness—which are in conflict—Good and Evil. These tattoos are in some way connected with it. So is the Serpent, which they sometimes tattoo and also draw on walls."[71]

Today, traces of these ancient tattoos continue to be found among a small

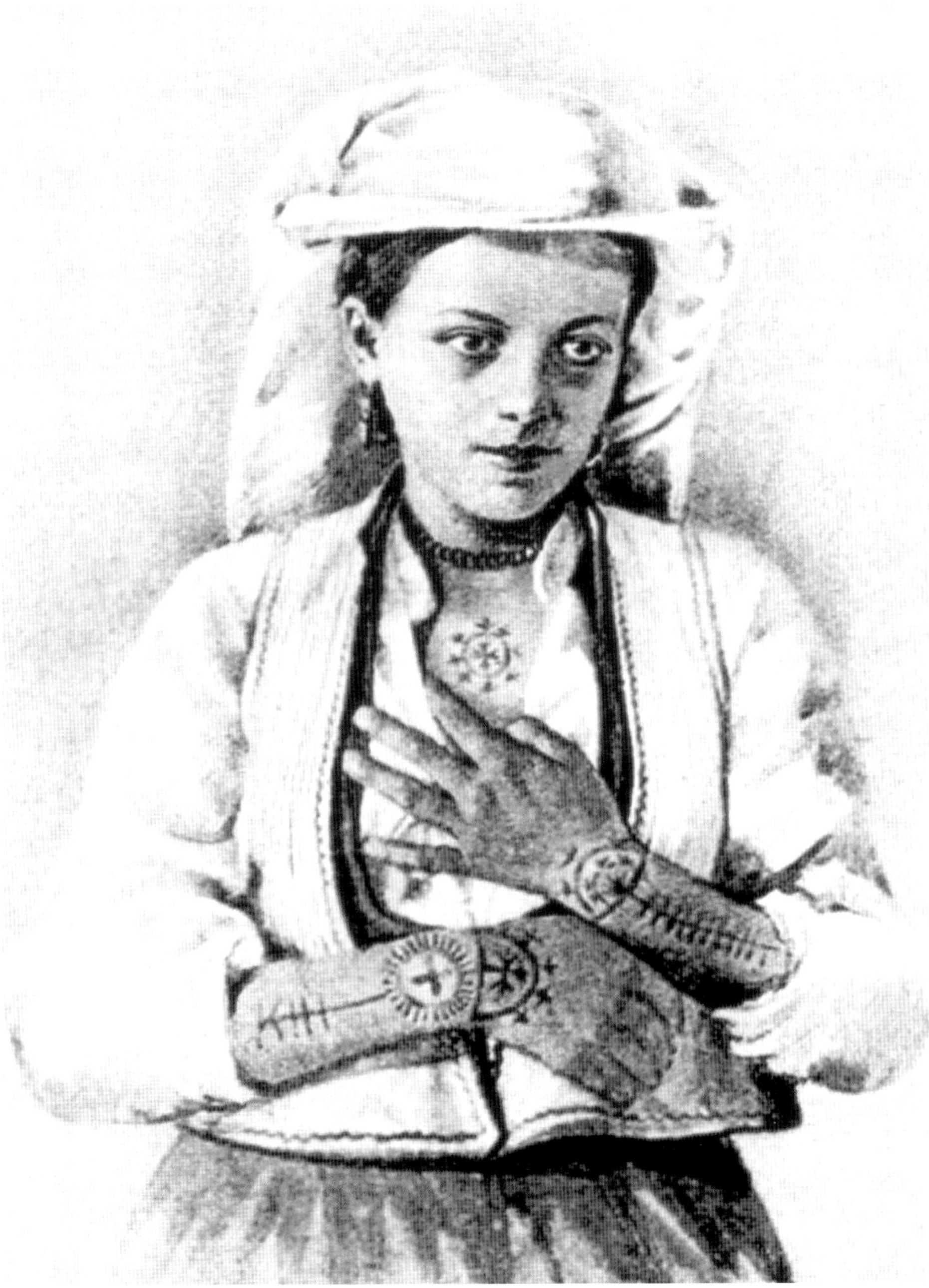

Bosnian Catholic body tattooing, late 19th century. After Glück (1894:456).

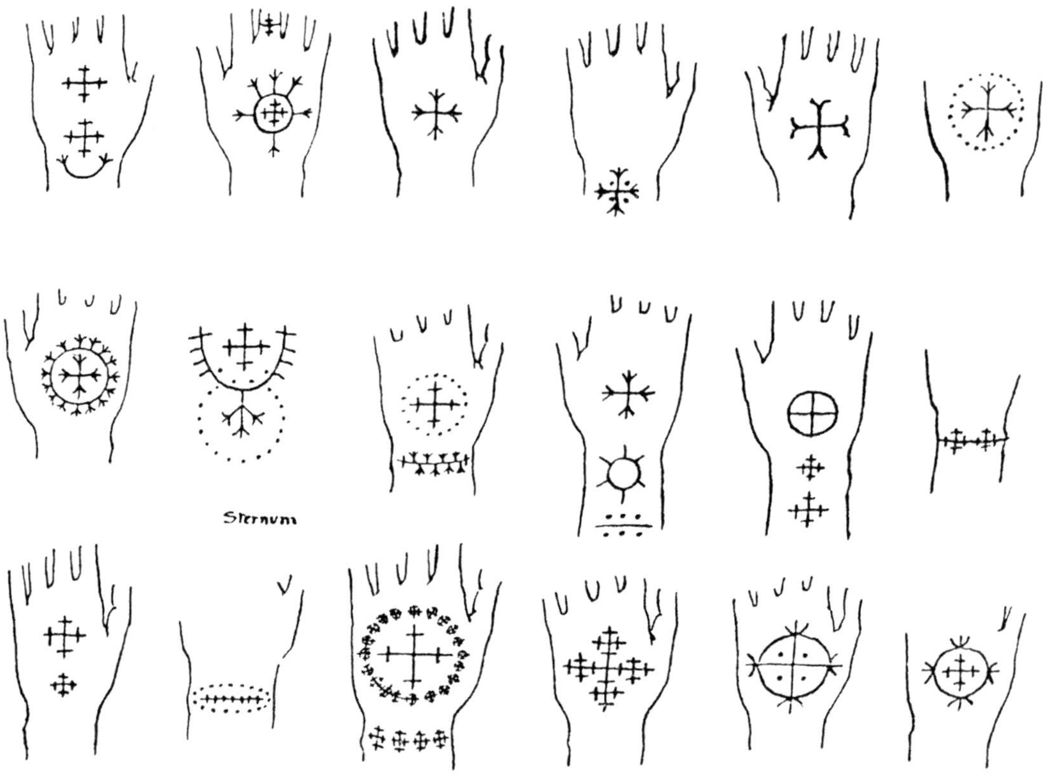

Bosnian Catholic tattoos, ca. 1908. Redrawn after Durham (1929: 103).

number of Bosnian Catholics,[72] although the majority of Bosnians are Muslim. Interestingly, Durham provided us with several illustrations of the Bosnian tattoos in the same work where she describes the Albanian ones, and it is noteworthy that many of her illustrations parallel several salient elements that continue to be worn as tattoos by contemporary Bosnian women.

Bosnians called the tattooing process *sharati* ("to color") and many patterns were as follows: *kolo* ("the circle"), named after the traditional dance of the region,[73] *klas* ("ear of corn"), *ograda* ("ring-fence"), *narukvotza* ("bracelet"), *grancica* ("small pine twig"), *eliza* ("fir tree"), *krizh* or *krizhevi* (cross, crosses) and more importantly Sun, Moon, and Star.[74]

Old Bosnian Catholic women who knew the tattoo patterns worked as tattoo artists and tattoo pigment consisted of the soot of resinous pinesap collected on a plate, then combined with honey and water, saliva and mother's milk.[75] Sometimes tattoo designs were carved into a piece of willow bark and stenciled on the skin as a guide.

Certain days of the year were better for tattooing than others. Annunciation Day (March 25th) and Palm Sunday were tattooing days, but March 19th (St. Stephen's Day) was the most common.[76] According to Durham's informants, tattooing was connected to fertility, springtime, new life, religion, and the position of the sun.[77]

Not surprisingly, sun worship in the Balkans was an ancient pre-Christian phenomenon: the cross as a sun symbol, the four spokes representing the four quarters of the heavens and the wheel as a whole represents the movement of the sun through the heavens.[78] Many of the Bosnian and Kurdish tattoos depict this symbol, as well as the Albanian Catholic motifs, however abstract they may be.

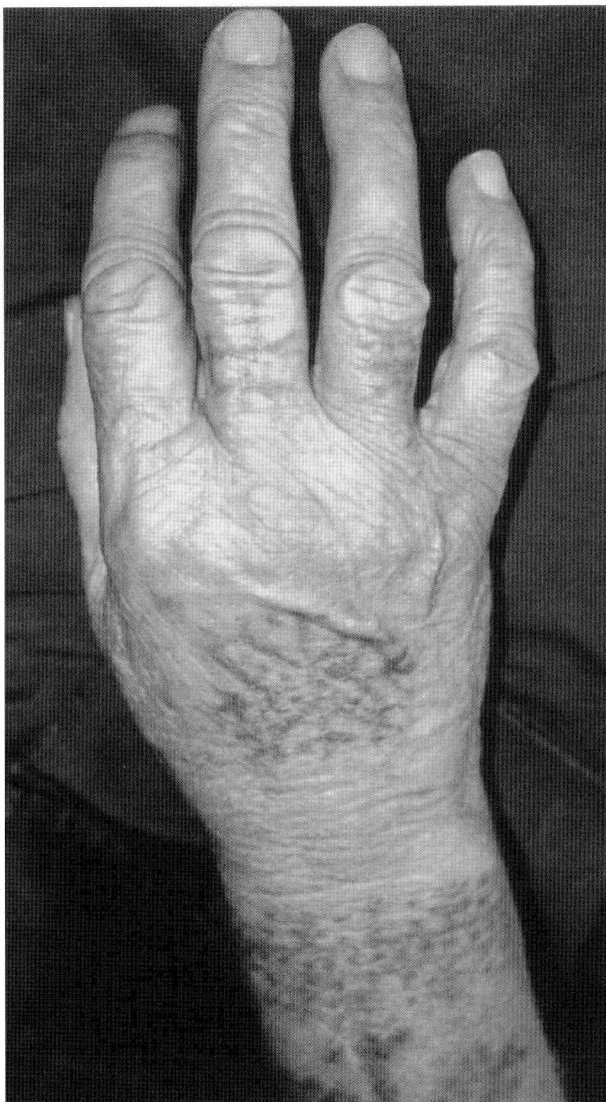

Bosnian woman's hand tattoos, 2000. Courtesy of Michael Laukien.

The Romans, who exacted their rule over the Balkans for centuries, brought a variety of cults to the area, especially that of Mithras.[79] A capital doctrine of Mithraism was fatalism, where the destinies of humankind were bound to the planets. The sun, the greatest of them, influenced kings and emperors. Each day of the week was sacred to a

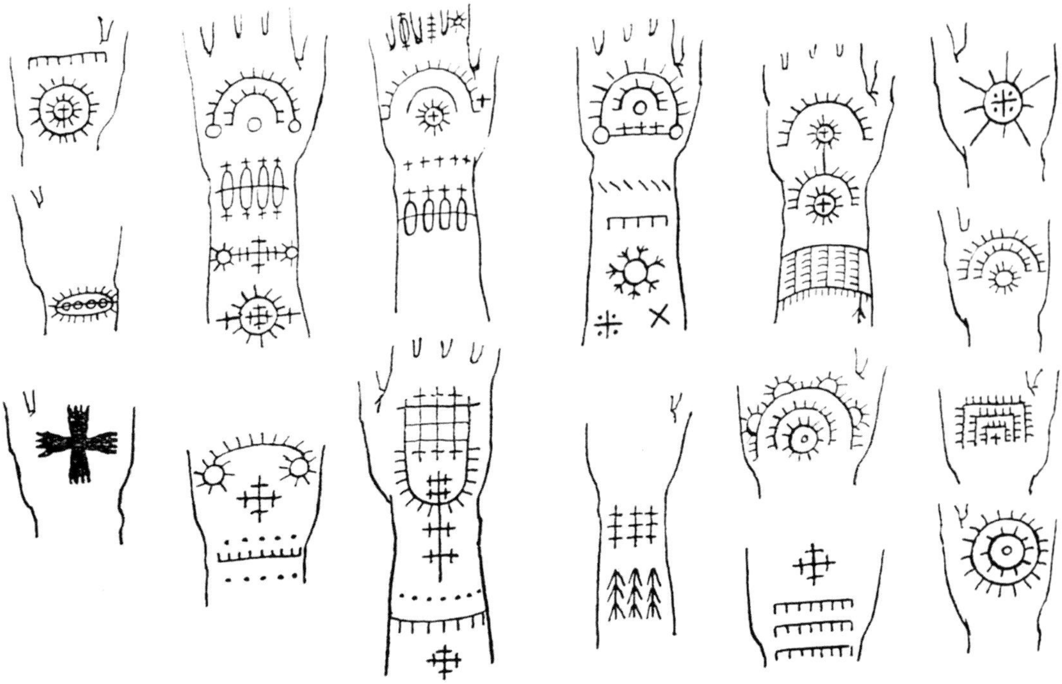

Bosnian Catholic tattoos, ca. 1908. Redrawn after Durham (1929: 105).

planet and December 25, the birthday of *Sol Invictus* ("Invincible Sun"), was especially holy and is now fêted as Christmas.[80] An immense mountain towered above the sun, moon, and stars and was the home to the immortals. After death, the spirits of light and darkness struggled for the soul, which, if it escaped darkness, rose first to the moon and then passed to the six other planets to be cleansed before reaching eternal bliss.[81]

After Constantine the Great (ca. 280-337 A.D.) moved the seat of the Roman Empire to Byzantium (Istanbul) and adopted Christianity as the religion of the state, Mithraism nearly fell out of favor. However, Constantine, before taking this step, was a follower of Mithras, which accounts for the fact that his standard, the labarum, bears a striking resemblance to the sun-wheel: it was even marked on Byzantine coins until the 7th and 8th centuries.[82] In these coins, the cross, which began as a sun-wheel, is the most prominent, and a small sun appears at the end of each—or a crescent-like object, which may represent the moon or be a broken sun-wheel.[83] It is these combinations of moon, sun and cross that the Arab, Albanian, Bosnian, and Kurdish tribeswomen tattooed on their arms and bodies.

Although Mithraism eventually died out, it is obvious that specific symbols associated with that religion did not. In the 9th century, Manichaeism, a strange compound of sun worship, Zoroastrian Dualism, Babylonian folklore, Buddhist ethics and Christianity, entered the Balkans and spread rapidly throughout districts where Mithraism had once flourished.[84] This new religion purported to be the true synthesis of all the religious systems then known, and the essential part of this faith was a belief in two antagonistic powers of Light and Darkness, spirit and matter. Durham stated:

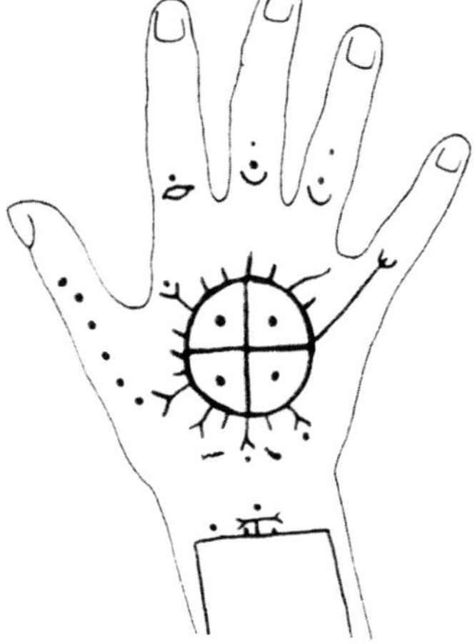

Arab woman's hand tattoo from Iraq, ca. 1930. Redrawn after Field (1958: Fig. 26).

> Man was created by the powers of Darkness, but contains some stolen particles of Light. Woman contains no particles of Light and is, therefore, an instrument of destruction. Christ was the efflux of the Power of Light and had His dwelling place in the sun. To the sun were drawn those souls in whom the principle of Light prevailed, and they passed onward for ablution in the pure water that formed the moon. When the moon was full of souls, they passed from it, thus accounting for the waxing and waning of the moon. Finally, the souls dwell in a column of light, because it is filled with perfect souls. The celestial bodies were witnesses of the great strife and took part in it. The spirits of evil were caught and bound to the stars. Hence the maligning influence of the constellations and the destructive force of the elements.[85]

The Vlachs

The indelible tradition of tattooing in the Balkans also permeated a small number of indigenous groups living in northwest Greece. In the remote vastness of the Píndhos Mountains lives a population of Orthodox Christians called the Vlachs or Roumaní.[86] The origins of the Vlachs are obscure, shrouded as they are by time, and most historians agree that they are the last remnants of the Latin speaking population that existed in the Balkans since the incorporation of ancient Macedonia into the Roman Empire in 148 B.C. Their unwritten language—*Arouman*—has Latin origins and can be described as a proto-Romance language mutually comprehensible to modern Romanian.[87]

During Roman times the *Via Egnata*, an old Roman road and trade route

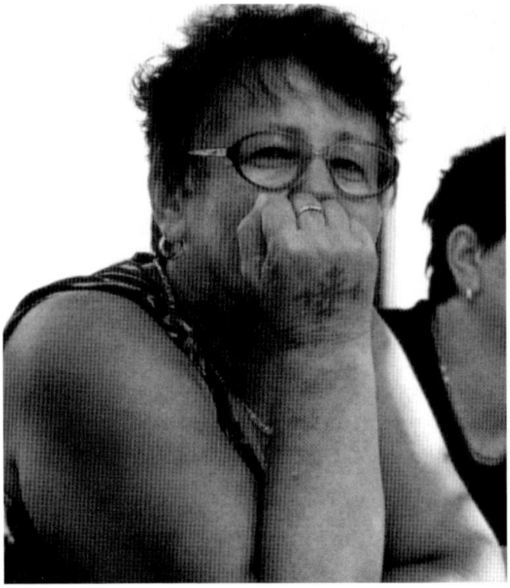

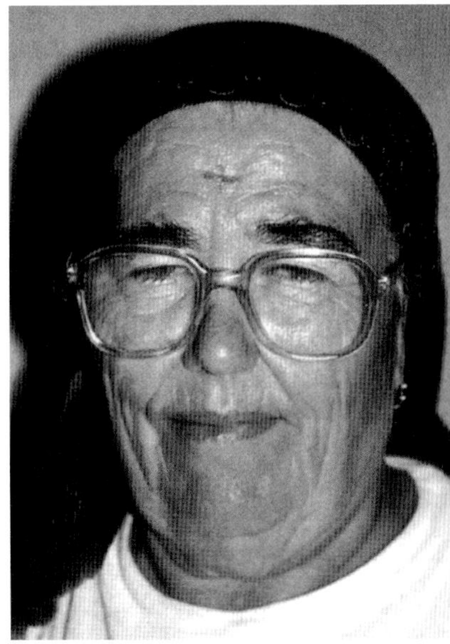

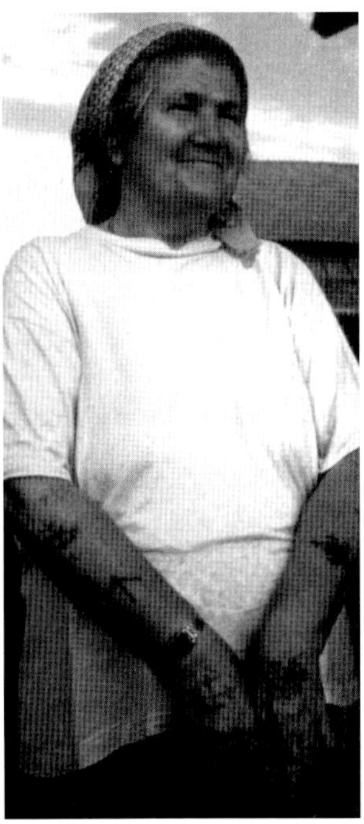

Tattooed Bosnian Catholics, 2000. Courtesy of Michael Laukien.

connecting Constantinople to the Adriatic, was heavily guarded by Legionnaires who in turn trained indigenous shepherds and herdsmen along its route for military work in the high mountain passes. Greek Vlachs probably learned Latin through these working associations and down through the millennia preserved it in undisturbed form in the highlands of the largely inaccessible Píndhos.

As late as the early 15th century, the Vlachs were a powerful independent kingdom in parts of Bulgaria and Greece.[88] But within a century the Ottoman Turks conquered the Balkans and most of Eastern Europe eventually collapsing Vlach autonomy in their core area for the next 600 years.

Today, the Vlachs are a minority population in an overwhelmingly Greek state. But they continue to retain their traditional dress, language, and indelible customs—including tattoo.[89] Although increasingly rare, traditional Vlach tattoo exists on only a handful of elderly women in the Píndhos region. These marks, tattooed on the skin by old Vlach

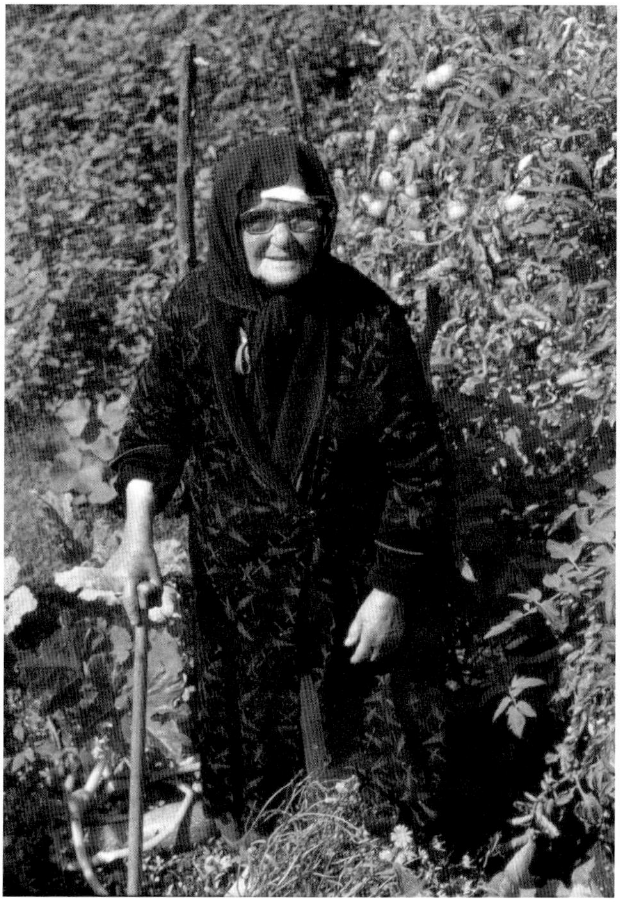

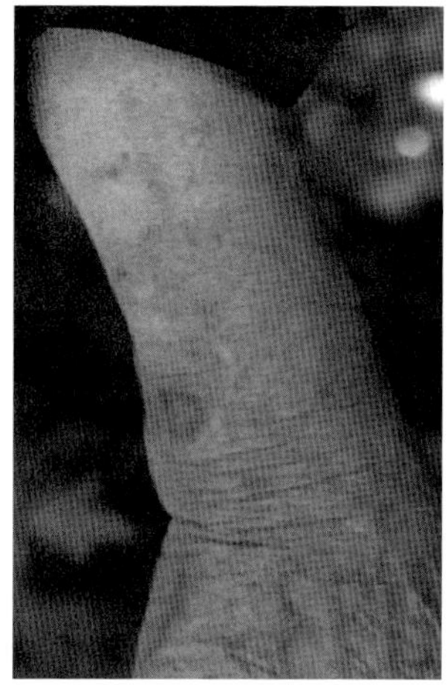

Tattooed Vlach woman. Giannoula Giannaki was born in Albania and moved to northern Greece. At the time of this photograph (2002) she was 94 years old and one of only a handful of tattooed Aromanian Vlachs still living in Greece. Giannoula wears a large, faded cruciform design on her right forearm. She also wears a faint cross tattooed upon her forehead. Her mother wore five cruciforms on her forehead. Photographs by Lars Krutak.

women, not only reaffirmed their Orthodox Christian belief, but also affected powerful charms against the evil eye and other disease spread by spirits encountered while herding sheep and other domesticates in the wilderness.[90]

Lampblack, the finely powdered soot derived from charcoal, was chosen as tattoo pigment because it was believed to have purificatory power. Charcoal was utilized at Vlach funerals to not only repel the spirit of the recently deceased, but also to prevent spirit possession.[91] Through such associations, it would seem that Vlach tattoo pigment perhaps held *baraka*-like power, acting to both purify and protect the physical body from disembodied metaphysical forces met in the local landscape.

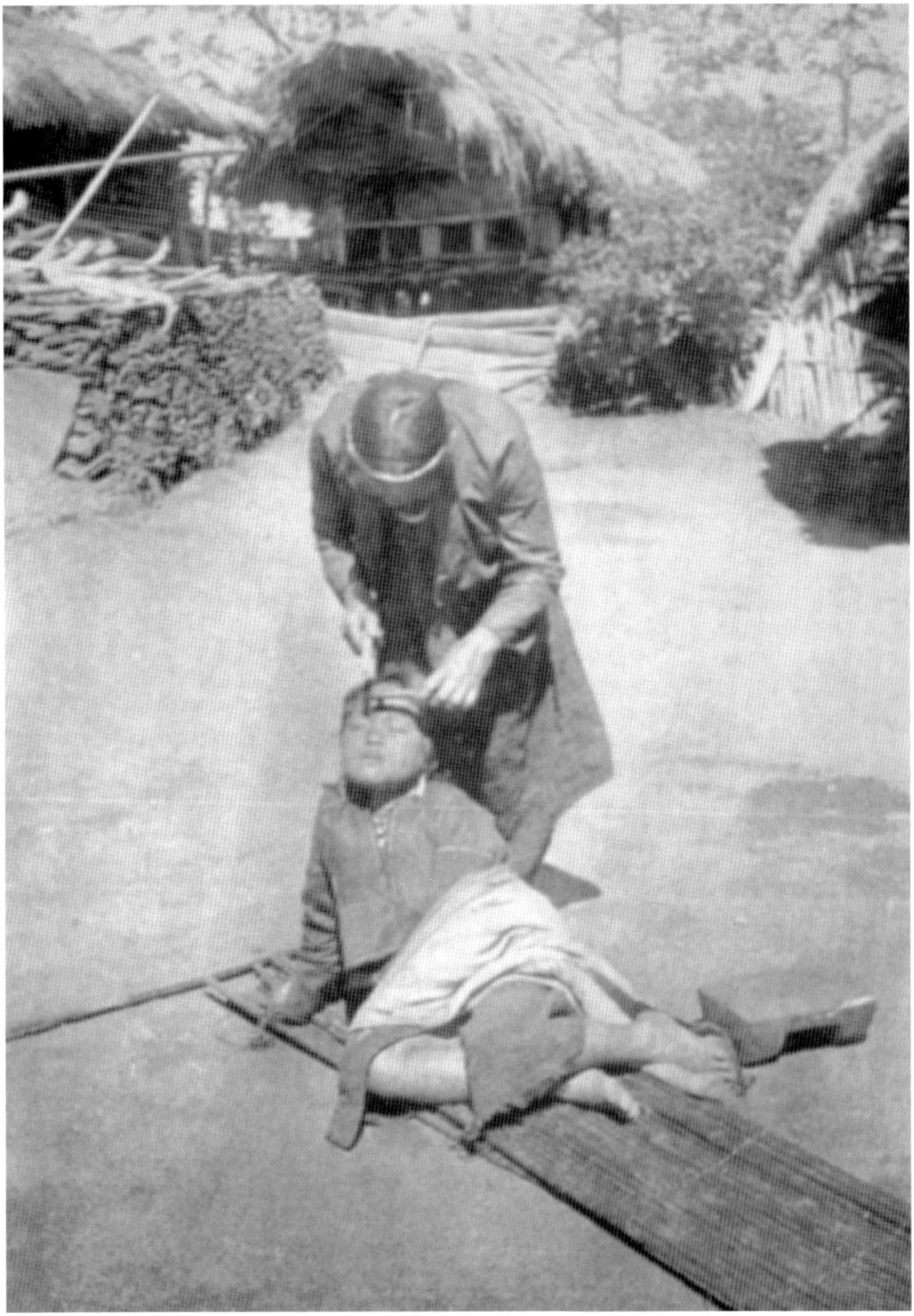

Atayal tattoo artist at work, ca. 1910. After Formosa Bureau of Aboriginal Affairs (1911: 3).

Taiwan and Borneo

Taiwan, formerly known as Ilha Formosa (Portuguese, "Beautiful Island"), is a mountainous island lying approximately one-hundred miles southeast of Mainland China. Today perhaps less than five percent of the total population is indigenous occupying the central mountainous region, a portion of the coastal plains, and a large portion of the southeastern hill country.[1] Traditionally, twelve, or more than one-half, of the aboriginal groups here practiced tattooing.[2] They included both plains and mountain tribes.

Three-hundred years ago, aboriginal Formosans lived in all districts of Taiwan until large inmigrations of Han Chinese forced the "barbarian tribes" to withdraw from the coastal regions and into the central mountains.[3] This trend towards isolation continued through the early years of Japanese colonial rule (1895-1945) when aborigines living in the central regions still remained relatively undisturbed from Western contact.[4]

By the beginning of the 20th century, however, the indigenous mountain strongholds of the Atayal, Paiwan, and other tattooed peoples were threatened by the expanding camphor tree industry—a development that increased the flow of outsiders into the interior, and eventually contributed to widespread rebellion and bloodshed.

Growing in immense groves in the Central Mountains of Taiwan, slow-growing camphor trees were utilized in the early 20th century for ship building and in the manufacture of mothballs, perfumes, and more importantly celluloid: a material that could be used to make drugs, combs, tobacco pouches, and billiard balls.[5] Since the method of collecting camphor necessitated the clear-cutting of the forest, contacts and conflicts with indigenous peoples inhabiting the camphor groves increased, forcing the Japanese government of Formosa to take up defensive measures to protect their economic interests.

Expanding on the existing Chinese defensive system of the *aiyu-sen*, or guard-line, the Japanese basically encircled the indigenous territories with military outposts connected by battle fences that were constantly being advanced as the Japanese conquered new camphor groves.[6] One Western traveler to Taiwan in the 1920s described the *aiyu-sen* as follows:

> The *aiyu-sen*, or guard-line, is a cleared space, from fifty to a hundred feet wide, climbing over hill and dale completely around the uncontrolled territory. It is started by cutting a road along the crest of a mountain, then destroying the vegetation on either side of this far enough back so that the guards can see attacking savages in time to defend themselves. This system dates back to the reign of Ch'ien-Lung, toward the middle of the 18th-century, when the Chinese paid tamed savages to protect them against the others . . .
>
> The Japanese have constructed bullet-proof, loopholed forts, barbed-wire entanglements, mines, and wire fences, the latter in some places locally electrified by harnessing mountain streams; hand-grenades, sometimes mountain—and field—guns, are used; on the east coast war-ships have occasionally been called upon to subdue belligerent villages . . . To-day the guard-line is about three hundred miles long.[7]

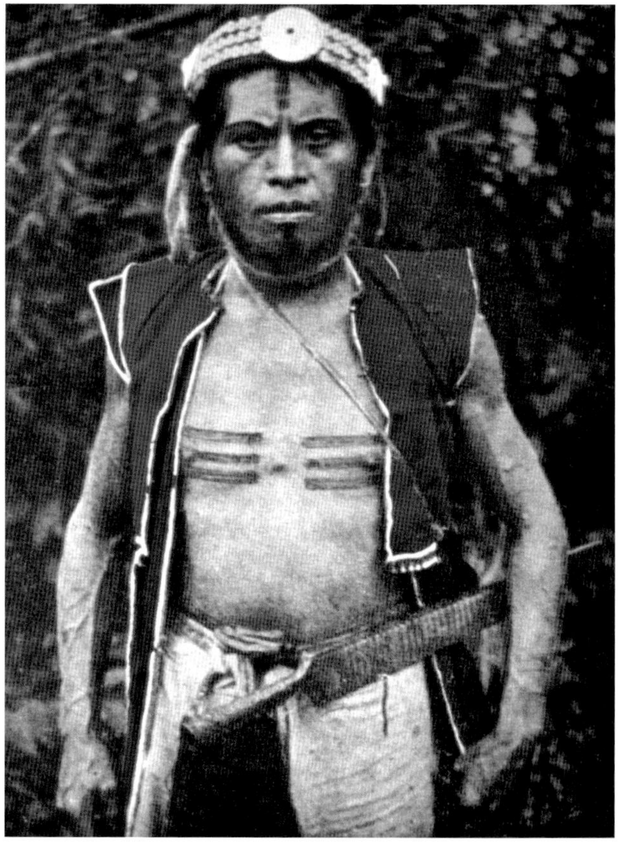

Tattooed "Saiset Barbarians, Formosa." Japanese postcard, ca. 1930. The earliest account of the tattooing custom in Taiwan was recorded in the Chinese History of the Sui Dynasty dating to the 7th century A.D. (Ho 1960: 44). Postcard from the collection of the author.

Incredibly, between 1903 and 1908 the Japanese pushed forward this guard line on seventy separate occasions.[8] But the military campaign did not entirely suspend indigenous raids into Japanese territory. Rather, indigenous headhunters in search of human heads often came over or under the *aiyu-sen* barrier at nightfall to lay waiting in ambush for unsuspecting victims.[9]

Headhunting, the primary ritual component of the Atayal, Paiwan, Saiset, Rukai, and other groups, was a traditional custom considered indispensable to human existence. Successful headhunting communities enjoyed enhanced status and could assert their territorial claims to land by challenging rival villages through armed conflict. Headhunting also served to maintain several religious functions including agricultural and community fertility through blood sacrifices that propitiated the deities and ancestors.[10] More specifically, one Atayal elder recounted in the 1940s that headhunting was believed to induce rapid growth in village children which was a desirable outcome:

> After our young men return from killing, they tattoo their foreheads and chins. Even when they went to kill someone our ancestors took many people, even their children, with them. Then, from the head taken, they distributed one hair to each of the children. After they returned, these people who went out to kill were all tattooed. As a result of this, the children grew with the speed of the wind. According to the Atayal custom, a man who has killed many men tattoos his chest. A man who has killed only a few does not tattoo his chest.
>
> When we return from killing, we return with our voices raised in the war cry along the road. When we get home we all go to the place for the heads and sing. On the following day we assemble and dance, and put the heads in the head stockade. We always place rice flour cakes, which our wives have pounded, into the mouths of the heads. Taking them out again, we let the children of those of us who have returned from head-hunting eat them. We make *owao* [millet wine] in celebration, and also go hunting. When our *owao* is mature, we always invite everyone in the whole village. Then everyone comes and drinks our *owao*.[11]

As noted, the Atayal marked success on the headhunt by deliberately tattooing their faces and bodies. Yet those headhunters who acquired more than five heads with their machete-like beheading knife might also have

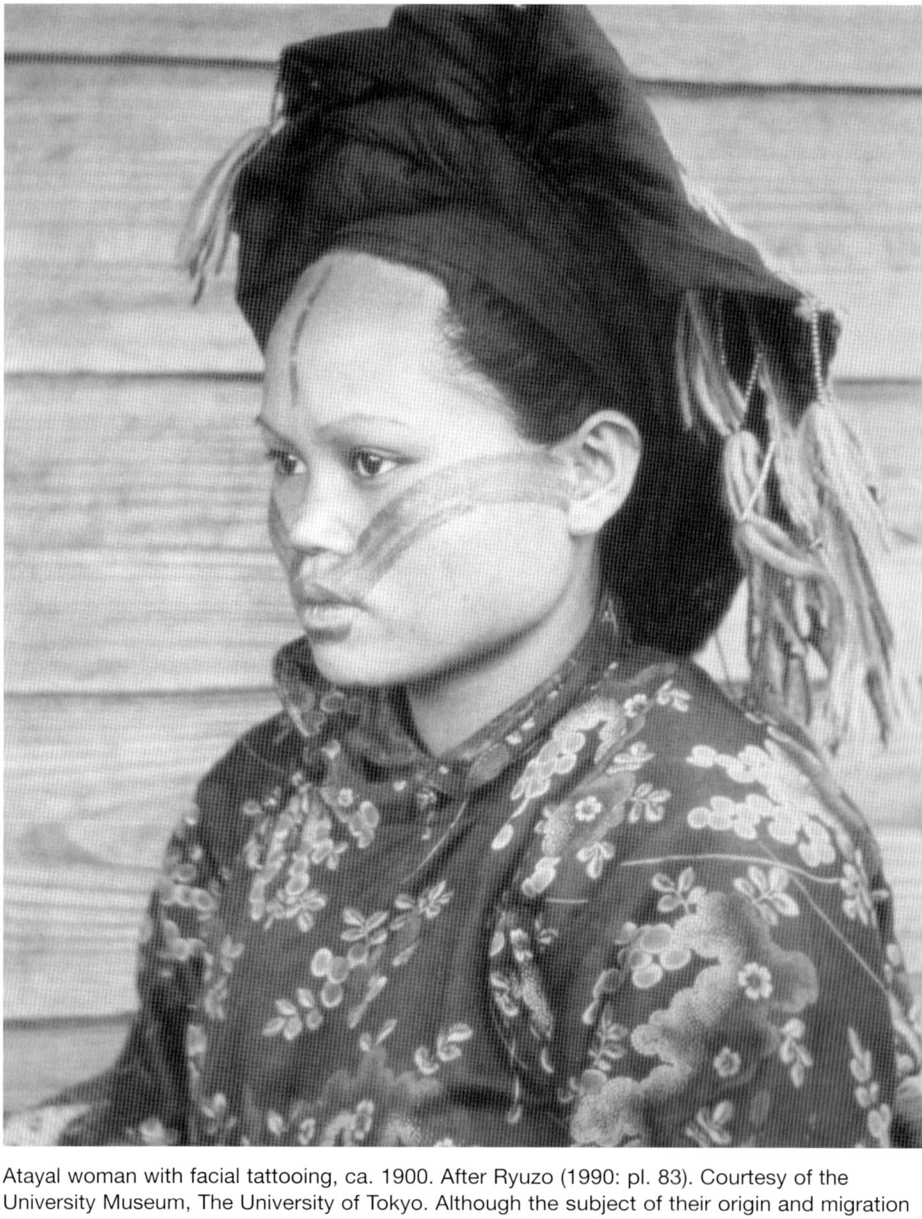

Atayal woman with facial tattooing, ca. 1900. After Ryuzo (1990: pl. 83). Courtesy of the University Museum, The University of Tokyo. Although the subject of their origin and migration to the island continues to be debated, the indigenous peoples of Taiwan probably have occupied the region for at least 3,500 years (Hsü 1991: 9-10). Particular cultural traits such as swidden agriculture, the utilization of the backstrap loom, nose flutes and bamboo harmonicas in musical traditions, a social organization based on a ruling gerontocracy, and practices of headhunting and tattooing linked each group to other Austronesian-speaking populations inhabiting Southeast Asia, especially the Dayaks of Borneo, the Li of Hainan Island (China) and the Bontoc of the Philippines (Hose and Shelford:1906; Hsü 1991: 10; Ho 1960: 47-48; Yang 1995/96, 1997).

tattooed their chests or the backs of their hands.[12] Among the Paiwan, it was believed that the spirits of ancestors dwelled in their beheading knives, which were held in the possession of the tribe for several generations.[13] However, the Paiwan were not necessarily tattooed after having taken the head itself; instead, the successful warrior was also denoted by the wearing of a certain kind of cap which was woven by women of the tribe.[14]

More generally, tattooing could also be administered to the foreheads of unmarried Atayal boys and girls in their teens. Yet apart from the tattooed foreheads of these girls, only those who were skillful in weaving could tattoo their cheeks and other parts of their bodies.[15]

Besides the beautiful cloths they wove on the loom, Atayal weavers also

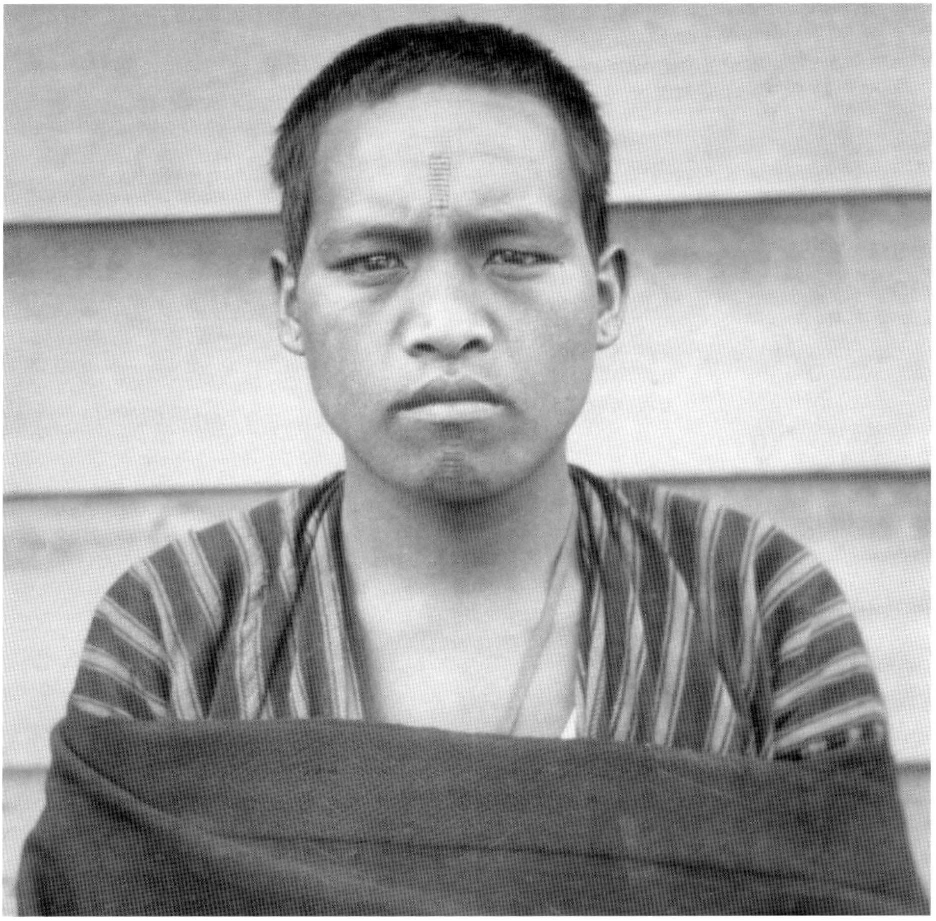

Tattooed Atayal man, ca. 1900. His facial markings indicate success on the headhunt. After Ryuzo (1990: pl. 62). Courtesy of the University Museum, The University of Tokyo.

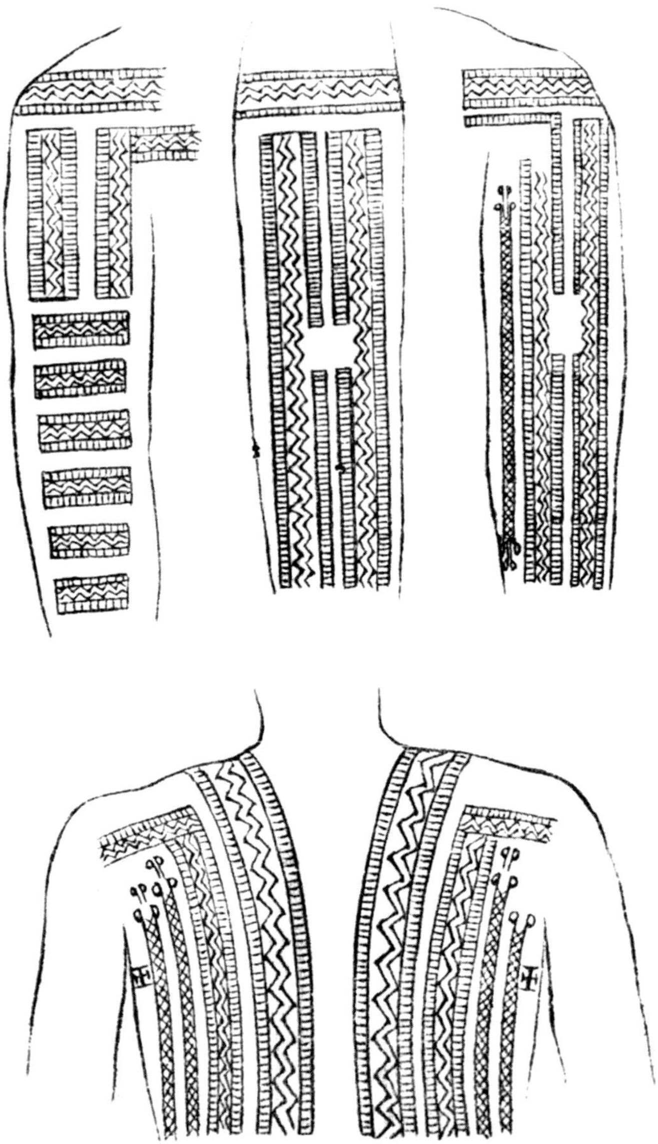

Rukai chief and headhunter's tattoos, ca. 1900. After Inō (1910). Like the Paiwan, Rukai shamans—who were usually female—worked as the tattoo artist. Before the first marks were laid upon the skin, prayers and offerings, consisting of glass beads and betel nuts, were given to guardian spirits in order to protect the tattoo client from evil spirits attracted by the bloodletting. Other ceremonial taboos tied to the tattooing included: no sexual relations immediately before the operation; no tattooing while a corpse lay in the village or when a woman was menstruating; no ingestion of animal blood before the tattooing; and no use of red-colored clothing during the operation (Ho 1960: 46).

manufactured net bags which their headhunting husbands used to carry severed human heads. Next to his beheading knife, these bags were a warrior's most treasured possession.[16]

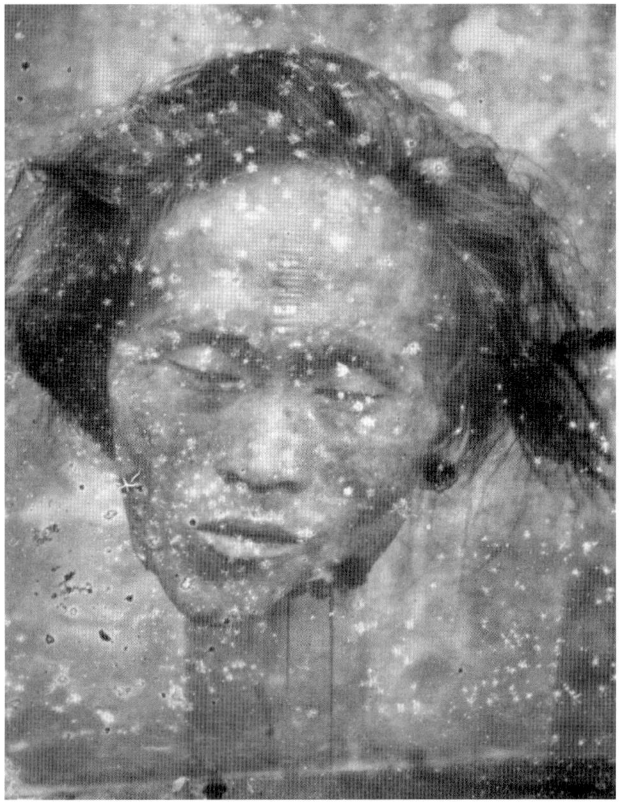

Atayal war dead with facial tattooing, ca. 1900. After Ryuzo (1990: pl. 30). Courtesy of the University Museum, The University of Tokyo.

Interestingly, the Atayal believed that only those women who were proficient weavers and those men who were successful headhunters could pass safely into the afterlife.[17] According to the 17th century Dutch missionary Georgius Candidius, who spent sixteen months among the indigenous people of Taiwan, individuals who had not thus lived honorable lives were destined to meet a terrible fate after death:

> According to their belief, an exceedingly narrow bridge, made of bamboo, leads across [the] river [of death], over which the souls of deceased must pass before they can reach the *Campum Eliseum*, or Land of Promise. Moreover, those who have led a bad life, and who attempt to cross the bridge, will find it suddenly turning round; and, instead of entering the Land of Promise, they will fall into the filthy stream [below], there to suffer great torment and pain.[18]

Remarkably, a very similar myth is told among the Toradja and neighboring peoples of the Celebes,[19] the Maori of New Zealand,[20] the Kayan, Punan[21] and Murut[22] of Borneo, among other peoples.[23]

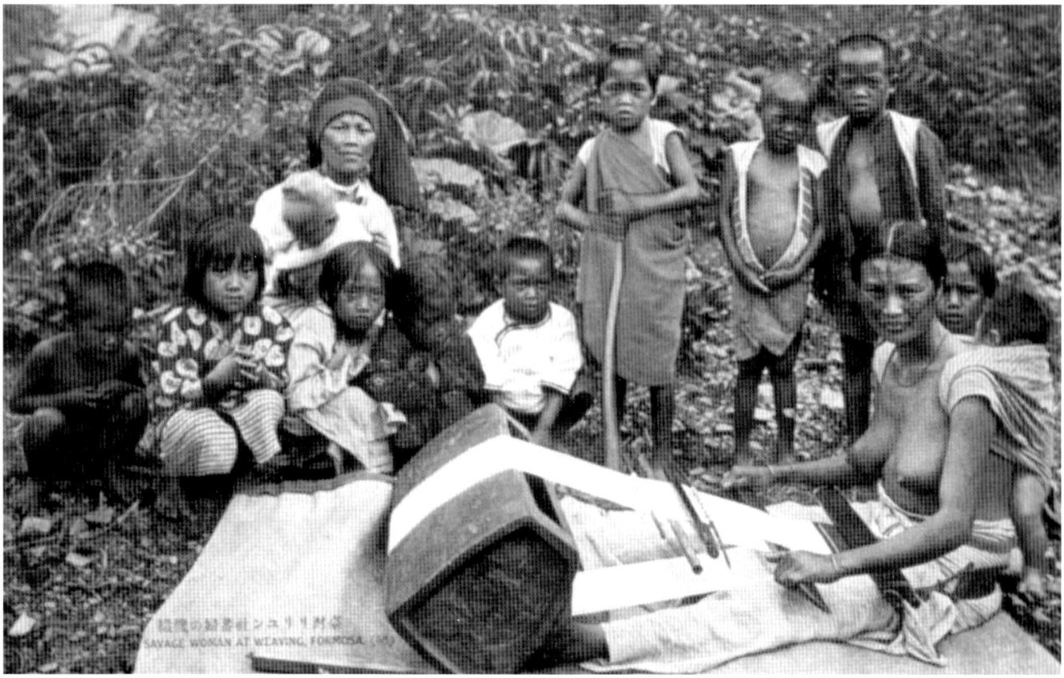

“Savage Woman at Weaving, Formosa,” ca. 1930. This Japanese tourist postcard draws heavily on poetic metaphors of nature to create a mythical and dreamlike landscape whereby indigenous Atayal “savages” become tamed by the gaze of the camera. Postcard from the collection of the author.

Atayal tattoo artists

Atayal tattoo artists, called *patasan*, were women.[24] They had to be of high virtue and most of them inherited their profession from their mothers, though some learned it by apprenticeship. Usually there were not many tattoo artists in any one particular region, so if one did not reside in an Atayal village, one was invited from the outside. Tattooists commonly charged a piece of cloth or two strings of beads for an individual’s first tattoo; but, for one who had married or committed adultery, she would charge more—sometimes one or two beaded skirts.[25] According to one male Atayal informant interviewed ca. 1930, the tattooer’s fee for a simple design was equivalent to seven *bunun*; that is, five sickles and hatchets wrapped in a bundle equivalent to the price of seven Japanese yen at that time. More complex patterns fetched slightly higher prices.[26]

Tattoo artists first stenciled their designs upon the skin with a linen thread soaked with black soot. The tattoo instrument resembled a

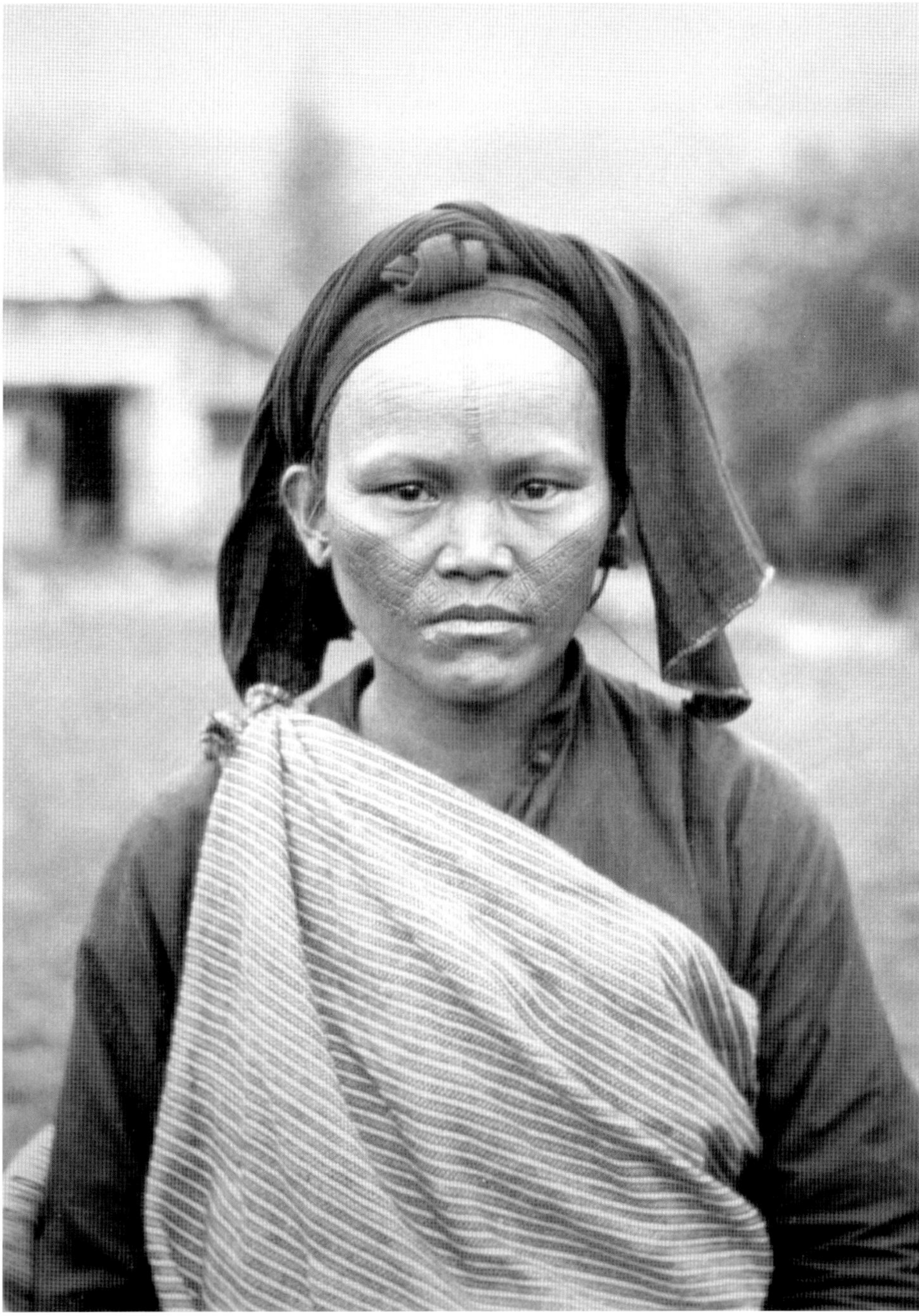

Atayal woman with facial tattooing, ca. 1900. After Ryuzo (1990: pl. 50). Courtesy of the University Museum, The University of Tokyo. This woman's extensive tattooing denotes her prowess as an expert weaver.

toothbrush with four to sixteen needles (*atok*) arranged in rows and fastened to a wooden handle about 1.5cm in diameter and 15cm in length.[27] Before iron was introduced to the indigenous Atayal, thorns of orange or tangerine trees were used. The hammer, which pounded the tattoo instrument into the skin, was called *totsin* and was constructed of a single piece of wood about 2.5cm in diameter and approximately 17cm in length. Excess blood was removed with a scraper (*quwar*) made from a rattan splint that was bent and bound at either end with linen thread. Lampblack (*ihoh*) was used as pigment but occasionally soot from charred pinewood resin was collected, to be stored in a gourd or small iron case.

Tattooing operations were almost always performed in a small hut located away from the living quarters. Most tattooing took place in winter, since the cold weather was believed to facilitate the healing of the tattoos and prevent scabbing. Interestingly, the Atayal linked suppuration to the lack of virtue of the client.[28]

The tattoo client lay down with a folded cloth under her head. The tattoo artist usually sat on a low stool behind her or stood hunched over the patient with her tool. She took the needle instrument and knocked it home with several forceful blows of her hammer and scraped the blood-stained face with the *quwar*. Oftentimes a block of wood was held in the tattoo artist's hand, and with this the tattooing implement was struck after it had been laid upon the area of application. Of course, this action ensured a stronger blow and one more accurately placed upon the forehead.[29] Afterwards the tattooist washed the hammered area and rubbed it with black soot.

The client prepared herself for the rite by observing various taboos before the operation including: no sexual relations, no imbibing of any animal blood, and especially no wearing of red-colored clothing, since this was believed to cause her blood to flow unabated. The parents of the client chose a favorable day for the tattooing by dream divination, and on that particular day they observed various bird-omens and offered sacrifices to the spirits of their ancestors for a safe and successful operation.[30]

Familiar spirits

In the Atayal tradition, the spirits of the ancestors (*rutux* or *kutux*) were believed to guide all of their descendants in their daily affairs. Most ancestral commands came to family members through dreams, and those descendants who strictly followed their ancestors' orders were given glory in war, health in life, and fertility in agriculture.[31]

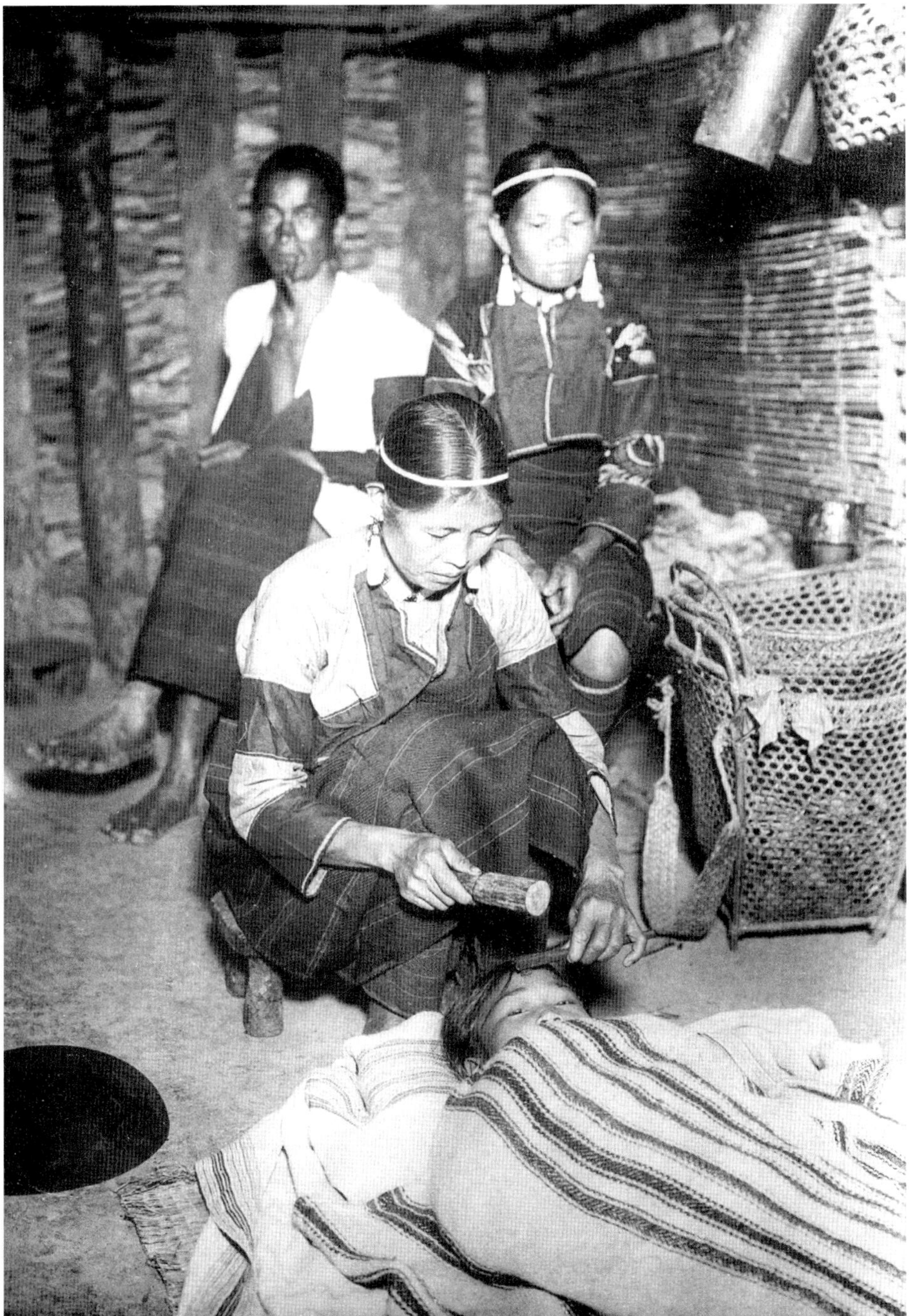

Atayal tattooist at work, ca. 1930. Postcard from the collection of the author.

Paiwan tattoo artists

Men and women's tattoo marks differed according to the social status of the wearer and tattooing was generally a privilege of the Paiwan nobility, but a commoner could purchase the right from a "big chief."[32]

Paiwan tattooists were mostly professional women who inherited the occupation through the family line. Each village had one or two artists, but most were aristocrats by birth and at the same time shamans.[33] Paiwan tattoo artists received payment from all clients, except members of the ruling chief's family. The amount of reward differed according to the complexity of the design chosen. For example, the cost for tattooing a man's chest, back, and

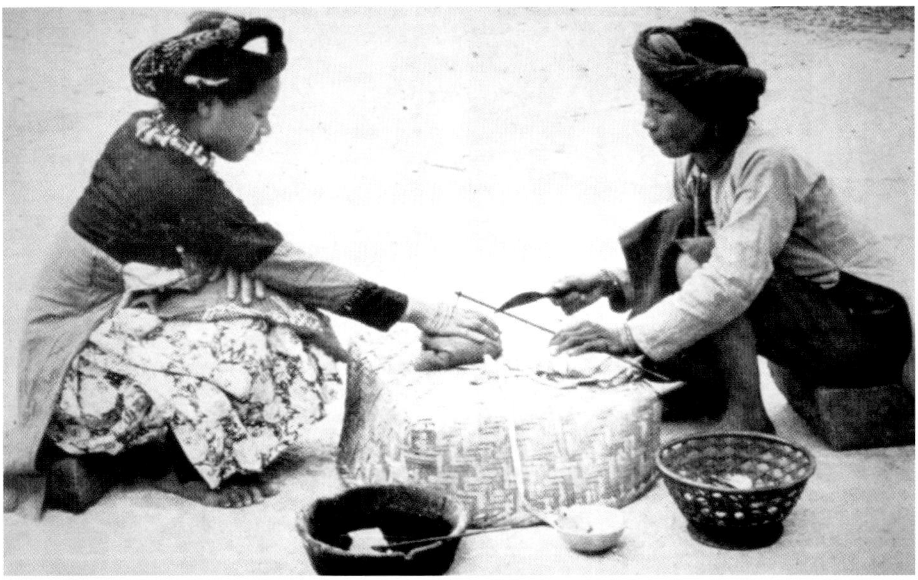

Paiwan tattoo artist at work. After Ho (1960: pl. 7). Photograph courtesy of John T.J. Ho.

both arms was high: one pig, two iron rakes, four waist knives, one axe, one roll of cloth, one porcelain bowl, and a bottle of wine.[34]

Paiwan tattoo artists used bamboo splints or grass stems as rulers, and the back of a knife covered with soot as a pencil to draft the desired motifs. Tattoo needles were made by binding a pair of steel needles with linen thread on a bamboo stick about 40cm in length. The needles were again wrapped with linen thread, and only about 2-3mm of the point could be seen. A small knife was used to tap the needles with soot pigment into the skin, and the handle of this instrument was also used to scrape away excess blood. Before the introduction of steel needles, the Paiwan, like the Atayal, used thorns of the mountain orange as a tattoo needle.[35]

According to Chi-Lu[36] and Ho,[37] most Paiwan men and women were tattooed in the winter. The ritual operation was performed in a small hut specifically built for the purpose. To prevent intruders, a bamboo stick was erected in front of the hut. The client usually reclined during the operation, but women who were to receive hand tattoos sat upright. Tattooing proceeded according to a certain order, usually the hands first, and the chest (for men) last. Each unit of the design was punctured repeatedly, up to three or four times.

Prior to the operation, the tattoo client had to present the ruling chief with ceremonial beverages: for it was the chief who decided the appropriate day of the tattooing. Offerings were made to the spirits of the ancestors and various taboos were observed. During the operation, the tattooist spat betel nut juice on the tattooed area to stop excessive bleeding.

Paiwan women tattooed their arms, the backs of their hands, their knees, and the calves. The designs consisted mainly of lines or dots. Paiwan men tattooed the chest, arms, knees, and calves. Sometimes the motifs were realistic consisting of human heads, human figures, snake or sun designs.[38] Serpent designs, especially that of the "hundred-pace viper," are especially significant and recount mythological origins. The hundred-pace viper "is the spirit of life, the greatest of all the spirits" and represents the guardian spirit of all Paiwan.[39]

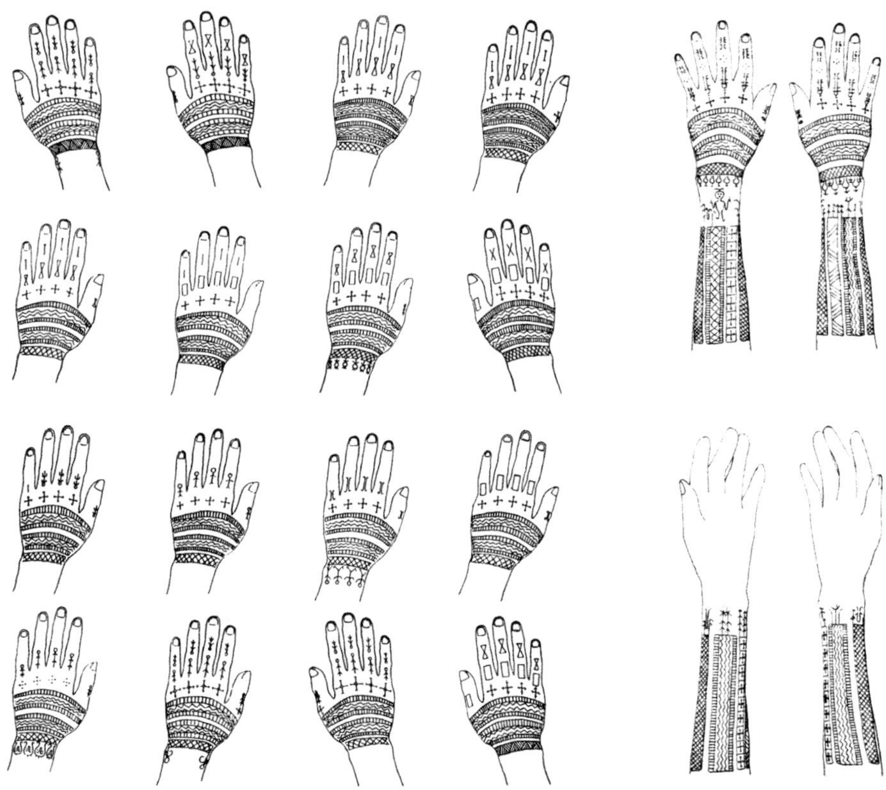

Paiwan women's arm and hand tattoos. After Ho (1960: pls. 3, 4). Drawings courtesy of John T.J. Ho.

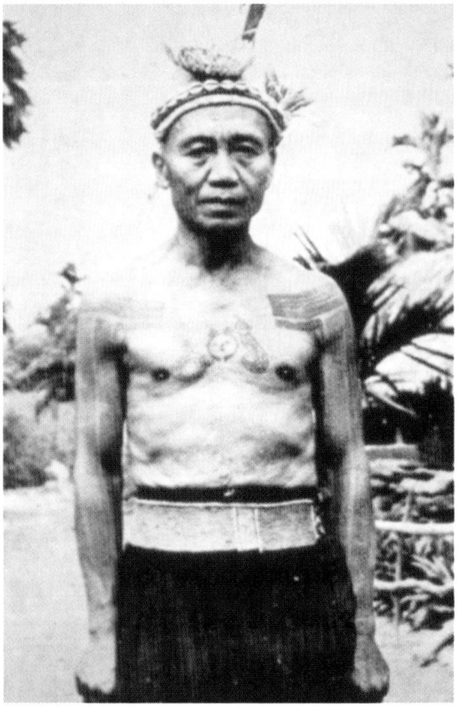

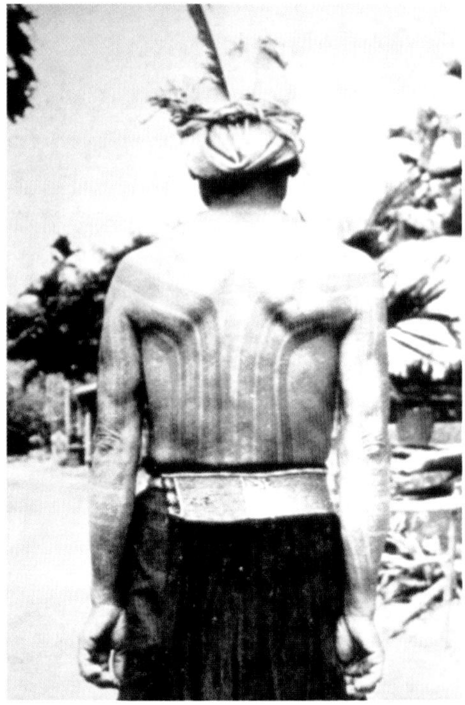

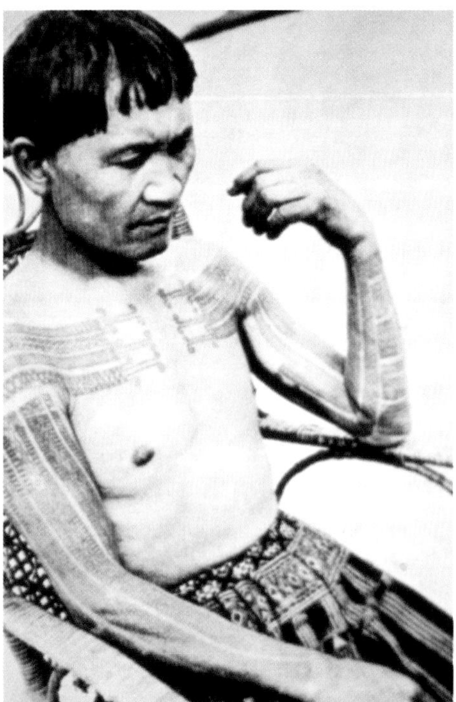

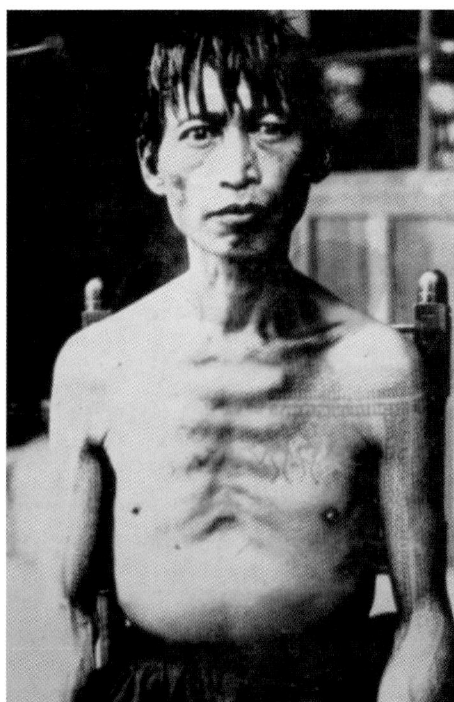

All of the descendants of an ancestor were grouped together in a religio-economic social institution called *gaya*. Within the *gaya*, family members worked together in common ritual and labor to procure the favor of their ancestors. However, it was commonly held that the unity and harmony of the *gaya* could be jeopardized when only one of its members offended an ancestors' command, such as abstaining from weaving while warriors were away on the headhunt.[40]

Ancestral commands sometimes manifested themselves in the form of bird omens. Bird omens were consulted prior to most ceremonial occasions and especially before a hunting or war/headhunting campaign.[41] The efficacy of a bird omen lay in the fact that particular birds were in communication with the spirits of ancestors who, in turn, guided the pursuits of their descendants (*gaya*). The anthropologist Janet McGovern, who spent two years in Taiwan during 1916 and 1918, noted that it was the responsibility of the Atayal priestesses to read the omens and guide their people:

> All groups of Taiyal hold sacred the small bird . . . whose cry is regarded as an omen of good or evil, according to the note, and followed accordingly. The flight of this bird is also noted when starting on either a hunting expedition or one of warfare (head-hunting) . . . the tribes-people seem to regard it as the spokesman of some ancestor—one who was in his day a famous warrior, and who thus, through the medium of the bird, continues to guide his descendants, and all members of the tribal group to which during his lifetime he had belonged. Sometimes it is the spirit of a priestess which is supposed thus to contribute to guide and guard her people.[42]

Atayal priestesses were the spiritual leaders of their communities. The position was not a hereditary one; rather it was an elected office with the community choosing those women who were particularly successful in driving away evil spirits or in interpreting omens that lead to successful headhunting expeditions.[43] Priestesses also led prayer sessions to honor, propitiate, and "feed" the spirits of the ancestors at seasonal ceremonies, especially on the nights of the full moon at seeding time and later at the millet harvest.

Facing page: Paiwan men's tattoos. After Ho (1960: pl. 10). Photographs courtesy of John T.J. Ho. Note the hundred-pace viper or "guardian spirit" tattoos at top left (chest). The hundred-pace viper motif can also be seen zigzagging between the horizontal bars tattooed on the arms or hands of Paiwan men and women. The anthropomorphic tattoos (chest) at bottom right indicate the warrior's headhunting victims.

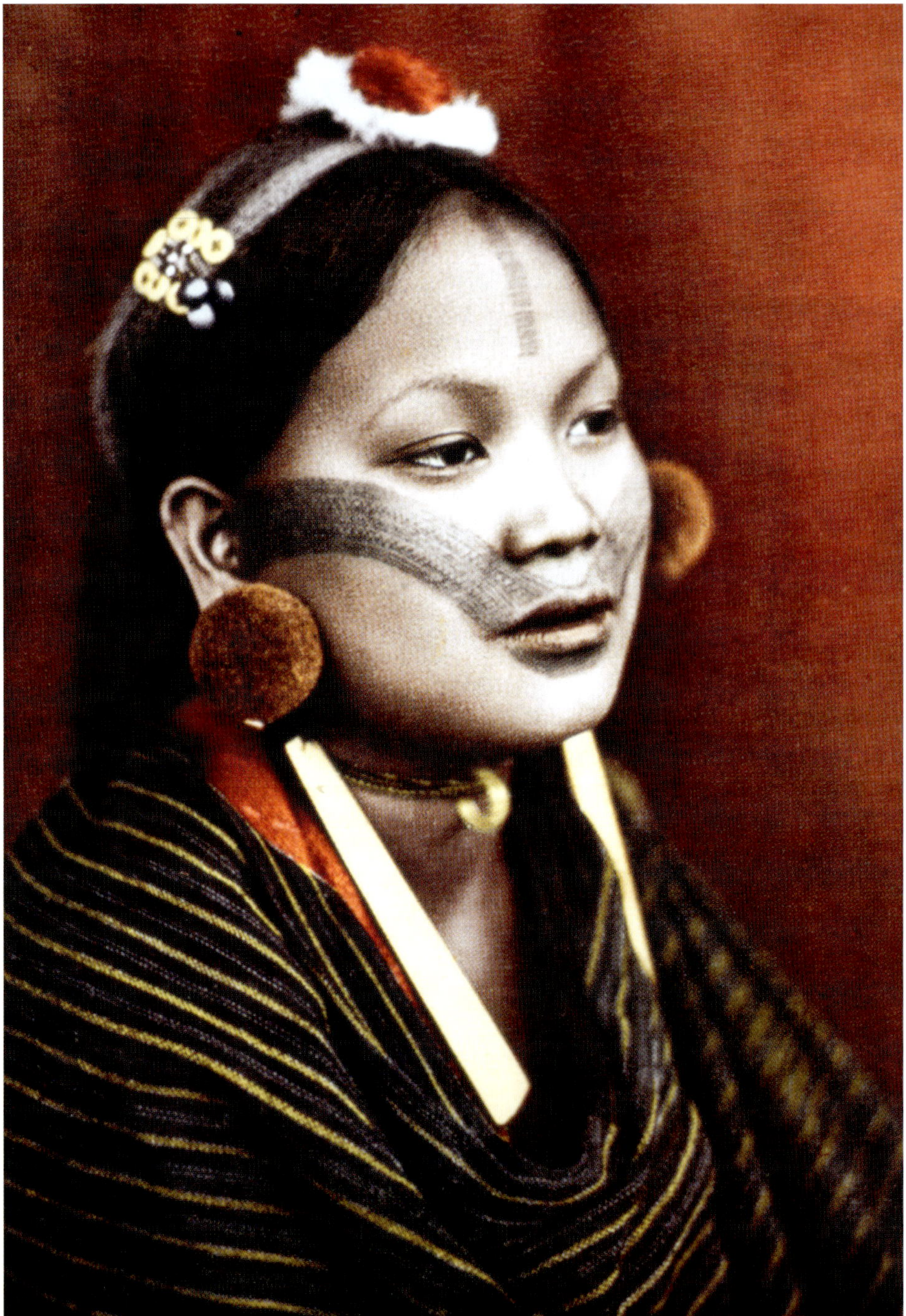

Atayal woman, ca. 1930. Postcard from the collection of the author.

Father Candidius, writing before 1630, also witnessed the practices of priestesses and recorded them in graphic detail:

> All other nations that I have ever known have male priests, popes, or teachers, who instruct the people and are priests of their gods; but this nation has only priestesses, whom they call *Inibs*. The public service these *Inibs* perform in a religious capacity is twofold; calling upon their gods and bringing sacrifices to them, which sacrifices are chiefly offered in their temples, and consist of slaughtered pigs, cooked rice, pinnang [areca nut], and a great quantity of their beverage [*owao*], as also the heads of stags and swine.
>
> After offering sacrifice, one or two of the priestesses generally arise and call upon the gods in a long sermon or address. While so doing, these prophetesses roll their eyes, fall down upon the ground, and scream most hideously; then their gods appear to them. The priestesses lie like corpses upon the ground, and cannot be raised from it, even by five or six persons. When at last they recover consciousness, they tremble and shiver as if in extreme distress, which is a sign that the gods upon whom they called have really made their appearance. In the meantime the people who surround them do nothing but cry and weep. I have been witness of this ceremony, but have never seen any of their gods nor been able to find out what the prophetesses had seen. After this ceremony has lasted an hour, the prophetesses climb on the roof of the temple, stand each on a corner, and again make long speeches or orations to their gods. At last they take off their garments, and appear to their gods in their nakedness, strike their naked bodies with their hands, cause water to be brought, and wash their entire bodies, now perfectly naked, in presence of all the people; but the greater part of the bystanders are women; who, however, are so intoxicated that they can hardly stand. Never have I seen their gods or any apparitions appear. This service or ceremony is public, and takes place in their temples.
>
> . . . It is the office of these *Inibs* to prophesy good or evil, whether it will be rain, or whether fine and beautiful weather may be expected. They judge concerning unclean places, and banish evil spirits or devils; for, as they say, many evil spirits or devils dwell amongst the people, and these spirits the *Inibs* banish with much noise and clamour. They also carry hatchets in their hands, and chase the devil till he jumps into the water and is drowned.[44]

Dayaks of Borneo

Borneo—for many outsiders the name has been synonymous with a forbidding and isolated wilderness, a steamy rain-soaked place, dangerous and

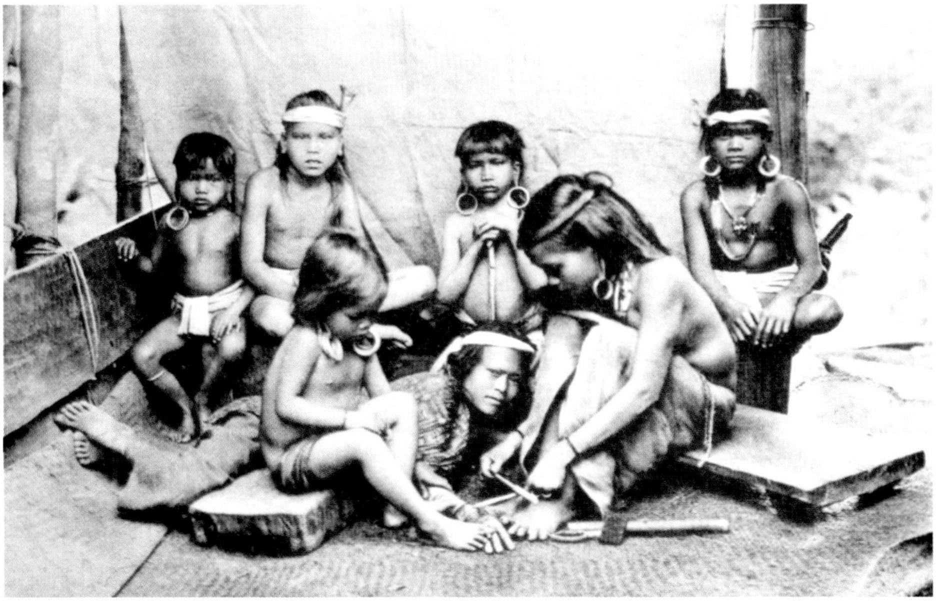

Kayan girls of Borneo hand-tapping tattoo in the traditional method, ca. 1896. After Nieuwenhuis (1904: pl. 77). All Kayan tattooists were female. They worked under the spiritual guidance of their tutelary and protective patron, Bua Kalung, who was propitiated with blood sacrifices before each tattoo operation. In some cases, Kayan shamans, who were usually women, encouraged their sick female patients to become tattoo artists, because the omnipotent Bua Kalung offered spiritual protection and good health to all of her disciples (Hose and Shelford 1906: 68).

forlorn. While it was among the first lands in Asia to be visited by Europeans, it remained among the last to be mapped.[45]

Borneo is the third largest island in the world. Six major, and numerous minor, navigable rivers traverse the interior and function as trade and communication routes for the indigenous peoples who live here, namely the Dayak.[46] Dayak, meaning "interior" or "inland" person, is the term used to describe the variety of indigenous native tribes of Borneo,[47] each of which has its own language and separate culture. Approximately three million Dayak—Ibans, Kayans, Kenyahs, Kelabits and others—live in Borneo.[48] Most groups cultivate rice in shifting or rain-fed fields supplementing their incomes with the sale of cash crops: ginger, pepper, cocoa, and palm oil.[49] However several hundred nomadic hunter-gatherers, the Penan, continue to follow a traditional subsistence lifestyle in the jungle, one that is rapidly vanishing.

Aside from a few scattered reports of missionaries, traders, and a handful of explorers, little accurate ethnographic research focusing on the Dayak had been conducted by the mid-1800s. This can be attributed partially to

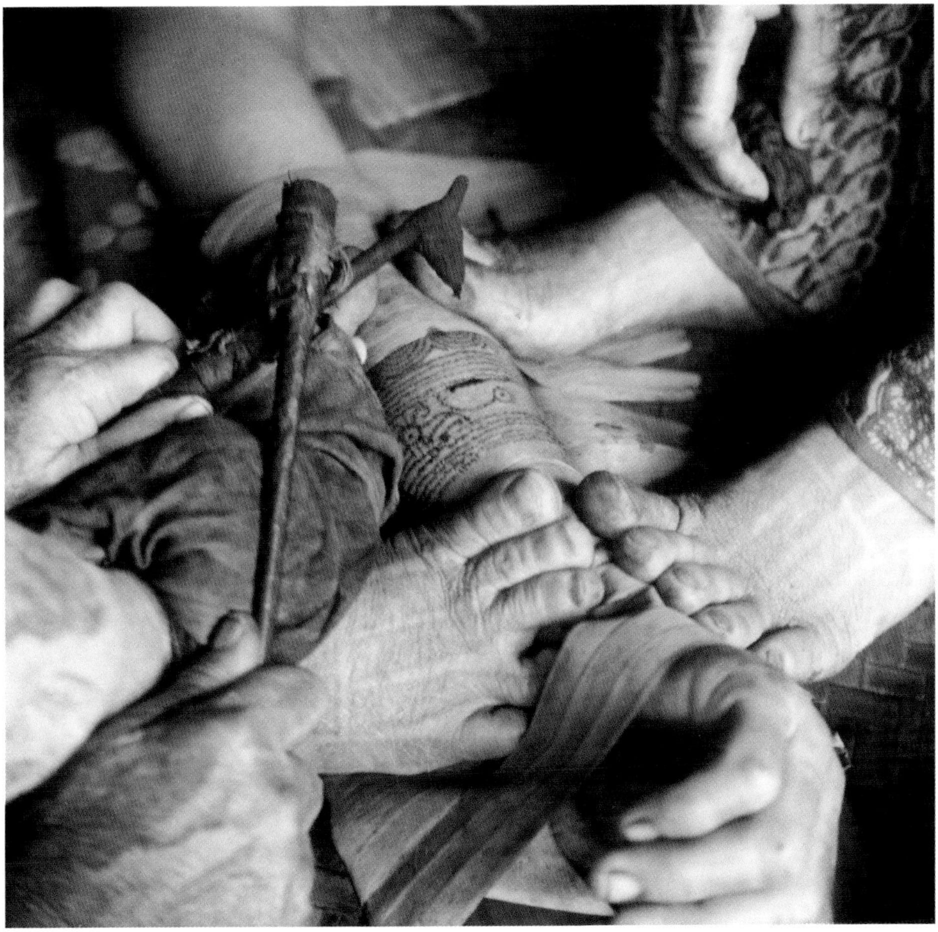

Close-up of traditional Kayan tattooing, 1951. Courtesy of the Sarawak Museum Archives.

the reputation of some indigenous groups, like the Iban, whose exploits in the headhunt incited fear in many Europeans as well as other indigenous groups inhabiting Borneo.[50]

By the 1890s, however, a more systematic anthropological approach to field study was initiated and the island became the focus of several museum expeditions by the Dutch and British. With the many ethnological accounts that followed, some of the most interesting material that was generated at this time focused upon the traditional tattooing practices of the Dayak, particularly the Iban and Kayan. Tattooing was believed to be a sacred activity that was connected to many aspects of traditional Dayak culture, especially spirit worship and headhunting.[51]

Spirits, gods, ancestors, and the circle of life

Among the Dayak, all life—whether animal, vegetable, or human—is believed to be endowed with a spiritual aspect.[52] Spirits living in the rainforest must always be propitiated and never offended. Even when an individual wishes to urinate, he or she must first ask the spirits living there in order to give them an opportunity to move, because no one knows which tree or bush is somebody's house.[53] Iban spirits (*antu*), both good and bad, exercise many powers; they provide the techniques of rice cultivation, the techniques of textile weaving, and the techniques of tattooing.[54] Spirits usually come to individuals through dreams and even tattoo artists are under the protection of a particular spirit.[55] Dreams are revelations sent by the gods, sometimes by deified ancestors, and all Dayak are guided by them in their daily affairs.[56]

The spiritual cosmos of the Dayak is a place filled with spiritual energies that charge with life-power most existing beings and things. This realm, removed from secular time and the laws of this world, is the abode of gods and ancestors who grant privileges to those who maintain the proper balance of life throughout all of its stages.[57]

The Dayak, living their lives in strict moral accordance to the divine norms and commandments by which the gods and ancestors had lived theirs, relied upon human sacrifice to propitiate the good will of their masters. Headhunting, the ritual component, served to maintain the prosperity of the group by ensuring agricultural and community fertility.[58] The taking of fresh heads also ended periods of mourning, affirmed the prestige of particular chiefs, and enhanced the standing of communities in relation to others.

In the eyes of the gods and ancestors, the taking of fresh heads was not only pleasing; it was duly rewarded with many gifts. For example, the divine indicated locations in the forest where fields should be cleared and planted; they protected the rice fields against crop failure; they lent their diagnosis in illness; and they accompanied men in war or on the headhunt to insure success. Headhunting was therefore an institution believed to maintain balance and harmony in the cosmos and oftentimes a man's status was not established until he had proven success in headhunting itself.[59] This proof usually came in the form of a severed head that would come to hang from the rafters of the longhouse, and later, from the completed tattoos that were lasting symbols of his success in the human hunt.

The most important symbol marking participation in the headhunt was tattoo (Iban, *pantang*; Kayan, *tedek*). Among the Iban and Kayan fine tattoos, sometimes anthropomorphic, were tattooed onto the finger digits and were known as *tegulun*.[60] Although they denoted having taken one or more heads, *tegulun* possibly represented a sacrifice to a helper spirit that in former times was propitiated by killing a slave upon the construction of a new longhouse.[61] Similar anthropomorphs, termed *engkeramba'*, were carved on house posts to repel evil from the longhouse; but they also appear in women's woven textiles and hand-crafted beaded objects, in addition to shaman's baskets.[62] According to Haddon, the Kayan carved a monumental pole called *tegulan* in front of the longhouse facing the river which "keeps off sickness from people, and by means of this image you can either curse a man or prevent him from cursing you."[63]

Other headhunters' tattoos included fantastic motifs that covered the entire surface of a man's body. For example, an elder Dayak man photographed in 1896 and depicted here (see page 75) possesses a

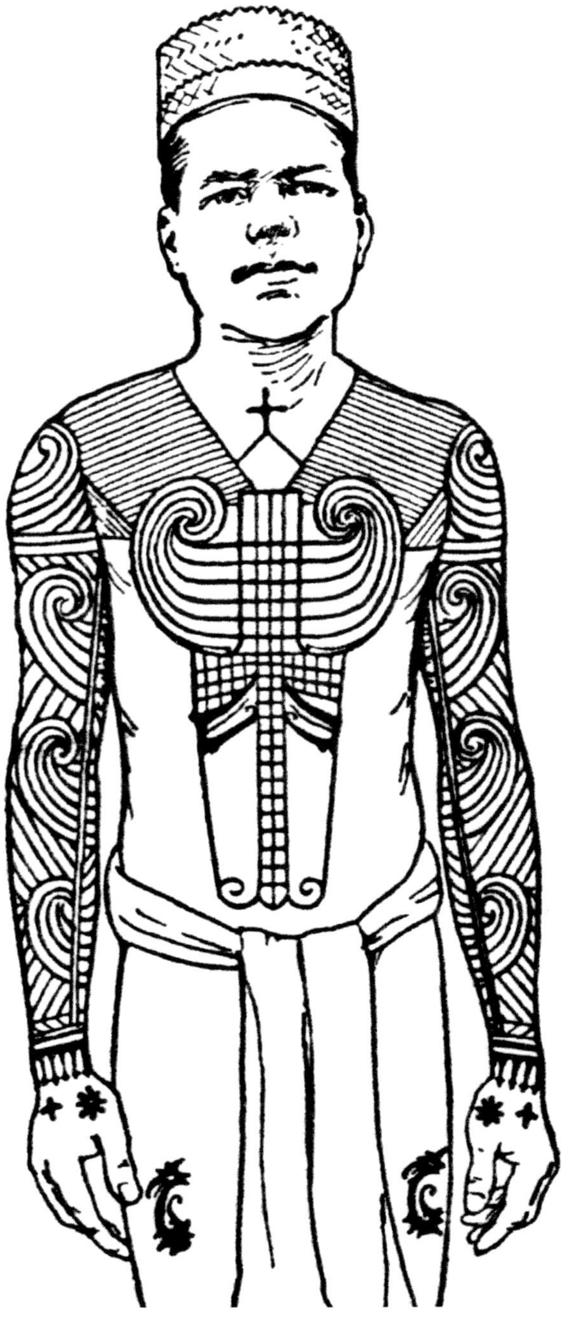

Dayak man of the lower Katingan River with intricate tattooing, ca. 1920. Redrawn after Lumholtz (1921).

tattoo style no longer seen today. The central motif on his chest represents the trunk of the Garing tree; adjoining it above are two outstretched wings of the hornbill; and finally the tattooing that appears down the arms and over the shoulders represents the leaves of the areca palm.[64]

Garing trees were believed to be immortal and invulnerable[65] and areca leaves were used in curing rites by Iban shamans to repel evil spirits.[66] The hornbill, marking rank and prestige, was believed to provide protection against the intrusion of evil spirits living in the jungle. Interestingly, figures of the hornbill (Iban, *tenyalang*) were often carved and propitiated with sacrifices of pigs and human heads before they were mounted on display poles.[67] The spirit of the figure was thought to leave its wooden body, fly to the longhouse of the enemy, and weaken the spirit of the headhunters living there.[68] Kayan warriors wore hornbill feathers in their war hats, an honor bestowed only on those men who had previously taken heads.[69]

Thus, Dayak men of this time were tattooed with a symbolic canopy of the plants and animals that lived within their jungle domain. However, and when combined together, these markings worked as an indelible form of camouflage acting upon the malevolent forces encountered in the jungle—namely enemy headhunters and evil spirits.[70] But at the same time, the tattooed integument was worn as a garment of power, one that exuded so much magical efficacy that it physically and psychologically transformed the perceived self-identity of its owner.

Iban

Just as a great Iban warrior was tattooed to mark his achievements in headhunting, Iban women were tattooed as proof of their accomplishments in weaving ceremonial fabrics.[71] Although many Iban women were accomplished weavers, gaining prestige and enhanced status through their labor-intensive work, only a few were truly "experts," able to produce the *pua kumbu'* blanket that contained the most powerful and intricate designs and colors.

The most important of Iban fabrics was the ritual blanket or *pua kumbu'*.

Facing page: Dayak man of the Kahajan River with a virtual "canopy" of the jungle tattooed on his skin, ca. 1896. After Nieuwenhuis (1904: pl. 81). Many of the origin myths surrounding tattoo in Borneo (e.g. Kayan and Iban) are nearly equivalent to others told among indigenous groups living in the northern Philippines and Hainan Island, China. In each of these tales, one or two particular species of bird created tattooing for the indigenous peoples of the area to appropriate for their own use (Hose and Shelford 1906: 65; Ganjing 2001: 12-14; Jenks 1905: 224-225; Nieuwenhuis 1904, I: 456; Salvador 2004: 5; Stübel 1937: 35).

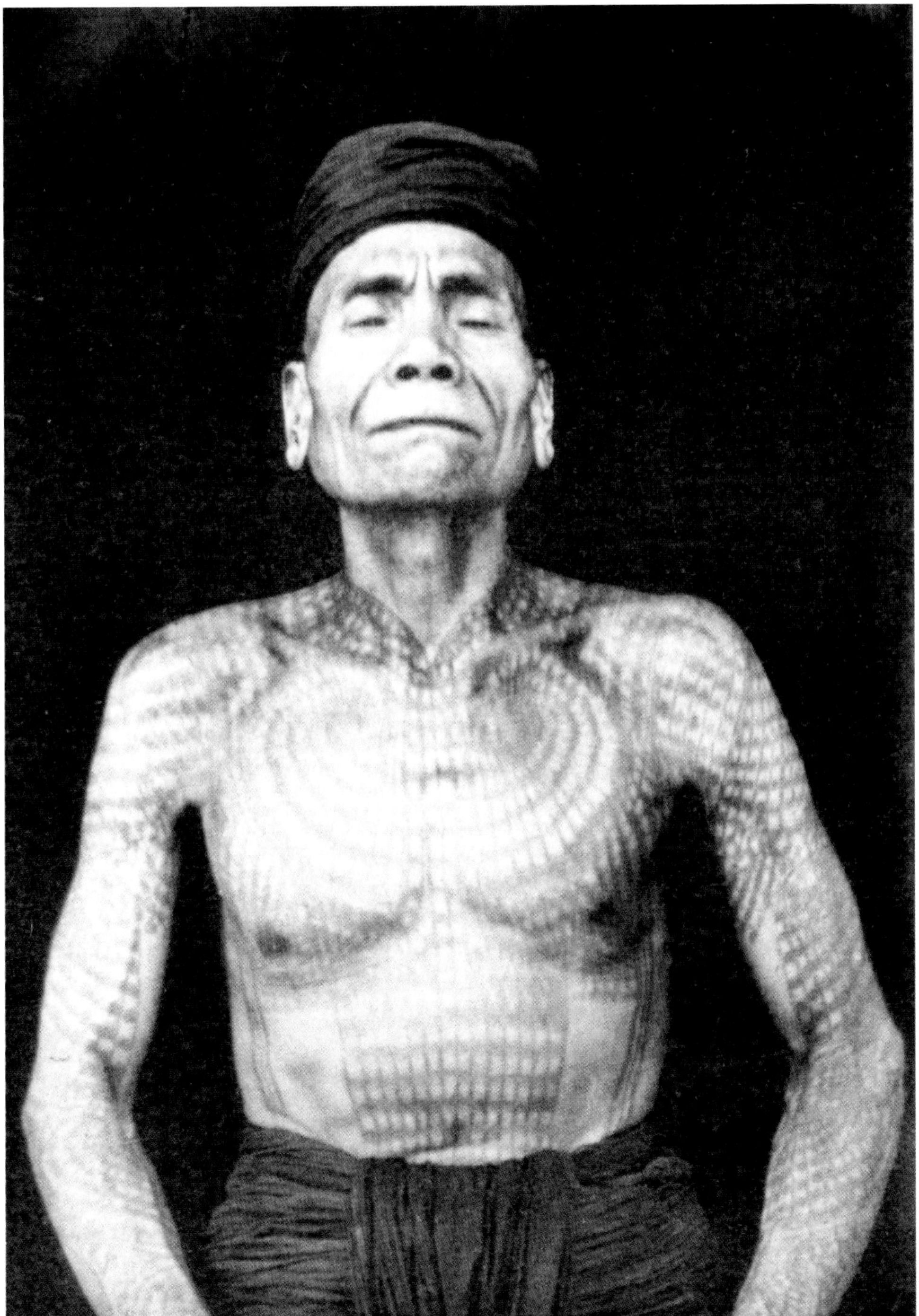

Puas had several uses, the most significant being to receive the freshly severed human heads captured by Iban warriors on the headhunt.[72] Iban shamans or *manang* and warriors also used *puas* to create sacred enclosures. They sat under the fabrics to wait for the arrival of their spirit helpers called *petara* for guidance and success.[73] *Petara* were summoned before wars, headhunts, and healing ceremonies since it was "futile to attempt any operation of importance without the assurance that *Petara* sanctions it . . . this approval can only be ascertained by the messages that [are conveyed] through omens."[74]

The entire process of crafting a *pua* required great mastery and patience not to mention ritual knowledge and actions, including the sacrifice of a pig or chicken whose blood appeased the spirits.[75] Each woven design was vested with its own meaning and spiritual energy and weavers were compelled to follow a type of ritual etiquette when conducting their work to avoid personal or collective disaster.[76] If a weaver created a *pua* with anthropomorphic "spirit figures" (*engkaramba*) in the central panel, these had to be carefully "fenced-in" with protective centipede (*kemebai*) bands and strong top, bottom, and side designs.[77] Otherwise, the spirits might break loose from the cloth and cause disharmony and misfortune in the longhouse. Haddon clearly noted the Iban's "psychic attitude" towards textile production in the following statement:

> The designs and patterns on the cloths clearly indicate this psychic attitude towards everyday life. They might be regarded in some cases as being protective, to ward off dangers of various kinds, in others as being a means to obtain blessings and good fortune. Thus they express a constant reliance upon supernormal power, and it is probably no exaggeration to say that these attractive people are literally clothed with prayers.[78]

Like Iban tattoo artists, weavers employed the use of many protective charms in their work, usually small sacred stones, porcupine quills, or even meteorites.[79] Generally speaking, the locations of these objects were revealed to weavers by their ancestors in dreams. Weavers also fortified themselves against evil spirits by biting on pieces of steel to strengthen their souls.[80] Furthermore, they communicated with spirit helpers (*antu nulong*) in their dreams to prevent irritating spirits that were to be represented in a new weaving[81] and to advance their "psychic strength," especially if the *pua* was related to headhunting.[82] These supernatural communications also

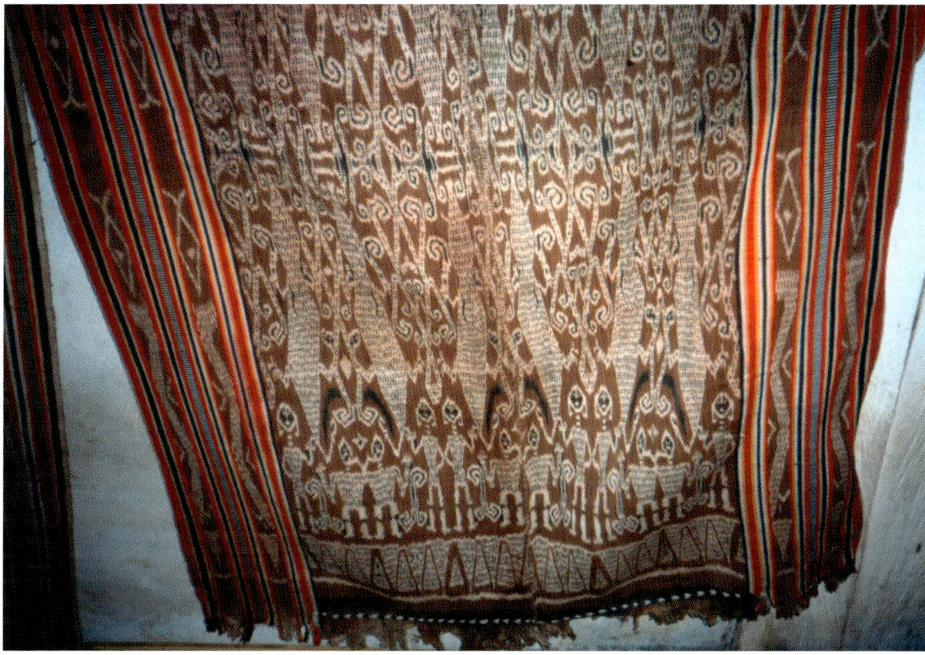

Skrang River *pua kumbu'*, 2002. Photograph by Lars Krutak. Woven by a master some 100 years ago, this *pua* is considered to have a life of its own. Although water-damaged from numerous floods, the design motifs are bold in their abstraction and show a headhunting scene: spirit figures holding skulls (near bottom), crocodiles, water serpents (side border), and centipedes (bottom) dominate the pattern. Some of these creatures were believed to repel evil spirits and were worn as tattoo designs on both men and women. The mixing of the blood-red dye used in *pua* production was difficult in itself, and perhaps only one in fifty women knew the procedure (Howell 1912: 63). For this, the dyer was paid a small jar, a sacred stone, a small bell, and a brass ring. Expert weavers worked under the protection and direction of several Iban female deities (Howell 1912: 63).

protected weavers from spirits attracted to the blood-red dye used in their *pua* creations which was nearly equivalent to human blood.

Obviously, *pua* weaving was a hazardous physical and spiritual undertaking. And for this reason it was considered complimentary to headhunting; especially since weavers of high repute played important roles in the ceremonies for receiving the fresh heads which were enveloped in their spiritually-charged *puas* after arrival at the longhouse. In this way, expert weavers not only participated metaphorically in "war," they also gained prestige and enhanced status for their spiritually charged works: not to mention attention from bachelors living in the longhouse community.[83]

Weavers, and women in general, had a vested interest in encouraging headhunting, since the fortunes of their husbands directly affected their own future and community status. An extreme example of the Iban women's penchant for heads was recorded in a 1909 contribution to the *Sarawak Gazette*:

> The women, in their cruel and bloodthirstiness are the cause of this head-hunting. At every festival the old skulls are taken from the fire place, where they are preserved and smoked from generation to generation, and carried through the house by some women. A monotonous song is sung by the women in honour of the hero who cut off the head, and in derision of the poor victims whose skulls are carried around; and again and again the infernal chorus is heard, '*agi ngambi, agi ngambi*' (bring us more of them).[84]

On a similar note, the Iban believed that some textile designs even had the power to incite (*merangsang*) men to go on the warpath: "The pattern of the iron hook is crying, weeping and softly pleading, proudly demanding the ribs and both flank for bait."[85] Interestingly, the hook was widely used throughout Borneo as a tattooing motif, and recently I have seen such designs tattooed on the legs of Iban men. Among the Bakatan and Ukit of Borneo, women wore tattooed hook (*gerowit*) designs on their metacarpals and forearms,[86] and Bakatan men wore elaborate hook tattoos on their chests.

Haddon, traveling in Kayan country in 1899, noted that "[w]ooden hooks (*kawit*) are hung up near the skulls, with the idea that they will help the head-hunters to obtain more skulls on their forays. It is an example of sympathetic magic, the object of the wooden hooks being to hook in fresh heads."[87] On another occasion, Haddon sought to purchase hook-like stones which were held in very high esteem by the locals: "but these he could not by no means be persuaded to sell, as he gave us to understand that they, as it were, hooked his soul to his body, and thus prevented the spiritual portion of him from becoming detached from the material."[88]

Notwithstanding, the Iban called *pua* weaving "women's war" (*kayau indu'*) and women who excelled in this work were both socially and ritually marked—like headhunters—with small tattoos on the fingers or with others that covered the thumbs. However, master weavers, or those who possessed the highest power, were afforded another form of tattoo which

Facing page: 80-year-old Iban woman of the Skrang River with *pala tumpa'* tattoos, 2002. Photograph by Lars Krutak. The words *pala tumpa'*, meaning "head of bracelets," refer to the traditional Iban practice of women wearing bangle bracelets from the wrists to the elbows (Krutak 2006b).

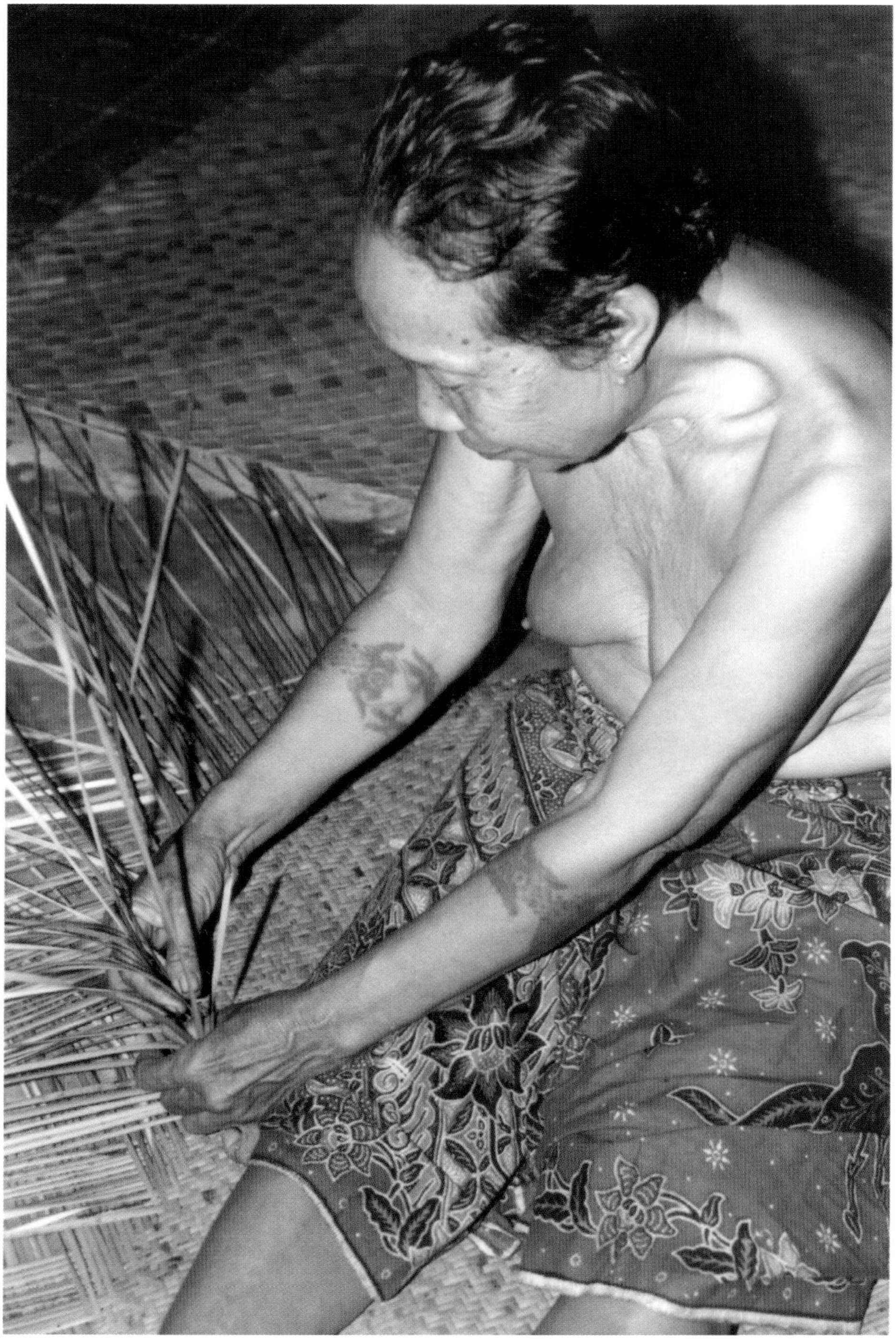

specifically conveyed spiritual protection to its owner: the *pala tumpa'* or "head of bracelets" tattoo.

Although extremely rare today, *pala tumpa'* is both tattoo and sometimes heirloom, passed from mother to daughter.[89] The tattoo takes its name from the position on the body where it is placed: usually on the forearm where successive rows of traditional bracelets are worn. The motifs that dominate *pala tumpa'* are the scorpion (*kala*) and centipede (*kemebai*), and each is considered a protective or apotropaic symbol—as they are among other indigenous peoples of Indonesia, Papua New Guinea, the Philippines, and Polynesia.[90]

However, with changing lifestyles and

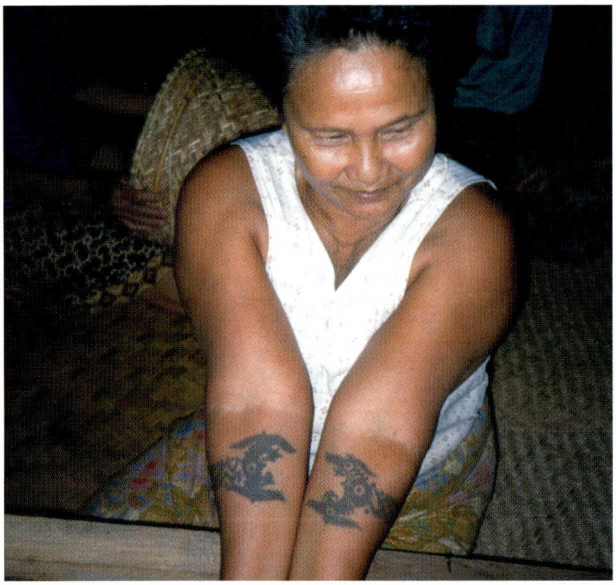

65-year-old Iban woman of the Skrang River with *pala tumpa'* tattoos, 2002. Photographs by Lars Krutak. The pincher-like motif that terminates at the mid-forearm is *kala* or scorpion. The zigzagging band that circles the arm is the *kemebai* or centipede. Both are protective symbols widely used in Iban art.

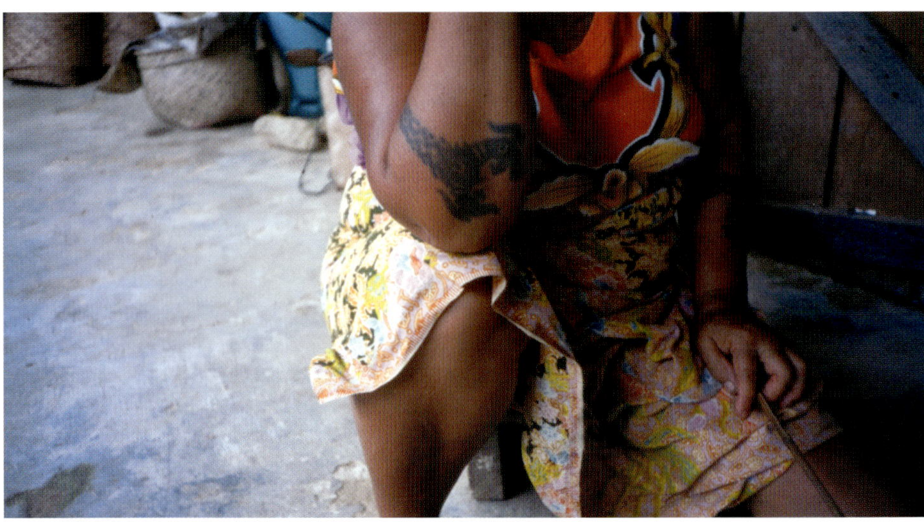

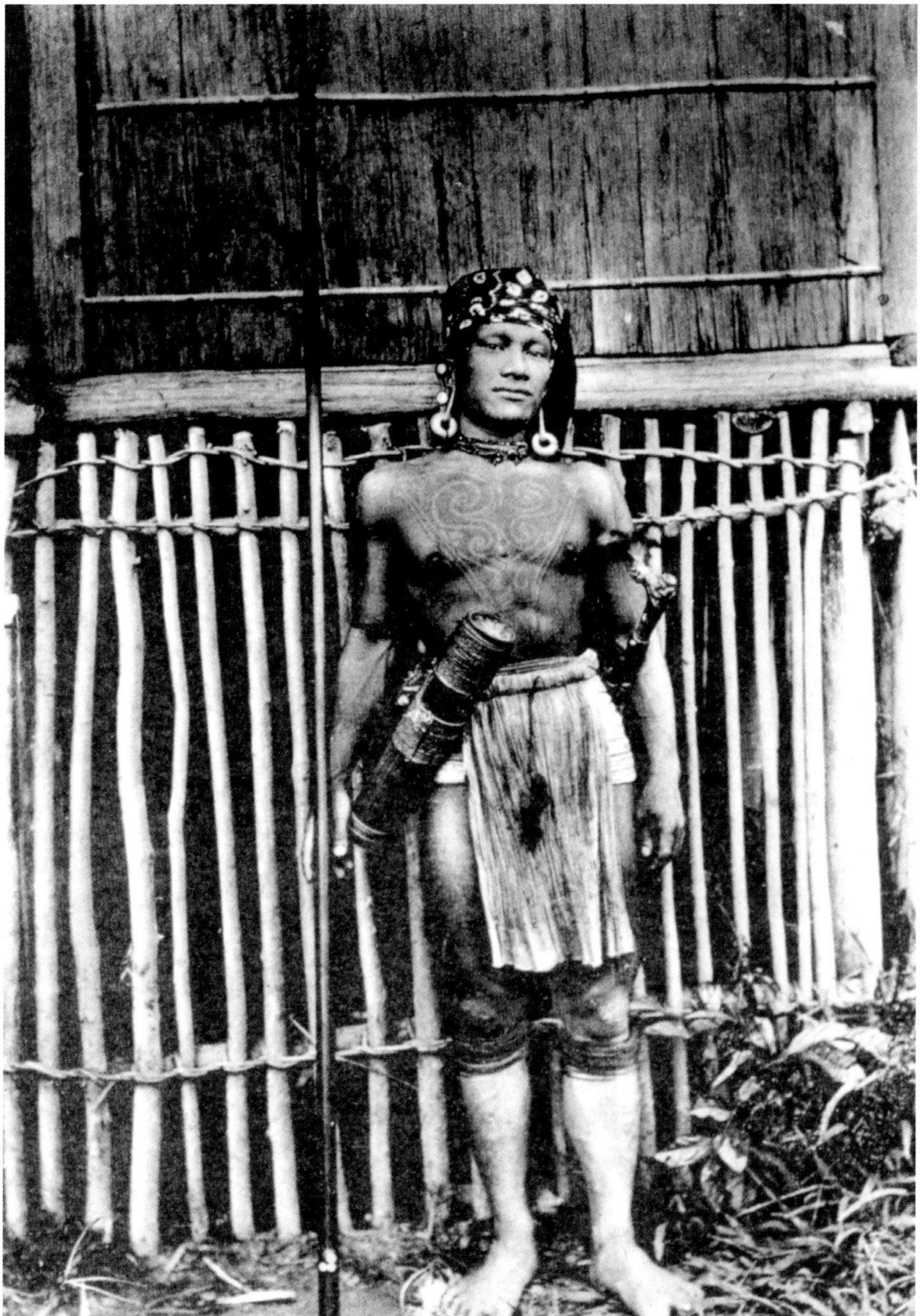

Bakatan warrior with elaborate *gerowit* chest tattoos standing with blow gun. Ukit men wore similar designs. After Nieuwenhuis (1904: pl. 80).

values, the most powerful *puas* and tattoos associated with weaving have become obsolete. Modern day weavers are converting to commercial ready-dyed yarns and tourist motifs, and *pala tumpa'* tattoos are now only worn on the arms of the few elderly experts. Sadly, "women's war" and the tattoos associated with it are being invaded by changing times.

Orang Ulu of the Rejang River

The Kayan, Sihan, and Lahanan are three of numerous other Dayak groups of central Sarawak (Malaysian Borneo) living on or near the Rejang River. Together all of these tribes are called Orang Ulu or "upriver people" and most of them tattooed. Unlike Iban tattooing which was done by male artists, Orang Ulu tattooists—whether working for male or female clients—were strictly women.[91]

Orang Ulu tattoo is stunning in its simplicity yet powerful in its abstraction, and, until recently, it has remained relatively unrecognized from an artistic standpoint. But for the small group of talented female artisans who plied the human skin, tattooing was a form of spiritual artistry. Their tattoo kits consisted of natural objects—wood, thorns, grass fibers and pigments—that came from the jungle, a place where all things, animate and inanimate, have a life and spiritual energy of their own.

Kayan

At the turn of the 20th century, the tattooing of a Kayan girl was a serious operation, not only because of the considerable amount of pain caused, but

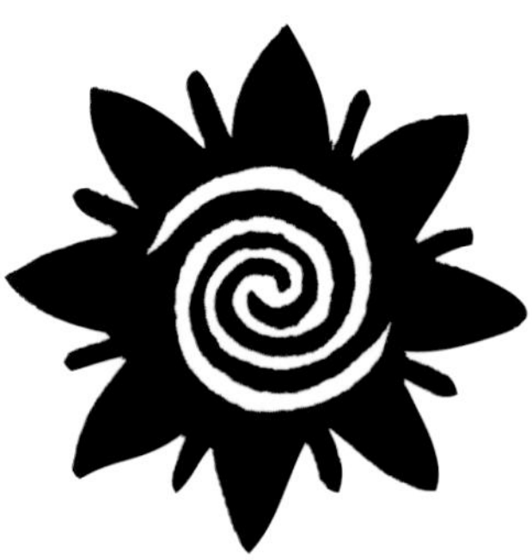

Kenyah rosette pattern. After Hose and McDougall (1912: pl. 140). Rosettes like this are worn on either shoulder by many elderly Dayak men today. Among the Iban, the center swirl represents the underbelly of the tadpole (NHNZ 2004), and frogs are believed to be the earthly manifestation of the Iban creator god Selempandai who is the "maker of men" (Richards 1997: 332). Stylized designs of frogs were woven by high ranking Iban women into *kalambi gajai* jackets and it is said that the croaking sound of the frog represents "the spirit's children as they are born into the world…[frogs are] somewhere near the [long]house whenever a child is born" (Haddon 1936: 131). The frog was also tattooed on the necks of Iban headhunters as a form of protection. Among the Kayan of Borneo, it is believed that the frog revealed the secrets of headhunting to warrior society (Furness 1902a: 59).

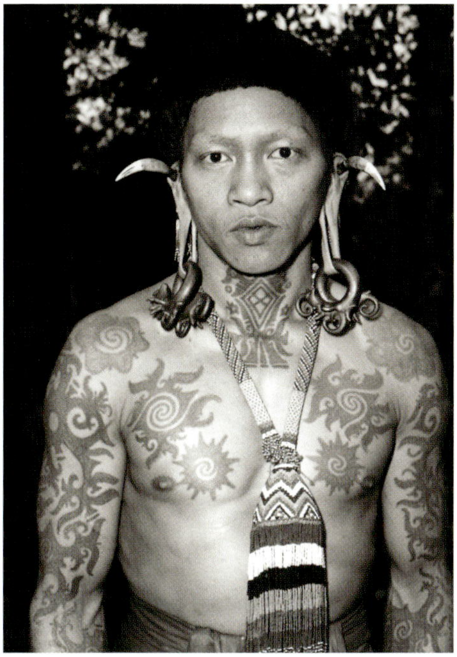

Penan man with complex rosette and other hook-like tattoo patterns, ca. 1950. He also wears a frog tattoo on his neck. Courtesy of the Sarawak Museum Archives.

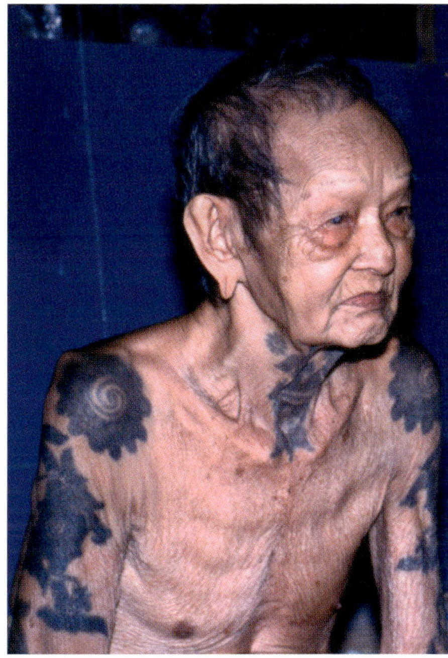

Iban man of the Skrang River with rosette (*bunga terong*) and throat tattoos (*lagu*), 2002. Photograph by Lars Krutak.

also on account of the elaborate ceremonial attached to this form of body ornamentation. The process was a long one, lasting sometimes as much as four years, since only a small piece could be tattooed at a sitting and several long intervals elapsed between the various stages of work.[92] The program of tattooing was initiated at a specific juncture in the cosmological cycle, and "the time at which to begin tatuing [sic] a girl is about the ninth day after the new Moon, this lunar phase being known as *butit halap*, the belly of the *halap* Fish (*Barbus* bramoides)."[93]

A girl received her first tattoos when about ten years old. She would have had her fingers and the upper part of her feet tattooed first, and then about a year later her forearms were completed. The thighs were partially tattooed during the next year, and in the third or fourth year from the beginning all the tattooing was completed.[94]

Kayan women endeavored to have their tattoos completed before they were married and especially before they became pregnant, as it was considered immodest to be tattooed after having become a mother.[95] If a woman

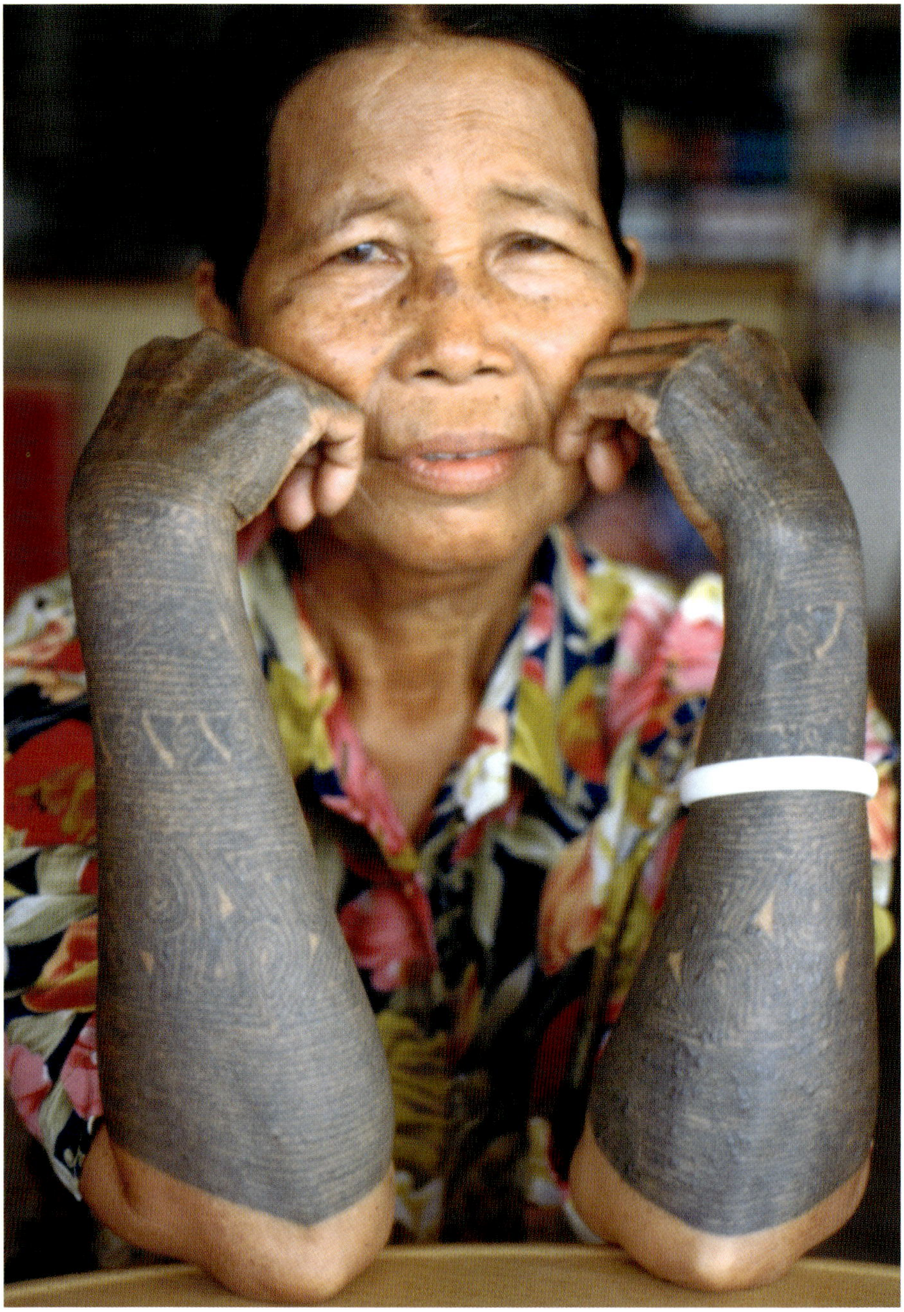

Kayan woman of the Rejang River, 2002. Photograph by Lars Krutak. Many of the tattoo motifs seen here warded off evil spirits encountered in the jungle or worked as fertility symbols. Most Kayan stopped tattooing over 40 years ago and I could find no living traditional tattoo artists on the Rejang River in 2002.

had a severe illness after any portion of her body had been tattooed, the work was not continued for a short period. Additionally, woman were prohibited from being tattooed during seeding time or if a dead person was lying unburied in the longhouse, since it was taboo to let blood during these occasions.[96] In addition, girls could not be tattooed during their menses, because it was believed that the flowing blood attracted evil spirits. Bad dreams, such as those of floods, metaphorically foretold of much bloodletting during the forthcoming tattoo rite and in these cases the tattooist would also interrupt her work.

Most Kayan tattooists were restricted by other social taboos.[97] If her children were of young age, she was debarred from the practice of her profession because they were susceptible to spiritual encounters. Tattooists were also prohibited from eating certain foods, especially meat and fish. Fasting was construed as form of ritual purification that prevented spirits from attaching themselves to particles of food that caused illness when ingested. If an artist transgressed any of these and other ritual mandates, by disregarding the prohibitions imposed upon her profession, it was believed that she herself would sicken and perhaps die,[98] because the tutelary spirit of tattoo artists, Bua Kalung, would deny her spiritual protection.[99]

Tattoo (*tedek*) amongst Kayan women was universal. They believed that the designs acted as torches after death, leading them through the darkness of the afterlife to the longhouses of their dead ancestors.[100] Women, never men, performed the tattooing, and it was always the women who were the experts on the significance and quality of the tattoo designs, though the men actually carved the stencils on wooden blocks. The office of tattooist was a hereditary position,[101] and the artist, like blacksmiths and carvers, worked under the protection of a tutelary spirit who was propitiated with sacrifices before each tattoo session.[102]

The tools used by the tattoo artist were simple, consisting of two or three thorn prickers, *ulang* or *ulang brang*, and an iron striker, *tukun* or *pepak*, kept in a wooden case, *bungan*.[103] The prickers were wooden rods with a short pointed head projecting at right angles at one end; to the point of the head was attached a lump of resin in which were embedded three or four short needles, their points alone projecting from the resinous mass. The striker was merely a short ironwood rod, half of which was covered with a string lashing. The pigment consisted of a mixture of soot, water, and sugar-cane juice, that was kept in a shallow cup of wood. The best soot was obtained from the bottom of a metal cooking pot, but that derived from burning resin or dammar was also used.[104] The tattoo designs were carved in relief on blocks of wood (*klingé*) that were smeared with the ink and then pressed on the part of the body to be tattooed. In effect, these blocks worked as a type of stencil.[105]

The tattoo client reclined on the floor, and the artist and a female assistant squatted on either side of her. The tattooist then dipped a piece of fiber from the sugar palm into the pigment and, pressing this on to the limb to be tattooed, plotted out the arrangement of the rows or bands of the tattoo design; along these straight lines the artist tattooed rows of additional lines (*ikor*), then taking the tattoo block carved with the required design, she smeared it with pigment and pressed it on to the limb between two rows of *ikor*.[106] The tattooer or her assistant stretched with her feet the skin of the body part to be tattooed—this sped up the process—and then, dipping a pricker into the pigment, the tattoo artist tapped its handle with the striker as she worked along a line, driving the needle points into the skin. Of course, the operation was quite painful, and the client could rarely restrain her cries. But the artist was always quite unmoved by such reactions and she proceeded methodically with her task.

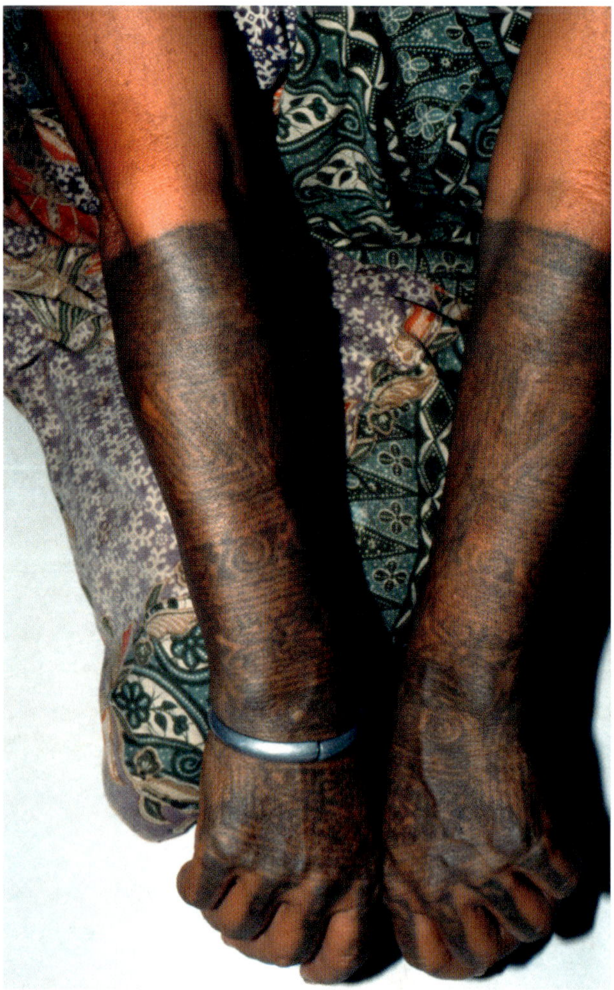

80-year-old Kayan woman with bold forearm tattoos, 2002. Photograph by Lars Krutak.

Kayan woman. After Tillema (1938: 175, pl. 123). Copyright National Museum of Ethnology (Rijksmuseum voor Volkenkunde), The Netherlands. This Kayan woman photographed around 1920, was tattooed with snake-like motifs called *aso'*. The design at the bottom of these vertical bands, the coil that looks similar to an abstract letter "A," is the *tuba* root pattern. Both the *aso'* and *tuba* motifs are ones which evil spirits dread and it is interesting to note that the *tuba* plant, when crushed, produces a poisonous juice used to stupefy fish. In mythology, the *tuba* was given to the Kayan by the snake deities. *Silong lejau* ("tiger's faces") were other important and powerful tattoo symbols used against the spirits. They are related to a famous story in which a shaman, clothed in a ceremonial garment with designs of crocodiles and tigers, blocked the entrance to his longhouse to scare away the evil spirits plaguing the community.

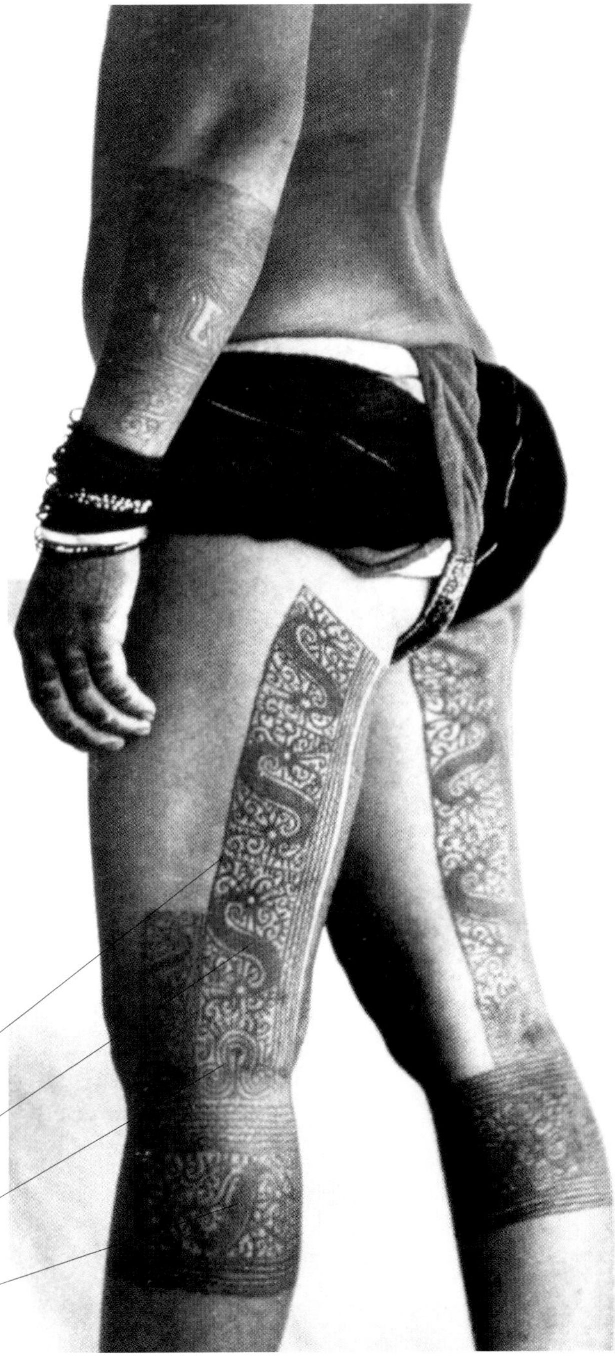

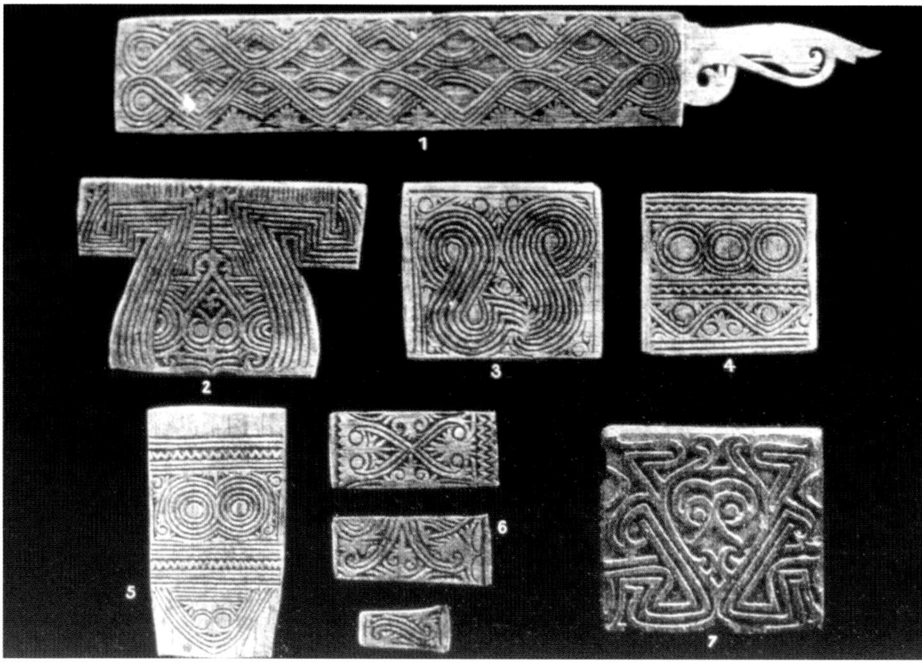

Kayan tattoo stencil blocks (*klingé*), ca. 1895. After Nieuwenhuis (1900: pl. XXVIII).

According to one account of 1900, the fees paid to the artist were more or less fixed; for the forearms a gong, *tawak*, worth from eight to twenty Sarawak dollars, according to the workmanship required, was paid; for the thighs a large *tawak* was paid, worth as much as sixty Sarawak dollars if the very best workmanship was demanded, from six to twenty dollars if only inferior workmanship was required.[107] For tattooing the fingers the operator received a *parang* or short sword. Furness, writing around the turn of the 20th century, suggested:

> All these [tattoo] instruments are usually kept in a cob-webby, sooty, blood-smeared box; but as heirlooms and tools they are of almost priceless value . . .
>
> As an indispensable preliminary, before the skin is touched, several beads must be given the operator, who may not keep them all, but must hand over some to the 'Toh'—the demons who are always lurking about to see that the rules of the house are obeyed. It is *lali* [taboo] to draw human blood in a house unless the Toh be previously informed that it is for a lawful purpose. Some of the beads are, therefore, flung broadcast out of doors, for the Toh to gather up at their leisure.

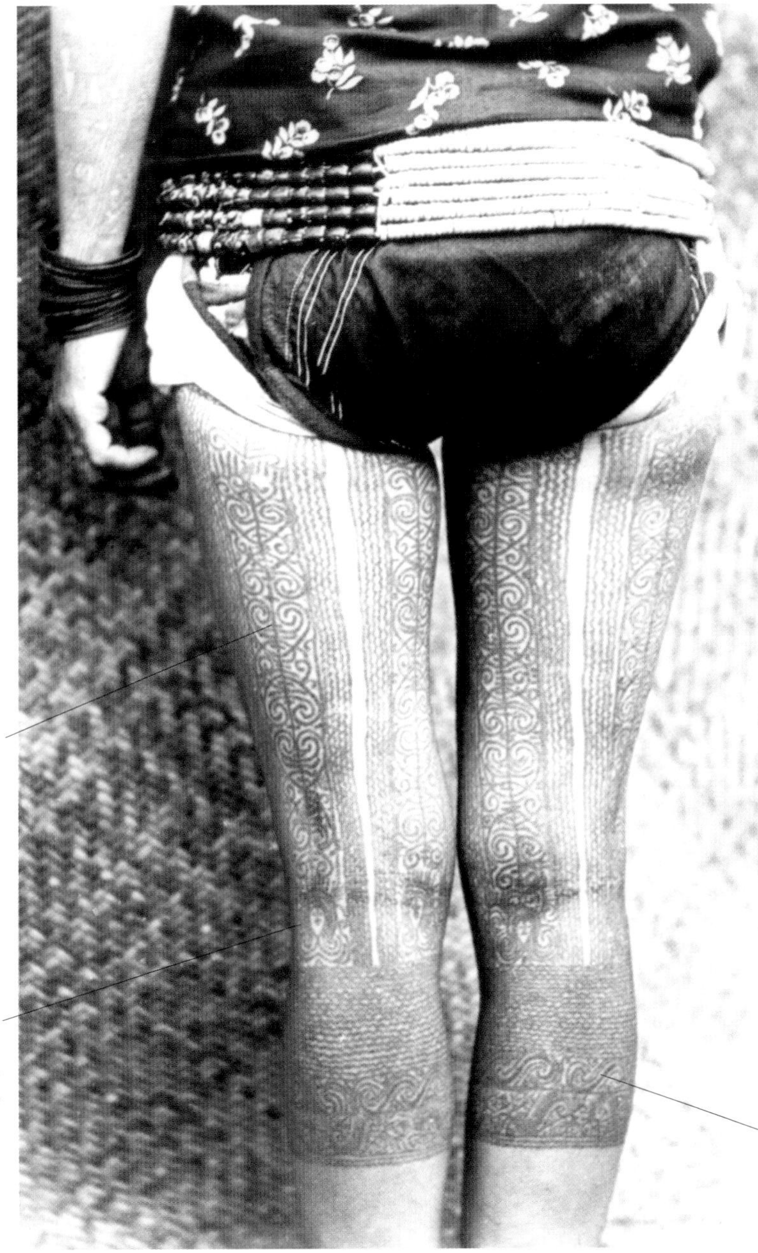

Kayan woman's leg and thigh tattoos. After Tillema (1938: 176, pl. 125). Copyright National Museum of Ethnology (Rijksmuseum voor Volkenkunde), The Netherlands. A woman's social position is indicated by the number of rings around the calves of her legs (Thomas 1968: 210; Tillema 1989: 164). This Kayan woman is of high position. It was believed that if the slivers of undecorated areas on the back of the legs were tattooed, the woman's legs would become gangrenous and she would be denied passage to the afterlife.

> . . . I say that the pain of the Kayan operation, even for an hour, it becomes torture. Having also experienced for many consecutive hours the Japanese method, I can affirm that in comparison the Kayan verges on the inhuman.[108]

One Kayan woman I interviewed in 2002 stated that her thigh tattoo (*kulan higo*) cost one gong, several strands of old trading beads, two pigs, and one *parang*.[109] She said that the artist would die in one year or less if her charges were excessive.

Kayan priestesses

According to Rousseau,[110] the client's family was also expected to feed the tattooer and to brew rice-beer for her consumption. Both the client and tattoo artist had to be purified (*ngaping*) by a Kayan priestess or priest before the tattooing commenced and afterwards at the harvest festival, in order to cleanse them from the spiritual dangers inherent in the tattoo patterns.

Like the headhunter or Iban weaver, Kayan priestesses (*dayong*) performed dangerous work. They needed to be strong physically, emotionally, and spiritually if they were to effectively interact with the various deities and spirits in curing, purification, naming, and agricultural rituals.[111] It was

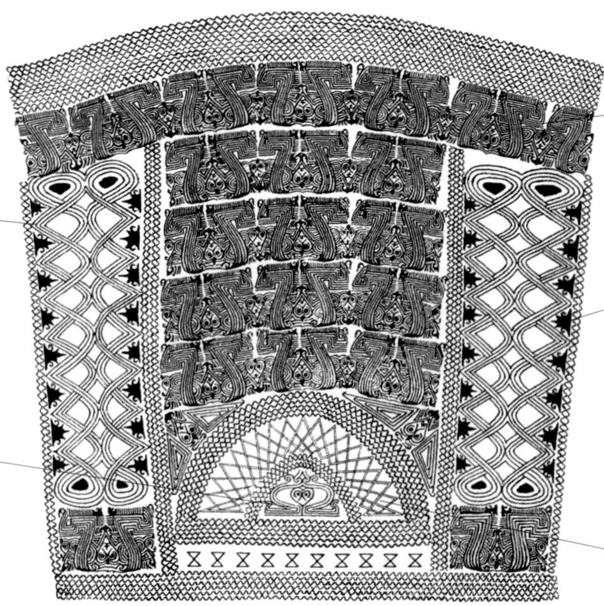

Thigh tattoo of a Kayan chief's daughter, ca. 1900. After Nieuwenhuis (1904: pl. 84).

the priestess who could nullify the effects of a headhunter's ill-omened dreams; it was the priestess who had mastered the ritual language and ceremonies necessary to ensure the warriors' safe return to the longhouse; and it was the *dayong* who had the power to attempt to reclaim the lost souls of her patients with the assistance of spiritual "helpers" or familiars that could be both male or female.[112] Furness relates the following event concerning a *dayong* who attempted to retrieve the soul of a dying woman. Like the tattooist, she received a payment of old beads for her work:

> A female Dayong was then summoned to find out whither the soul had gone, and to lure it back to the body; to this end she made several successful demands of valuable beads from the husband, as a fee, and the agonized, headlong haste with which he ran to get them from time to time, was truly [alarming] . . .
>
> A flickering dammar lamp was placed on the floor near the body, and within the circle of its light the Dayong, chanting [to her familiars] in a monotonous

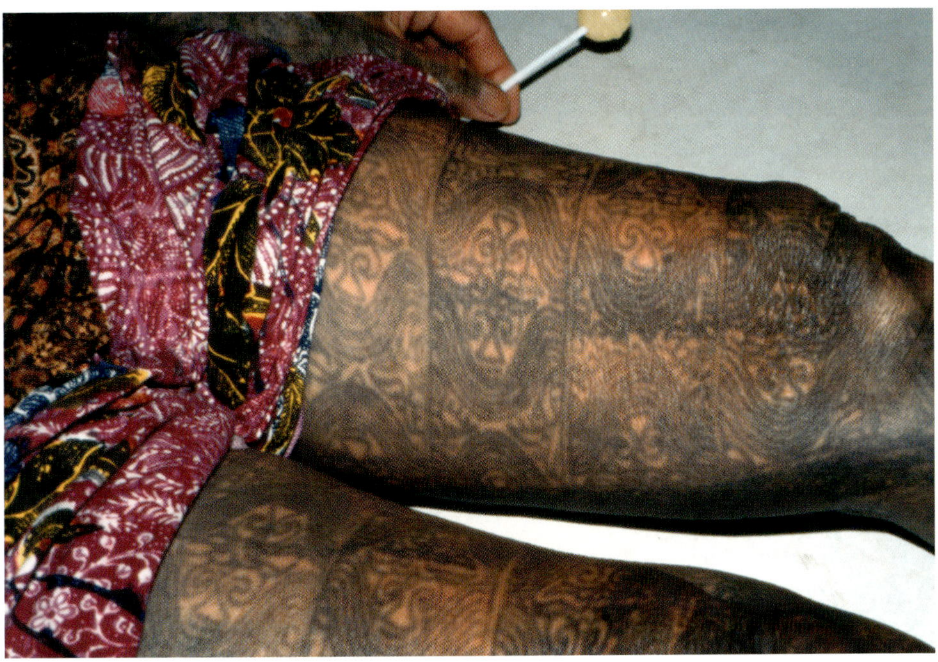

Thigh tattoos of an elderly Kayan woman (80+ years of age) of the Upper Rejang River, 2002. Photograph by Lars Krutak. The anthropomorphic faces worn upon her skin are protective ancestral spirits. Thigh tattoos were expensive and generally restricted to those aristocratic women who could afford them. The motifs thus represented carried powerful apotropaic magic which only aristocratic women could manipulate to their benefit. Today, thigh tattoos (*kulan higo*) are rarely seen on women under 70 years of age.

minor key, strutted backward and forward with a shield on one hand and a parang [sword] in the other, and many strings of beads about her neck and waist. Twice she paused to ask for a young chicken, and when it was handed to her, she seized its head in her mouth and bit it off, sucked a mouthful of blood from the neck and spat it on the floor, closely scrutinizing how it splattered. Throughout this scene the grief-stricken, wailing reiteration of the dead woman's name echoed through the veranda, now but dimly lit with dammar lamps; every sound of mirth and gaiety was hushed; the only noise, except the wailings of the Dayong, came from dogs and pigs beneath the [long]house, where they snarled and fought over the remnants of the feast that had fallen through the floor.

When the female Dayong had done her utmost to recall the soul, and had

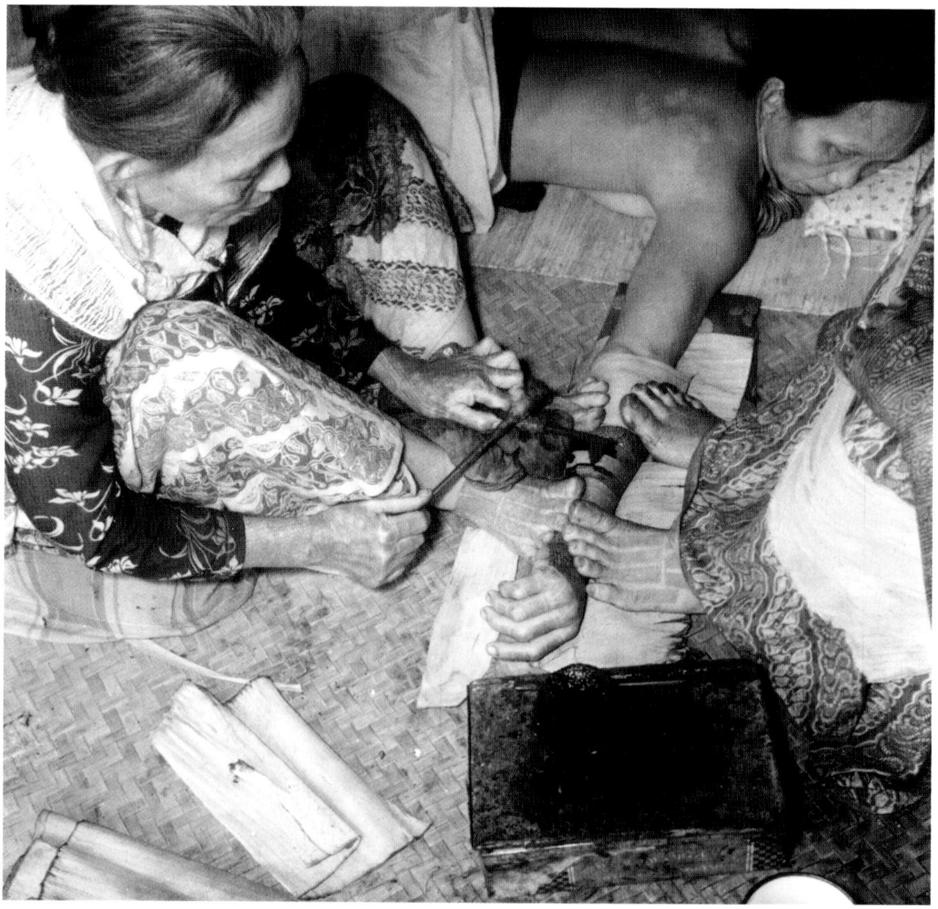

Kayan women tattooing, 1951. Courtesy of the Sarawak Museum Archives.

failed, our good, faithful friend, Tama Talun, volunteered to try his power . . .

[Afterwards] the group suddenly realised that the woman was veritably dead, beyond all hope. With a scream the husband and the brother snatched up the body and rushed into the family room with it; some of the group followed, and some crept silently away into the dark corners of the veranda.[113]

Sihan and Lahanan

The Sihan, numbering approximately one hundred and fifty persons, are one of the smallest indigenous groups living in the Rejang Basin.[114] They speak a dialect of Kayan and their tattooing traditions are very similar. The Sihan, however, carried their indelible arts further into the present than the Kayan, only abandoning them thirty years ago; the Kayan stopped tattooing altogether approximately fifty years ago.[115]

Konok, a 50-year-old Sihan woman told me she received her first tattoo

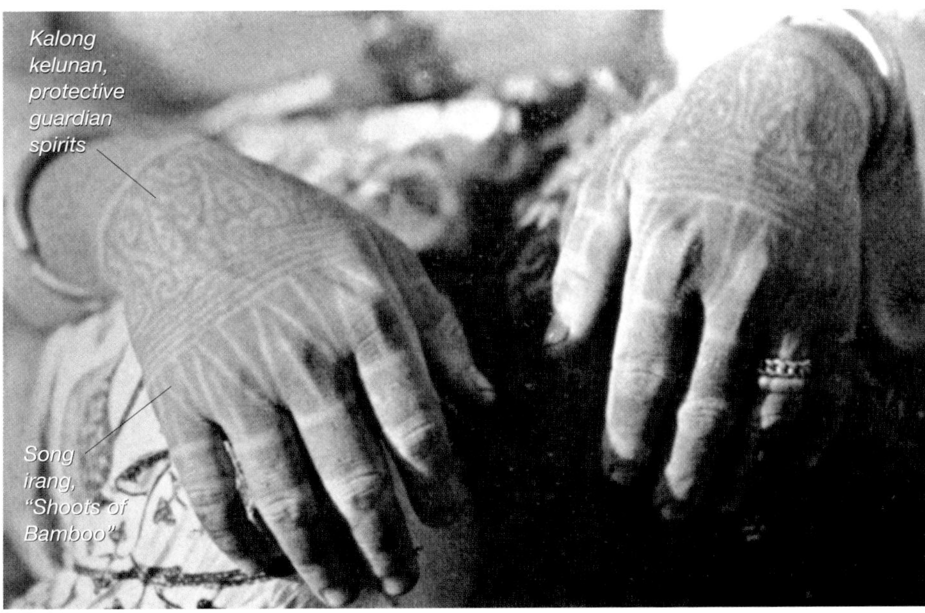

Kayan hand tattoo, ca. 1920. After Tillema (1930: 195). Copyright National Museum of Ethnology (Rijksmuseum voor Volkenkunde), The Netherlands. Among the Kayan, tattoo was hand-tapped onto the fingers of women in various patterns, although black spikes running from the knuckles to mid-digits was a fairly common design. This motif, called *song irang* ("shoots of bamboo"), expresses a connection between plant life and fertility while the anthropomorphic designs above her wrist represent protective ancestor spirits (Hose and Shelford 1906: 67). Floral imagery, symbolizing spiritual powers and relationships, permeates every facet of Kayan life. Plants are regarded as a major kind of living thing, sharing the same fundamental properties of life and death as humans.

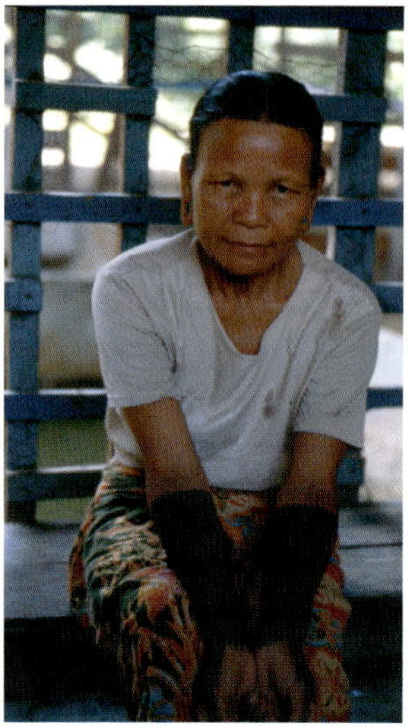

Lahanan woman with arm tattoos, 2002. Photographs by Lars Krutak.

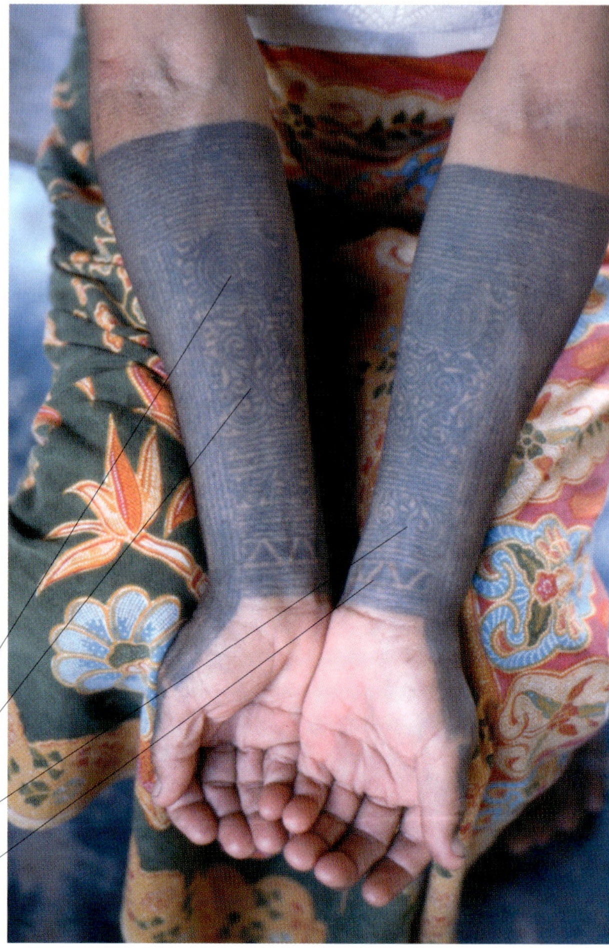

(arm) at eighteen years of age. Her tattoos were pricked-in with a thorn implement and were requisites for marriage; men would not marry a Sihan woman without them.

Old Sihan women were the tattoo artists and they generally employed the same methods and motifs as the Kayan. The position of tattooist was hereditary, usually passed from mother to daughter. At death, the tattoo artist was buried with her equipment.[116]

The neighboring Lahanan also excelled in tattooing. Lahanan tattooists were always women and the profession was hereditary in the female line. One 65-year-old woman, Bangu, gave me a vivid account of her ca. 1950 tattoo experience and the price list for each tattoo in Sarawak dollars (SD). "Several women held me down, each took a limb, and another woman

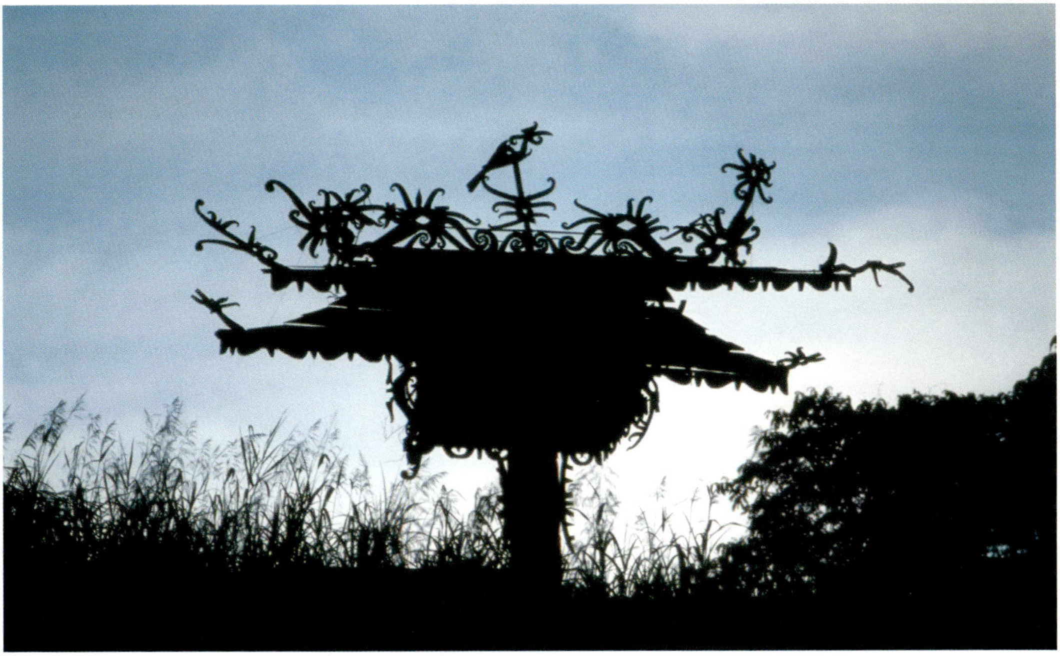

Above: Only aristocratic women were allowed the privilege of wearing *kalong kelunan*, because only they could resist any negative magic associated with the design. In the distant past, the motif may have represented a ritual offering, depicting a slave sacrifice, or a guardian spirit. Sometimes this and other tattoo motifs such as *aso'* (dragon-dog) and *tingan* (hornbill) adorn the elaborately carved graves of aristocratic Orang Ulu women. The photograph above depicts a Kayan gravehouse lying on the banks of the Upper Rejang River.

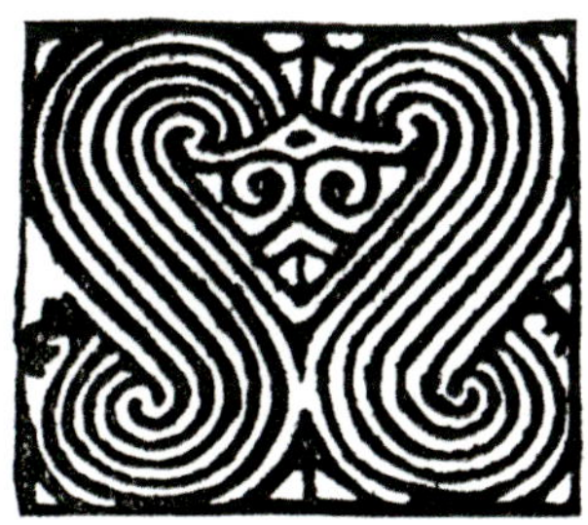

Right: *Kalong kelunan* woodblock tattoo print, ca. 1900. After Hose and McDougall (1912: Fig. 71).

stretched the skin for the tattooist who began working once I was calm. I wanted to get through it because I wouldn't get a husband if I didn't. It took four days to tattoo one arm (60 SD) and four for the other (60 SD); four days for one foot (3 SD) and four more for the other (3 SD). I was fifteen years old at the time and we did all the tattoos in those sixteen days!"[117]

Two Lahanan men, who were tattooed by women, mentioned that if you had no money, you paid for your tattoos with a gong or a *parang* (short sword). One of these men, 80-year-old Pugwun Bapai, told me he was tattooed for a 25 Sarawak dollar fee at the age of fifteen. A special party was held in his honor after the ritual because he was no longer a "boy," but a "man."

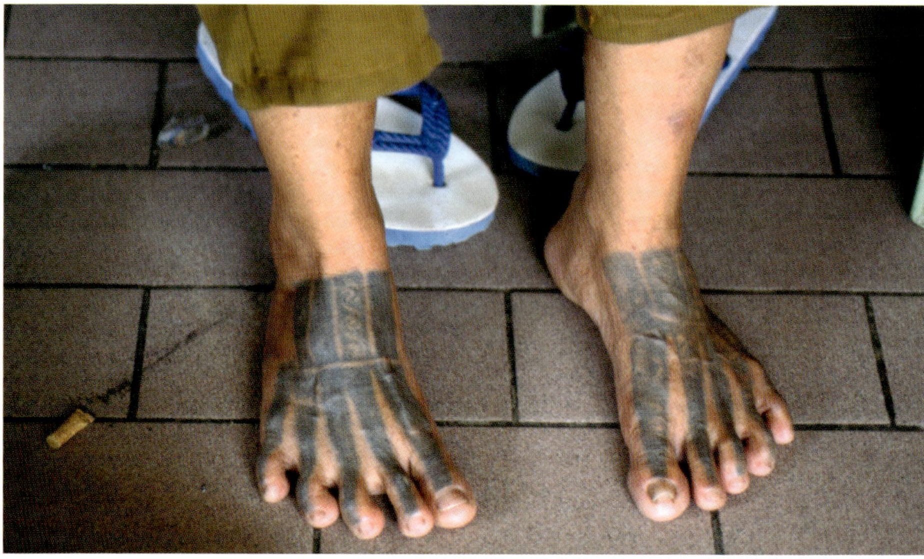

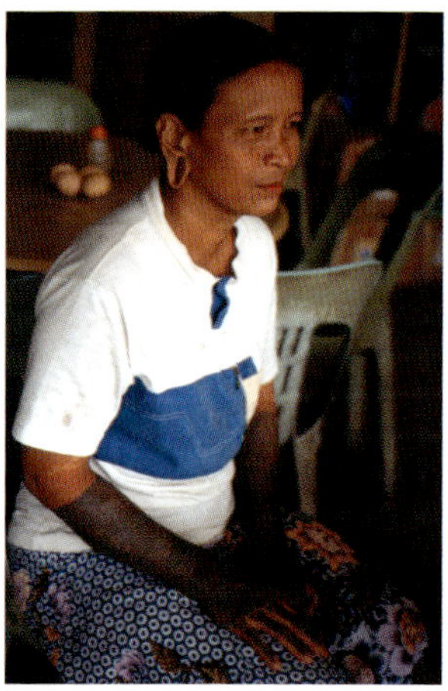

Above: Sihan foot tattoos (*panyat*). *Panyat* means "to stretch," 2002. Photograph by Lars Krutak.

Left & below: Sihan woman with full compliment of hand and arm tattoos, 2002. Photographs by Lars Krutak. A good friend points out her highly abstract markings and a close-up reveals her inner forearm tattoos.

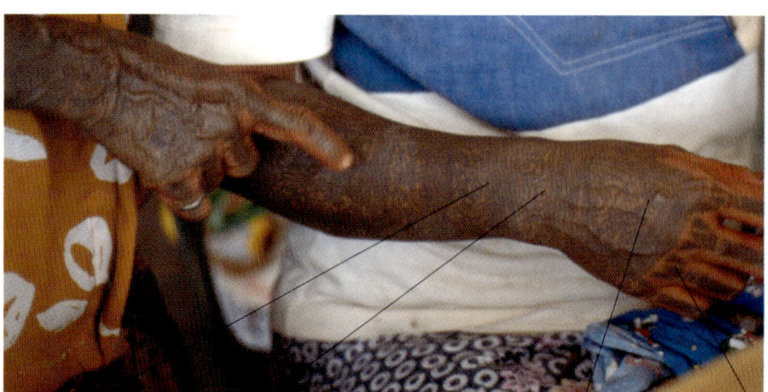

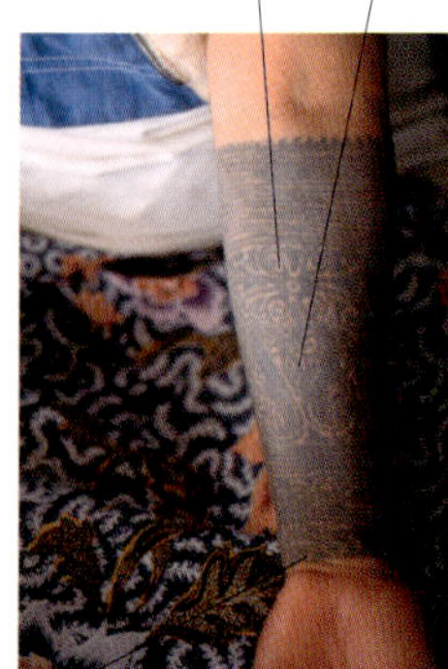

Prelude of change

Today, Orang Ulu tattoo is a dying, if not already dead, traditional practice. Disruptions to indigenous Kayan, Sihan, and Lahanan culture as a result of missionization and modernity continue to pave the way for a relinquishing of ancient customs. One Lahanan man said, "This generation of Orang Ulu are not interested in old ways. They have no desire to get the older traditional tattoos," and are drawn to urban centers, logging camps, or frontier towns where they can find work and become more open to other cultural influences, including fast, accessible, and more Western-style tattoos: tattoos which are oftentimes seen on popular American videos of World Wrestling Federation wrestlers. Missionaries continue to convert and compel Orang Ulu to literally "bury" their traditional customs and material culture, especially charms and other "pagan devices" like tattooing instruments.[118]

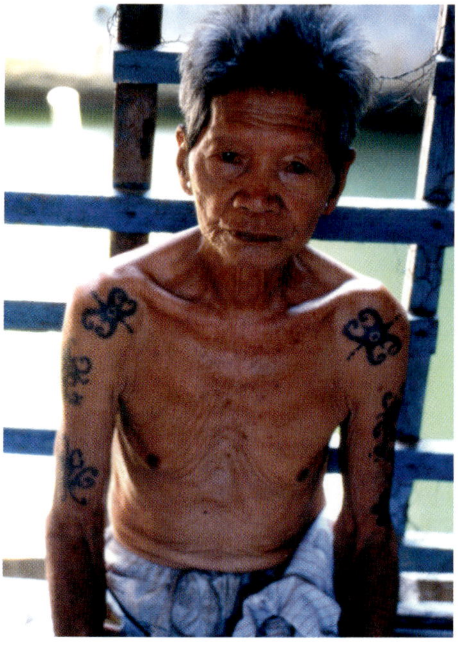

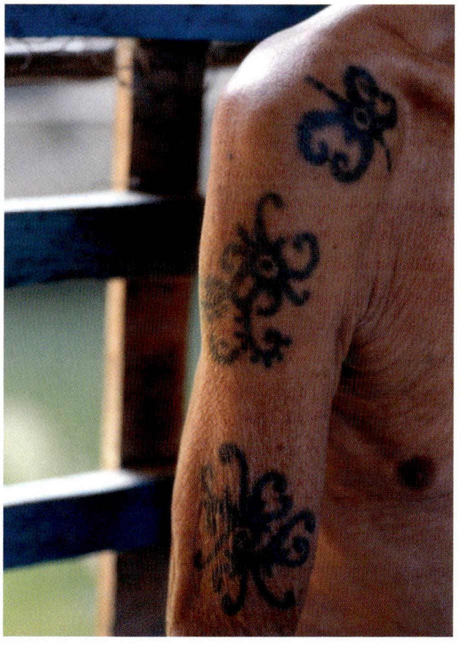

Elderly Lahanan man tattooed by female tattooist approximately 60 years ago, 2002. Photographs by Lars Krutak. His tattoos represent a stylized combination of hornbill and *aso'* (dragon-dog) motifs. Some art historians insist that these designs are neither bird, dog, or dragon (water spirit), but tigers (Mashman 1989: 217-220). Tigers never lived in Borneo, but their teeth and skins, which were believed to have special powers, came to the Orang Ulu through trade with other Indonesian islands. Different Orang Ulu groups associated the tiger with high rank and the male qualities of strength and bravery which were certainly needed during the headhunt. Regardless of the associations, this tattoo design represents a protective symbol.

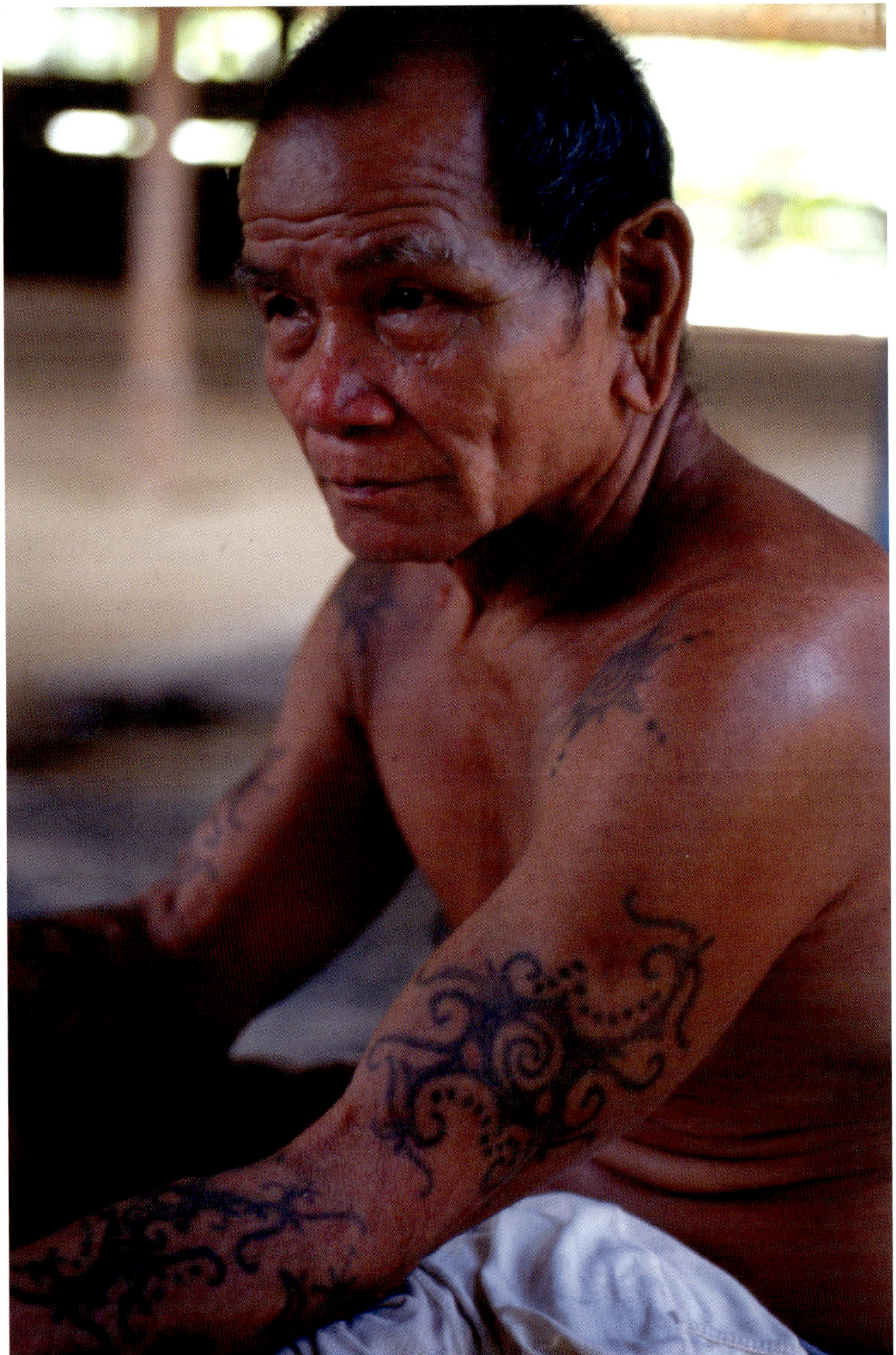

Facing page: Lahanan man with intricate *aso'* and hornbill tattoos on arms, 2002. He wears a durian motif on his shoulders and was tattooed by a woman. Photograph by Lars Krutak. Despite its sickly smell, the durian is a cherished fruit for many Dayak peoples in Borneo and was chosen as a tattoo motif by some. According to legends still told on the Upper Rejang, the progenitor of all aristocratic Kayan families fell from the heavens encapsulated in a durian (Sandin 1975: 63-66).

Right: Frontal view of durian tattoo motifs, 2002. Photograph by Lars Krutak.

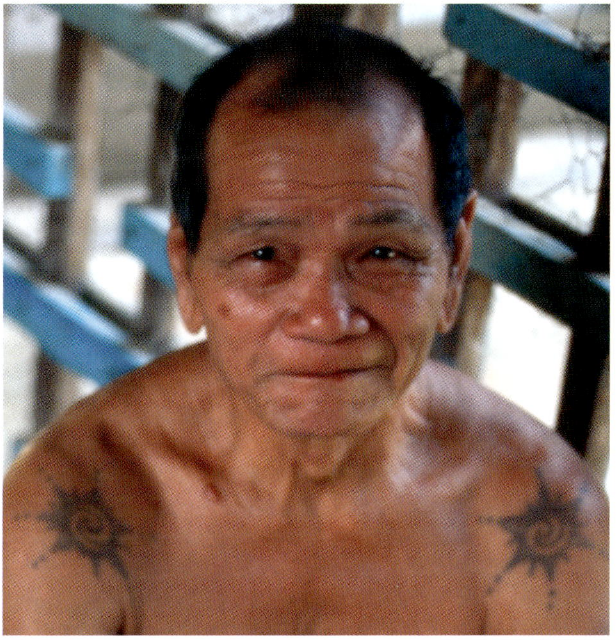

To compound these and other problems, the Malaysian government is in the process of building the largest hydroelectric damn in all of Southeast Asia on the Upper Rejang.[119] The Bakun Dam has already displaced ten-thousand Kayan and other Orang Ulu living in a dozen or more longhouses: longhouses that have stood on ancestral lands for centuries, if not millennia. Eventually the Bakun will flood a tract of virgin rainforest that supports over forty species of endangered mammals and birds. Understandably, and poised on the fragile prelude of change, the Orang Ulu have not yet folded to modernity; but as the jungle slowly disappears underneath the ensuing canopy of water, so too will that which gave life—and tattoos—to all of its peoples.

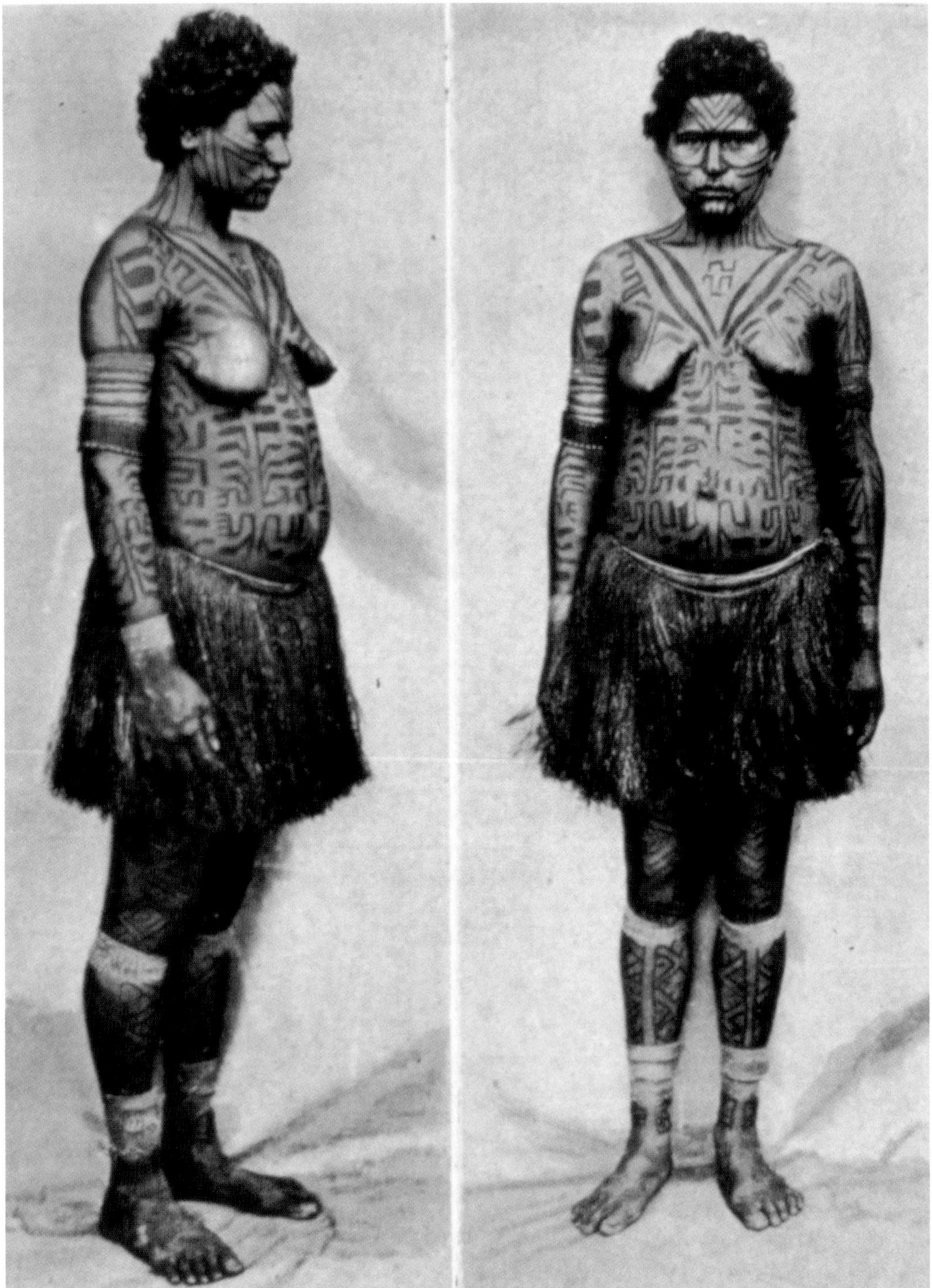

Papua New Guinea and Easter Island

As far back as the old men and women can remember, tattooing has been a custom of several Austronesian-speaking peoples of coastal Papua New Guinea. Among the Motu, Waima, Aroma, Hula, Mailu, Mekeo, and other neighboring groups, women were heavily tattooed from head to toe with abstract geometric forms of iconography while men displayed chest markings related to their exploits in the headhunt.

By World War II, however, tattooing largely disappeared in Papua for a variety of reasons; head-hunting was outlawed; missionaries discouraged initiation ceremonies; and tattoos associated with the Hula and Motu trading voyages (*lakatois*) became obsolete,[1] especially since motorboats had replaced sailboats, making these trips much less dangerous.[2] Today, only the Maisin and a few neighboring peoples like the Tufi of Collingwood Bay in southeastern Papua remain as the last coastal people to carry tattooing on their bodies and faces.[3]

According to the relatively sparse ethnographic record of tattooing in the region, tattoos were generally inked upon women in a fixed order among all coastal Papuans.[4] First, girls between five to seven years of age were tattooed on the backs of their hands to the elbows and further along to the shoulders; next, girls between seven to eight years of age were tattooed on the face and lower abdomen to below the navel. Then the waist down to the

Facing page: Waima woman wearing full body tattooing. After Barton (1918: pl. II). Courtesy of Blackwell Publishing. The V-shaped tattoo on this Waima woman's neck was called "frigate bird," and the branching elements on her abdomen "centipede." Her entire body, including the inner thighs, has been tattooed except the deltoid region of her arms and portions of her belly. The photographer doctored this and many subsequent photographs by painting along the tattoos so they would show more clearly. This was not an uncommon practice in Papua, because tattoo pigments did not show up well on dark complexions (Fraser 1909: 288; Haddon 1894: 172). The subject has been posed in front of a white canvas sheet to provide contrast.

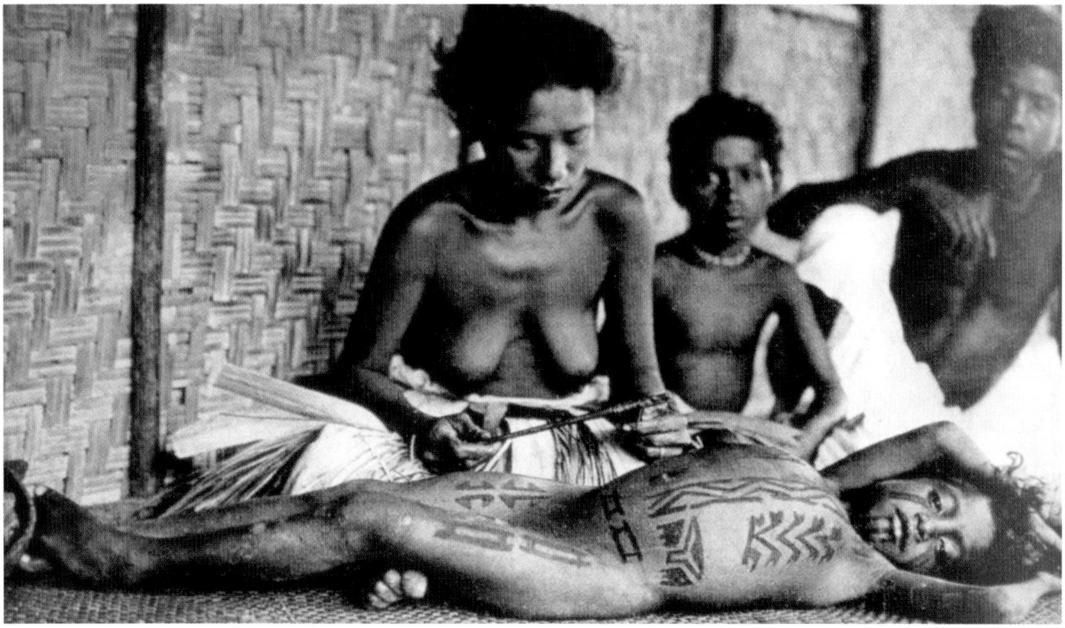

Motu tattoo artist hand-tapping client. After Oldham (1934: 270).

knees and the outside of the thighs were marked. At ten, the armpits and areas extending to the nipples were tattooed with the throat done shortly thereafter. When the first menses appeared, the back from the shoulders down, then the buttocks, back of the thighs and legs were inked. When a girl was ready for marriage, V-shaped designs from the neck down to the navel were tattooed.[5]

Among the inland Sinagoro and other groups, girls were marked with a special pattern on either side of the vulva (*bunegoala*) which signaled a completed transition into womanhood.[6] This custom was followed by the Motu and Hula,[7] but it occurred earlier in the Aroma region: perhaps as early as seven to eight years of age for girls.[8] Sometimes special tattoos could be added to the girl if her father, brother, or a close relative killed another man, or if any of these family members displayed prowess in fishing or trading expeditions. Some tattoos were prerequisites for marriage, while other arrangements of tattoos indicated clan affiliations and specific links to female family members.[9]

All coastal Papuan tattoo artists were women and the technique employed to apply the markings was a form of hand-tapping. Tattooing kits were fairly simple, and among the Motu the wooden "hammer" was called *iboki* and the needle-like *gini* was a lemon branch twig with a thorn projecting out at one end.[10] The Motu first painted the desired tattoo motif on the skin and allowed it to dry. With the *gini* held in the left hand, the point of the thorn almost touching the skin, and the *iboki* held in the right hand by the small end, the *gini* was tapped with enough force to cause the thorn to pierce the skin.[11] For finishing the tattoo design, the *gini* may have had three or four thorns tied together to fill in the design more quickly.

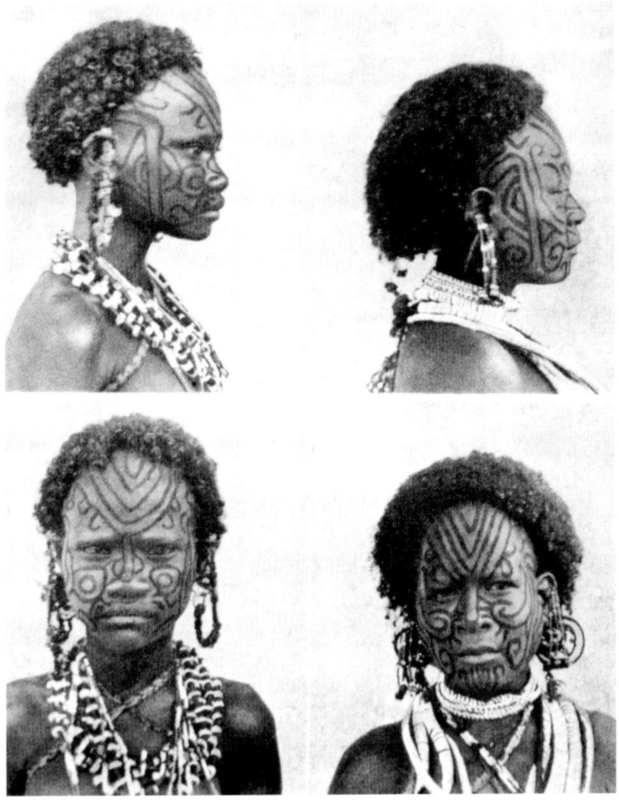

Maisin women of Collingwood Bay, Oro Province who are among the last coastal Papuans to wear tattoo today. After Barton (1918: pl. XV). Courtesy of Blackwell Publishing.

Usually tattoo pigment came from the charred remains of the candlenut. Candlenut (*Aleurites moluccana*) was also utilized in Hawaii (*kukui*) and other Pacific islands in Polynesia as pigment.[12] Interestingly, the leaves of the candlenut tree, and the sap from the tree itself, was used throughout Polynesia, the Philippines, China, and Indonesia in the treatment of arthritic joints or as a healing application for chapped lips, cold sores and sunburn.[13] Even in Papua the Sinagoro tribe specifically utilized several types of "medicinal" tattoos to treat rheumatoid arthritis.[14] These marks were often grouped around aching joints on the back, neck, or shoulders. Triangular motifs seen under the left breast of a Sinagoro man ca. 1900 appeared to one anthropologist as "hav[ing] been tattooed for palpitations or uneasy sensations in the region of the heart."[15] Other marks on the forehead were believed to remedy headache.

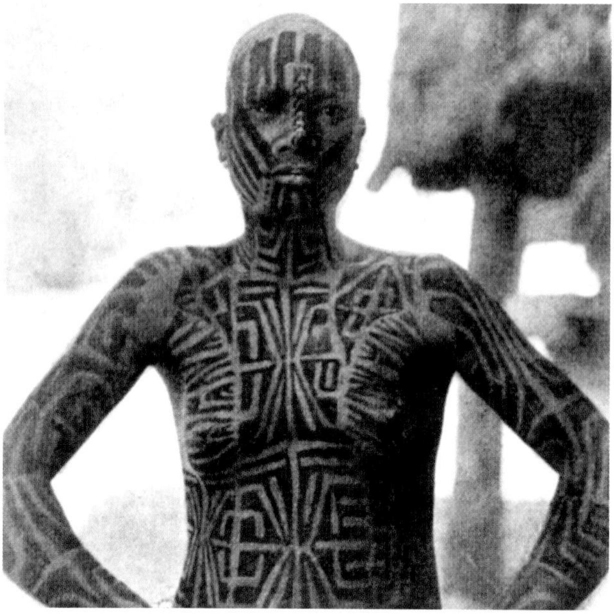

Left: Aroma woman, ca. 1915. After Barton (1918: pl. XIII). Courtesy of Blackwell Publishing. All portions of the body are tattooed with various designs. *Pau-lo*, or bamboo motif on chest, is reminiscent of the design found on Aroma beheading knives (Barton 1918: 54); frigate bird motif on nose; centipede (*aivamele*) pattern on lower right abdomen.

Below: Group of Waima girls with frigate bird motif on sternum below neck, centipede motif on sides of the abdomen. After Seligmann (1910: pl. XXXVIII).

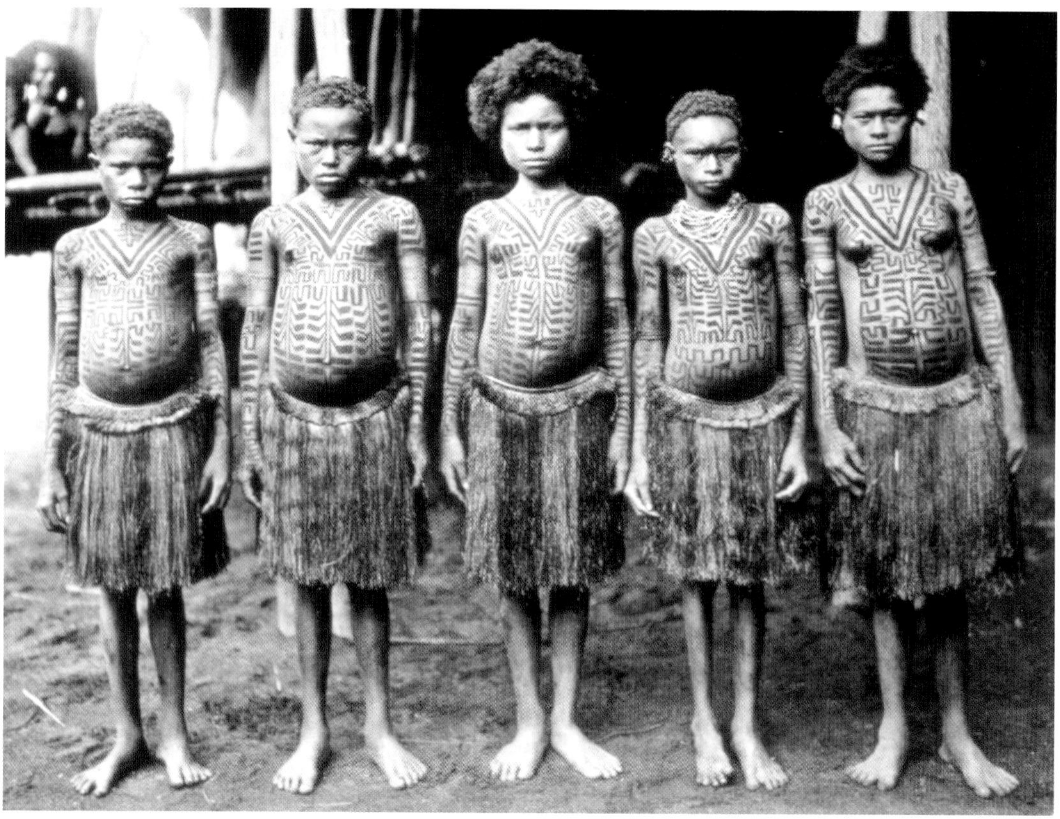

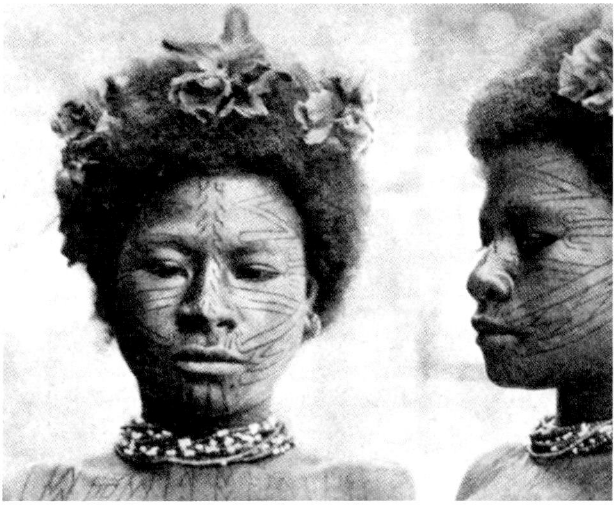

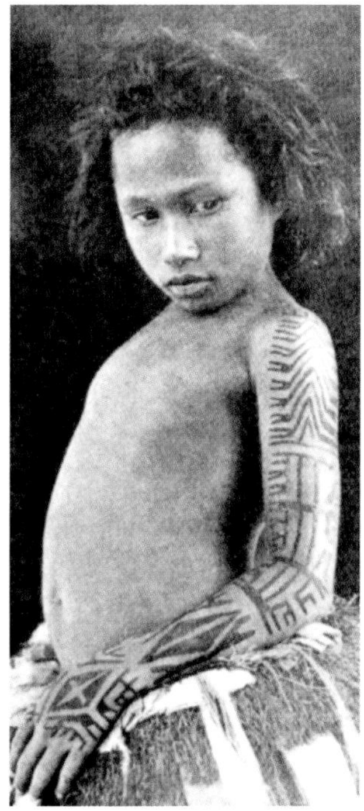

Above: Mailu girl with frigate bird tattoos (*aisava*) on either side of forehead with each extending to the cheek. After Barton (1918: 70). Courtesy of Blackwell Publishing. Interestingly, the etymology of the word *aisava* possibly means "bird which is the host of the spirit of the dead" (Barton 1918: 58).

Right: Hula girl with *ialata* pattern on shoulder. After Barton (1918: pl. VII). Courtesy of Blackwell Publishing. The *ialata* design represents the spinal column of a local fish. Throughout Polynesia and the Pacific, spinal or zigzag motifs are symbolic of genealogical relationships likened to a "family tree" of ancestors. She wears a hornbill (*bina*) mark on the back of her hand.

For the Sinagoro, all sickness, no matter how serious, was attributed to supernatural agency[16] and this belief extended to most, if not all, Austronesians living in coastal Papua.[17] Even dead ancestors were believed to "deal out sickness, or death, to anyone who may displease them."[18]

Generally speaking different women were employed for tattooing specific parts of the body.[19] Among the Mailu, facial tattoo artists seem to have been paid more as this work was the most painful and dangerous. Around 1900, a typical payment for facial work included: two strings (pairs) of arm shells, quantities of cockatoo and parrot feathers, and a string bag. If other parts of the body were tattooed, the tattooist may have only received a small payment of cooked food.[20]

Hula women who had completed the final phase of their tattooing, namely the receipt of marks below the navel, were celebrated at an initiation feast called *kapa* that was held annually at the ceremonial house (*dubu*) in the village center.[21] At the climax of this two-day ceremony, known as *kuiriga*, the freshly tattooed initiates ascended to the *dubu* platform to prepare themselves for the forthcoming public display of their newly transformed bodies:

> Seven recently tattooed girls . . . ascended the *dubu* and stood in a row facing the village square. Two men then carried [a] pig, which was tied on a pole, and stood in front of the girls. An old woman came and stood in front of the girls. An old woman came and stood beside them; she was not ornamented in any way, whereas the girls wore numerous swagger petticoats; round their neck were as many necklaces and ornaments as they could must, and some had wonderful shell head-dresses. [Only a girl, providing her father has taken life, may wear his bird of paradise plumes]. The girls next took off all their petticoats and were anointed by the old woman, who dabbed each girl with a mixture of coconut oil and water by means of a bunch of wild thyme. As soon as the anointing was completed a drum was beaten, and the girls quickly dressed themselves and jumped down from the *dubu*.[22]

Linguistic concepts of tattooing: the raw and the cooked

Interestingly, and in a shift from the previous description of Papuan tattooing practice itself, we begin to observe through the analysis of linguistic data that various coastal Papuans modeled notions of being (personhood) metonymically to wider cosmological perceptions of nature through their tattooing. For example, in the Motu language the condition of being non-tattooed is called "*kasiri vahoro*," "*kasiri*" means raw, uncooked, or unripe and in duplicated form, "*kasiri-kasiri*," denotes something that which has a dull red color.[23] Thus, a transition from *dull red* to *raw* (indicating the idea of uncooked flesh, immaturity, thus infertility) is connoted for the literal definition(s) of *kasiri*, and from this to *unprepared*.[24] In far-away Mangareva, some 1,200 miles to the east, the word for untattooed, according to Barton, "is *roro tea*, and this word is apparently compounded of *roro*, the milk of coconuts, and *tea*, meaning unpolished or dull."[25]

Among the Austronesian Maori of New Zealand, girls who reached puberty were often tattooed on their lips with soot because the Maori considered "red" lips unsightly,[26] perhaps because they had not yet been "cooked." The Maori called tattooing *ahi ta moko*, "the fire (or oven) of tattooing,"[27] and anyone who has had a large amount of tattooing work will not forget the distinctive "burning" sensation felt when the skin is incised. Jackson has noted that the color red was important in Maori symbolism for the following reasons:

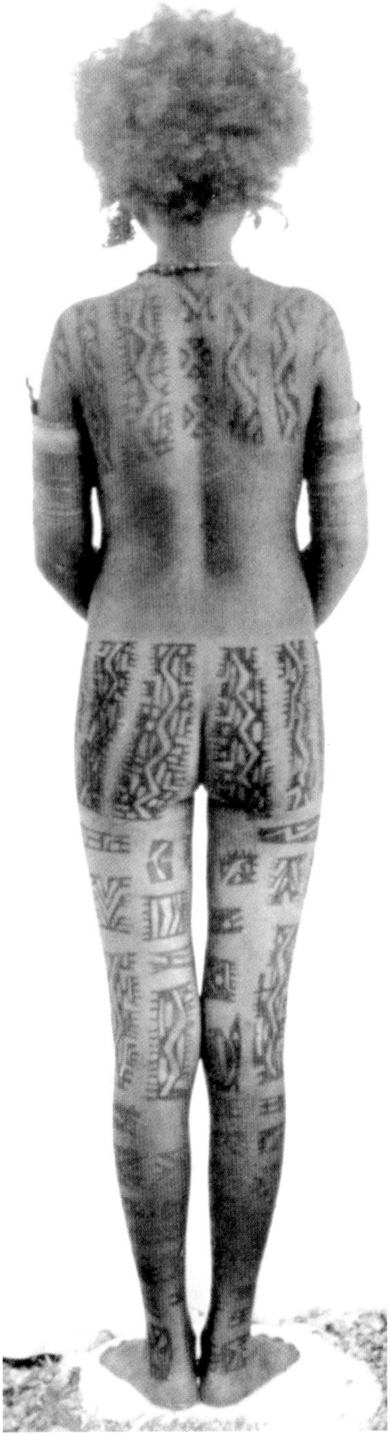

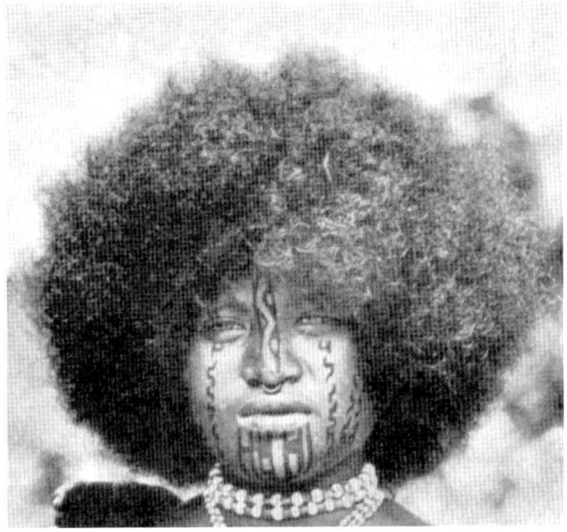

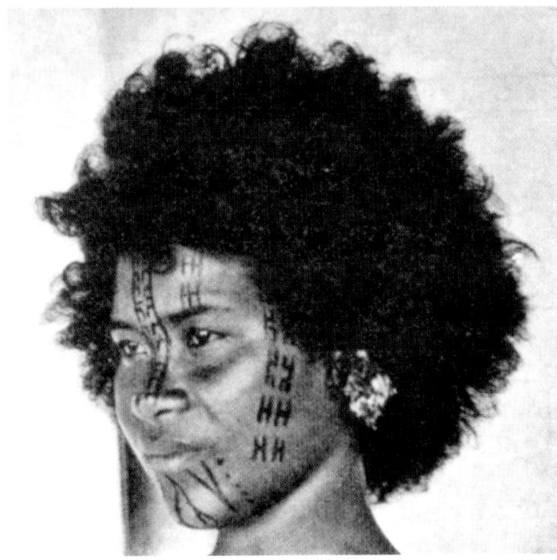

Above: Two Motu women with facial tattooing. Above: *neneva* motif on nose; Below: frigate bird on nose. After Barton (1918: pl. VI). Courtesy of Blackwell Publishing. In the Solomon Islands, it was believed that the guardian of the land of the dead inspected each dead person for his or her frigate bird tribal mark. If the deceased did not have the tattoo, they were not allowed to pass into the afterlife (Codrington 1891: 257).

Left: Motu woman with back tattooing. *Gado* designs predominate on the shoulder, back, and buttocks. After Barton (1918: pl. XII). Courtesy of Blackwell Publishing.

The symbol of death and birth is red and relates to the ambiguous position a person occupies *en passage* between the social world outside the house and the social world within the house . . .

Menstrual blood equivocally refers to both processes in so far as it signifies the death of latent life and the potentiality for bearing life . . .

In many myths and stories the colour red, and also the arts of tattooing and carving, originates in the underworld . . . Thus the death-in-life symbolism of red.[28]

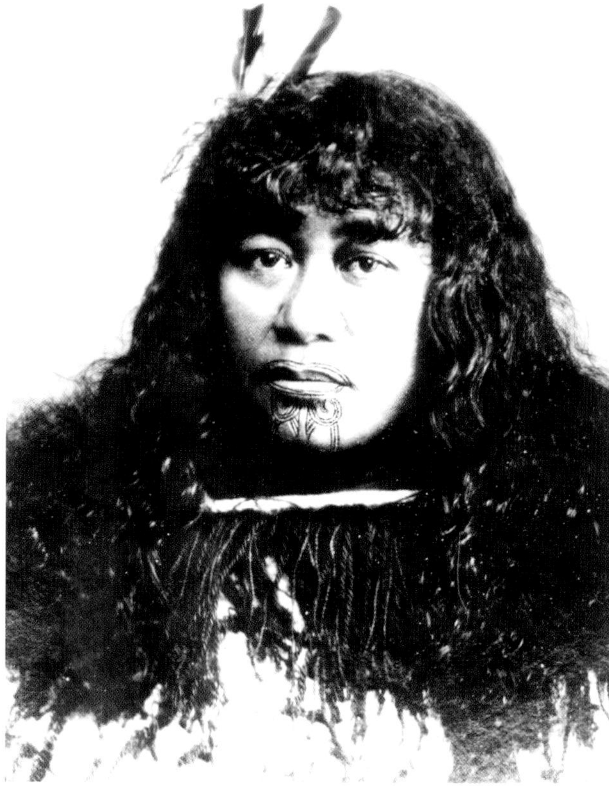

Maori women's facial tattooing, ca. 1915. Postcard from the collection of the author. Maori tattoo pigment was made from a sooty black carboniferous substance obtained from burning the resin of the *kauri* pine tree and combining it with other elements (Best 1952: 237). According to a chant performed for a Maori woman about to be tattooed in 1920, pine ash, as an agent of fire, was considered to be a sacred transformative substance: "My ash is sacred ash / From you, lo Tikiti-o-Rangi; / These are your elementary students, / These are your more advanced students; / The sacredness is great, the sacredness is extensive, / Held together with large strands, / Strands of knowledge, / The strands of unique mystical knowledge, / The lore of paramount chiefs, / The lore of the gods, / Derived from the heavens, / From the ancient source, from the special source, / From the main source! To you, Ruatua! / To you Tane, Provider of Good Health!" (King 1972: n.p.).

Returning to Papuan perceptions of "the raw" vs. "the cooked," the Mekeo and neighboring related peoples trace all of their clan customs (*kangakanga*) to the myth of their culture hero Akaisa and his younger brother Tsabini.[29] According to Mosko, these heroes have the ability "to produce specifiable or desired effects or transformations in the world, including interrelationships between humans, living and dead,"[30] through agentive properties that are custom and which the Mekeo charac-

Hula woman. After Barton (1918: pl. X). Courtesy of Blackwell Publishing. The stepped tattoos (*lakatoi*) on her cheeks and nose note that her father participated in several successful trading voyages. However, it has been postulated that this design perhaps evolved from the concept of an elbowed bird's wing, possibly a predatorial bird (Barton 1918).

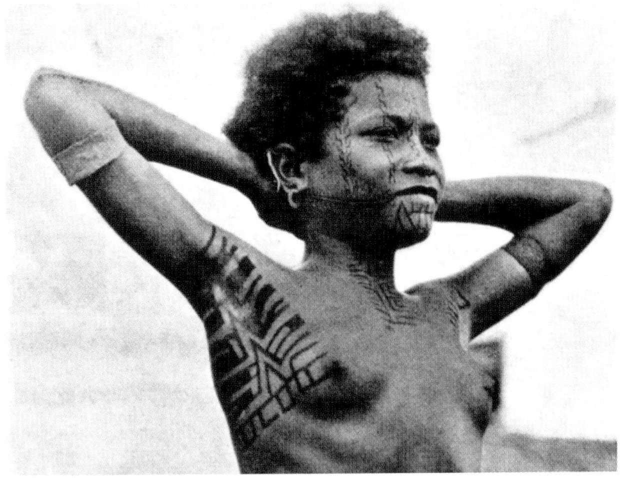

terize as "hot" (*tsiabu*). Thus, fire is *hot* for cooking food, a stone axe is "hot" for chopping down trees, and today even money is "hot" because it allows men and women to gain personal renown and fame.[31] Hence, all customs, whether practiced in the past (e.g. Mekeo tattooing) or in the present, are generally regarded as embodying the transformative properties associated with heat, or in Mosko's words, "the 'hot' personal *qua* bodily/spiritual efficacy of their celebrated culture-hero[es]."[32]

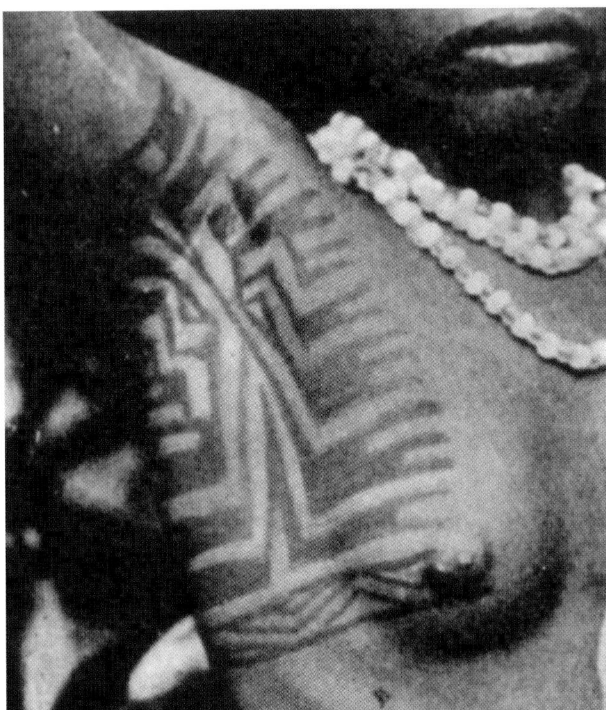

Hula girl with "armpit" (*kadidiha*) tattooing. After Barton (1918: pl. VIII). Courtesy of Blackwell Publishing. With this design, the girl completes her third stage of the tattooing ritual.

Important as it was to the overall logic of Papuan and Maori tattoo customs, heat in its various aspects obviously had other symbolic referents,

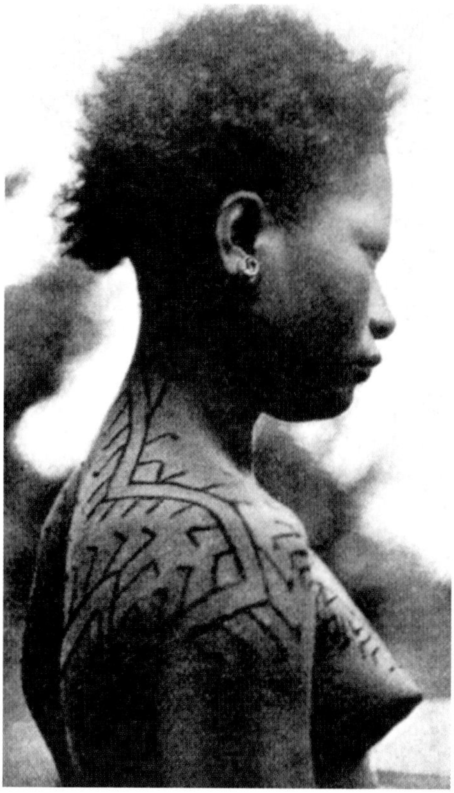

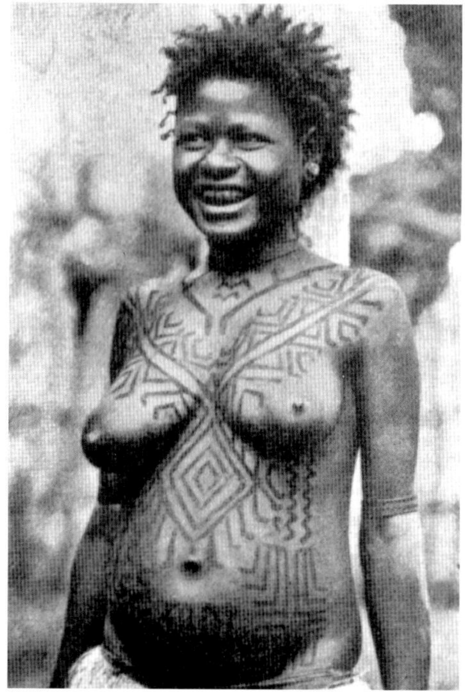

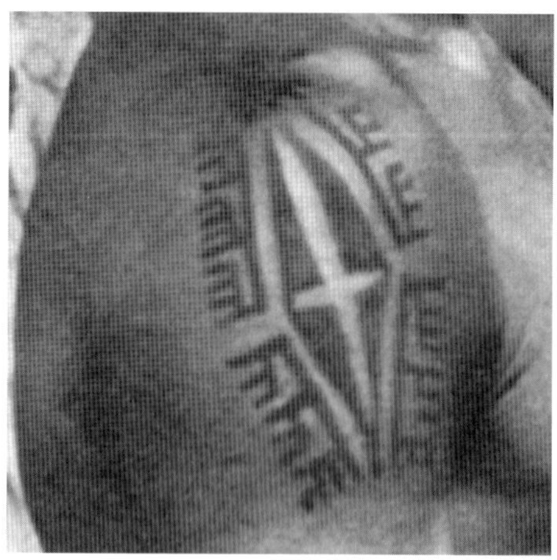

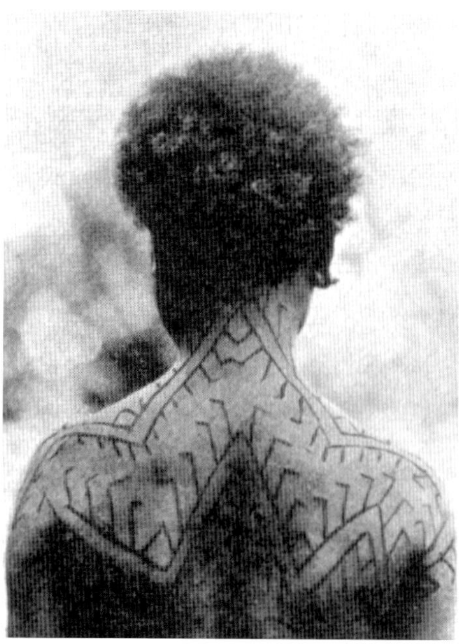

Views of two Mekeo women and one Hula woman with *bina* (hornbill) tattoo on shoulder. After Barton (1918: pl. IV). Courtesy of Blackwell Publishing. Upper right shows the V-shaped motif on the chest that signifies marriage while the small elbowed designs on the throat are frigate birds. The zigzag motifs under her breasts are centipedes. The *mangeau* pattern adorns one Mekeo woman's back; it represents a bird soaring upwards.

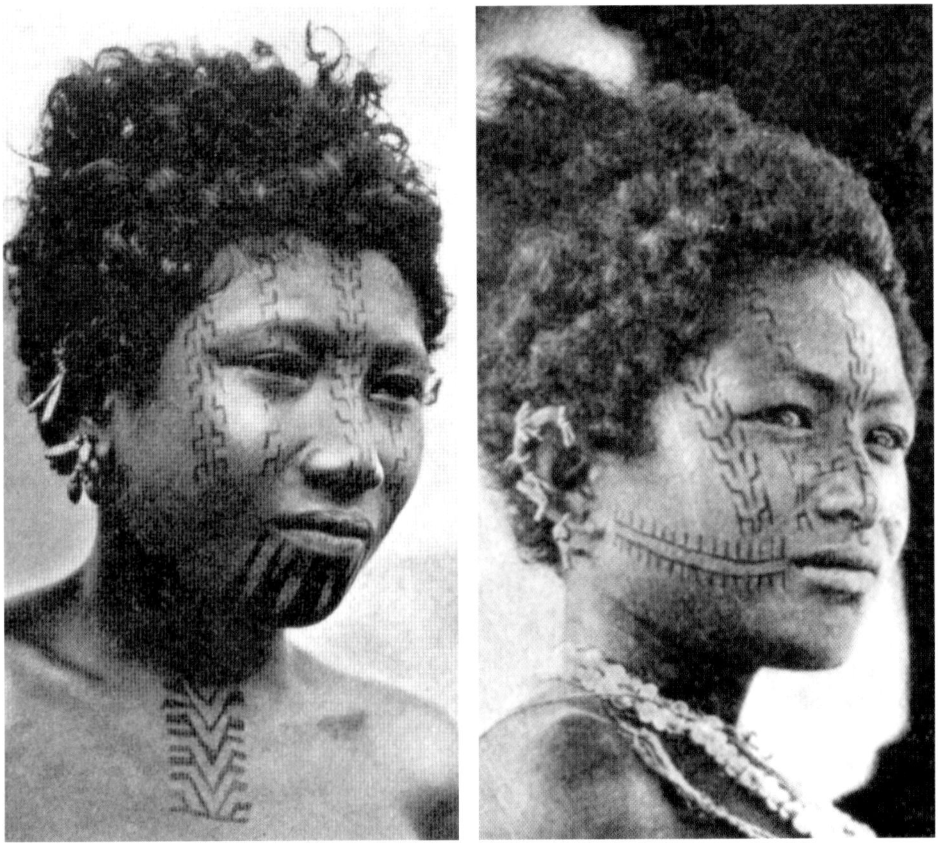

Views of two Hula women with *lakatoi* and other facial markings. After Barton (1918: pls. VII, VIII). Courtesy of Blackwell Publishing.

especially in its connection to fire. Through its transformative capacities, the fire of the domestic hearth changes food, like raw and bloody meat into an edible meal. Fire cooks the flesh, definitively separating the "raw" from the "cooked," as does the tattoo, separating the "girl" from the "woman," when it is placed on a girl's skin after her first menstruation. More than simply enhancing life, tattoo also enabled life, since it was the heat that "cooked" the woman until she had achieved maturation. Thus, it is precisely in this sense that tattooing provides the central metaphor for the conjugal and reproductive dimension of female personhood; it transformed the initiate, whose immaturity (e.g. infertility) originated in her "raw" body, into a reproductive agent by making her maternal flesh warm.[33]

However, the transformation that occurred in tattoo ritual was not completed until the initiate was properly "cooled down" with coconut oil or milk. As noted, Barton[34] and others observed that in some of the tattoo nomenclatures of Melanesia and Polynesia word roots, like *oro*, were used in conjunction with other terms to signify the "untattooed" (Motu, *kasiri vahoro*; Mangareva, *roro tea*). More specifically, the term *roro* and its dialectical cognate *lolo* is used throughout Polynesia (New Zealand, Samoa, Hawaii, Tonga, Fiji, Mangereva) to express the verb "to oil," usually the milky oil of coconuts.[35]

Barker and Tietjen,[36] Guise,[37] Haddon,[38] Ison,[39] and Seligmann[40] recorded that coastal Papuan girls were anointed by old women with coconut oil over their entire bodies (including genitals) after the tattoo ritual. Even in Samoa, Marquardt stated that the tattoo ceremony was brought to its conclusion when priests sprinkled "the milk of a coconut [upon] all those who had been tattooed."[41]

Coconut oil, or "milk," I suggest, is cool, like water, and beneficial because it is a symbol of life and fertility; it is imbibed by some Papuan women to increase the production and flow of their own breast milk.[42] As a cooling substance then, coconut oil and milk are antithetical to heat and by extension fire, and would be suitable substances used to "cool" a woman down after the tattoo ritual. Therefore, it would seem to follow that coconut products worked symbolically to "solidify" a girl's transition into womanhood.

Papuan tattoo patterns

Yet it remains to comment on the ritualized tattoo patterns used by the coastal Papuans. As seen in the illustrations, there are numerous recurring designs and motifs, and many of these were found among different indigenous populations, suggesting particular efficacies for specific tattoos. Generally speaking, the tattooed peoples of coastal Papua seemed to have preferred abstract motifs of natural subjects, and those of falling objects (stars), flying birds, especially predatory birds (frigate bird, hawk), or other creatures associated with rapid movement and predatory habits (like centipedes or serpents) were quite common.[43] It could be argued that some of these animals were tattooed onto living skin because they were able in nature to straddle diurnal and nocturnal lifestyles, thus mastering the worlds of both light and darkness. Perhaps for the Papuans this otherworldly existence was perceived in abstract reality as "life" on the supernatural plane of the living and the dead. Therefore it should come as no surprise that most—if not

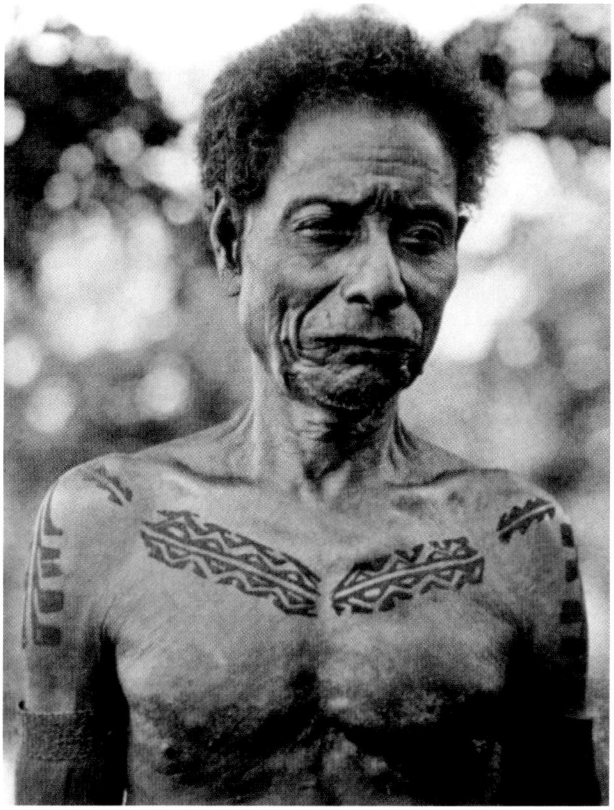

Motu man with headhunter's tattoos. After Seligmann (1910: pl. XIV). The motif on his chest is called *gado* and probably represented a tally of his victims. According to Haddon (1894: 177-178), the chief Vaburi had: "both upper arms tattooed, and two zigzag stripes down the middle of the back. They indicate that he has killed three people, two men and two women. Hila, the deposed chief of the Motu, and quite the modest man in Anuapata, is richly tattooed on the breast and on the arms down to the wrists. He bears on his chest the double obtuse-angled stripes, like the *gado* of the women. Sometimes zigzag stripes are found only on young people. They are, in that case inherited from the father, and by no means signify that the party in question has killed any one." (see Finsch 1885).

all—of these animal emblems (birds, serpent, fish, or even plants) were believed to either repel evil spirits, since they were powerful spirits themselves,[44] or were considered tutelary spirits that were sometimes tabooed from being eaten,[45] because they were highly revered "clan" or even individual "insignias."[46] These types of family crests were also carved upon clan houses, canoe prows, pottery, and practically all wooden utensils.[47]

Among Hula, Motu, and Mailu headhunters, some of the most popular tattooed emblems were abstract hornbill (*bina*) designs.[48] Hornbills practice a peculiar nesting habit which may have something to do with their symbolic importance. For example, female birds enclose themselves within the confines of tree trunks to nest, with their male counterparts visiting regularly to provide sustenance for the family. Female hornbills only emerge after their young have hatched and this behavior may suggest the symbolic oppositions between light and dark, life and death. It should be noted that Hula and Motu women also wore the *bina* tattoo design.[49]

Similarly, the Iban, Kenyah, Kayan and Lahanan of Borneo, utilized the great-beaked hornbill as a tattoo ornament; it was placed on headhunter's chests and arms because it was thought to provide protection against the intrusion of evil spirits; it was also associated with the Upper World and was a sacred omen bird. For the Iban, the hornbill was the primary messenger of the war god Singalong Burong.[50] Kenyah, Kayan, Sihan, and Lahanan women also wore the motif on their forearms.[51]

In Papua, the association between man, woman and bird, was also expressed in mimic bird dances, songs, and the wearing of hornbill feathers and beaks on dancing regalia as symbolic ornament.[52] Among the Hula of the 1880s, warriors who had taken human life wore white cockatoo feathers in their hair, the mandibles of the hornbill on their foreheads, other plumes as headdresses, not to mention serpentine and avian tattoos on their legs and chests.[53] Even the sons, daughters, and the wives of those men who had taken heads were entitled to hornbill tattoos worn on their skins. Mailu men wore the white feathers of the hornbill to signify that the wearer had killed one or more men. Mailu warriors also wore a tattoo on either shoulder to mark success in the headhunt, and this design "was taken from the peculiar curve and corrugations of the huge beak of the same familiar bird, and bears the name of the bird, *bina* [hornbill]."[54] Based on this description, it can be presumed that the Motu *gado* motif worn on headhunters' chests carried a similar symbolism.

However, other avian creatures, like the frigate bird, seemed to have ranked as high on the tattoo motif map.[55] Characterized in folk belief as a rapacious, ravenous, and voracious seagoing predator, frigates were widely associated with Papuan headhunting mysticism; somehow lending power to the wearer, or even to the family of the tattooed, acting as a sort of spiritual "assistant."[56] This belief was widespread, and many other headhunting groups inhabiting Melanesia, Indonesia, and Polynesia tattooed the frigate emblem, including the Easter Islanders who lived some 6,000 miles across the Pacific Ocean.[57]

Easter Island

On Easter Sunday, 1722, the Dutch navigator Jacob Roggeveen was cruising the vastness of the South Pacific when he sighted a small volcanic island in the distance. Landing at a rocky cove, his crew marveled at colossal seven-meter high stone statues (*moai*) standing in silent rows along the shore. Perhaps at that moment his men began to wonder just who lived in this mysterious place cut off from the entire world. It seemed that Easter

Island had developed in complete isolation for centuries.

The Easter Islanders, who today refer to themselves and to their homeland as Rapa Nui, are the easternmost of some thirty-six Polynesian peoples whose ancestors discovered and settled the islands of the central and eastern Pacific.[58] They share a common ancestry with other Polynesians, such as the Hawaiians, Tahitians, and the New Zealand Maori,[59] and their tattooing traditions retain particular features that link them to other Austronesian speakers of Melanesia.[60]

The ancestors of the Polynesians began to migrate from Southeast Asia around 1500 B.C. and by 600-800 A.D. they arrived on Easter Island.[61] According to Rapa Nui legend, the island was settled by Hotu Matu'a, a powerful chieftain who arrived with a group of colonists in two large sailing vessels.[62] At this time, dense palm forests and stands of small trees covered the island, and the coasts were visited by seabirds, sea turtles, and marine mammals. Over time, however,

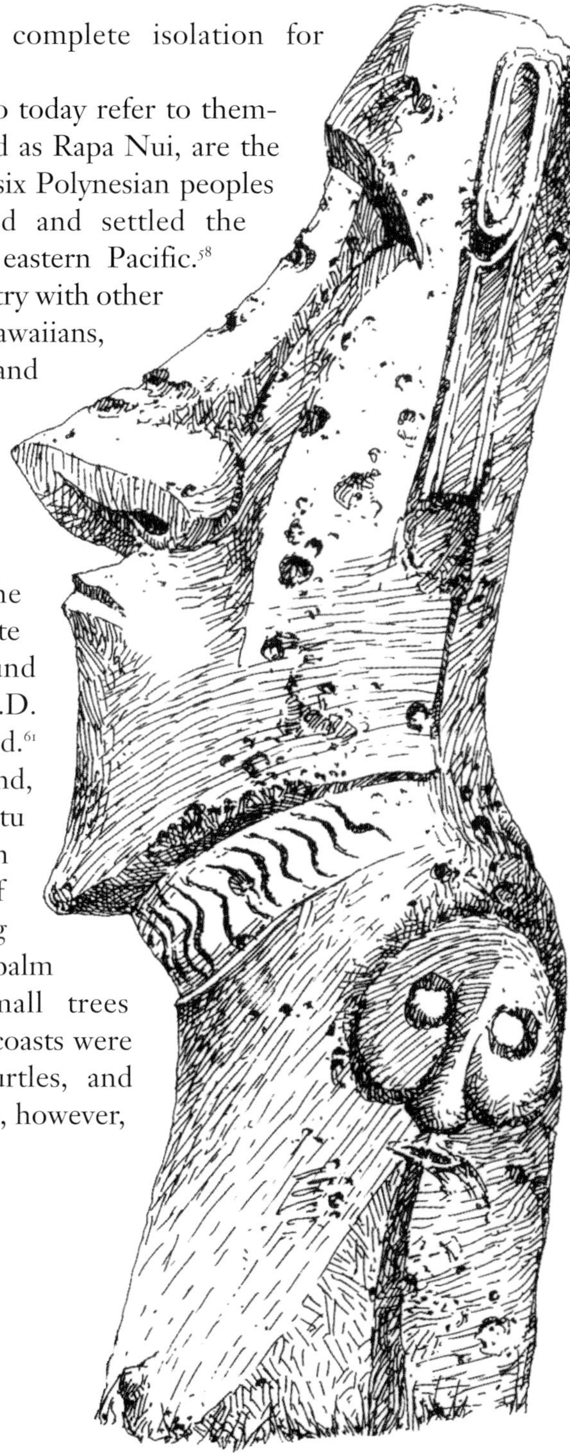

Profile view of a *moai*, showing superimposed carved tattoo designs on the neck. Other tattoo motifs have been seen on the chests and faces of several *moai* around the island. Redrawn after Van Tilburg (2001: 31).

the trees were cut and by the close of the 19th century, Rapa Nui was virtually a barren landscape.

Down through the centuries, a distinctive form of art developed on the island blending anthropomorphic and zoomorphic imagery into superbly crafted and almost surrealistic forms. The power of this aesthetic tradition revolved around perceptions of life experienced in an unforgiving insular environment, one devoid of trees and land mammals (except perhaps for one lizard species), which led Rapa Nui artisans to focus their energies completely and entirely on the few fragments of wood they could find.

Although wood for carving was rare, barkcloth objects (*tapa*) made from mulberry trees were rarer still and perhaps even more important.[63] Where Hawaiian chiefs wore red feather cloaks to assert their high, god-like status, the Rapa Nui chiefs wore *tapa* cloaks and tattoos on their backs, suggesting that these ornaments were considered as high-status substitutes.[64] Furthermore, the ruling elite may have utilized anthropomorphic figures covered with barkcloth to assist them in communicating with their divine ancestors. These objects are exceedingly rare and only three of these figures (*manu uru*) are known to exist in museum collections.[65] Because all are decorated with paintings representing tattoos, they can be associated directly with the ruling class; since only they were sacred enough to control the supernatural power (*mana*) manifested in these types of objects.[66]

On Easter Island, tattoo was widespread and often associated with chiefly or warrior status.[67] The face, neck, torso, back, legs, arms, and top of the head were tattooed and Rapa Nui tattooing implements (*ta kona*) were similar to those found elsewhere in Polynesia: a comb of bird bone lashed at a right angle to a wood handle.[68] The comb was dipped in a prepared pigment of charred ti leaves (*Cordyline terminalis*) mixed with black nightshade (*Solanum nigrum*) juice and struck with a mallet into the skin.[69] In Hawaii, ti was considered sacred to the god Lono and to the goddess Laka.[70] Ti leaves were emblems of high rank and divine power and they were carried to ward off evil spirits and bring good fortune.

The vanishing Rapa Nui tattoo

Sadly, there is very little pictorial evidence of Rapa Nui tattooing today. In fact, perhaps only one photograph survives of traditional Rapa Nui tattooing. This 1870s postcard, shot by Tahitian photographer Madame Hoare, portrays Juan Tepano, a Rapa Nui nobleman, with neck and facial tattoos.[71]

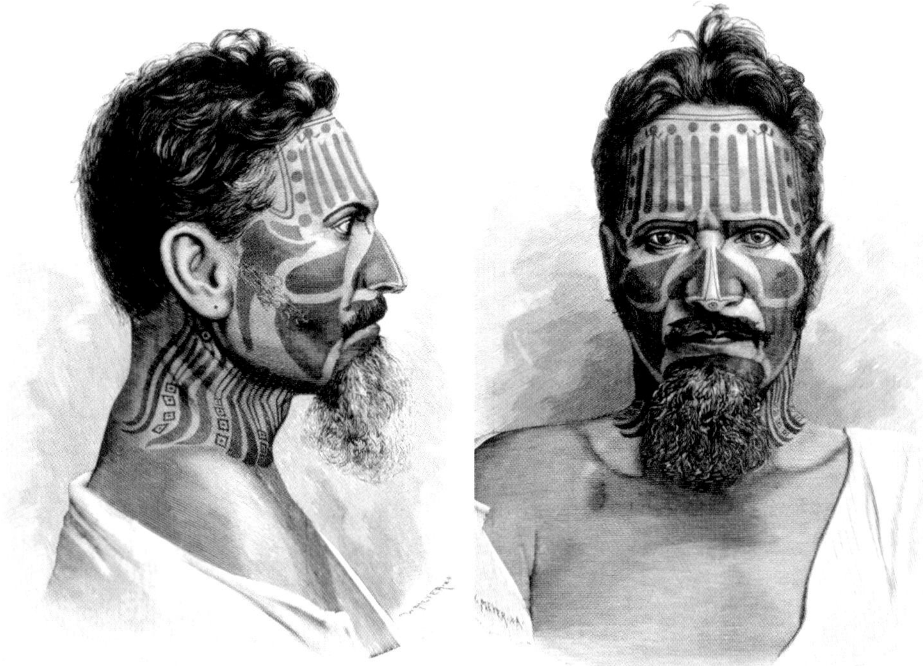

Above: Profile and portrait view of Juan Tepano, ca. 1880s. Engravings after drawings by Hjalmar Stolpe (1899: figs. 4 & 5).

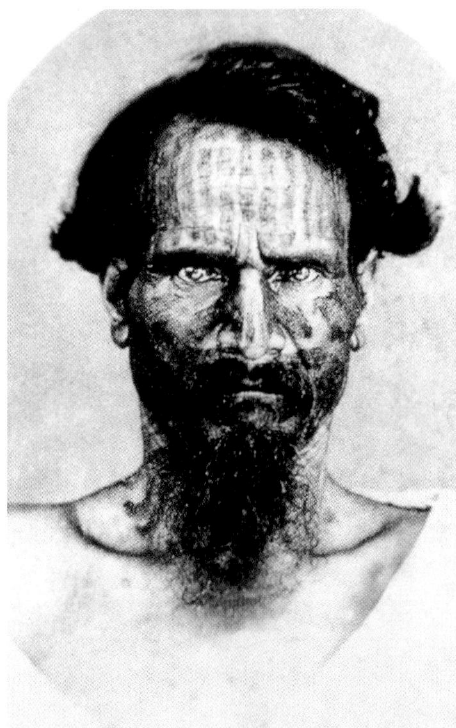

Right: *Carte de visite* of Juan Tepano by Madame Hoare, ca. 1870s.

The Swedish ethnographer Hjalmar Stolpe who traveled the Pacific in the 1880s also illustrated Tepano in portrait and profile views,[72] but by 1911 only four islanders out of 228 wore traditional tattoos, and these were women.[73] By 1930, only two tattooed women survived: Juan Tepano's mother, old Viriamo, and Ana Eva Hei, the wife of Atamu Te Kena, one of the last "kings" of Easter Island.[74] Both women were incompletely tattooed and Viriamo said she refused to submit to further sittings because the tattooing operation was too painful. Ana Eva Hei, who was younger, was tattooed by one of the last "experts."[75]

As in most of Polynesia, tattoo artists were men and on Rapa Nui they were specialists—like wood and rock carvers—and their work was supervised by the *ariki mau*, or ruling king.[76] Being *maori* ("expert"), tattooists likely constituted a class of *tufunga*, or a kind of priesthood or guild, "charged" with sacredness, because they had mastered their ritual craft.[77] Certainly, tattooists, as members of the *tufunga* brotherhoods, worked under strict religious codes that dominated their respective professions. Because as Thomson noted, *tufunga* were exempt from performing any laborious activity not associated with their work, indicating their divine status in the eyes of the community.[78]

Symbolic dimensions of women's tattooing

Generally speaking, Rapa Nui tattoo was comprised of fundamental motifs preserved and passed from one generation to the next. It is true, however, that personal taste varied and perhaps different clans had favorite designs, but little else is known of the symbolic import of tattooing: except that certain designs were more common than others.[79]

Women and men very often had heavy lines on their faces which crossed their foreheads or extended from one ear to the other. These lines were curved and combined with a series of large dots (*humu* or *puraki*) that marked the forehead and temples.[80] These designs are also seen on existing barkcloth figures, but in smaller detail.

On the cheeks of women below the ears was a motif called *pagaha'a*, "something that hangs heavy,"[81] formed by the meeting of two designs, one triangular and the other fusiform (tapering at each end). An old spelling of this word is *tangehua*[82] or *pangehúa*[83] and based on the root *hua*, it can be suggested that these were fertility markings: *hua* means "testicle," or more figuratively, "son."[84] Other motifs included tattooed rings (*ngutu tika*) surrounding the mouth of women, possibly akin to the Maori tattoo custom,[85] and three vertical lines descending the mouth sometimes crossing the chin.[86] These motifs also appear on some of the barkcloth figures.

On the back of old Viriamo, between the shoulder blades, is a motif called *'ao* ("dance paddle") with conventionalized eyes and nose.[87] Along the lower part of her back, and under the *'ao* is a stripe which winds back and forth. These bands, or "dancing torsos,"[88] are tattooed in one continuous design around the body. On one barkcloth figure, the same tattoo design

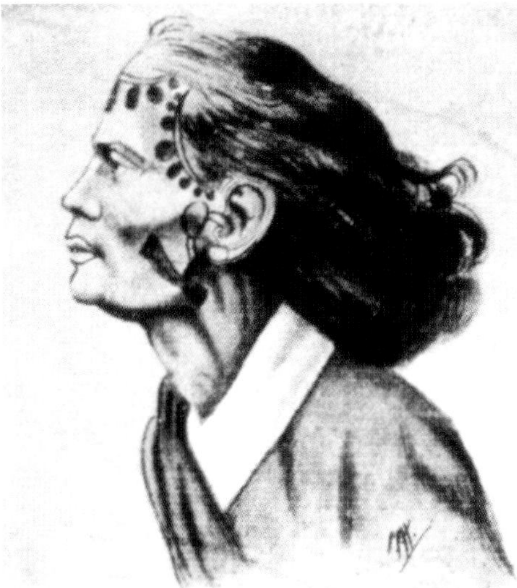

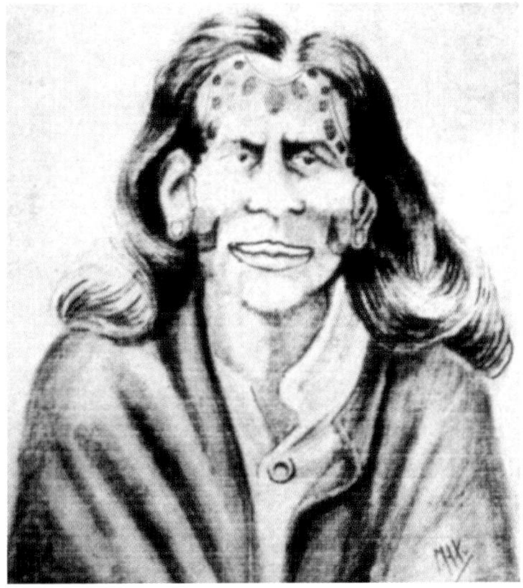

Above left & right: Profile and portrait views of Ana Eva Hei. Note the tattooed mouth ring. After Knoche (1912: figs. 7 & 8).

Left & below: Back and profile view of Old Viriamo, Tepano's mother, 1911. After Knoche (1912).

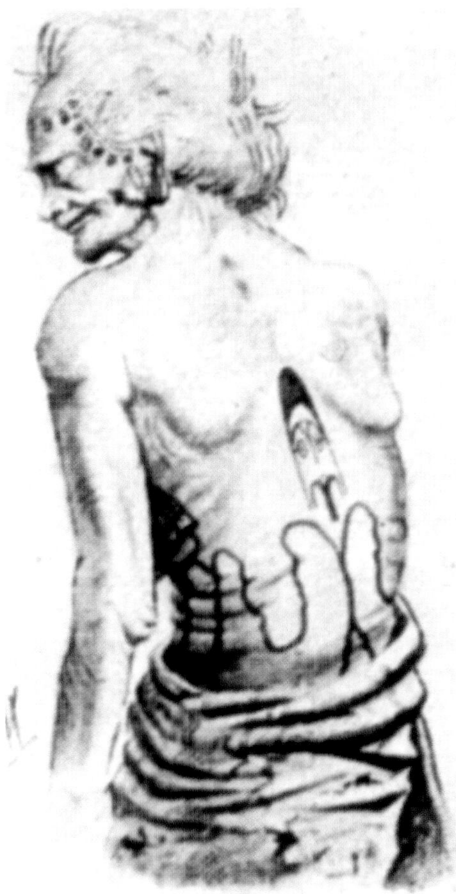

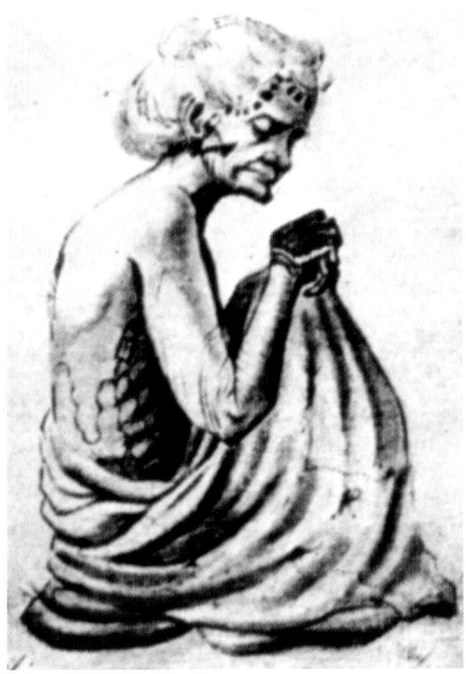

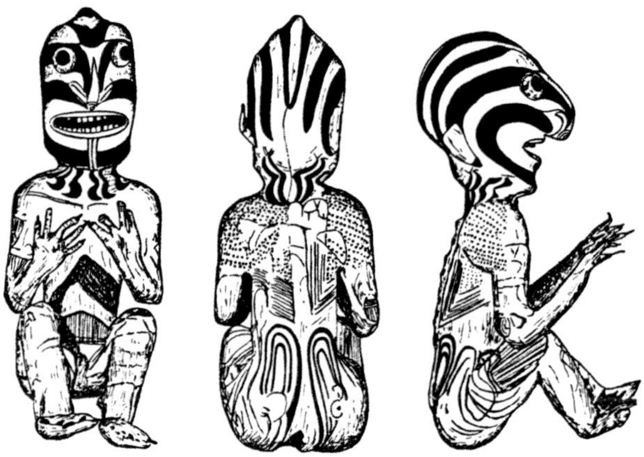

Two sketches of fully tattooed tapa figures. Redrawn after Métraux (1940: 238-239). From top; swooping, plunging frigate bird tattooed on back above buttocks (center view) is symbolic of war and headhunting. From bottom; *ao'* or *mata'a* motifs on torso, back and buttocks are suggestive of warfare. Feather-like tattoos appear on the neck and three lines adorn the chin.

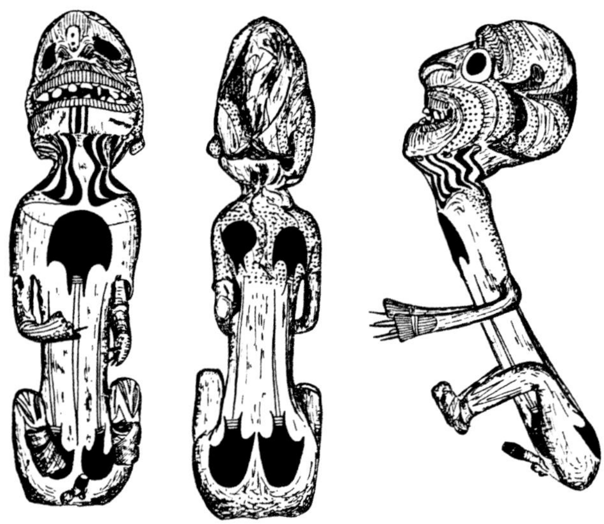

covers the buttocks and the waist region, and the band terminates at a bird design with a beak joined by two concentric rings.

It is possible that the *'ao* motifs have an ancestral importance, especially since the word *'ao* also refers to the ruling elite,[89] suggesting that only aristocrats could wear these tattoo motifs. However, the *'ao* designs perhaps have a deeper symbolic significance. In 1770, Spanish explorers to Easter Island noted that a pair of tattoos called *pare* marked the abdomen: "they depict two fearsome monstrosities . . . and I believe they look on them with veneration, but they do not like one to touch them with the hand."[90] Routledge also gave the name *pare-pu* to the anthropomorphic tattoos on the abdomen of her informant,[91] which raises some issue over what was *ao*' and what was *pare*? Métraux recorded that the word *pare* was given to him as meaning a motif tattooed around the waist[92]—one that I would suggest was similar to that which Viriamo wore on her torso.

Gleaning linguistic evidence from Rapa Nui dictionaries, Fuentes notes that *pare* is an obsolete word, meaning "a kind of sculpture made of wood" or "tattooing on the arms."[93] Englert gives *pare* as "a wooden figurine representing a human head with arms."[94]

What seems clear from this discussion is that some sort of affinity existed between particular forms of Easter Island tattooing and woodcarving. Looking towards New Zealand, the same pattern follows since the culture hero Mataora introduced tattooing

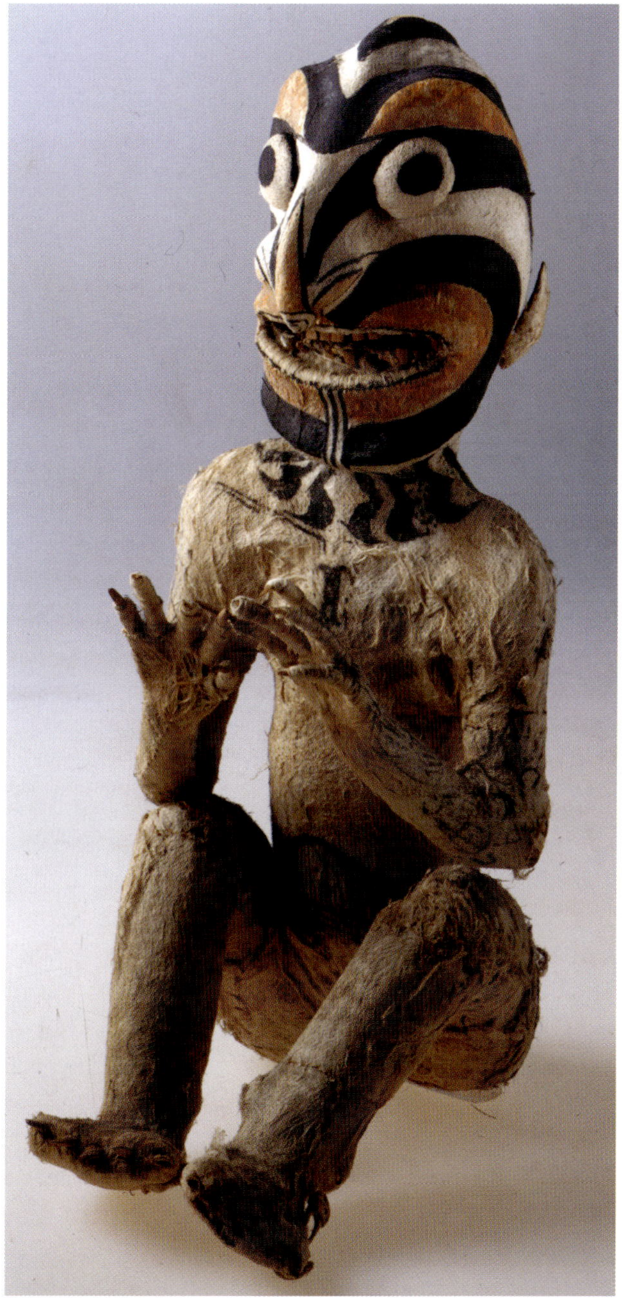

Tapa barkcloth figure with facial, neck, and sternum tattoos. Reeds, barkcloth and paint, 19th century. 40 cm. in length. Copyright 2006 Harvard University, Peabody Museum of Archaeology and Ethnology, Photo 99-12-10/53543 T2816.2.

and wood carving to the Maori.[95] More specifically, the Maori maintained a rich tradition of wood carving and one particular form, called *pare*, adorned the lintel above the entrance door of the house. Of course, as Easter Island became devoid of trees circa 1850-1900, we can be fairly certain that even before that time large pieces of wood were scarce,[96] and certainly those needed to carve lintels must have been rarer still. Indeed, we have no archaeological evidence that this custom was ever practiced on Rapa Nui,[97] although carved wooden images of lizards (*moko*), possibly in the form of clubs, stood on either side of doorways to ward off intruders or to protect the dwellers of the house against evil spirits.[98] For the Maori, lizards were symbolic of death and it was necessary to employ a ritual specialist to avert their evil omen.

Jackson has commented extensively on the "symbolic system" of Maori *pare*, where "[t]here seems little doubt that the *pare* composition reveals a symbolic connection with the Maori conception of birth and death, creation and dissolution."[99] For example, over the door of the Maori house, female genitalia were carved in deep relief on *pare* lintels, sometimes with a small stylized anthropomorphic head being situated in place of the genitalia suggesting parturition.[100] Best, however, tells us that in Maori mythology, the vagina symbolized destructive energy,[101] thus crossing the threshold of the Maori house brought an individual dangerously close to the great *mana* (supernatural power) contained and displayed within it.[102] In this sense, *pare* sculptures exemplify a double-sided function whereby the female, who has the power to transform life by destroying it and then reforming it (by giving birth), symbolizes the fundamental division of the Maori mythological universe; one that is displayed in the carved lintel, which by surmounting the dwelling house, embodies all social life within and outside of its door.[103]

Similarly, the mouth tattoos of Maori and Rapa Nui women also evoke this cosmological relationship. *Waha*, the Maori word for mouth, also referred to the vagina,[104] and the tattooed mouth ring of Rapa Nui women, called *ngutu tika* or "mouth marking," probably embodied similar concepts, although a related term *ngutu tiko* translates to "menstrual opening."[105] Because it is the death and rebirth of symbolic forms that is at the essence of our inquiry, it is obvious that menstrual blood equivocally refers to both processes insofar as it signifies the death of latent life and the potentiality of bearing life.[106] Curiously, the main facial tattooing of Maori women besides the labial markings placed around the mouth were chin markings called *whakatehe*, from *tehe*, "the penis in an erect state."[107] Although the term for these tattoos has been forgotten on Easter Island, the chin was crossed by three vertical stripes descending from the mouth.[108] If we are to read the female mouth/chin-tattoo as a manifestation of the phallus probing towards its predestined (open) orifice, a view proposed by Gell,[109] then I would suggest that this form of tattoo was perhaps conceived of as a kind of fertility symbol.

Notwithstanding these considerations there are other comparisons that suggest themselves. When Knoche interviewed Viriamo in 1911, she said she received her *'ao* torso markings "after the first sexual intercourse."[110] From a compositional standpoint, her "dancing torsos" were purposefully placed and according to an early Spanish account similar tattoos were marked "with so much skill that it excited our wonder, not a dot nor a line from right side to left side wanting in regularity."[111] Upon re-examination of the Knoche drawings,[112] the anthropomorphs adorning Viriamo's skin were placed on either side of her torso under her armpits, with a larger central figure placed at the mid-back between the shoulder blades. The symmetry generated here reveals a composition created by the insertion of a central figure that mediates between two neighboring ones, very similar to the aesthetic structure of the Maori *pare* that in effect carries "the eye of the beholder with great rapidity from part to part, and from element to element."[113] However, a symbolic reading of this composition can be offered. Best, in his discussion of Maori perceptions of the body, noted that:

> The right side of the body is the male side, the tama tane, the strong and lucky side. It stands for vigour, health, virility, life. The left side is the female side, the tama wahine, the weak, listless, unlucky side, and represents misfortune, [and] death . . . [114]

As such, it is possible that Viriamo's tattooed body may have carried this dual meaning of life and death.

Men's tattoo motifs

Besides the tattooing which was done for women, however, many elaborate and symbolic forms were received by Rapa Nui men. Juan Tepano, Viriamo's son, wore forehead tattoos (*retu*, "to stand") consisting of six to ten solid vertical stripes.[115] The parallel lines across the top of the forehead and the fringe of dots around his hairline were the first motifs tattooed on the face. This pattern was the most general, since it was the one commonly recorded by early voyagers.[116]

But of considerable interest are the tattoos that you cannot see. Beneath Tepano's chin and beard (on the throat) is a stylized bird with head turned down, elongated body and wings reduced to four small tattoo lines.[117] This motif, also seen in other abstract versions on barkcloth figures, is that of the frigate bird.[118] The frigate, a predatory bird that flies swiftly and cunningly, is widely associated with the tattoo traditions of several indigenous peoples of Polynesia, Melanesia, and Indonesia, and is symbolic of headhunting and warfare.[119] Although rarely seen on Easter Island today, frigates "acquired a special mystique as a symbol of invasion and aggression . . . [They were] a symbol of the warrior class" who overthrew the ruling nobility during the Decadent Period (1500-1722 A.D.): a time when Rapa Nui was characterized by intertribal warfare, cannibalism, and the disintegration of society.[120]

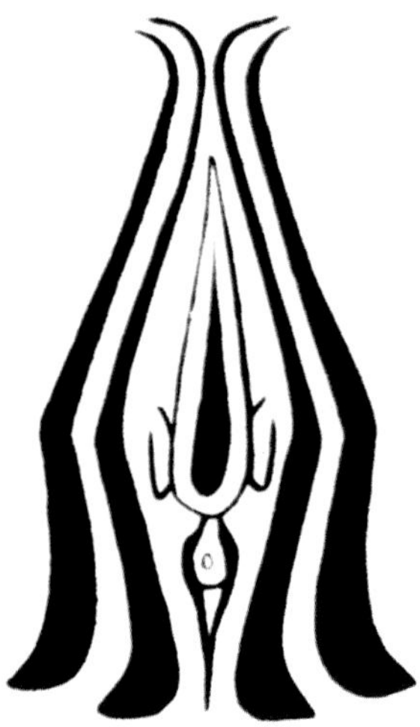

Stylistic frigate bird tattoo appearing on Tepano's throat and barkcloth figures. After Stolpe (1899: fig. 6).

Tepano's other tattoos reinforce this avian symbolism. On the right side of his spine is a set of nine parallel lines, running vertically and bending to the right at the bottom, reminiscent of a bird swooping downwards with wings outstretched.[121] The fundamental decoration of the neck (*ua*), which was essentially masculine, consisted of four pairs of broad and wavy stripes.[122] Also appearing on large stone *moai* around the island,[123] these tattoos look like bird feathers, and when combined with Tepano's other markings they transformed him into a powerful predatory "birdman."

As early as the 15th century, a series of annual religious ceremonies developed on Rapa Nui that were centered on the creator god Makemake, whose earthly manifestation was the *tangata manu* or birdman.[124] The rise of the cult of Makemake marked a radical shift from the old religion of ancestor worship and "seems to have evolved from a postulated earlier bird ritual that arose in response to the warrior class's need to justify and legitimize its anarchistic rule" over the secular and declining authority of the ruling elite.[125] Born from a floating skull that was washed from a temple into the sea, Makemake created the first humans and with his companion, the goddess Haua, brought the first flocks of migratory seabirds to the island.[126]

The continuous cycle of war that plagued Rapa Nui during the Decadent

Period has been supported by archaeological findings: obsidian spearpoints (*mata'a*) have been uncovered in large quantities.[127] Likewise human bones that display cut marks have been unearthed suggesting cannibalism. For the Maori of New Zealand, warfare was also endemic and provided a constant source of terrifying reality.[128] It is probable that Maori *pare* sculpture embodied this reality because some of the forms carved into these lintels (e.g. female genitalia) were symbolic of death and destruction. Other design elements, which have not been alluded to until now, were called *manaia*, and they closely resembled some of the existing Rapa Nui barkcloth figures, especially in their bird-like appearance.[129] Jackson provides evidence that *manaia* forms "were symbolic of death, evil influence, and imperfection."[130]

The concept of death among the Maori was called *mate*. *Mate* is also the Rapa Nui word for death and the derivative *mata'a* means a spearhead made of obsidian in both the Maori and Rapa Nui languages.[131] Interestingly, *mata'a* appear on two of the barkcloth figures from Easter Island suggesting in all likelihood that they were a traditional tattoo motif of the *matatoa*—the warrior class.

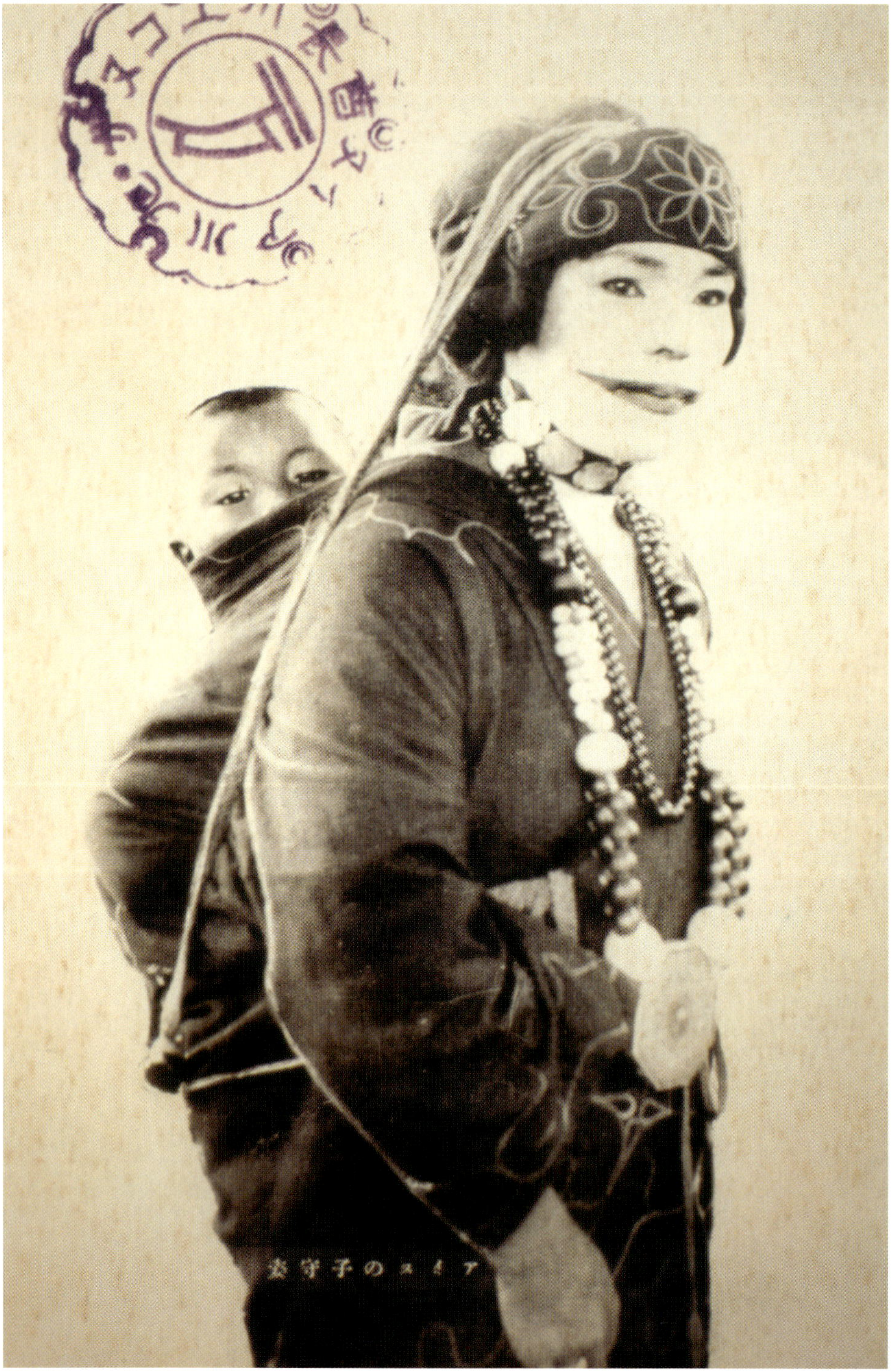
アイヌの子守姿

Japan, Northwest Coast, and Arctic

The indigenous people of northern Japan (who also formerly occupied the Kurile Islands, southern Sakhalin, and parts of the southern Kamchatka peninsula) call themselves "Ainu," meaning "people" or "humans" in their language.[1] Recent DNA evidence suggests that the Ainu are the direct descendents of the ancient Jomon people who inhabited Japan as early as 12,000 years ago.[2] Astonishingly, the Jomon culture existed in Japan for some 10,000 years, and today many artistic traditions of the Ainu seem to have evolved from the ancestral Jomon. As such, this artistic continuum represents one of the oldest ongoing cultural traditions in the world, spanning at least ten millennia.[3]

Jomon culture, like that of the Ainu, was based on a hunting-and-gathering economy. Exploiting natural resources from riverine, terrestrial, and marine ecosystems, the Jomon achieved stasis through active and continual engagement with their surrounding environments. Archaeological evidence in the form of ceramic sculpture supports this view, but it also suggests that particular animals (bears, whales, owls) were highly revered and possibly worshipped as deities.[4] Among the contemporary Ainu, all natural phenomena (including flora, fauna, and even inanimate objects) are believed to have a spiritual essence, and particular animals (e.g. brown bears, killer whales, horned owls) continue to be honored in ceremony and ritual as "spirit deities" (*kamuy*).

Apart from zoomorphic sculpture, Jomon artisans also created anthropomorphic figurines (*dogū*) that were probably used for protection against illness, infertility, and the dangers associated with childbirth.[5] Markings on the faces of many of these *dogū* likely indicate body painting, scarification,

Facing page: Portrait of a Chikabumi Ainu woman with child, ca. 1930. Postcard from the collection of the author.

or tattooing,[6] and similar figures, carved as masks or rock art in the lower Amur River basin of the Russian Maritime Region,[7] suggest an ancient and unbroken tradition of personal adornment and ritual practice.

Until very recently (the last fully tattooed Ainu woman died in 1998), Ainu women retained a tradition of facial tattooing, lending support to the argument that the ancient Jomon also employed the custom in the distant past. For the Ainu, however, tattooing was exclusive to females, as was the profession of tattooist. According to mythological accounts, tattoo was brought to earth by the "ancestral mother" of the Ainu (Okikurumi Turesh Machi) who was the younger sister of the creator god Okikurumi.[8]

Because tattooing represented an ancestral custom derived from one common female ancestress (Turesh Machi), it was continued down through the centuries in the matrilineal line.[9] Viewing tattoo practices through the lens of kinship, it is not

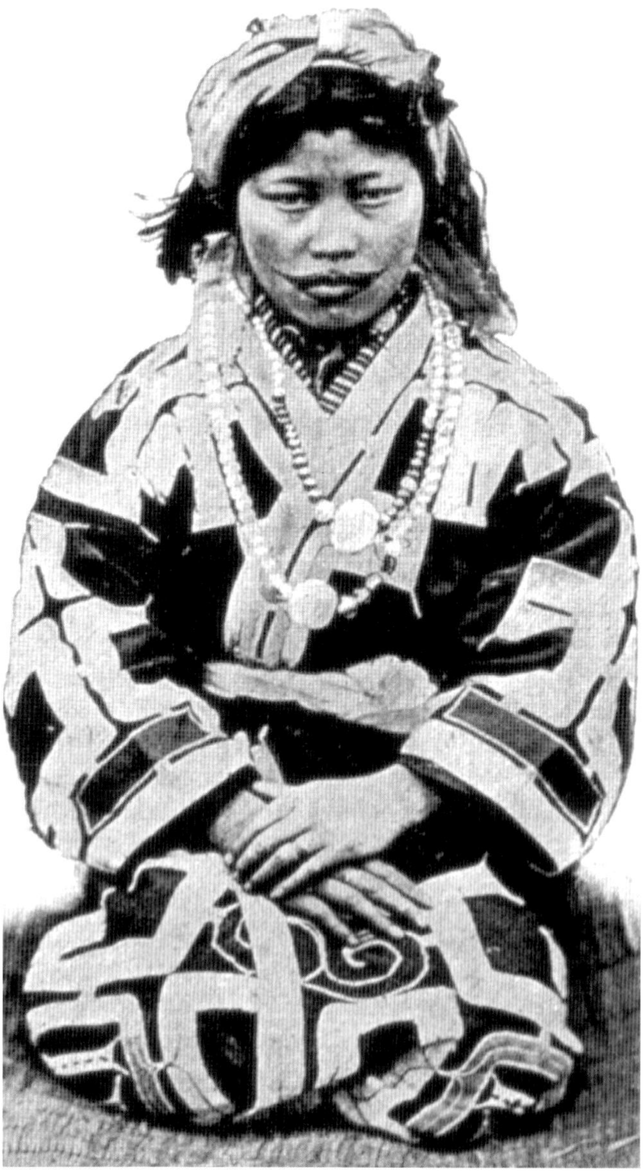

Ainu woman with tattooed mouth. After Fritze (1893: 45).

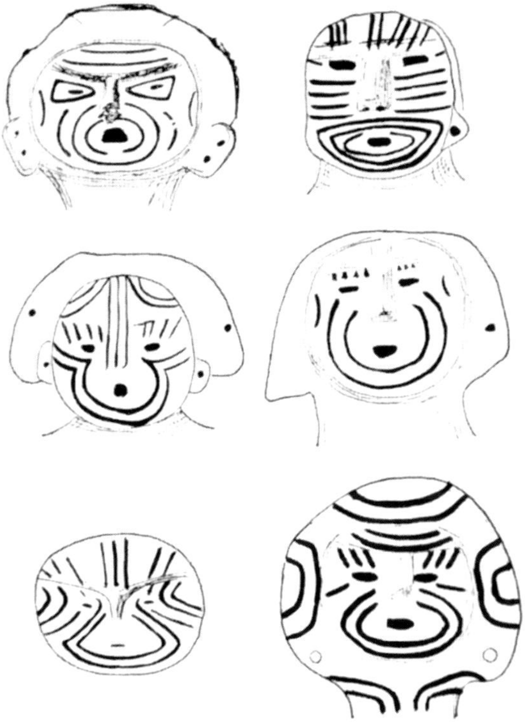

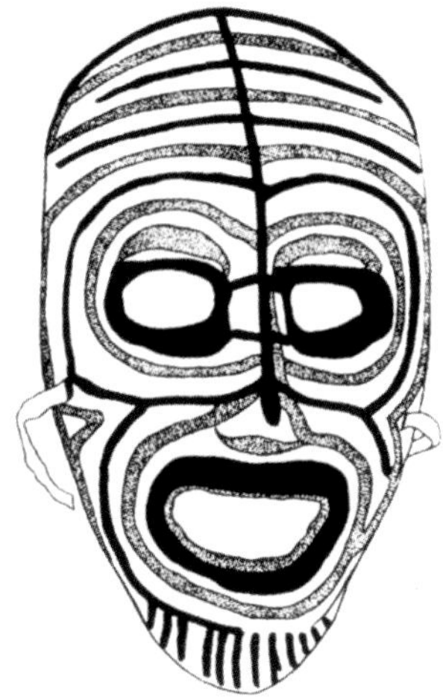

Above: Udege shaman's mask, Amur River basin, 19th century. Redrawn after Okladnikov (1971: 106).

Left: Facial markings of Jomon *dogū*. Redrawn after Esaka (1967: 309).

surprising that the position of tattoo artist was customarily performed by grandmothers or maternal aunts who were called "Tattoo Aunts" or more simply "Tattoo Women."[10]

At various times in history, Japanese authorities prohibited the use of tattoos by the Ainu (and other indigenous peoples under their authority like the Atayal in Taiwan) in attempts to dislocate them from their traditional cultural practices and prepare them for the subsequent process of Japanization. As early as 1799, during the Edo Period, the Ezo Shogunate issued a ban on tattoos: "Regarding the rumored tattoos, those already done cannot be helped, but those still unborn are prohibited from being tattooed."[11] In 1871, the Hokkaido Development Mission proclaimed, "those born after this day are strictly prohibited from being tattooed" because the custom "was too cruel."[12] To other observers, the Japanese attitude towards tattooing was necessarily disapproving since in their own system, "tattooing was associated with crime and punishment whereas the practice itself was regarded as a form of body mutilation, which, in case of voluntary inflictment, was completely averse to the prevalent notions of Confucian filial conduct."[13]

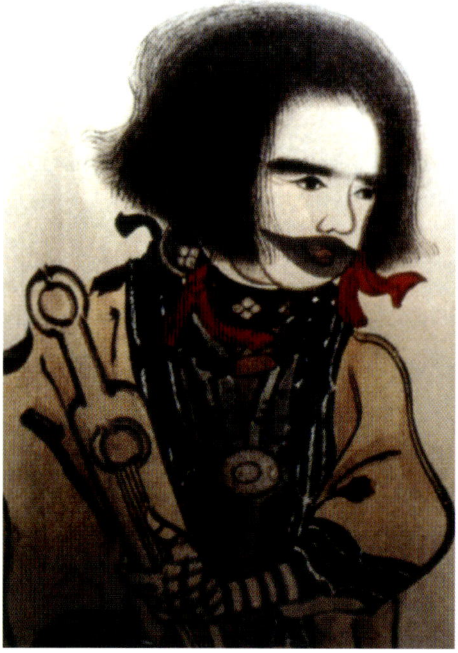

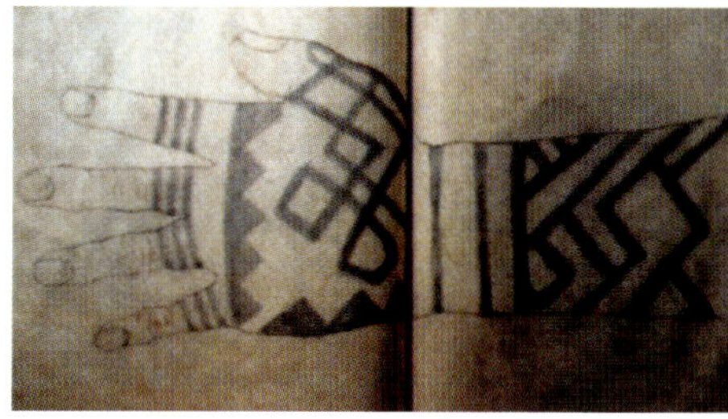

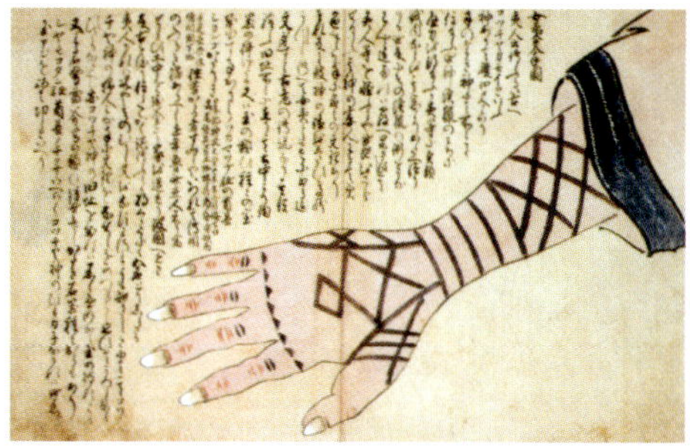

Edo Period drawings of Ainu tattooing, ca. 1800.

Of course, the Ainu vehemently evaded these laws because tattoos were traditionally a prerequisite to marriage and to the afterlife. One report from the 1880s described that the Ainu were very much grieved and tormented by the prohibition of tattooing: "They say the gods will be angry, and that the women can't marry unless they are tattooed. They are less apathetic on this than on any subject, and repeat frequently, 'It's part of our religion.' "[14] One Ainu woman stated in the 1970s, "I was twenty-one years old before I had this little tattoo put on my lips. After it was done, my mother hid me from the Japanese police for five days. I wish we could have retained at least this one custom!"[15]

Ainu tattoos, girdles, and symbolic embroidery

Traditional Ainu tattooing instruments called *makiri* were knife-like in form, and sometimes the sheaths and handles of these tools were intricately carved with zoomorphic and apotropaic motifs.[16] Before the advent of steel tipped *makiri*, razor sharp obsidian points were used, which were wound with fiber allowing only the tip of the point to protrude so as to control the depth of the incisions.[17] As the cutting intensified, the blood was wiped away with a cloth saturated in a hot ash wood or spindlewood antiseptic called *nire*.[18] Soot taken with the fingers from the bottom of a kettle was rubbed into the incisions, and the tattooist would then sing a *yukar* or portion of an epic poem that said: "Even without it, she's so beautiful. The tattoo around her lips, how brilliant it is. It can only be wondered at."[19] Afterward, the tattooist recited a kind of spell or magic formula as more pigment was laid into the skin: "*pas ci-yay, roski, roski, pas ren-ren*," meaning "soot enclosed remain, soot sink in, sink in."[20]

While this invocation may not seem important at first glance, it was symbolically significant nonetheless. Every Ainu home was constructed according to plan with reference to the central hearth and a sacred window facing a stream.[21] Within the hearth was kindled fire, and within the fire was the home of an important deity who served as mediator between all Ainu gods—Fuchi. The fire goddess Fuchi was invoked prior to all ceremonials because communication with other *kamuy* (deities and spirits) was impossible without her divine

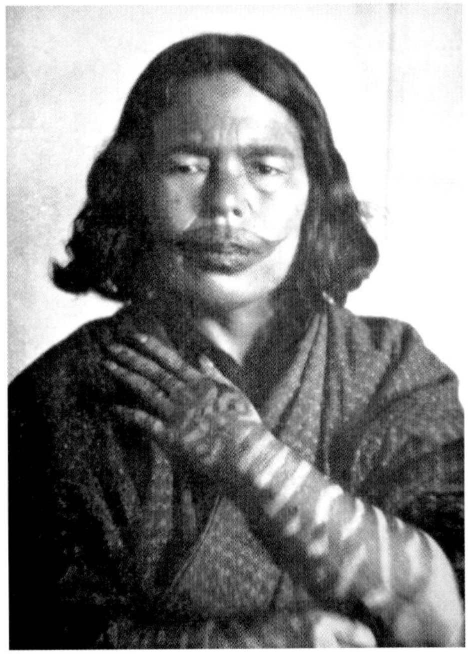

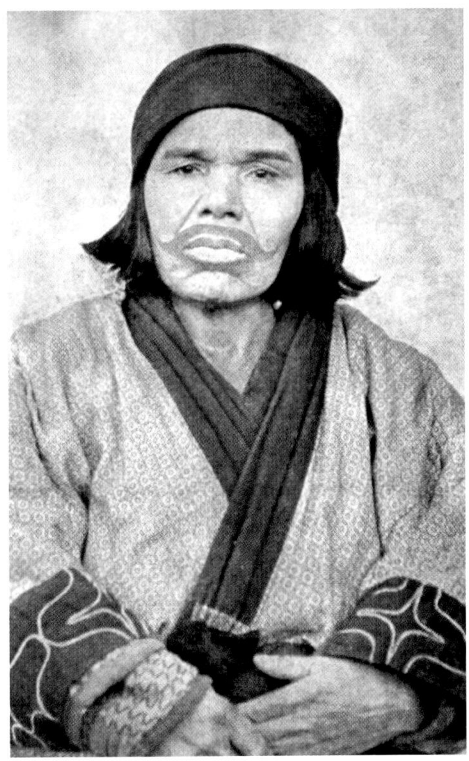

Above: Ainu woman. After Batchelor (1901: 21). The modern Ainu term for tattooing is *nuye* meaning "to carve," and hence "to tattoo" and "to write" (Shabatani 1990), or more literally, *sinuye* "to carve oneself" (Van Gulik 1982: 188). The old term for tattoo was *anchi-piri* (*anchi*, "obsidian"; *piri*, "cut") (Batchelor 1927: 49).

Below: Ainu woman. After Starr (1904: 69).

intervention.[22] Fuchi guarded over families and lent her spiritual support in times of trouble and illness or at times of birth and death.[23] In this respect, the central hearth was a living microcosm of the Ainu mythological universe. Because as a ritual space it replicated and provided a means from which to actively intervene in the cosmos. However, it was also a space where Ainu and the gods grew wary of one another, especially if the fire was not burning at all times.

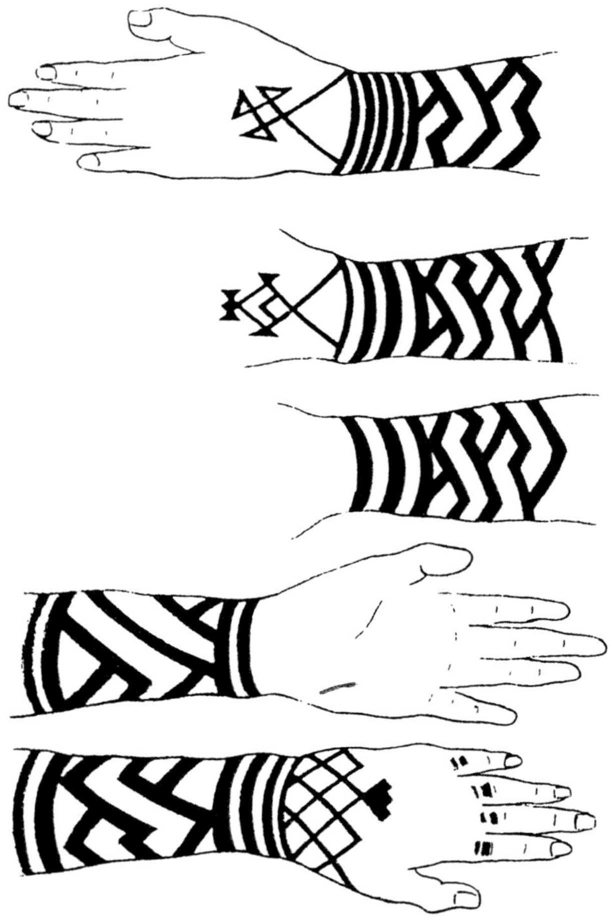

Ainu women's hand and arm tattoos. After Scheube (1882: fig. III). Other marks were placed on various parts of the body as charms against diseases like painful rheumatism (Kodama 1970: 124).

According to Romyn Hitchcock, an ethnologist working for the Smithsonian Institution in the late 19th century, Ainu tattoo was laid upon the skin at specific intervals, the process sometimes extending over several years: "The faces of the women are disfigured by tattooing around the mouth, the style of which varies with locality. Young maidens of six or seven have a little spot on the upper lip. As they grow older, this is gradually extended until a more or less broad band surrounds the mouth and extends into a tapering curve on both cheeks towards the ears."[24] Of course, the tattooist encouraged her client to remain still throughout the painful ordeal. But if the pain was too great, one or more assistants held the client down so that the tattooist could continue her work.

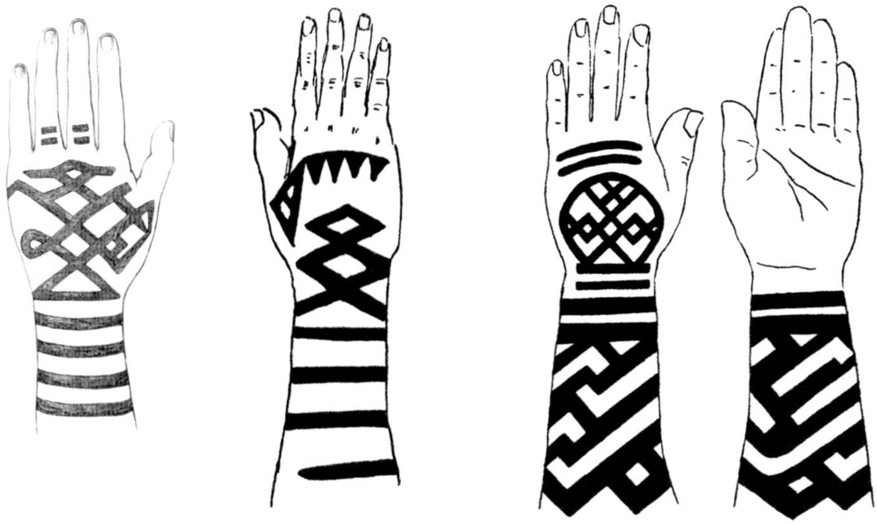

Ainu hand and arm tattoos. Top left after Fritze (1893: 46); top right after Montandon (1937: 143); bottom left redrawn after Montandon (1937: 142); bottom right after von Siebold (1881: fig. II). Occasionally, the abstract hand patterns resemble degraded anthropomorphs.

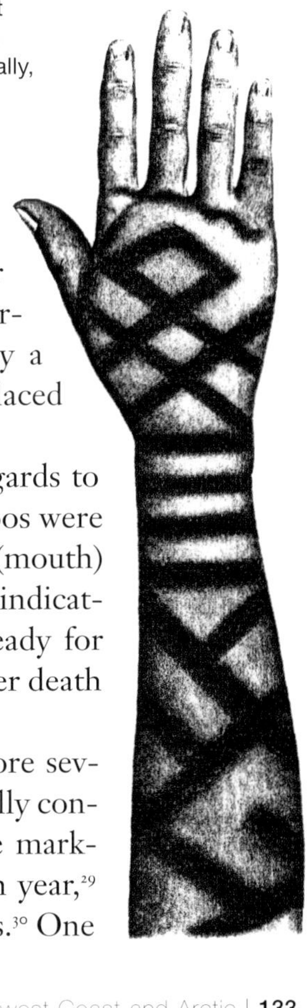

After the mouth tattooing, the lips would feel like burning embers. Oftentimes, the client became feverish and the pain and swelling would keep her from getting much sleep. Food became an afterthought and when the tattoo client became thirsty a piece of cotton grass was dipped in water and placed against her lips for sucking.[25]

The completed lip tattoos were significant in regards to Ainu perceptions of life experience. First, these tattoos were believed to repel evil spirits from entering the body (mouth) and causing sickness or misfortune.[26] Secondly, they indicated that a woman had reached maturity and was ready for marriage.[27] And finally, lip tattoos assured her life after death in the place of her deceased ancestors.[28]

Apart from lip tattoos, however, Ainu women wore several other tattoo marks on their arms and hands usually consisting of curvilinear and geometric designs. These markings, which were begun as early as the fifth or sixth year,[29] were intended to protect young girls from evil spirits.[30] One motif, the braidform pattern, consisting of two rectilinear stripes braided side by side linked to a special design, represented a kind of band also used for tying the dead for burial.[31]

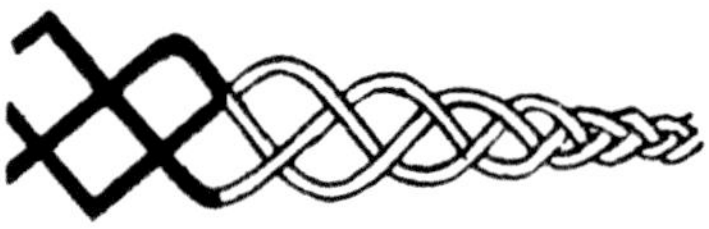

Structure of three-strand *upsor* braid. Redrawn after Tosabayashi (1948).

As with burial cords, the braid-like weave structure of women's plaited girdles called *upsor-kut* ("bosom girdles") were also embodied with a powerful supernatural "magic" symbolizing not only a woman's virtue, but her "soul strength."[32] First discussed by the Western physician Neil Gordon Munro, who with his Japanese wife operated a free clinic in Hokkaido in the 1930s, *upsor-kut* were objects worn underneath the woman's outer garment (*attush*) and kept "secret" from Ainu men.[33] They were made of woven flax or native hemp varying in length and width and in the number of strands.[34] Composed of either three, five, or seven plaited cords (sometimes alternating with intersecting or overlapping lozenges or chevrons), they closely resemble the tattoo motifs that appear on the arms of Ainu women.[35]

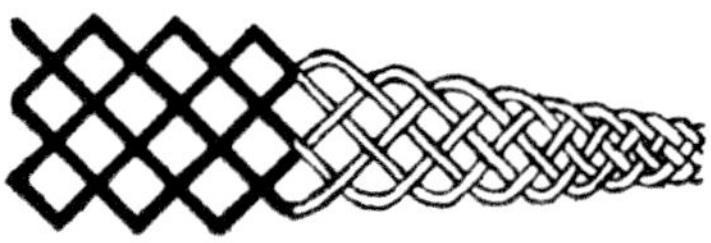

Structure of five-strand *upsor* braid. Redrawn after Tosabayashi (1948).

Interestingly, girdles were received upon completion of a girl's lip tattooing just before or on the occasion of marriage.[36] The design specifications of the girdle were passed down by the girl's mother; she instructed her daughter how to make the girdle and warned that if it was ever exposed to any male, great misfortune would come to her and the family. In Ainu epic poetry and song (*yukar*), the importance of the *upsor* is emphasized:

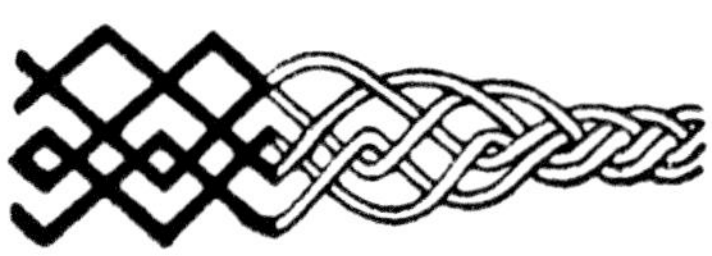

Structure of five-strand *upsor* braid with alternating twine. Redrawn after Tosabayashi (1948).

> For a man to see a woman's body, or perhaps her girdle, was tantamount to raping her, and he would have to marry her or kill her (or she kill him). In some epics, when there has been a shipwreck and bodies are washed ashore, other

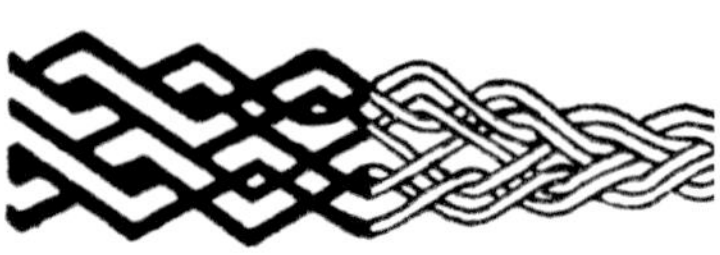

Structure of seven-strand *upsor* braid. Redrawn after Tosabayashi (1948).

women will run ahead to cover up the bodies of the women who may be lying injured or unconscious so that they will not accidentally be seen by the men.[37]

According to Munro, all women were compelled to keep a spare *upsor* ready for their burial.[38]

Munro recorded at least eight types of *upsor*. Each form was related to a different line of matrilineal pedigree and associated with several animal and spirit deities (*kamuy*), such as the killer whale, bear, and wolf crests.[39] Thus aristocratic women, especially the daughters of chiefs *(kotan)*, wore more powerfully charged girdles than common women, because their ancestry connected them more closely to the *kamuy*. Munro also observed that the daughters of Ainu chiefs were tattooed on the arms before any other women in the village, suggesting that these types of tattoos conferred prestige and social status to the wearer.[40] In this sense, tattoos and girdles appear to be functionally related.

However, tattoos and girdles were connected on yet another, more metaphysical level. The Ainu believed that the fire goddess Fuchi provided Ainu women with the original plans for constructing the sacred *upsor* girdles.[41] As noted earlier, Fuchi was also symbolized by the soot used in tattooing practice thereby linking the traditions of tattooing and girdling to Ainu mythological thought. And because each type of girdle was associated with a particular *kamuy*, it can be suggested that particular tattoo motifs were associated with specific deities: "the wives of the deities were tattooed in a similar fashion as the Ainu women, so that when evil demons would see it, they would mistake the women for deities and therefore stay away."[42]

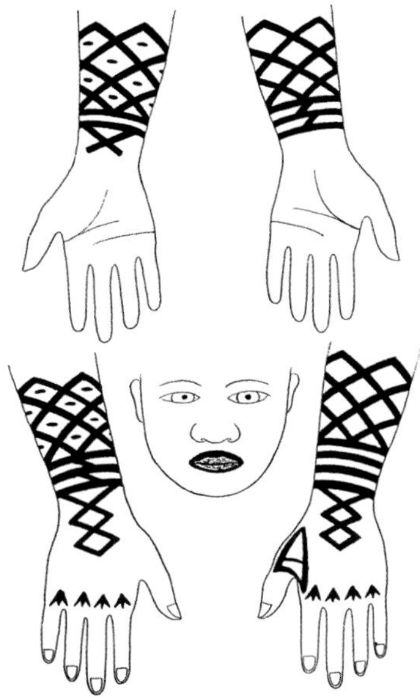

Ainu forearm tattoos with five-strand network pattern. Redrawn after Kodama (1970: 127).

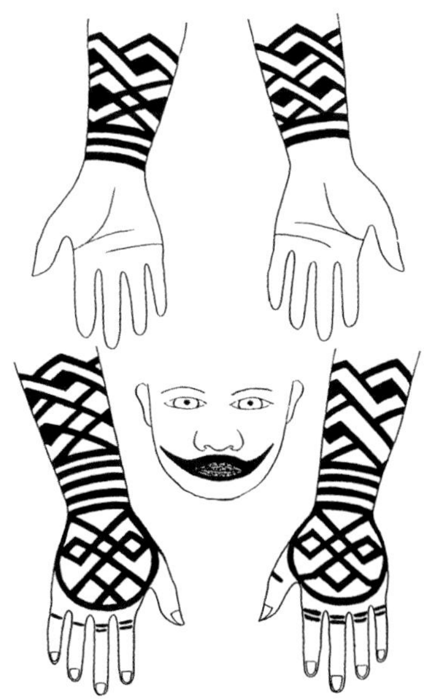

Ainu forearm tattoos with seven-strand braid pattern. Redrawn after Kodama (1970: 127).

But the symbolic fortification of the body did not end with tattoos and girdles; it also extended to clothing. For example, Ainu embroidery seems to have had a related functional efficacy. Women embroidered simple double-stranded braid-like brackets around the neck, front openings, sleeves, and hem on the earliest Ainu salmon skin and elm bark garments (*attush*) to keep evil spirits from entering the apertures of the body.[43] The original designs, resembling braided rope, were nothing more than a solid color, usually dark blue similar to the color of tattoo pigment.

Early scholars argued that these embroidered design forms were highly abstract zoomorphic renderings of a stylized bear's head with outstretched ears.[44] Yet one could just as easily assign these cryptic designs to that of the fish owl. Both brown bears and the long-eared fish owl rank as the highest *kamuy* in Hokkaido and are honored in ceremony and ritual. More specifically, the owl is identified by some Ainu groups as the "god" or "guardian of the village" (*kotan-kor-kamuy*),[45] and today it is sometimes seen surmounting non-traditional totem poles displayed outside of Ainu villages. Furthermore, its usage in the indigenous art of Japan is ancient as its image has been found on ceramic sculpture dating from the terminal Jomon culture of 1000 B.C.[46]

Among the indigenous peoples of the lower Amur River Basin (with whom the Ainu traded), similar design conventions embroidered and appliquéd onto traditional fish skin garments provided the wearer protection from evil spirits.[47] Design motifs were placed on the borders around every opening in traditional robes (neck, arms, legs, front closure, and hem) and all borders had symbolic referents. For instance, the upper borders represented the Upper World and the patterns placed there offered protection in that direction; the hem represented the underworld or underwater world; and the middle parts stood for the world inhabited by humans.[48] On one old Nanai fish skin robe, avian designs represent the Upper World, fish patterns symbolize the lower realms and a Chinese inspired dragon completes the center.

Ainu crests

In what would seem as a contradiction to the previous discussion, the Ainu adhered to a rigid set of artistic rules in their depictions of animals. Perhaps animal figures were highly abstract because incorporating any of the animal gods in realistic compositions was taboo for fear of angering the *kamuy* they represented.[49] Of course, there were some exceptions to the rules that governed artistic production, especially in the manufacture of men's objects:

ikupasuy (prayer sticks) and *sapaunpe* (men's ceremonial headdresses). Within these objects crest (totem) animals such as bears, killer whales, wolves, and owls were realistically depicted in naturalistic form.[50] According to the art historian Chisato Dubreuil, Ainu crests were carved into prayer sticks because they were necessary for communication to the gods:

> Humans are incapable of expressing themselves directly to the *kamuy*, the gods, in a proper manner. The *ikupasuy* not only acts as an intermediary between *kamuy* and worshipper, it also has the power to translate human prayers into hallowed prayers that will honor the intended recipient. Through the use of the *itokpa*, the ancestral crest carved into the design, the stick also identified the worshipper, because without identification, *wen-kamuy*, the evil gods, could misdirect the prayer.[51]

Perhaps this is why women's *upsor* girdles were, as previously noted, associated with crest animals; because they identified the wearer to the gods so that no misfortune would befall them.

The traditional use of crests in carving, however, was shared with other Pacific Rim cultures, especially among the Tlingit and Haida people of the Northwest Coast of North America. The highest value and importance of crest objects there rested in their roles as embodied symbols of a clan's origin, history and identity.[52] Like those among the Ainu, crest objects comprised the social and spiritual element that held the Tlingit and Haida people and the land together. Crest objects, including human bodies tattooed with crest animals, were inseparable from life itself and the Tlingit and Haida could not conduct their traditional ceremonies or make speeches in a spiritual context without them.[53] Crests harbored associated oral traditions, songs, and names representative of clan intellectual property.[54]

Tlingit and Haida of the Northwest Coast

The Tlingit and Haida, as well as other Northwest Coast peoples, used animal emblems as crests (totems) to identify the different social divisions among their society. Crests were also employed to affirm a group's territorial claims.[55] One's moiety, clan, and house (lineage) each owned a crest or several crests.[56] Crests included, for example, land animals (Bear, Wolf), sea animals (Killer Whale, Halibut, Shark), birds (Eagle, Thunderbird, Owl), as well as geographical features (Mountain, Iceberg), celestial bodies (Sun, Big Dipper, Moon) and natural materials (Copper, Clay, Yellow Cedar).[57]

The possession of these crests by moiety, clan, subclan, or house derived from events that the Tlingit recount in their oral traditions, events that account for their unique identity as a distinct group. Oberg succinctly describes the nature and function of crests for the Tlingit as ways of explaining the existence of their world.[58] Crests are honored as an individual's and group's link to the wider world in which they live, linking them to creatures or things in the natural environment and to other Tlingit clans and their membership via the demarcation of rank and group identity in the social milieu.[59] Furthermore, crests chronicle the origin of supernatural and significant events in the history of the clan. They serve as title to the object on which they are placed and to the site and geographic region where these events occurred. Crests symbolize the special relationship a clan member has to the animal depicted on the crest since the crest embodies the spirit or being depicted in the crest. Thus, the crest, and the right to use it in stories, sets the group apart from other groups while defining its position with respect to other groups. Therefore, the ownership of a crest, the right to *use* the emblem, was more valuable than the possession of a particular physical object, an heirloom or crest object itself.[60]

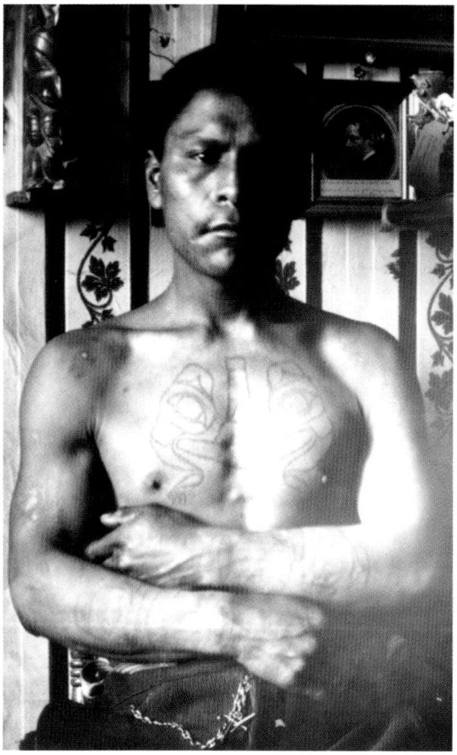

Haida Johnny Kit Elswa of Skidegate, Queen Charlotte Islands, 1886. A bear is tattooed on his chest and dogfish on each forearm. Photograph by James G. Swan. Copyright National Anthropological Archives (N-SI-4117).

The concept of *at.óow* among the Tlingit describes this special form of possession not only of physical things, but also of the identity of a house or clan by its members. *At.óow* literally means "an owned or purchased thing,"[61] and also refers to both tangible and intangible property embodied within crest objects themselves, such as personal names, stories, songs, spirits, or even geographical features/locations. For example, the Chookaneidi

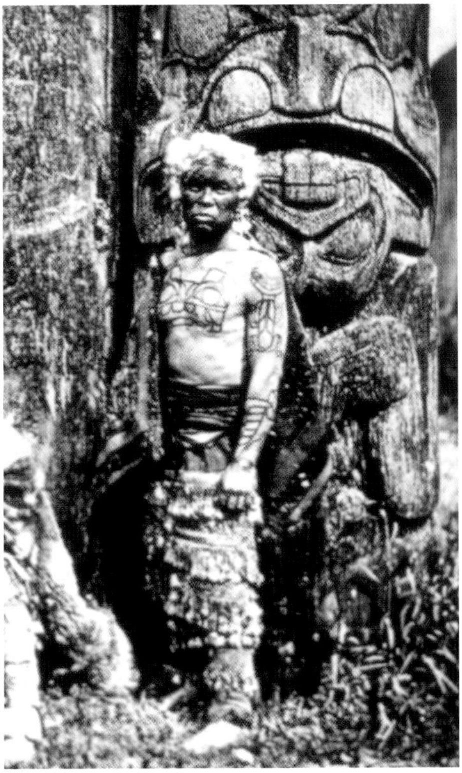

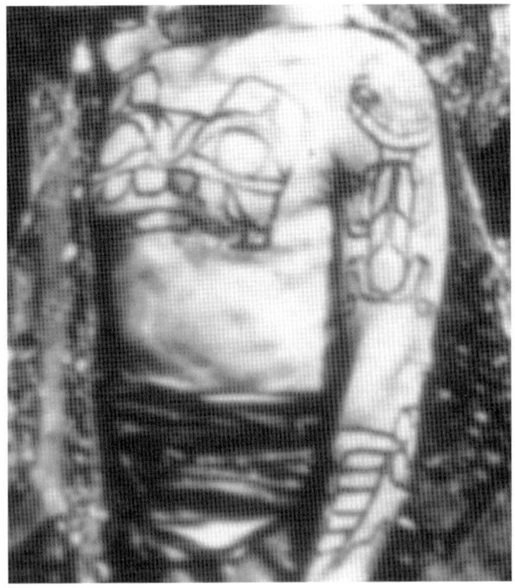

Left: Haida Chief Xa'na of Grizzly Bear House with tattooed hereditary crests, Masset, British Columbia, 1881. Photograph by Edward Dossetter.

Above: Close-up of Chief Xa'na's tattoos: grizzly bear on chest, seated bear on shoulder, and possibly a killer whale on his forearm.

clan of Hoonah, Alaska uses a glacier as their crest. They refer to the land of Glacier Bay, the glacier itself, the visual image of the Woman in the Ice (their ancestor who was covered by the glacier, "purchasing" it with her life), the story and the songs explaining the origin of the crest, and the physical and spiritual ancestor herself as *at.óow*.[62]

The right to a crest was not necessarily exclusive, however. Claims to a crest were contested and evaluated by the Tlingit, so that one clan might be perceived to have more of a right to a particular crest than others. Because crests were so closely linked to a group's identity, and because other clans validated one's own right to a crest, wars occasionally resulted from attempts by competing clans to gain status over the other: to become the highest ranking owners of the crest.[63] Appropriating a crest sometimes forced the payment of a debt or it intentionally shamed a rival clan.[64] This was in part due to the fact that these objects were group property; they could not be transferred, conveyed, or alienated unless all members of the clan agreed.[65]

Clans sometimes possessed the use of more than one crest. Wealth, of course, played an important role in the number of crests a house or clan could own, since "some families were too poor to have an emblem, and on the other hand it is said of some of the great ones . . . that they were so rich that they could use anything."[66]

The social functions that crest objects served, however, are inseparable in Tlingit thought from their role as sacred objects. Clan crests both symbolize the spirit of the being depicted on objects and embody the spirit that resides with them.[67] Crests symbolize kinship and a spiritual relationship of its clan members to the physical wildlife, and they bond the Tlingit to their ancestors who paid for the crest with their lives or deeds by holding the object through the generations.[68]

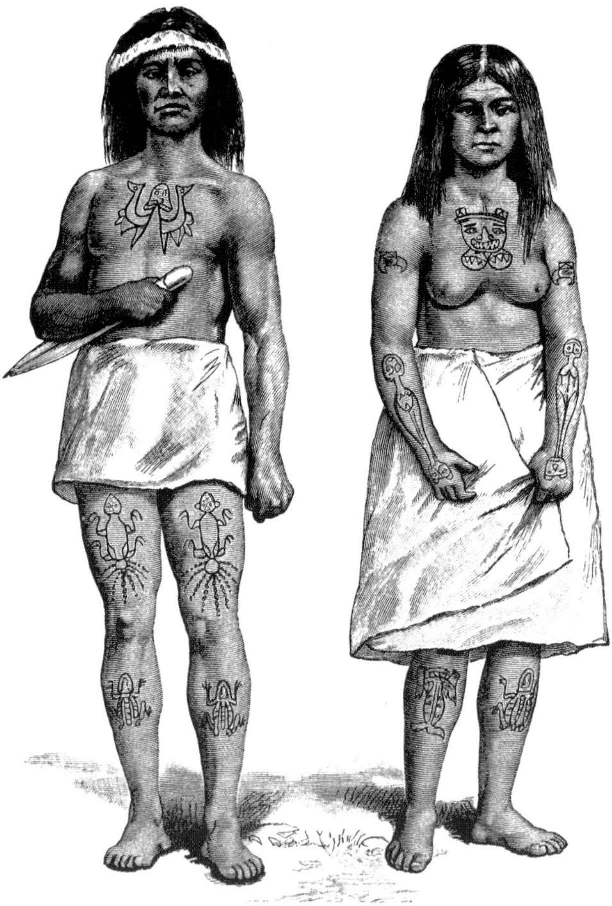

Haida couple with crest tattoos. After Swan (1886: 69). On the man's breast is a codfish split head to tail and laid open; on each thigh is an octopus, and below each knee is a frog. On the woman's breast are the head and forepaws of a beaver; on each shoulder is the head of an eagle; on each arm is a halibut; on the left leg is a sculpin, and on the right is a frog.

As crests and crest objects served to unify the people to their ancestors, to each other, and to the natural forces around them, the Tlingit treated them with great respect and reverence, for it was through them that they defined themselves. Although the Tlingit did not worship crests or the creatures they represented, they did cast spiritual meaning to the people and crests were represented on a wide variety of a clan's objects and in many different materials, including blankets, tools or weapons, crest (totem) poles, rock art, hats, body paint, and tattooing kits.[69] All crest objects were made by a member of the opposite moiety and at the first potlatch or ceremonial party, the public display and witness of the crest by the attendees imparted great value to the object.[70] The guests were appropriately compensated for their attendance because it validated the prestige and importance of the crest object, especially if it were the newly tattooed body of the Tlingit host's son or daughter.

Tlingit and Haida tattooing was performed in conjunction with the potlatch.[71] Generally speaking, potlatches were typically held to honor the dead and their exploits, but they also served to enhance the prestige of the living.[72] Tlingit individuals of rank were greatly concerned that others should recognize their clan's claims, status, and history. For the purpose of maintaining the clan's standing, the clan hosts publicly distributed great amounts of property at the potlatch, both tangible and intangible, which was necessary to validate and uphold the social ranking and position of the clan and its leaders relative to other clans in Tlingit society. Names, ranks, privileges, and honors of the lineage inheritance were meaningless without this formal ritual of hospitality and the acceptance of gifts by the guests:

> The memorial potlatch . . . lasted four, eight, or more days, involving as hosts or guests all members of the community, as well as a guest clan invited from another tribe. Within this series, the potlatch proper was the climax, when the host clan, in honor of their deceased relatives, repaid in full the members of the opposite moiety (their guests) for their services during the funeral feast. While only a wealthy man (or woman) could give a potlatch, the occasion enabled his poorer clanmates to contribute wealth and so pay off their own funeral debts, so that a single ceremony concluded the rights for several deceased persons in the same clan. At this time, the heir and new house master assumed his title, exhibited his crests, bestowed honorable names on the juniors of his clan, or had the ears of his own children pierced. Payments were made to the guests not only for their work but also for being witness to the honors and prerogatives claimed by the hosts, which might include territorial rights symbolized by crest objects displayed.[73]

Potlatching was a method of publicly acknowledging and validating a clan's status during memorial and other rites. The costs associated with the distribution of property were great, especially as a thousand people might be in attendance at any one time.[74] Groups of related families mustered all available resources to make the occasion memorable, for their standing and influence in the tribe depended on such display and wealth. Oftentimes, they erected a lasting symbol of the occasion—a totem pole.

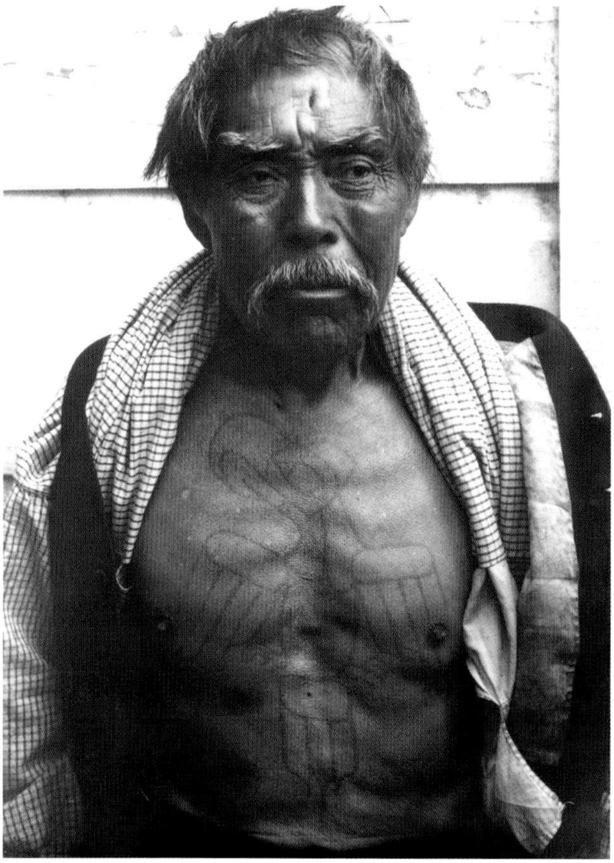

Haida man (David Yelthmow) from Masset, Queen Charlotte Islands with thunderbird tattoo on chest, 1897. Copyright American Museum of Natural History (N-11693).

However, other types of potlatches were given by very wealthy chiefs to ennoble their children.[75] These ceremonial events, practiced by both the Tlingit and Haida, were primarily held for the oldest child, although other children of the same house or lineage were included. For major potlatches of this kind, guests belonging to the father's moiety, but of different clans, would be invited from neighboring villages or tribes.[76] After several days of feasting and dancing, guest chiefs or noble women pierced the ears of the children and tattooed their bodies.[77] According to Olson, the Tlingit followed a ritualized pattern when it came time for the piercing and tattooing of the noble children at the potlatch:

> The next day the ear-piercing and tattooing of the children are done, one of the children being seated in front of each guest chief. The host's eldest son sits in front of the highest visiting chief, the eldest daughter in front of the highest guest chief of the home village. At a signal each of these chiefs takes

hold of the lobe of an ear of the child in front of him and pinches it. Everyone now gives a loud and long "sh." This is repeated three times. At the fourth "sh" the ear is pierced. The same is done for the other ear of each. For some children, tattooing is a substitute for the ear piercing. Girls are tattooed on the hands, boys on the chest or hands. This may take several days. A day or two later the property is given out.

At the beginning of the giving, some or all of the honored children are given new names. Each naming is accompanied by a speech giving the history of the name, the great deeds of those who formerly bore the names, and so on . . .

The host then distributes the property, most of it going to the chiefs [or noblewomen] who did the ear piercing or tattooing. An average would be fifty blankets for ear piercing or tattooing the hands, one hundred blankets for a chest tattoo.[78]

George T. Emmons, a knowledgeable collector and fastidious observer of Tlingit culture who also served as an officer in the U.S. Navy in the Alaska Territory from 1882-1896, recorded that these tattoos generally represented the whole body or some part of the crest animal of the clan.[79] They were emblems of rank and expensive luxuries which only the wealthiest could afford; especially since slaves were prohibited from tattooing altogether.

One of the last Haida potlatches to feature tattooing occurred in the winter of 1900-1 in the village of Skidegate in the Queen Charlotte Islands. It was witnessed and described by the anthropologist John R. Swanton, and it followed the same ritual pattern as its Tlingit counterpart:

[On the second day] they called them to put the tattoo-marks on. At once they painted their faces. Those in the house shouted to the people to come in and look on. When the spectators were all in, they began dancing, and sang property-songs. Those who were to be tattooed began dancing. The wife [of the house chief] stood at the end of the line, wearing a painted [crest] hat. When they had sung four songs, they put eagle-feathers on the dancers [for purification]. The house was filled with eagle-feathers. Then they stopped. Those who put the feathers on them were given cotton cloth. When that was over, they had those who were to be tattooed sit down in front of the chiefs. Sometimes two took a fancy to be tattooed by the same [artist]. Now they beat the ground with a baton, mentioned the chief's name, and said, "so and so sits in front of you to be tattooed." Then they began to put the tattoo-marks . . . All that day they spent in tattooing, and finished it . . . The nose, lower lip, and ears were also pierced by members of the opposite clan. They were paid a blanket apiece for it."[80]

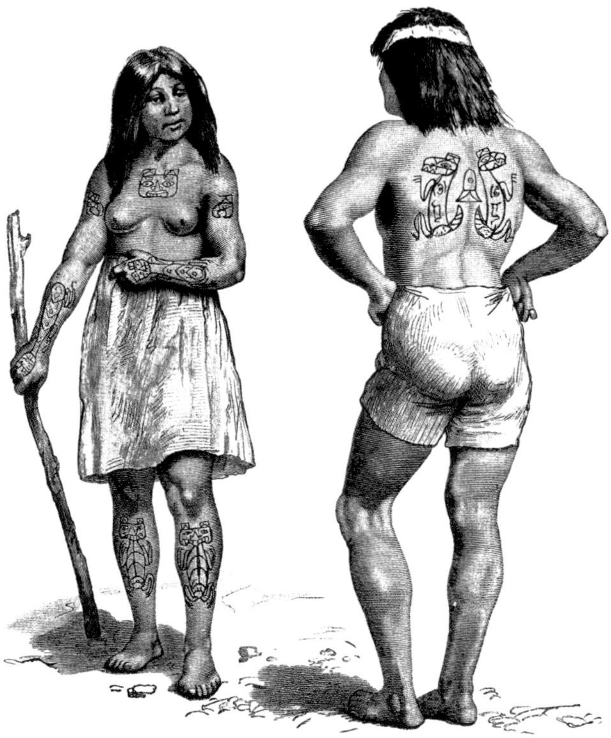

Haida couple with crest tattoos. After Swan (1886: 69). Haida woman with bear's head tattooed on breast, each shoulder adorned with head of an eagle. On her arms and legs are figures of the bear. Haida man with wolf spirit tattooed on back.

Traditional Haida tattoos (*ki-da*)[81] covered the arms, chests, thighs, upper arms, feet and sometimes an individual's back or cheek.[82] Tattooing kits consisted of a stone dish to mix magnetite (black) and hematite (red) pigments, cedar brushes with crests carved into each handle and four or five cedar batons with various configurations of needles, depending on the desired effect: shading, outlining, and fill.[83] Before the advent of steel needles, sharp thorns, spines of certain fishes or spicules of bone were used.

Thomas Lockhart of West Coast Tattoo in Vancouver, British Columbia has demonstrated that Haida tattoo instruments resemble those of contemporary Japanese hand-poking tools:

> Upon seeing photos of the Haida tattoo instruments, I was struck by the similarity to the Japanese tools, in particular, the paintbrushes. The Japanese used a stick at least a foot long with needles poking straight out, firmly attached to the end with thread. It would be grasped at the end with the right hand, laid across the web of the thumb and, using this as a fulcrum, jabbed into the skin.

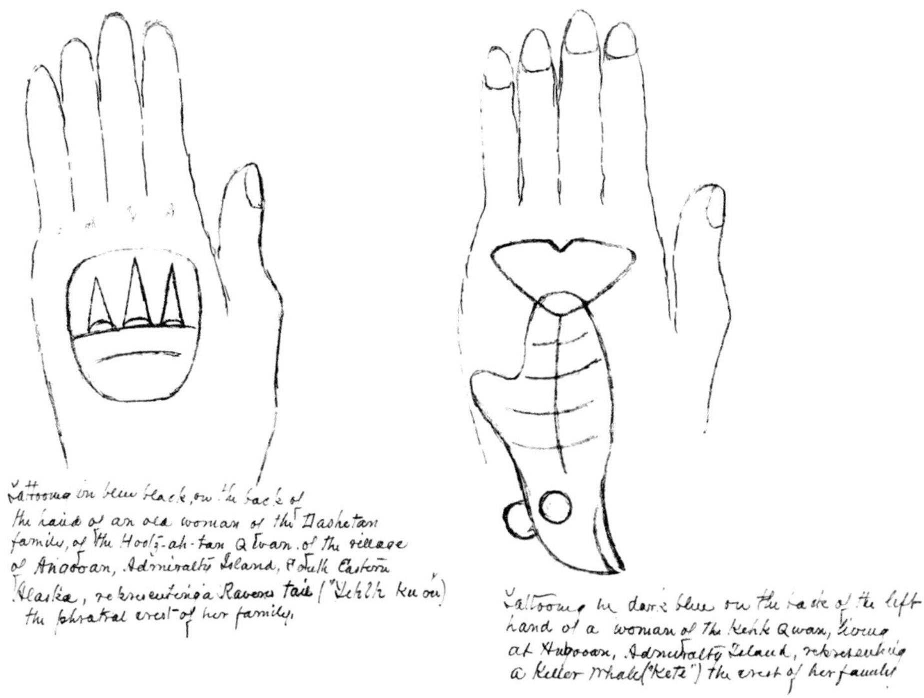

Tlingit women's hand tattoos drawn at Angoon, Alaska, 1889. After Emmons (1991: 253). Emmons's journal notes for these drawings read (from left to right): "Tattooing in blue black, on the back of the hand of an old woman of the Dashetan family, of the Hootz-ah-tah Qwan, of the village of Angooan, Admiralty Island, representing a Raven's tail ("Yehlh ku-ou") the phratral crest of her family." "Tattooing in dark blue on the back of the left hand of a woman of the Kehk Qwan, living at Angooan, Admiralty Island, representing a killerwhale ("Kete") the crest of her family."

> The paintbrush would be held under the middle joint of the left hand, bristles hovering over the tattoo and offering a fresh supply of pigment for the tattooist to work from. However, the sticks the Haida used appear much shorter than the typical Japanese tools—perhaps half the length—and the needles were in a looser grouping, not flattened out. I surmise the Haida would have held them in their right hand, much as we would hold a spoon, simply pricking the skin repeatedly using wrist action.[84]

Among the Tlingit similar tools were used, but only after contact with European traders: "After the acquisition of trade needles, a pricker was made with four of these placed close together in the end of a wooden handle."[85] This pricker replaced the more traditional Tlingit tattooing tool—a simple bone needle and piece of sinew thread.

Although we have no eyewitness accounts of Tlingit skin-stitching,

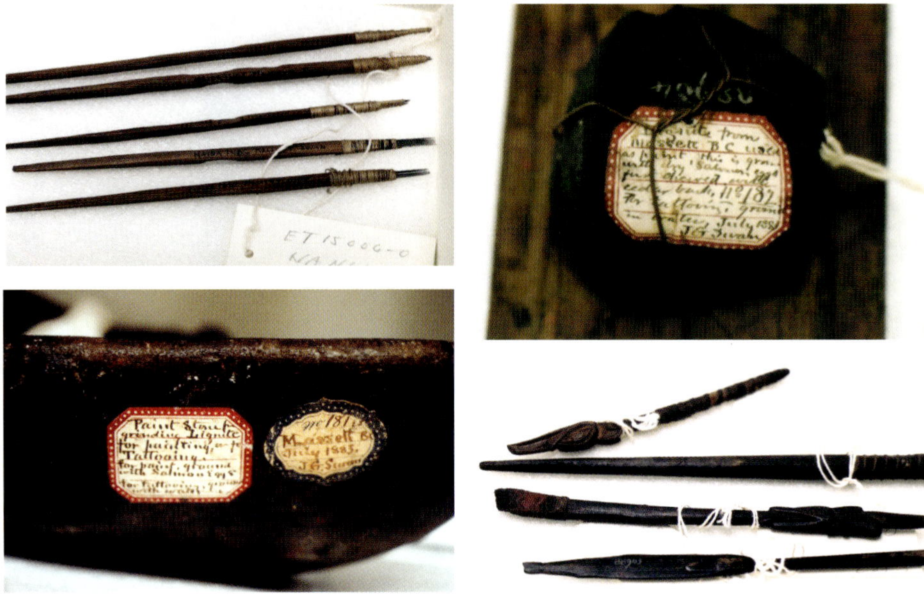

Haida tattoo kit, collected by James G. Swan at Massett, British Columbia, July 1883. Photographs by Lars Krutak, 2002. This Haida hand-poking kit consists of five cedar batons, a lump of magnetite for pigment, a stone dish to mix the tattoo pigment, and a set of carved cedar brushes – some still impregnated with pigment – adorned with crest symbols. I have searched other museum collections for similar examples and have found none. Thus, this assemblage of tools seems to represent one of the last, if not the only, authentic Haida tattoo kits remaining in the world. Today, it is housed at the Smithsonian Institution's National Museum of Natural History.

linguistic evidence supports the view that the Tlingit previously "sewed" in their tattoos with needle and thread. The old word for tattoo is *kuy-kay-chul* meaning "sewing on the body."[86] Although painful, skin sewing was a widespread method for tattooing, especially among more northerly Arctic peoples who practiced it for over three millennia.[87]

The Arctic: circumpolar regions

Archaeological evidence in the form of a carved human figurine demonstrates that tattooing was practiced as early as 3,500 years ago in the Arctic. Moreover, the remains of several mummies discovered in Bering Strait and Greenland indicate that tattooing was an element basic to ancient traditions.[88] This is corroborated in mythology since the origin of tattooing is symbolically associated with the creation of the sun and moon. The naturalist Lucien M. Turner, speaking of the Fort-Chimo Inuit of Quebec, wrote:

The sun is supposed to be a woman. The moon is a man and the brother of the woman who is the sun. She was accustomed to lie on her bed in the house [of her parents] and was finally visited during the night by a man whom she could never discover the identity. She determined to ascertain who it was and in order to do so blackened her nipples with a mixture of oil and lampblack [tattoo pigments]. She was visited again and when the man applied his lips to her breast they became black. The next morning she discovered to her horror that her own brother had the mark on his lips. Her emoternation knew no bounds and her parents discovered her agitation and made her reveal the cause. The parents were so indignant that they upbraided them and the girl in her shame fled from the village at night. As she ran past the fire she seized an ember and fled beyond the earth. Her brother pursued her and so the sparks fell from the torch [and] they became the stars in the sky. The brother pursued her but is able to overtake her except on rare occasions. These occasions are eclipses.

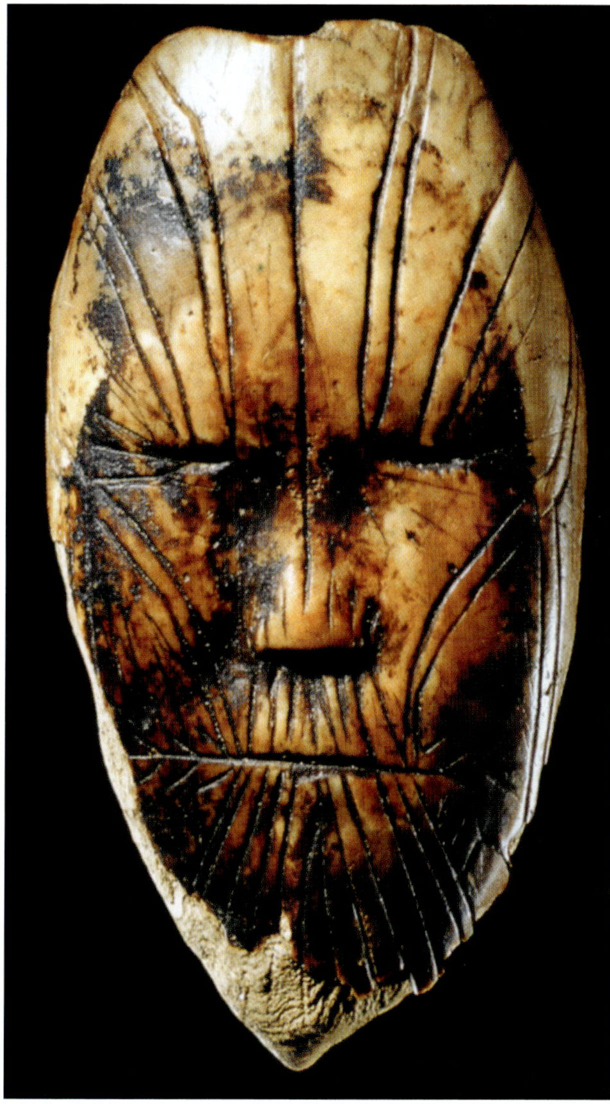

3,500-year-old ivory maskette from the Dorset culture representing the oldest known human portrait from the Arctic. Tattoos cover the face of the woman.

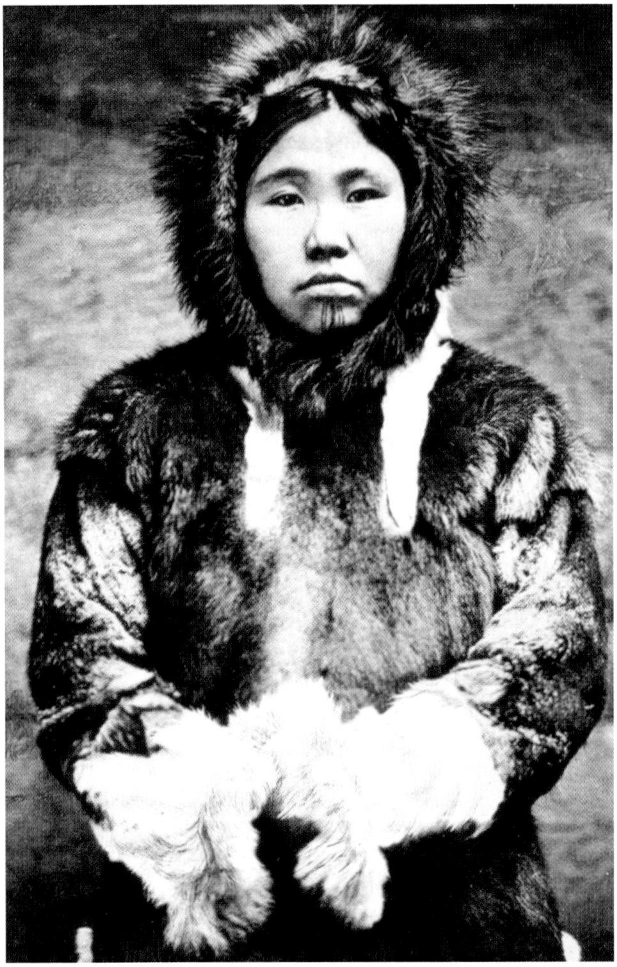

Tattooed Eskimo woman from the Bering Strait region, ca. 1910. Postcard from the collection of the author. At Point Hope, Alaska (*Tikigaq*) a girl's first tattoos were received after her first menstruation. And old woman (*aana*) drew a sinew thread soaked with lampblack (soot) through the eye of a needle. She then tattooed the girl's chin with three vertical lines, because it is said that "tattoos and sexual bleeding tie her to the celestial sister. Tattooing is soot smears, fire-sparks, speckles, the sun's streaking" (Lowenstein 1993: 70), and perhaps through such associations it symbolically transformed the initiate into a woman through a ritual process of "cooking" the flesh (cf. Saladin D'Anglure 1993: 29).

> When the moon wanes from sight the brother is supposed to be hiding for the approach of his sister.[89]

Tattoos and symbolic pigments

Ethnographically tattooing was practiced by all Eskimos and was most common among women.[90] While there are a multitude of localized references to tattooing practices in the Arctic, the first was probably recorded by Sir Martin Frobisher in 1576. Frobisher's account describes the Eskimos he encountered in the bay that now bears his name:

> The women are marked on the face with blewe streekes down the cheekes and round about the eies . . . Also, some of their women race [scratch or pierce]

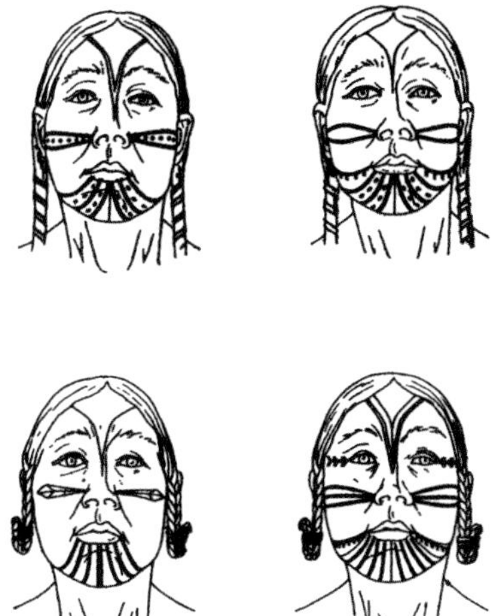

Above: Tattooed Inuit women from Baffin Island region. After Boas (1901-7: 108).

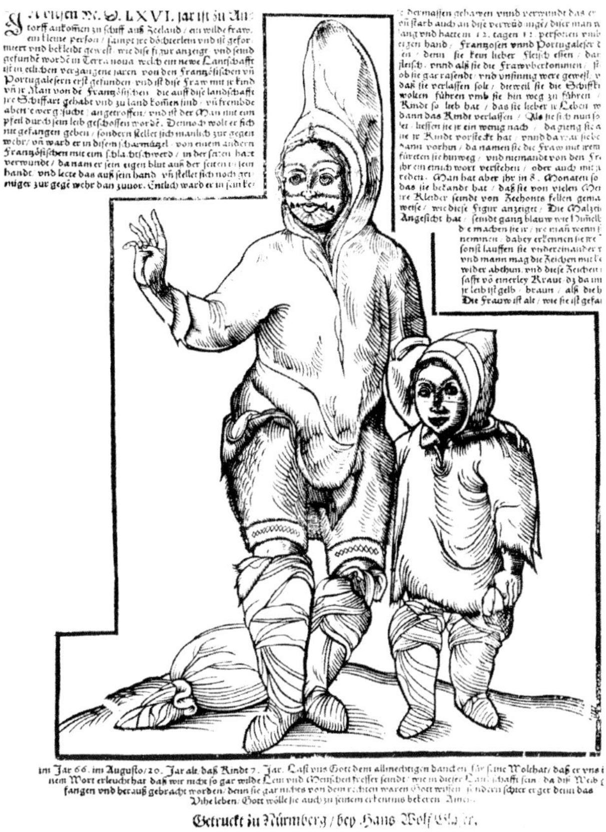

Left: These Canadian Inuit were kidnapped by French sailors in 1566. (Notice the tattoos that appear on the woman's face.) This woodblock print is the oldest known European depiction of Eskimos drawn from life. After Taylor (1984: 510).

> their faces proportionally, as chinne, cheekes, and forehead, and the wristes of their hands, whereupon they lay a colour, which continueth dark azurine.[91]

As a general rule, expert tattoo artists were respected elderly women. Their extensive training as skin seamstresses (parkas, pants, boots, hide boat covers, etc.) facilitated the need for precision when "stitching the human skin" with tattoos. Tattoo designs were usually made freehand but in some instances a rough outline was first sketched upon the area of application. A typical 19th century account provided by William Gilder illustrates the tattooing process among the Central Eskimo living near Daly Bay, a branch of Canada's Hudson Bay:

> The wife has her face tattooed with lamp-black and is regarded as a matron in society. The method of tattooing is to pass a needle under the skin, and as

> soon as it is withdrawn its course is followed by a thin piece of pine stick dipped in oil and rubbed in the soot from the bottom of a kettle. The forehead is decorated with a letter V in double lines, the angle very acute, passing down between the eyes almost to the bridge of the nose, and sloping gracefully to the right and left before reaching the roots of the hair. Each cheek is adorned with an egg-shaped pattern, commencing near the wing of the nose and sloping upward toward the corner of the eye; these lines are also double. The most ornamented part, however, is the chin, which receives a gridiron pattern; the lines double from the edge of the lower lip, and reaching to the throat toward the corners of the mouth, sloping outward to the angle of the lower jaw. This is all that is required by custom, but some of the belles do not stop here. Their hands, arms, legs, feet, and in fact their whole bodies are covered with blue tracery that would throw Captain Constantinus completely in the shade.[92]

Around Bering Strait, the tattooing method reveals continuity in application, as observed by Gilder, yet the pigments employed were more varied. In 1926, the University of Alaska archaeologist Otto W. Geist noted:

> Tattoo marks on arms and hands are drawn from life. Some of the St. Lawrence Island women and girls have beautifully executed tattoo marks. The pigment is made from the soot of seal oil lamps which is taken from the bottom of tea kettles or similar containers used to boil meat and other food over an open flame. The soot is mixed with urine, often that of an old woman, and is applied with steel needles. One method is to draw a string of sinew or other thread through the eye of the needle. The thread is then soaked thoroughly in the liquid pigment and drawn through the skin as the needle is inserted and pushed just under the skin for a distance of about a thirty-second of an inch when the point is again pierced through the skin. A small space is left without tattooing before the process is again repeated. The other method is to prick the skin with the needle which is dipped in the pigment each time.[93]

Tattooing an individual in the traditional manner required extensive knowledge of animal products, pigments, and natural substances suitable for indelible marking.[94] Lampblack was the primary pigment used to darken the sinew thread because it was believed to be highly efficacious against

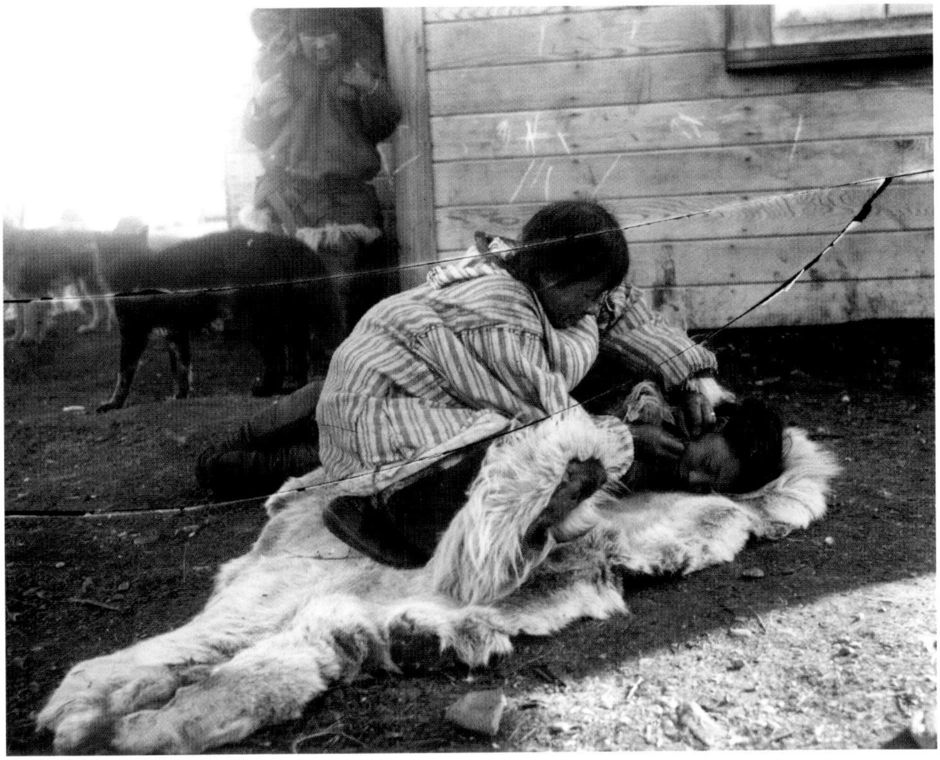

Lantern slide of Siberian Yupik woman "stitching the skin" at Indian Point, Chukotka,1901. After Bogoras (1904-9: pl. xxx, fig. 4). Copyright American Museum of Natural History (N-22323).

"spirits."[95] However, fine dark graphite (*tagneghli*) was also used. *Tagneghli* was a magical substance obtained through barter from the Siberians, and it was considered to be the "stone spirit" which "guards" humankind from evil spirits and from the sicknesses brought by them.[96] Traditionally, it was used to protect children from possessive spirits that were "awakened" as a result of a recent death in the village.[97]

Tattooing needles were made from slivers of bone, but as time passed, St. Lawrence Islanders (Sivuqaghhmiit) began using steel needles for "skin stitching." According to elder Mabel Toolie of Savoonga, one of the last women to wear traditional facial tattooing, a very small bag of seal intestine was used to hold the tattoo needle: "they don't use this needle for anything else, they just keep it in there and nobody else is supposed to touch it except the one who used it."[98] In unpublished fieldnotes, Geist described that the tattoo needle is laid aside and not used again until the tattoo heals. This seems to indicate that the tattoo needle was a dangerous object and "when any Eskimo is injured either accidently [sic] or willfully by any instruments, those instruments, including tattoo instruments [needles], are not used again until the wound is healed up again. If death occurs on account of the injury or if sickness results the instrument will be taken with the body of the dead or will be otherwise destroyed."[99]

The sinew (*ivalu*) used for tattooing usually came from reindeer tendons and sometimes from the tendons of sea mammals, like bowhead or gray whales.[100] Reindeer *ivalu* was made available by neighboring Siberians through trade. In the reindeer, a bundle of tendons (*ivalungelqughruk*) lie underneath the skin on either side of the vertebrae or along the muscles of the back legs.[101] These fine strands of reindeer *ivalu* were utilized in the tattooing of women. The *ivalu* procured from the back of the bowhead or gray whale was used in the tattooing of men, since, its coarseness was likened to that of a man's skin.[102] Sometimes whale *ivalu* was used to tattoo women, but only when they served as a pallbearer at a funeral.

Urine (*tequq*) was also considered to be an apotropaic substance suitable for tattooing, perhaps because it came from the bladder: an organ considered to be one of the primary seats of the life giving force of the soul.[103] Waldemar Bogoras, the late 19th century ethnographer of the Chukchi and Siberian Yupiit, recorded that if *tequq* was poured over a spirit's head, it froze upon contact immediately repelling the entity.[104] In this connection, it is not surprising that some St. Lawrence Island elders have said that *tequq* was poured around the outside of the traditional *nenglu* house to insure the same effect, because "many years ago, urine was . . . very special. It scared away the evil spirit."[105] Another St. Lawrence Island elder told me that, when he was a young man, he was walking one night outside of Gambell village. He heard a buzzing sound in his ears and was scared that a spirit was following him on the trail. He did not want to turn and look back, so he quickly began to urinate and the spirit disappeared immediately! But urine had other more practical uses. Because it has high ammonia content, it helped reduce the scabbing of a new tattoo and promoted healing.

Concepts of tattooing in the Arctic

Inuit (or, Eskimos generally) and St. Lawrence Island Yupiget, in particular, like many other circumpolar and indigenous peoples,[106] regarded living bodies as inhabited by multiple souls, each soul residing in a particular joint.[107] The anthropologist Robert Petersen has noted that the soul is the element that gives the body life processes, breath, warmth, feelings, and the ability to think and speak.[108] Accordingly, the ethnologist Edward Weyer stated in his tome, *The Eskimos*, that, "[a]ll disease is nothing but the loss of a soul; in every part of the human body there resides a little soul, and if part of the man's body is sick, it is because the little soul had abandoned that part, [namely, the joints]."[109] Thus, if one of these souls is taken away, the member or limb to which it belongs sickens and possibly dies.[110]

From this perspective, it is not surprising that tattoos had significant importance in funerary events, especially on St. Lawrence Island, Alaska. Funerary tattoos (*nafluq*) consisted of small dots at the convergence of various joints: shoulders, elbows, hip, wrist, knee, ankle, neck, and waist joints.[111] For applying them, the female tattooist, in cases of both men and

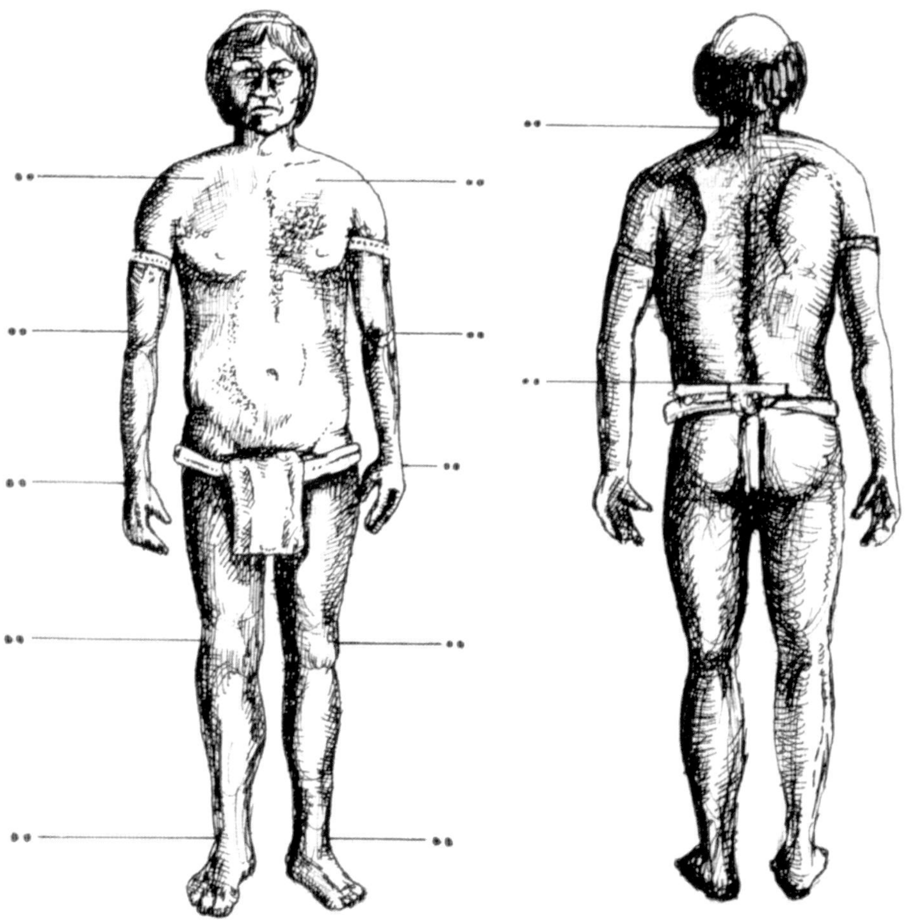

St. Lawrence Island joint-tattooing, ca. 1900. Sketch by Mark Planisek.

women, used a large, skin-sewing needle with whale sinew dipped into a mixture of lubricating seal oil, urine, and lampblack scraped from a cooking pot. Lifting a fold of skin she passed the needle through one side and out the other, leaving two "spots" under the epidermis.

Paul Silook, a native of St. Lawrence Island, explained that these tattoos protected a pallbearer from spiritual attack.[112] Death was characterized as a dangerous time in which the living could become possessed by the "shade" or malevolent spirit of the deceased. A spirit of the dead was believed to linger for some time in the vicinity of its former village.[113] Though not visible to all, the "shade" was conceived as an absolute material double of the corpse. And because pallbearers were in direct contact with this spiritual entity, they were ritualistically tattooed to repel it.[114] Their joints became the locus of tattoo because it was believed that the evil spirit entered the body at these points, as they were the seats of the soul(s).[115] Urine and tattoo pigments, as the nexus of dynamic and apotropaic power, prevented the evil spirit from penetrating the pallbearer's body.

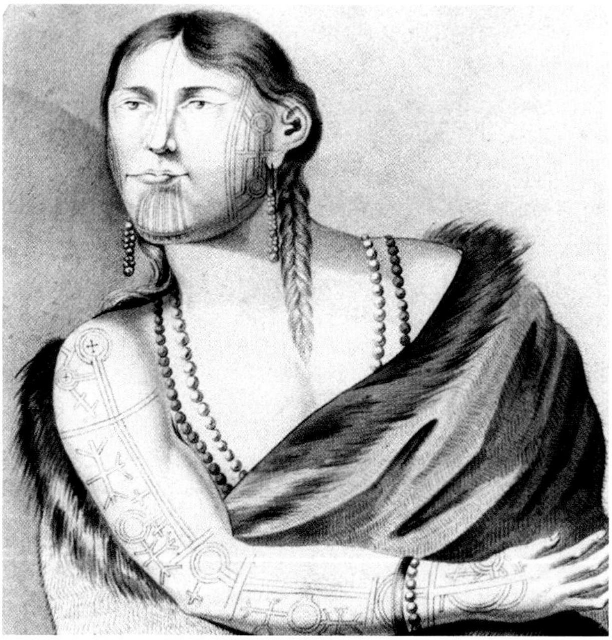

Oldest known European depiction of a Siberian Yupik woman, ca. 1795.

Similarly, nearly every attribute of the human dead was also believed to be equally characteristic of the animal dead, as the spirit of every animal was believed to possess semi-human form.[116] Men, and more rarely women, were tattooed on St. Lawrence Island when they killed a seal, polar bear, or harpooned a bowhead whale (*aghveq*) for the first time.[117] Like the tattoo of the pallbearer, "first-kill" tattoos (*kakileq*) consisted of small dots at the convergence of various joints: shoulders, elbows, hip, wrist, knee, ankle, neck, and waist. The application of these tattoos impeded the future instances of spirit possession at these vulnerable points.

However, *kakileq* were also important to other aspects of the hunt. One of the old hunters in Gambell village told me that "one reason for [the tattoos] is to hit the target, sometimes they don't [and] I think these are for that purpose, to hit the target."[118] This is not entirely surprising, since the anthropologist Robert Spencer remarked that tattoos on the North Slope of Alaska and other forms of adornment doubled as whaling charms, "serving to bring the whale closer to the boat, to make the animal more tractable and amenable to the harpooner."[119]

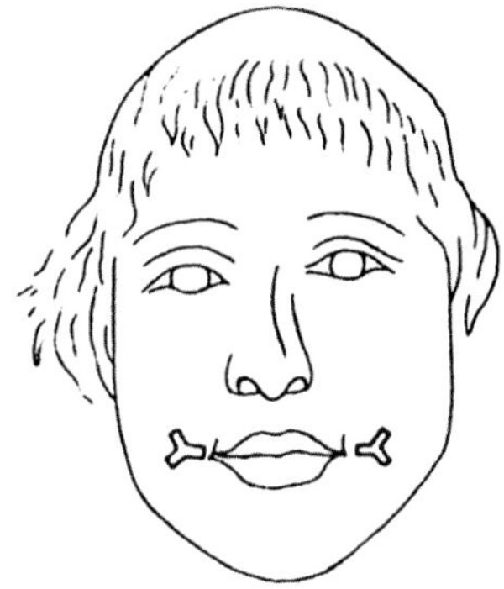

Men's fluke tail tattoos. After Gordon (1906: pl. ix, no. 3).

This type of sympathetic magic was also manifest in the stylized "whale-fluke" tattoos adorning the corners of men's mouths.[120] Fittingly, these symbols were applied as part of first-kill observances among the Yupiget of St. Lawrence Island and the Yupiit of Chukotka,[121] as well as by other groups in the Arctic.[122]

From the preceding remarks, it seems that the issue of death, whether human or animal, cast into symbolic tattooed relief important cultural values by which circumpolar peoples lived their lives and evaluated their experiences. As noted, physical contact with the dead, human or animal, was met with apprehension. This was because the spirits of great animals (e.g. polar bears, whales) or humans were believed to be imbued with a personhood that was considered to be equivalent or superior to that of the living.[123] As an individual matured, his or her education revolved around the increasing awareness of the natural and supernatural worlds, and the prescriptions and proscriptions for proper behavior within them.[124] The supernatural was met everywhere in the landscape and places along hunting or travel routes became sacred because they embodied local spirits or manifested the presence of higher divinities including animals and deceased ancestors.[125] Therefore, it was here, within the landscape of sea, ice, and frozen tundra, that the everyday, elusive and unobservable experiences, rituals and rites of passage took place circumscribing the identity of the people by linking them to a collectively shared and experienced sense of place.[126] Indeed, humans, animals and everything in the natural world shared the same fundamental spiritual essence,[127] and in this sense "persons" were

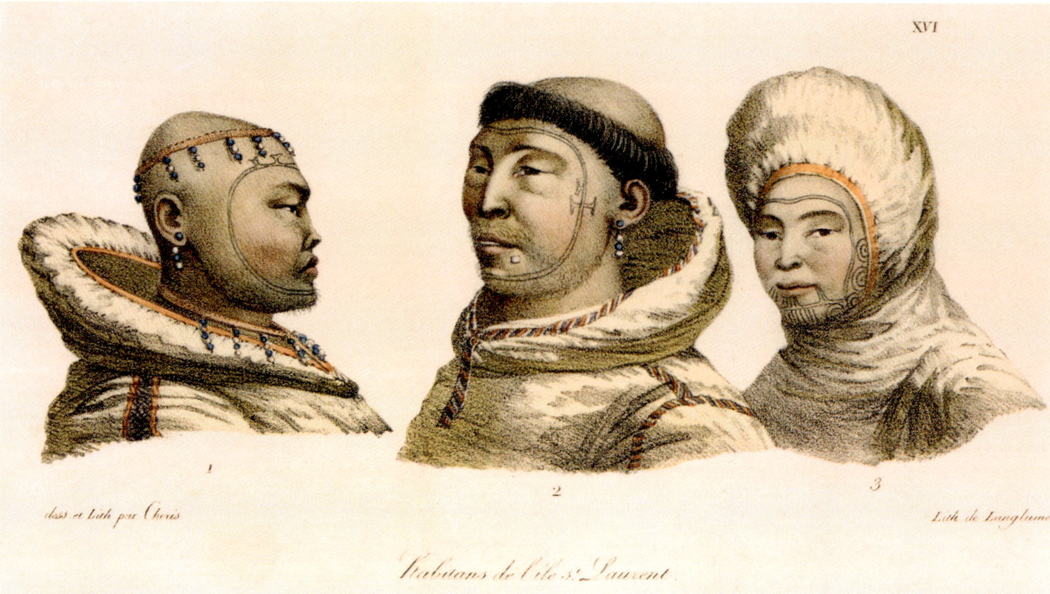

Inhabitants of St. Lawrence Island, ca. 1816.
After Choris (1822: pl. IX).

constituted of multiple personal attributes extending beyond the human domain. In this connection, specific forms of tattoos recalled an ancestral presence and could be understood to function as the conduit for a "visiting" spiritual entity, coming from the different temporal dimensions into the contemporary world.[128] For example, in many shamanistic performances in the Arctic, the human body was altered (via masking, body painting, vestments, or tattoo) to facilitate the entry of a "spirit helper."[129] Tattoos and other forms of adornment acted as magnets attracting a spiritual force—one that was channeled through the ceremonial attire and into the body.

The tattooing process involved iconographic manifestation of the "other side," acknowledgment of the manifestation's power, and harnessing that power within the corporeal envelope of human skin. On St. Lawrence Island, men and women tattooed anthropomorphic spirit helpers onto their foreheads and limbs.[130] These stick-like figures, sometimes appropriately named "guardians" or "assistants," protected individuals from evil spirits, disasters at sea, unknown areas where one traveled, strangers, and even in the case of new mothers, the loss of their children.[131] In Chukotka, murderers inscribed these types of tattoos on their shoulders in hopes of capturing the soul of their victim, thus transforming it into an "assistant," or even into a part of himself.[132]

Apart from such concepts, however, there seems to have been some relationship between labrets and tattoos, at least in the Bering Strait region. Adelbert von Chamisso, a naturalist with Kotzebue's expedition of 1815-1818, noted that labrets were rare among St. Lawrence Island men and often replaced by a tattooed spot.[133] Edward W. Nelson, a naturalist working for the U.S. Army Signal Service in the late 19th century, also suggested that these circular tattoos were a relic of wearing a lip-plug or labret.[134] Bogoras believed that this was probably true, though their position did not quite "correspond to the usual position of the labret. These marks are now intended only as charms against the spirits."[135] Dewey Anderson and Walter Eells, two sociologists from Stanford University who visited St. Lawrence Island in the 1930's, recorded that "a small circle on the lower lip under the corners of the mouth [was tattooed] to prevent a man who has repeatedly fallen into the sea from drowning."[136] Similarly, a Diomede Islander from Bering Strait was seen at the turn of the century with a mark tattooed at each corner of the mouth. He explained it as a preventive prescribed by his mother against the fate that had befallen his father—death by drowning.[137]

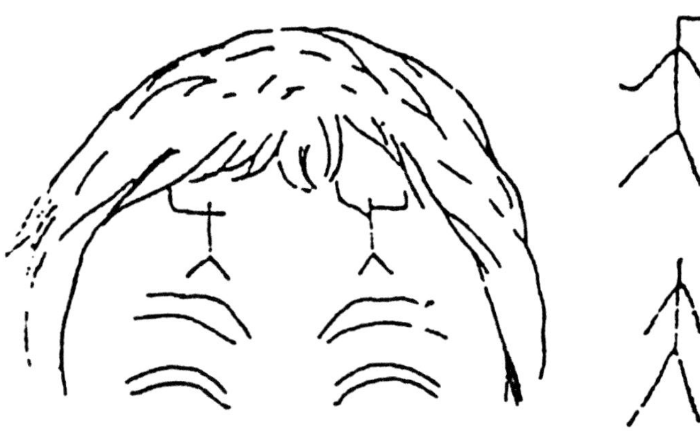

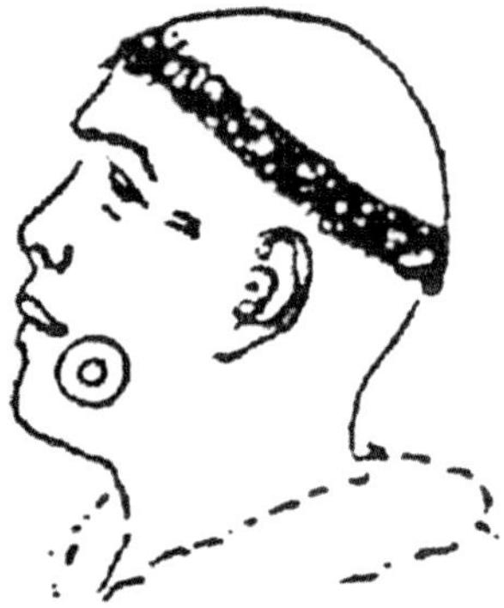

Above: "Guardian" or "assistant" tattoos. In the Siberian Yupik language these marks were called *yugaaq* or "powerful person." Drawing after Bogoras (1904-9: 343).

Left: Tattooed labret, ca. 1890. After Nelson (1899: 52).

Henry B. Collins, a Smithsonian archaeologist who worked on St. Lawrence Island in the 1930s, didn't necessarily believe that drowning was the danger. After interviewing Paul Silook, he was told that *angeyeghaq* (orphan walrus) was the problem:

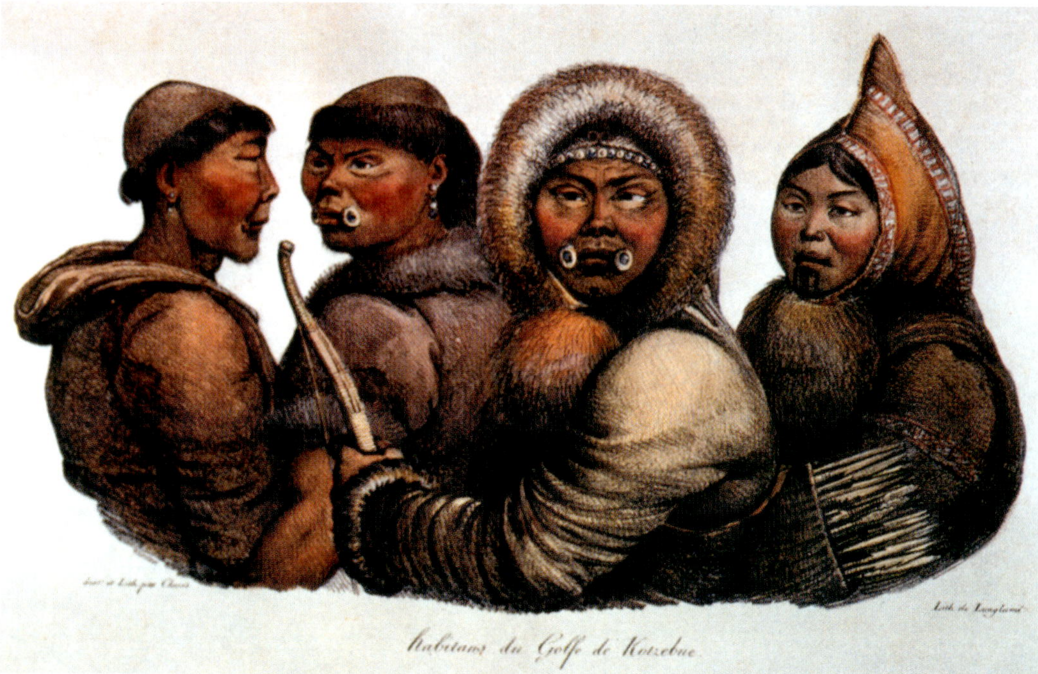

Eskimos wearing labrets from Kotzebue Sound, Alaska.
After Choris (1822).

> Walrus are believed to eat seals, and even humans, in addition to their usual food of seaweeds and mollusks. Paul Silook's father tells of two times he was chased by a walrus. It is believed that walrus that thus depart from their customary diet were left motherless when very young and so did not learn the proper method of eating.[138]

Maybe then, Bering Strait people designed labret-like tattoos to repel the aggressive orphan walrus called *angeyeghaq*? Aspects of St. Lawrence Island folklore recorded by Paul Silook suggest that labret-like tattoos recalled in symbolic form the appearance of a killer whale (*mesungesak*):

> Killer whales are said to have a white spot at each side of the mouth like the labrets of the mainland Siberian natives. [Killers] are said to have a white strip, ring, running obliquely from around the neck to beneath the flipper. Like the St. Lawrence Island leather strip with charms [*uyaghqutat*] worn by men.[139]

Therefore, if the concept of labrets, or labret-like tattoos, represented the killer whale, then the man that wore this tattoo might have believed he would become transformed into one, extending his safe passage through dangerous waters. On the other hand, the art historian Ralph Coe believes labrets, and by extension labret-like tattoos, mimicked walrus's tusks, especially since many labrets were carved from walrus ivory:

> The ivory seems to stand for the interchangeability of the animal or human, his soul[s], and the recipient, just the Eskimo himself thought of wood as a symbol of strength: 'to the Eskimo, dwarf willow is a symbol of strength and suppleness against an overwhelming Arctic background, where survival depends upon a man's ability to contend with the forces of nature, while at the same time yielding to them and conforming with them.'[140]

Adopting the anatomical characteristics of the walrus (tusks) through tattoo may have captured the essence of its aggressive behavior or transformed the hunter into this creature. This would not be surprising since the concept of transformation—men into men, men into animals, animals into men, and animals into animals—permeates all aspects of life in the Bering Strait area and is expressed on all kinds of objects including carved ivory sculpture.[141] No doubt this deceptive "tattoo foil" subverted the attention of the foe and safeguarded the hunter from malicious attack.

Tattoo foils, or "guardian" tattoos, were not only confined to labret-like tattoos. Instead, men and women were variably tattooed on each upper arm and underneath the lip with circles, half-circles, anthropomorphs, or with cruciform elements at both corners of the mouth to disguise the wearer from disease-bearing spirits. Paul Silook explained, "[y]ou know some families have the same kind of sickness that continues, and people believed that these marks should be put on a child so the spirits might think he is a different person, a person that is not from that family. In this way people tried to cut off trouble."[142] Similarly, Paul Silook's father had a small figure of a man tattooed on each upper arm. He put these on after four of his sons had

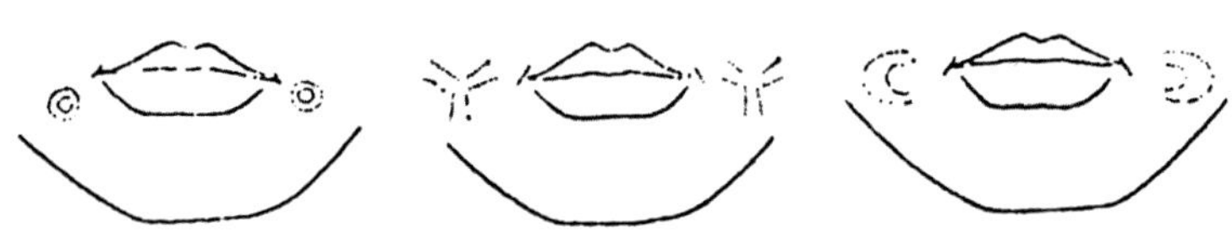

Tattoo foils. After Bogoras (1904-9: 255).

died, "to change his luck in this regard." Other families tattooed small marks at the root of a child's nose if he or she cried too much. Since a crying child was thought to be an indication of future misfortune: specifically that a family member would soon die.

The multiplicity of these types of "guardian" tattoos suggest, in all probability, that specific tattoo "remedies" were believed to differ from individual to individual, or more appropriately, from family to family. An account from a Siberian Yupik man visiting Gambell, St. Lawrence Island in 1940, reveals that this was the case, at least in Mainland Siberia:

> I was the oldest child in my family. In trying to save my brothers and sisters my father ask[ed] some woman to have me tattooed. The woman had all kinds of prayer when she tattooed me. While [a] woman [is] tattooing a person, every stitch as she goes has something to say with. My father[,] trying to save me as best he can, he put leather bands around my wrist and forehead, with beads hanging down all over my eyes, and beads on each sole of [my] stocking, stitched through . . . to save his child from death. Also on every joint beads are stitched, and sometimes little bells on elbows. My father sewed little pieces of squirrel's kettle on the band around my shoulders and under [my] arm. Part of parents' idea to save children.[143]

Women's facial and body tattoos

There seems to have been no widely distributed tattoo design among Eskimo women, although chin patterns or "stripes" were more commonly found than any other.[144] Chin stripes served multiple purposes in social contexts. Most notably, they were tattooed on the chin as part of the ritual of social maturity, a signal to men that a woman had reached puberty. Chin patterns also served to protect women during enemy raids. For example, fighting among the Siberians and St. Lawrence Islanders took place in close quarters, namely in various forms of semi-subterranean dwellings called *nenglu*. Raiding parties usually attacked in the early morning hours, at or before first light, hoping to catch their enemies while asleep. Women, valued as important "commodities" during these times, were highly prized for their many abilities. Not being distinguishable from the men by their clothing in the dim light of the *nenglu*, their chin patterns made them more recognizable as females and their lives would be spared.[145] Once captured, however, they were bartered off as slaves.

More generally, the chin stripe aesthetic was important to the Diomede

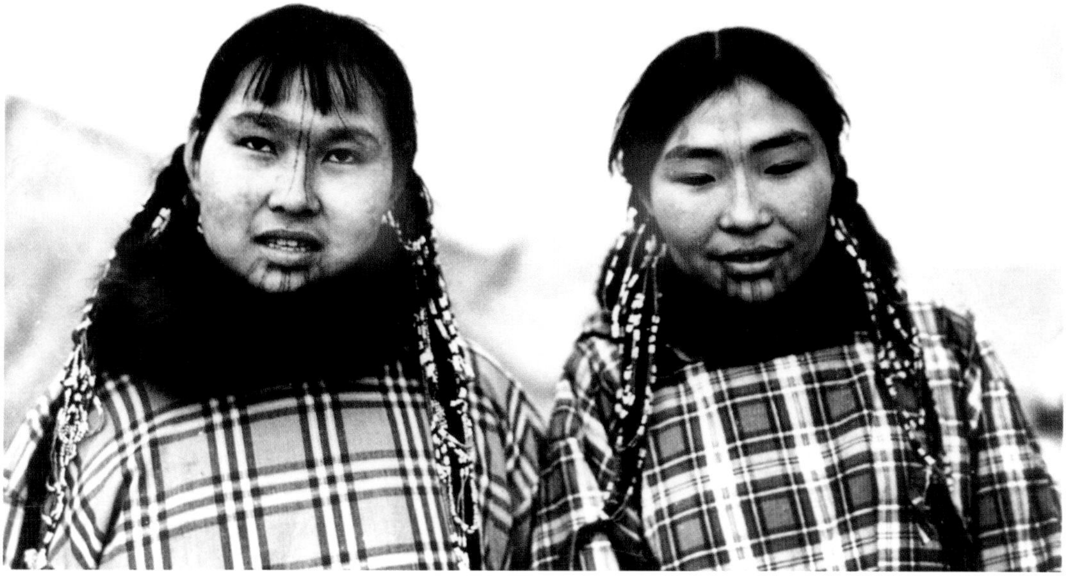

Two young girls from Savoonga, St. Lawrence Island, ca. 1930. Photograph by Dr. Leuman Waugh. Copyright National Anthropological Archives (N-95-9741).

Islanders living in Bering Strait. Ideally, thin lines tattooed onto the chin were valuable indicators for choosing a wife, according to anthropologist Sergei Bogojavlensky:

> It was believed that a girl who smiled and laughed too much would cause the lines to spread and get thick. A girl with a full set of lines on the chin, all of them thin, was considered to be a good prospect as a wife, for she was clearly serious and hard working.[146]

A full set of lines was not only a powerful physical statement of the ability to endure great pain, but also an attestation to a woman's powers of "animal" attraction. For example, in the St. Lawrence and Siberian Yupik area of the early 20th century, women painted and tattooed their faces in ritual ceremonies in order to imitate, venerate, honor, and/or attract those animals that "will bring good fortune" to the family.[147] Waldemar Bogoras added, "[i]t is a mistake to think that women are weaker than men in hunting-pursuits," since as a man wanders in vain about the wilderness, searching, women who "sit by the lamp are really strong, for they know how to call the game to the shore."[148] Moreover, it was through the performance of domestic activities—

butchering, cooking (turning hunted meat into edible "food") and sewing (creating sturdy and beautiful clothing that attracted game)—that a woman's ritual position as "wife the hunter" became solidified in Arctic culture.[149]

In this connection, it seems that a woman's facial tattoos assured a kind of spiritual permanency: they lured into the house a part of the land or sea, and along with that, part of its animal and spiritual life. Not surprisingly, an unusual event, such as the capture of a whale by a young woman's father, was sometimes commemorated on her cheek(s) by tattooed fluke tails, which advertised her father's prowess to members of Yupik society.[150]

Slightly sloping parallel lines, usually consisting of three tightly grouped bands on the cheek, were also tattooed on women. Bogoras mentioned that childless Chukchi women "tattoo on both cheeks three equidistant lines running all the way around. This is considered one of the charms against sterility."[151] There is a similar belief related in the story of Ayngaangaawen, a woman from the extinct St. Lawrence Island village of Kookoolok. Ayngaangaawen refused to get her tattoo-marks. She could not bear healthy children, and as a result, they all died as infants. Supposedly, "when she got some marks she had children" and they lived into adulthood.[152]

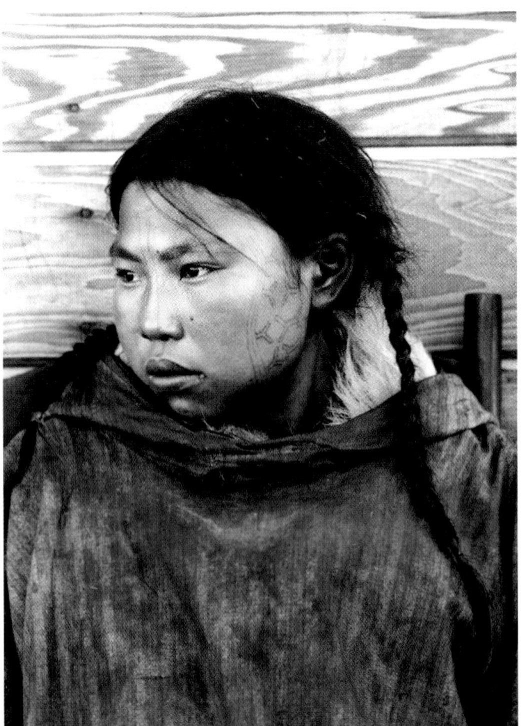

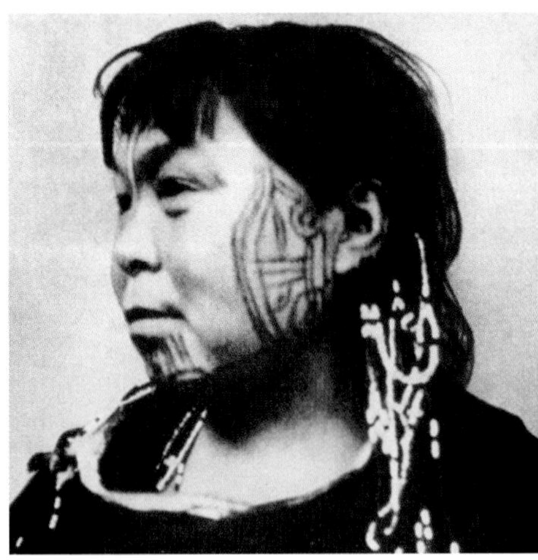

Above: St. Lawrence Island woman with intricate facial tattoos, 1901. Photograph by R.N. Hawley. After Jackson (1902: 28).

Left: Siberian Yupik woman with fluke tails (*veghaq*) tattooed on her cheeks, 1901. Photograph by Waldemar Bogoras. Copyright American Museum of Natural History (N-2533).

Other tattoos of St. Lawrence Island women have more cryptic functions. For example, two slightly diverging lines ran from high up on the forehead down over the full length of the nose. These tattoos were quite often the first ones to be placed upon pre-pubescent girls (six to ten years of age). Daniel S. Neuman, a doctor living in Nome, Alaska at the turn of the 20th century, wrote that these tattoos distinguished a woman "in after life from a man, on account of the similarity of [their] dress."[153] Chukchi myths illustrate that these same tattoos were the symbol *par excellence* of the woman herself.[154]

Tattoos also marked the thighs of young St. Lawrence Island women when they reached puberty. In Igloolik, Canada, some 2,500 miles east of St. Lawrence Island, the tattooing of women's thighs ensured that the first thing a newborn infant saw would be something of beauty.[155]

Intricate scrollwork found on the cheeks, and tattoos on the arms of women possibly form elements of a genealogical puzzle.[156] Most women of St. Lawrence Island say these tattoos are simply "make-up," beautifying their bodies. Dr. Neuman verified that this was the case, but he also believed that "[e]ach tribe adhered to their own design but with a slight modification for their own individual members. The designs on the hands

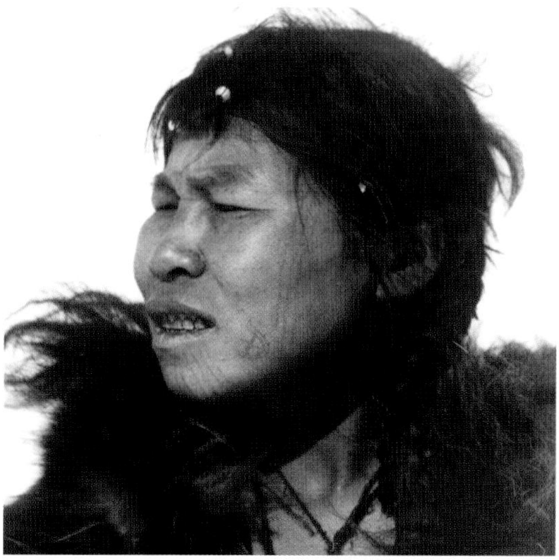

Above: Tattooed Chukchi woman with fertility tattoo on cheek and tattoo-foil near mouth, 1901. Photograph by Waldemar Bogoras. Copyright American Museum of Natural History (N-2459).

Right: Chukchi woman with fertility, chin, and nose markings. After Cantwell (1902: 212).

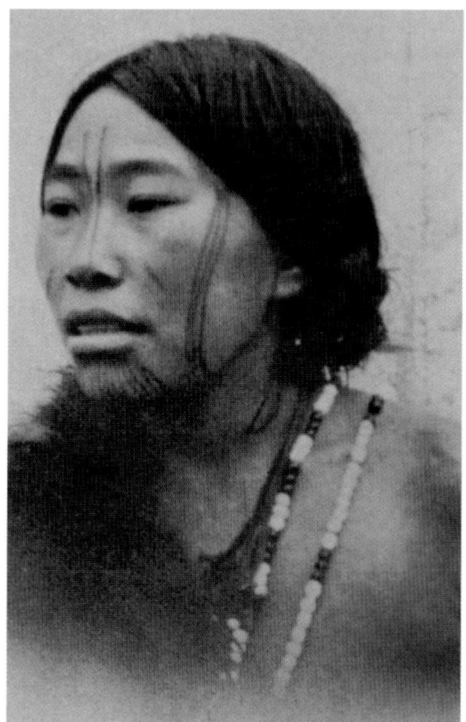

and arms often combined tribal and family designs and formed, so to speak, a family tree."[157] On the arms of one of my female informants, rows of fluke tails extend from her wrists to the middle of her forearms. These symbols represent her clan (Aymaramket), an honored lineage of great whale hunters.[158]

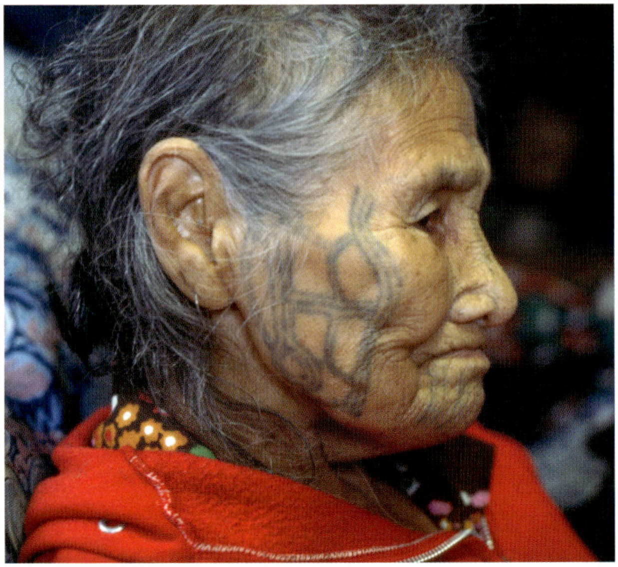

Facial tattoo of a St. Lawrence Island woman, 1997. Photograph by Lars Krutak.

Although it seems as though a woman's tattoo designs were individualistic, those tattoos found on the back of the hand (*igaq*) were not; possibly suggesting that these motifs marked the identities of women belonging to a cohort. For example, the last group of St. Lawrence Island women to have retained *igaq* had identical tattoo patterns and it is these women who were the last age group to be tattooed on St. Lawrence Island, ca. 1920.[159]

Medicinal function of tattoos

In the previous sections, the apotropaic aspect of tattoo has been discussed, specifically as a remedy against supernatural possession. In light of the indigenous theory of disease causation—dangerous spirits—it is not surprising that tattoo was considered as a form of medicine against a variety of ills. This medicine was believed to act as a curative or as a preventative one.

Paramount to these concepts was the role of the preventive function. Circumpolar peoples were socialized and trained from their earliest days to build their bodies into pillars of strength through running, weightlifting, wading into frigid waters, etc.[160] Therefore, when a biological disorder rose to life threatening levels, where "preventive" medicinal practice had failed the cure, it then became the responsibility of the shaman to summon his or her spiritual powers to safeguard and restore health. Disorders, as well as other inexplicable misfortunes, were attributed to supernatural agency and

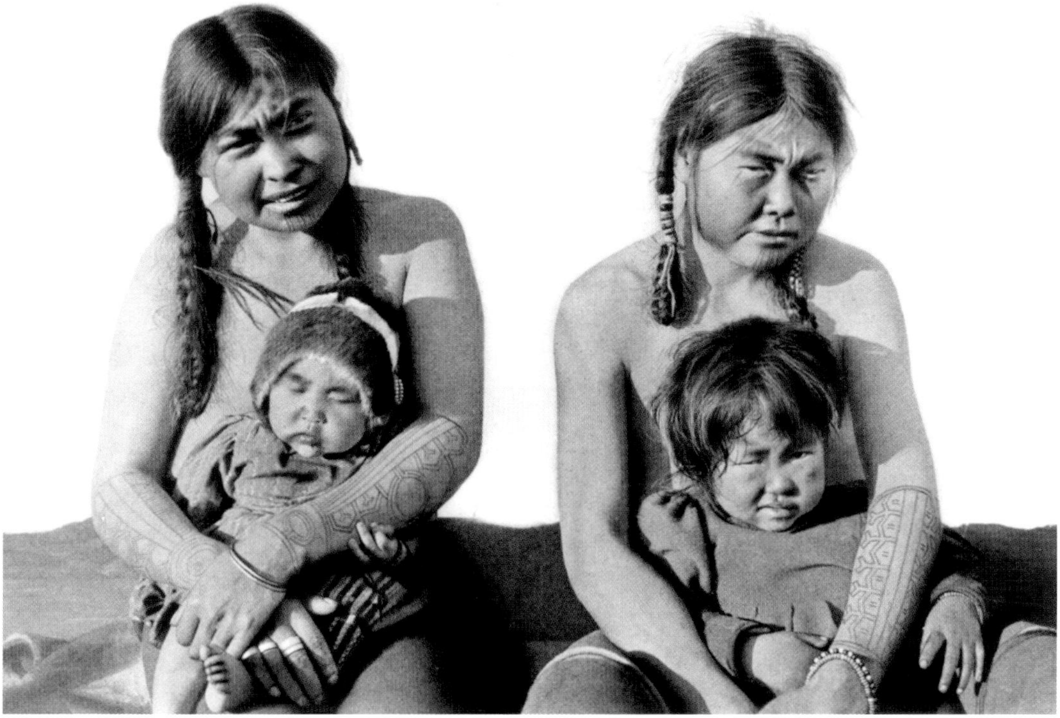

King Island women displaying arm tattoos, ca. 1900. After Gordon (1906: pl. XX).

were believed to be curable through the use of tattoo.[161] Oftentimes, shamans applied these types of medicinal tattoos, though not always.

Tattoo, as a curative agent, was often disorder-specific. Some maladies were cured with the application of small lines or marks on or near afflicted areas. Some examples from St. Lawrence Island are as follows:

> A mark over the sternum, which is the shaman's cure for heart trouble.
> A small straight mark over each eye, the cure for eye trouble.
> Various other small marks on the body used as remedies from time to time by the shaman.[162]

Thus, two lines placed near the eye of a man from St. Lawrence Island observed by the Smithsonian ethnologist Nelson in the 1880s represented one of these types of medicinal marking. Such markings are even seen on ancient Okvik/Old Bering Sea (500 B.C.-750 A.D.) and Punuk

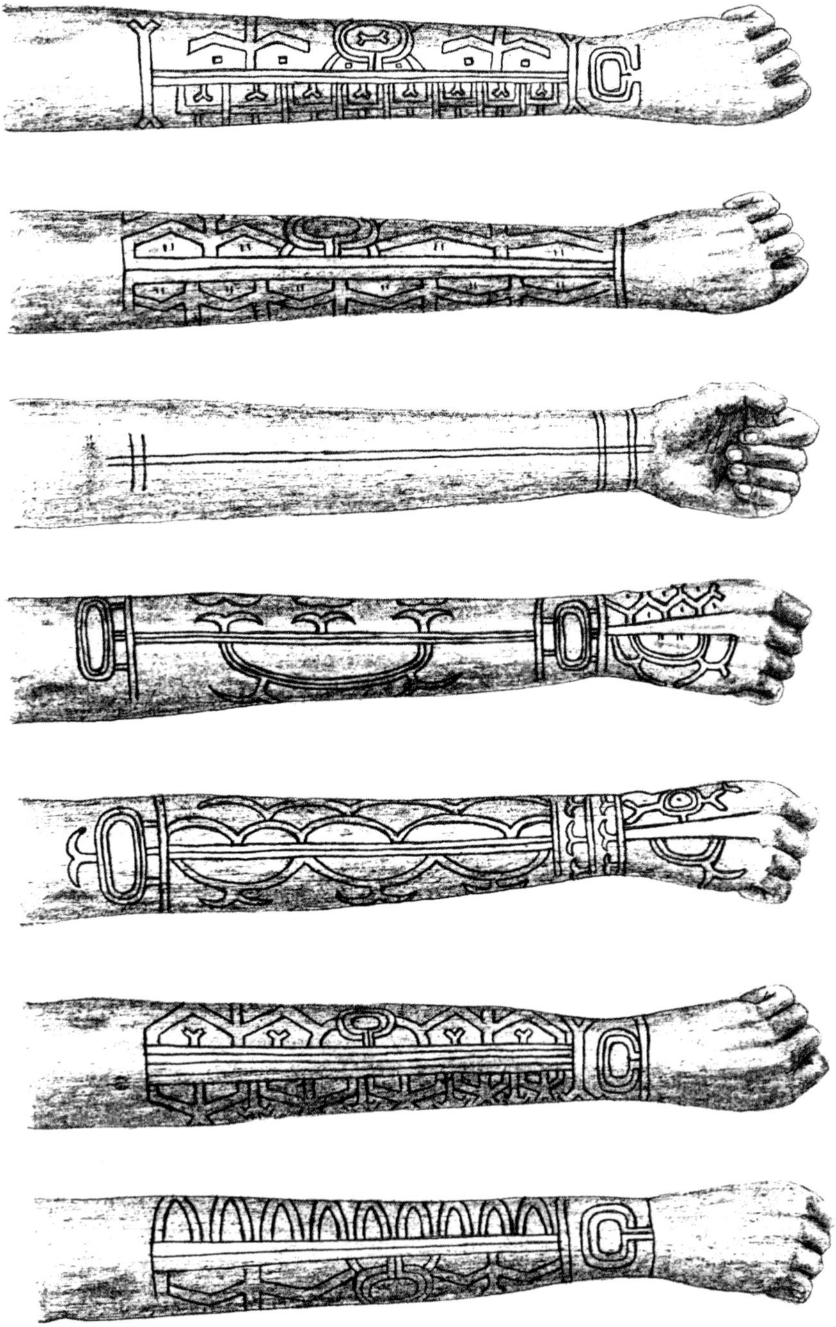

Reconstructions of Bering Strait arm tattoos, ca. 1900.
Sketches by Tim Sczawinski.

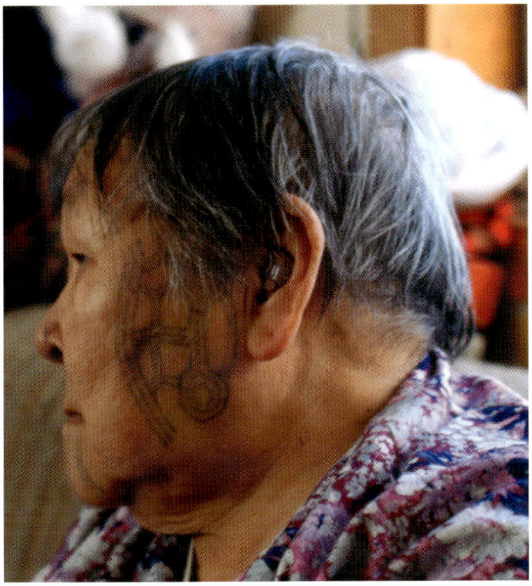 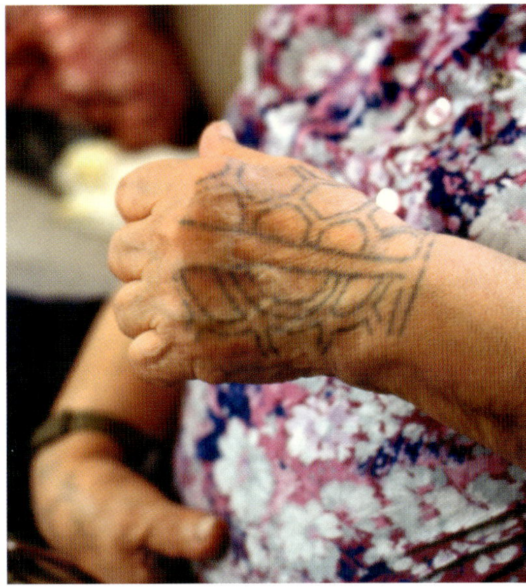

St. Lawrence Island Yupik facial and hand tattooing, 1997.
Photographs by Lars Krutak.

(750-1050 A.D.) culture ivory carvings from St. Lawrence Island. In the Bering Strait region, the ethnologist George B. Gordon observed a Diomede Island man with tattooed marks on either cheek, close to the mouth, others on the temple and two more on the forehead.[163] These three sets of marks on his face were explained as "medicine" and their presence was said to have directly benefited the wearer.

But tattoo medicine was not only confined to the simple placement of the markings themselves, since traditional practices of tattoo and ritually induced bleeding were oftentimes interrelated and may have even overlapped to some extent. Around Bering Strait, shamans commonly performed bloodletting to relieve aching or inflamed parts of the body. Nelson watched a shaman "lancing the scalp of his little girl's head, the long, thin iron point of the instrument being thrust twelve to fifteen times between the scalp and skull."[164] Similarly, the Alaskan Aleuts performed bloodletting as remedies for numerous ailments attributed to "bad blood."[165] On St. Lawrence Island, bleeding was resorted to in cases of severe migraine headache or as one elder said, "to release anything with a high blood pressure . . . the [ancestors] know that."[166] The Chugach Eskimo treated sore eyes by bleeding at the root of the nose or at the temples. Then the patient was made to swallow the blood, which affected the cure.[167]

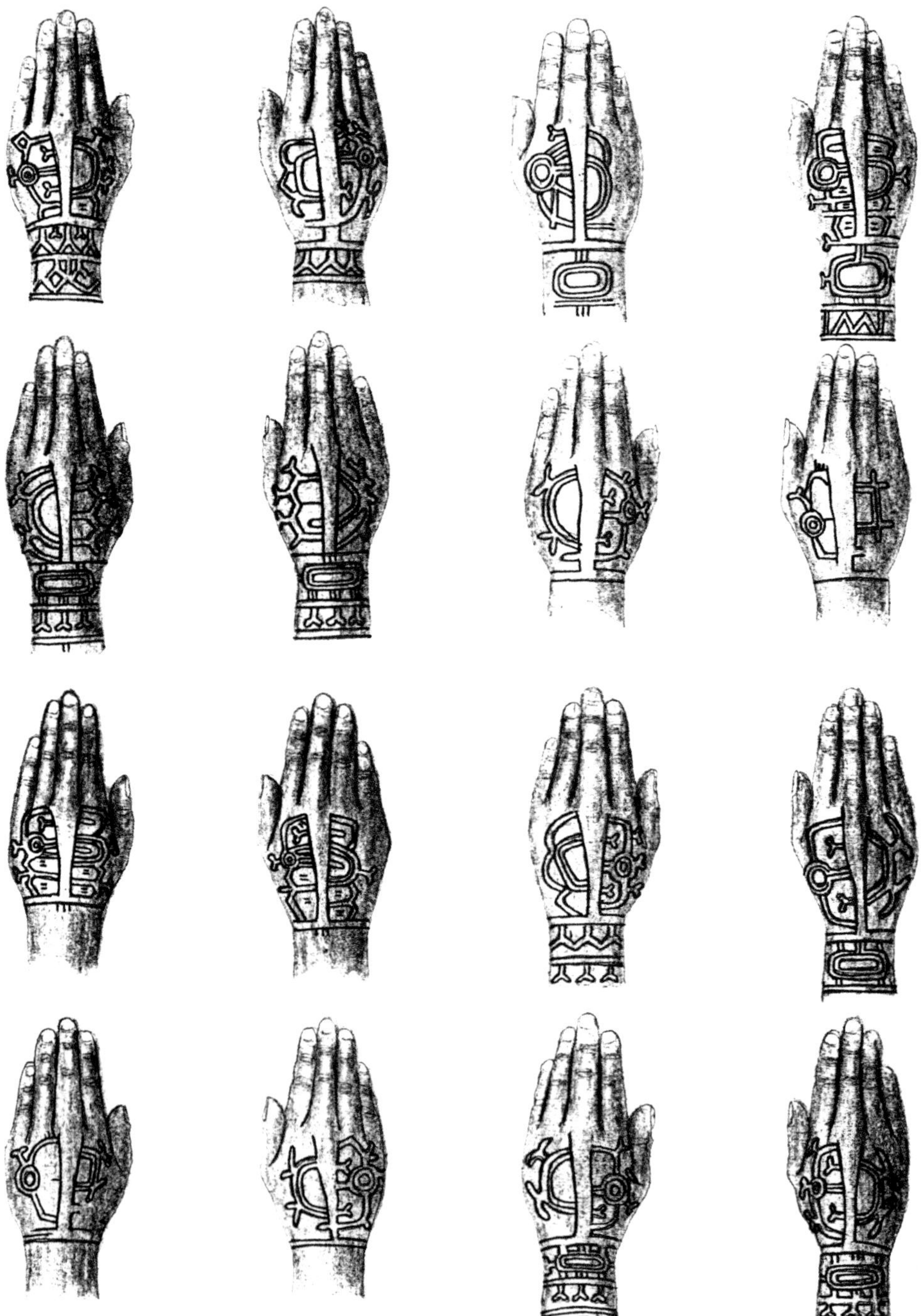

Siberian and St. Lawrence Island Yupik hand tattoos, ca. 1900.
Sketches by Tim Sczawinski.

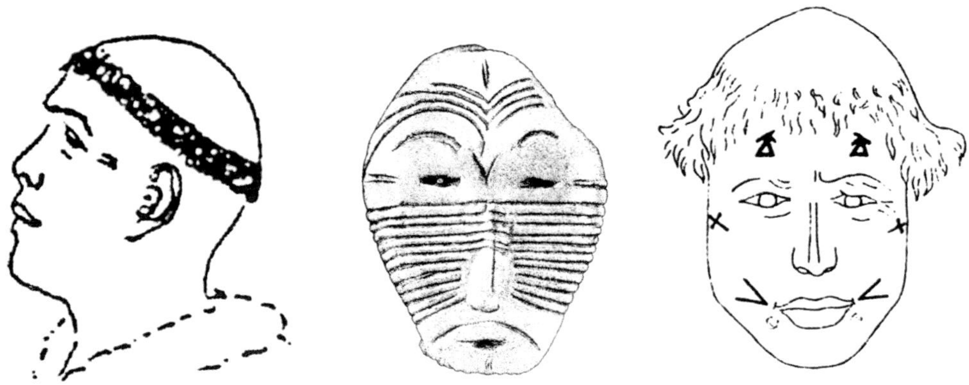

Left to right: Medicinal tattoos observed by Nelson (1899); Punuk sculpture with medicinal markings near eyes (sketch courtesy of the Rock Foundation); Diomede Islander with medicinal tattoos. After Gordon (1906: pl. IX).

It is also plausible that the release of blood functioned to appease various ills and spiritual manifestations. For instance, several St. Lawrence Islanders explained to me the importance of licking the blood that was released during tattoo "operations." According to one elder, the female tattoo artist, who performed the skin stitching, licked the blood that flowed from the punctured skin, "because that helps for them to have good sight."[168] Evidently, "bad blood" released from the tattoo rite acted as a kind of supplementary healing agent remedying specific ailments. Reliance on this cultural practice might seem to have grown out of the impression that the expulsion of the evil spirit would be facilitated through the escaping stream of blood.[169] Thus, by harnessing blood orally, and/or neutralizing it with saliva, the tattoo artist transformed it into a sanctifying substance.

Tattooing as a form of acupuncture

Surprisingly, the Arctic shaman's prophetic role in medicinal practice was closely paralleled by that of the Chinese acupuncturist.[170] Both were consulted to identify the causes of disease, by differentiation of symptoms and signs, to provide suitable treatments. In acupuncture, pathogenic forces are thought to invade the human body from the exterior via the mouth, nose or body surfaces and the resultant diseases are called exogenous disease.[171] In circumpolar cultures, and especially on St. Lawrence Island, the primary factor determining sickness was the intrusion of an evil spirit from outside the body into one of the souls of the afflicted individual. These types of malevolent actions of the spirit upon the body were traced to disordered behavior, possession, illness (rheumatism), and sometimes death.[172] Consequently, and as a form of spiritual/medicinal practice, St. Lawrence Islanders tattooed specific joints. As mentioned earlier, joints served as the vehicular "highways" which evil entities traveled to enter the human body and injure it. Thus, joint-tattoos protected individuals by closing down these pathways, since the substances utilized to produce tattoo pigment—urine, soot, and sometimes graphite—were the nexus of dynamic and apotropaic power, preventing an evil spirit from penetrating the human body.

In both Chinese acupuncture theory and St. Lawrence Island medicinal theory, it is believed that all ailments of the body, whether internal of external, are reflected at specific points either at on the surface of the skin or just beneath it. In acupuncture, many of these points occur at the articulation of major joints and lie along specific pathways called "meridians." Meridians connect the internal organs with specific points that are located either on or in the epidermis, often in close proximity to nerves and blood vessels.[173] Evoking the Chinese acupuncturists' yin/yang cosmology, the body is in a perpetual state of dynamic equilibrium, oscillating between the poles of masculine and feminine, man and animal, sickness and health.[174] Thus, relieving excess pressure at these points enables the body to regain its former state of homeostasis (harmony) within and outside of the body. As one can imagine, it is believed that there are many possible interrelationships and connections between organs, points, joints, and tattoos.

Analysis of traditional St. Lawrence Island tattoo practices suggests that several tattooed areas on the body directly correspond to classical acupuncture points.[175] In the recent past, these parallels were known to the St. Lawrence Islanders themselves. For example, one elder explained to me that one of the areas tattoos were placed upon coincides with the acupuncture point *yang pai*—utilized to remedy frontal headache and pain in the eye: "Grandparents, when they were pricking that [point when they] hurt from headache, when [they] thought that [the] eyes are bothering you . . . they use acupuncture."[176] Of course, this type of remedy is quite ancient. The earliest known reference to acupuncture analgesia of this kind is in a legend about Hua To (110-207 A.D.), the first-known Chinese surgeon, who used acupuncture for headache.[177]

The Aleuts also utilized acupuncture in medical therapy. Acupuncture was resorted to in cases of headache, eye disorders, colic, and lumbago.[178] Like the St. Lawrence Islanders, the Aleuts "tattoo-punctured" to relieve aching joints. The anthropologist Margaret Lantis observed that Aleut Atka Islanders, "moistened thread covered with gunpowder (probably soot in former times) sew[ing] through the pinched-up skin near an aching joint or across the back over a region of pain."[179]

Apparently, the efficacy of this potent medical technology was very great, because it was not only confined to the North Pacific Rim. For example, archaeological evidence in the form of tattooed mummies indicates that tattoo-puncture reached Greenland in the distant past.[180] Radiocarbon dated to the 15th century A.D., the mummies of Qilakitsoq have revealed that a conscious, exacting attempt was made to place dot-motif tattoos at important facial points.[181] Being that these dot-motif tattoos are suggestive of acupuncture points, and coupled with the fact that each actually designates a classical acupuncture point, cultural affinity must be suggested. Besides, Danish ethnologist Gustav Holm reported that Greenlanders "now and then . . . resort to tattooing in cases of sickness."[182] Although we are not entirely sure if Holm was specifically referring to "tattoo-puncture" in his statement, several intriguing 1,500 year-old ivory "doll-heads" excavated from

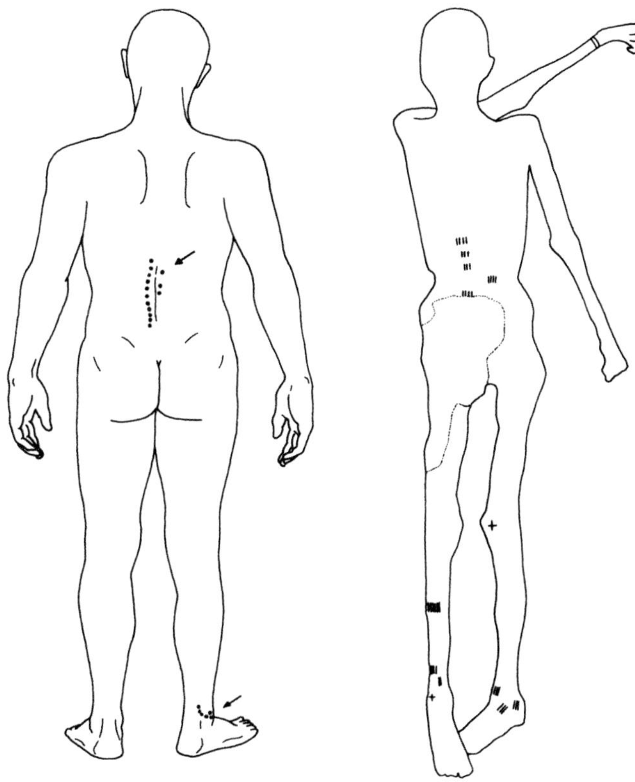

Right: The 5,000-year-old Iceman is the oldest known human to have worn medicinal tattoos akin to acupunture. Redrawn after Spindler (1994: 172).

Left: A 2,500-year-old mummy of a Siberian Pazyryk chief also sported tattoos; markings probably applied for therapeutic purposes (Krutak 1999). Redrawn after Spindler (1994: 173).

St. Lawrence Island illustrate ancient continuity spanning thousands of miles and hundreds of years.[183]

However, there are other similarities in the tattoo cultures of St. Lawrence Island and Greenland. In the early 1970s, beach erosion exposed the heavily tattooed, mummified body of an Okvik/Old Bering Sea woman radiocarbon dated to 1,600 years ago at Cape Kiyalighaq, St. Lawrence Island.[184] Her forearm tattoos were very reminiscent of those seen in late 19th century photographs of East Greenlanders at Ammassalik.[185]

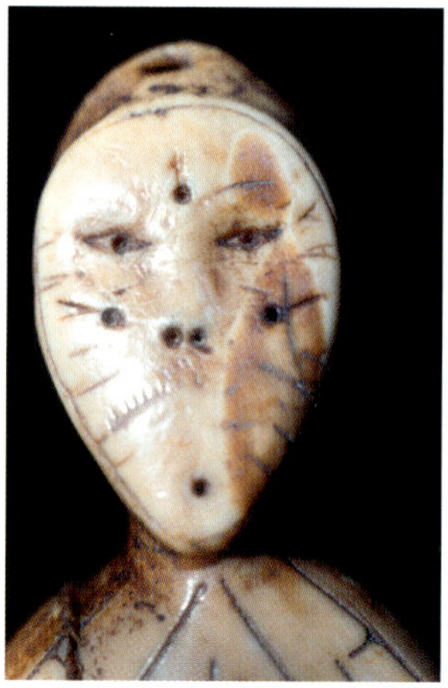

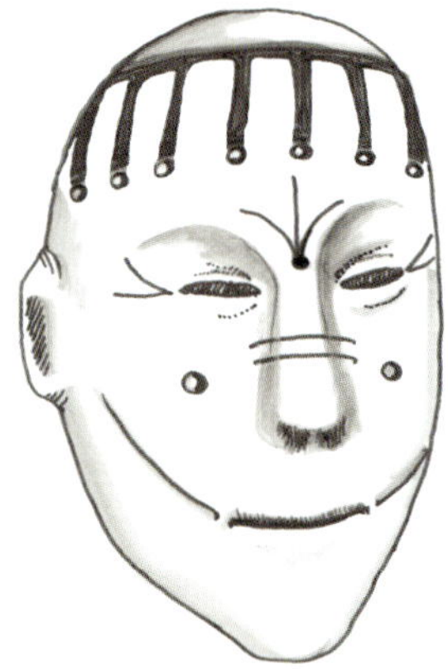

Left: Punuk doll-head with tattoo-puncture at facial joints, ca. 500-700 A.D. Courtesy of Rock Foundation.
Right: Okvik/Old Bering Sea doll-head with tattoo-puncture at facial joints, ca. 300-500 A.D. Drawing by Mark Planisek.

Other Ammassalimniut women displayed breast and arm tattoos similar to engraved female ivory figurines from the Punuk culture of St. Lawrence Island, suggesting that these practices not only persisted remarkably over the centuries, but stressed cultural unity for tattooing in the Eskimo area as a whole and, more specifically, of material culture from Greenland to ancient maritime cultures of St. Lawrence Island.

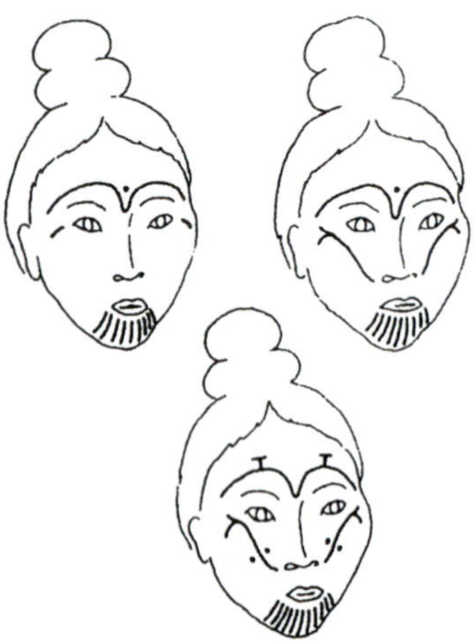

Reconstructions of the Qilakitsoq mummies, Greenland, 15th century A.D. Redrawn after Kapel et al. (1991: 105).

Considering the vast expanse of the Arctic culture area, the largest in the world, this may seem surprising. However, as circumpolar peoples were unified by environment, language, custom, and belief, the distinction is quite clear: as tattoo became part of the skin, the body became a permanent part of Arctic culture. Tattooing was a graphic image of social beliefs and values expressing the many ways in which circumpolar peoples attempted to control their bodies, lives, and experiences. As such, tattoos provided a nexus

Right: Kiyalighaq mummy's forearm tattoos, 4th century A.D. Redrawn after Smith and Zimmerman (1975: 435).

Far right: Ammassalik, Greenland arm tattoo, ca. 1897. After Holm (1914).

Below left: Ammassalik woman with faint breast tattooing on left bosom, ca. 1897. After Holm (1914).

Below right: Ivory figurine from the Punuk culture displaying arm and breast tattoos. After Collins (1929: pl. 16).

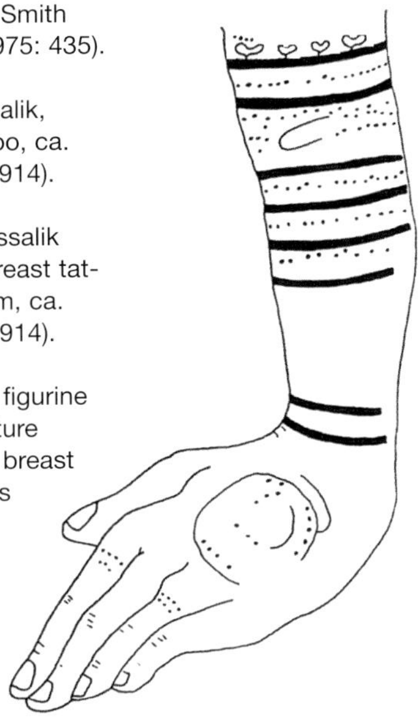

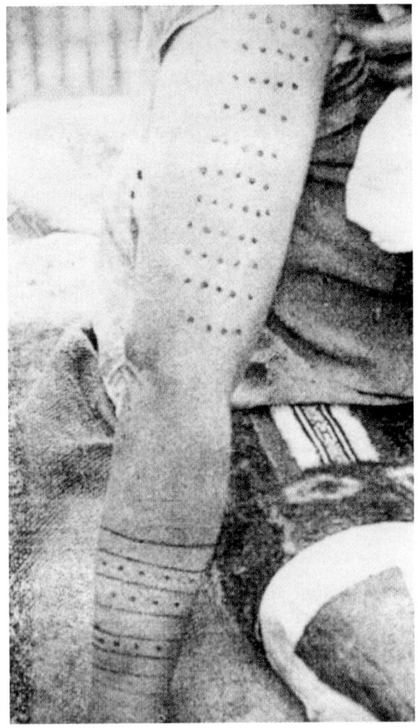

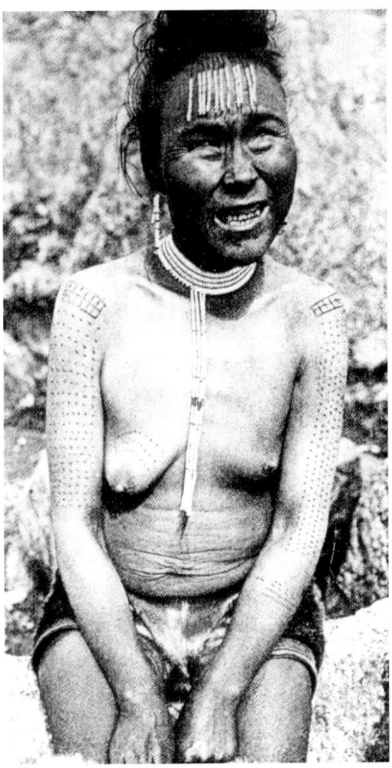

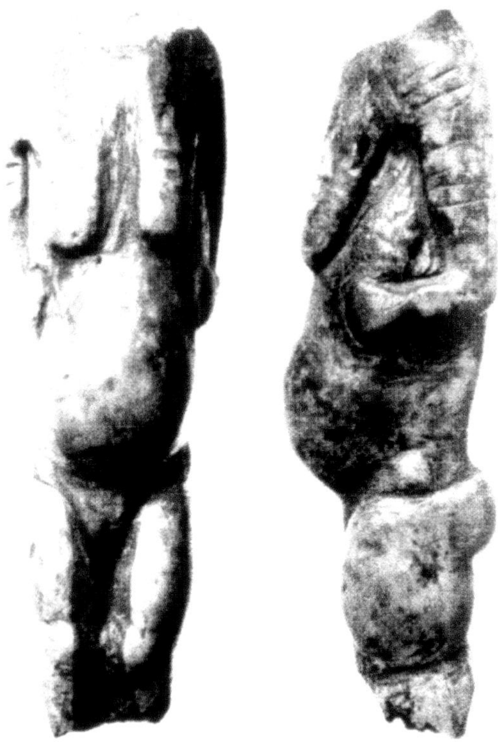

between individual, family, and communally defined forces that shaped perceptions of existence.

Aleut

In 1741, the German naturalist Georg Wilhelm Steller was sailing some 1,500 miles south of the Arctic Circle when he encountered Native Unangan or Aleuts on the Shumagin Islands. Steller, who became the first European to describe the Native peoples of Alaska, reported: "One man had a piece of bone three inches long struck through crosswise above the chin just under the lower lip. Still another had a bone like it fastened in the forehead, and another, finally, had a similar one in each of the wings of the nose."[186]

Stretching 1,500 miles from Kamchatka in Russia to the Alaska Peninsula, the Aleutian archipelago has been inhabited for about 7,000 years.[187] Traditionally, the term "Aleut" was used by Russian fur-traders to describe the indigenous peoples they met in this island chain. Today, the Unangan, who speak the Aleut language and inhabit several islands, and the Alutiiq, who inhabit Kodiak Island, see themselves as distinct from one another culturally and linguistically.[188] But with the invasion of the Russians in the 18th century, each group was gradually enslaved and organized into a collective force to labor for the Russian sea-otter fur trading empire.[189]

Besides the dramatic decline in populations due to the introduction of foreign diseases after European contact, the indigenous cultures were disrupted to the point where many traditional practices almost disappeared by the time of the American occupations in the mid-19th century. Whether fueled by the Russian distaste of the "hideous" customs of tattoo and piercing or the Christian missionary's efforts to eradicate aspects of dress, grooming, and ritual they found "deplorable" and "savage," body piercing, labrets and tattoos were rarely seen after 1800. The early 19th century explorer and writer Georg Langsdorff, speaking of the Unalaska Islanders, wrote:

> Tattooing was at one time very much in use among them, particularly among the women. The neck, arms, and chin were tattooed, and a sort of coal-dust mixed with urine rubbed in; at present these ornaments are rare, and chiefly to be seen among the old women; Russians have made the young women understand that they do not consider their beauty increased by them, and this has rather brought them into disrepute.[190]

According to most accounts, tattooing among the Aleut was first practiced when women reached maturity. On Kodiak Island, it not only signaled adolescence, but social standing as well:

> The tattoo at the chin the girls receive it at their first cleaning [menstruation]. (Menstruation is said to start late among these people, close to or after their twentieth year) . . . Women pierced themselves with needles made of seagull bones, and they blacken[ed] it immediately with coals.[191]

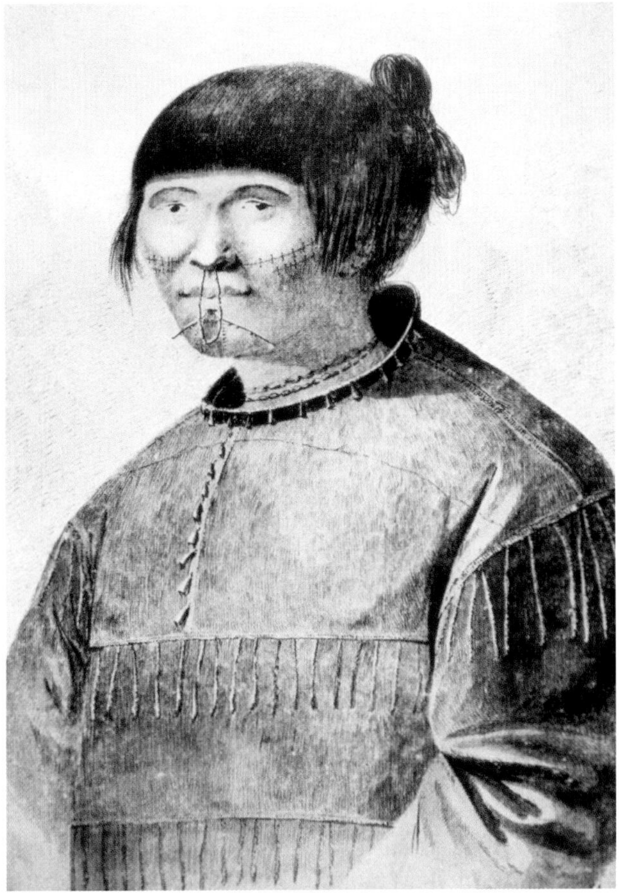

Tattooed woman of Unalaska Island, 1778. Drawn by John Webber of the Cook Expedition. After Bushnell (1928: pl. 12). One Russian explorer described tattoo practices on Unalaska Island in 1790. "The women sew in their cheeks, and rub with carbon, two lines, running from the lower part of the nose to the middle of the ears, and one broad band from the lower lip to the chin, which when they heal assume a bluish color" (Sarychev 1806-7, II: 117).

In the Unalaska Island district, The Russian priest Veniaminov observed that aristocratic women were more heavily tattooed than laypersons:

> The Aleut women had the habit of tattooing different designs, by 'sewing' or pricking . . . They tattooed the whole chin, two bands from cheek to cheek across the nose, two bands on the sides of the face, and one below the nose. But all did not have the same designs. The pretty ones and also the daughters of famous and rich ancestors and fathers, endeavored in their tattooings to show the accomplishments of their progenitors, as, for instance, how many enemies, or powerful animals, that ancestor killed.[192]

On the whole, ethnographic information on Aleut tattooing was limited to outside European observers. Just as tattoo methods and forms were widely scattered, so too were other forms of personal adornment. In an attempt to offer some rudimentary interpretation of the meaning and function of the tattooing, it is necessary to include in this discussion a description of the other forms of Aleut body modification including: nosepins, ear ornaments, and labrets. Aleut piercing and tattooing were natural symbols simultaneously linking nature, Aleut society and culture into one organic whole. Body adornment justified human existence by not only influencing the supernatural and the dead, but by influencing the wishes and actions of other living individuals in the community itself.

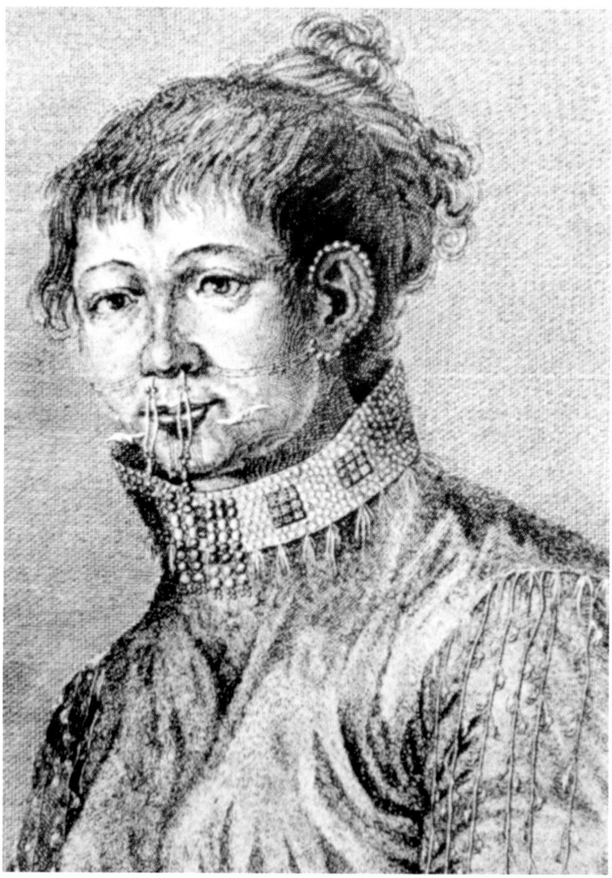

Tattooed woman from Unalaska Island, 1790. After Sarychev (1806-7: 18).

Nosepins

Nosepins were worn by all indigenous groups of the Aleutian chain, by both sexes, with the incision being pierced shortly after birth.[193] The ornament might be an eagle's feather shaft, a sea lion whisker, piece of bark, bone, or a leather thong with dentalium shells worn horizontally through the nose.[194] Sometimes women strung various beads of coral and amber on the nosepin and let them hang down to the tips of their chins.

More specifically, amber and dentalia were highly prized by both men and women.

Although there were natural outcroppings of amber in the Aleutian Islands, most of it was obtained through trade from other indigenous groups living to the east. Urey Lisiansky noted that the Aleuts esteemed amber and it was "held in as high estimation as diamonds in Europe."[195] Among the Chugach, "one pair of amber ornaments was worth two sea-otter skins ($90-100 a skin)."[196] Dentalia, however, were procured exclusively from indigenous traders living southeast of the Aleutian archipelago in the vicinity of Hecate Strait near the Queen Charlotte Islands. Here the indigenous traders of the shell immersed "in the water the body of someone who has died, or of a slave killed specially for the purpose," removing the worms that lived in the shell casings.[197] On Kodiak Island, a pair of dentalia was worth "an entire squirrel-skin parka" in 1805.[198]

Ear ornaments

Ear ornaments were another common form of adornment. Oftentimes, there were holes pierced all around the rim of the ear with dentalium shells, beads of shell, bone, and amber placed in each orifice.[199] An Unangan Attu Islander, before she was given to her husband in marriage, had ten sea lion whiskers pierced into each ear. Sea lion whiskers were considered to be very valuable and were regarded as trophies that indicated a good hunter, or the wife of a good hunter, since each animal has only four whiskers and "any number of them together must be a testimony of having captured a great many."[200] These whiskers also adorned the wooden hunting gear of Aleut men[201] or were used as ornaments in the nose.

A visitor to the Andreanov Islands in 1761 noted, "instead of earrings put into their ears the women wear eagles' and geese feathers behind the ears."[202] In the Kagamil Island burial caves, the Smithsonian scientist Aleš Hrdlička found numerous bird skulls, bones, the skins of hawks, dried bird wings buried with the mummies of children and even a bird feather "still stuck in the ear of one of the mummified heads."[203]

Certainly, particular birds were seen as protective animals in the afterlife and not surprisingly the Kodiak Islanders raised eagles as pets,[204] using their feathers in ritual festivals to honor the sun.[205] Their beaks not only represented the power of predation and killing but also stood for the male procreative power.[206] The speed, cunning, and accuracy of these birds were emulated by Aleut hunters who with their beak-like hunting visor, decorated with carved ivory "wings" and a "tail" of sea lion whiskers, became transformed into a powerful bird of prey whilst hunting upon the open sea in their kayaks.[207] The hunter's harpoon magically became a talon and bore sculptural forms of a fanged wolf-like creature that assisted in capturing game.

Labrets

When Russians first made contact with the peoples of the Aleutian archipelago, the one custom that intrigued them the most was the insertion of various types of labrets into the lower lip and cheek.[208] Captain Cook noted in the 1770s "what the men have thrust thro the hole in the underlip has the resemblance of 2 Boars tusk, and are 2 pieces of bone about 1 inch [25mm] long joining in the middle of the lip, & separating, by means of the tongue they can move these bones, & make them point up and down. Others have a single polished bone the shape and size of a large Stud."[209] Men perforated the lip by piercing several studs of walrus ivory into separate holes that appeared to Captain Cook as representing "another row of teeth immediately under their own."[210] This style of labretifery was common on the Turnagain River of mainland Alaska and on Kodiak Island where "men wear up to ten garnets—white in back, blue in front—underneath their lower lip."[211]

The Russian naval officer Gavrila Davydov said that Kodiak Island women made "several holes in their lower lip from which they hang a loop into which are placed beads and small white bones. These holes vary in number between two and six. Their lips are pierced by close relatives and there is a great deal of respect, therefore, for the girl islander who has the most."[212] Although labrets of this type were usually worn for decorative purposes, they also signified the social status, prestige, and age of the wearer.

Piercing medicine

Because tattoos, nosepins, earrings, and labrets were significant visual symbols tied to important realms of cultural experience, it is possible they were perceived as having medicinal value as well. The Aleut believed that a manipulable power resided in the body that persisted in the dead through mummification.[213] In life, this power was regulated at crucial periods, mainly though joint-binding with sinew cords. Joint-binding was practiced when a young girl had her first menses, and when a husband or wife died.[214] The Aleut also dismembered the bodies of enemies and dangerous persons at their joints as a way of protecting the living from the evil dead, because religious belief dictated that the soul of the departed remained on earth as long as the corpse was intact.[215] The practice even extended to honored birds,

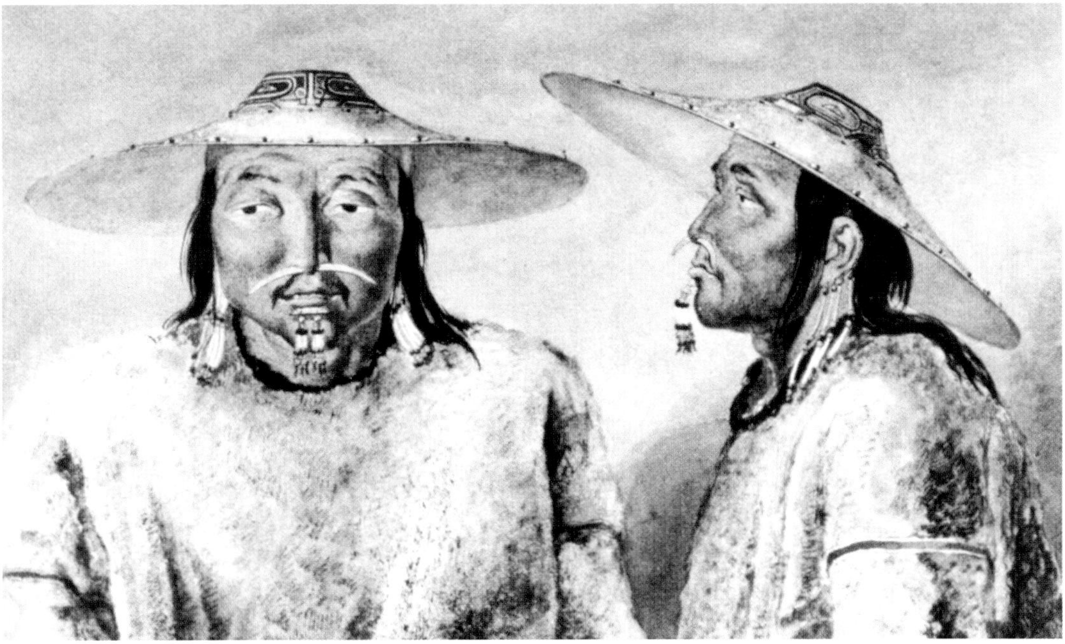

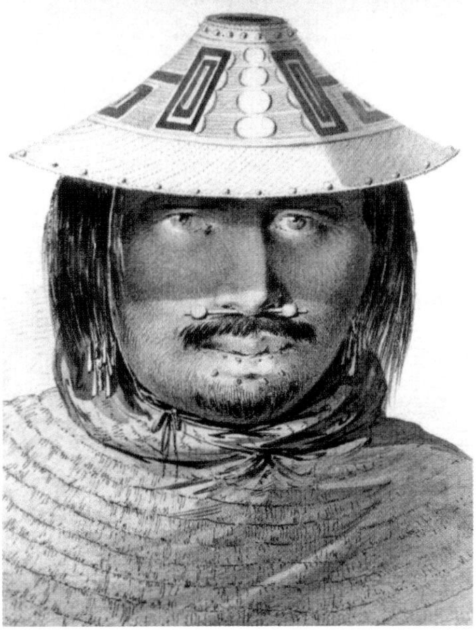

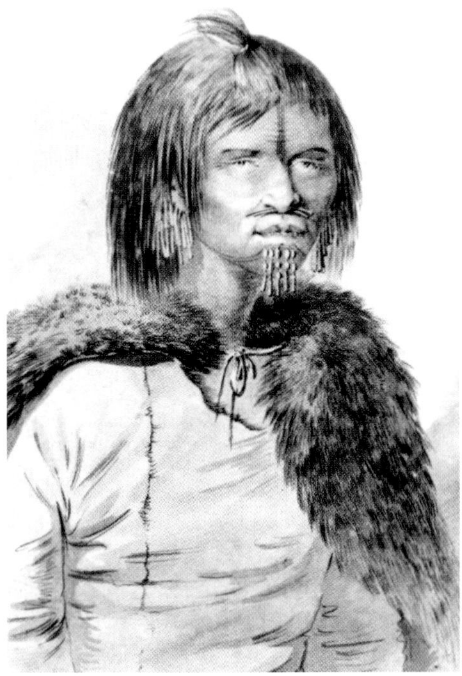

Top: Alutiiq man of Kodiak Island, 1817. Drawing by Mikhail Tikhanov.

Left: Chugach man of Prince William Sound, 1778. Drawing by John Webber.

A Chugach woman of Prince William Sound, 1778. Drawing by John Webber.

such as the hawk and owl;[216] creatures that were believed to embody supernatural power through their association with celestial bodies of both light and darkness.

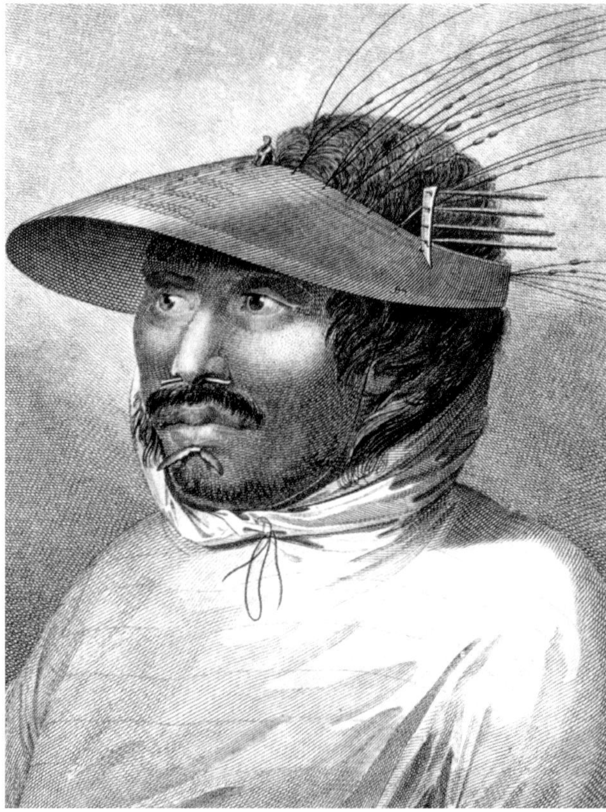

Man of Unalaska Island displaying labrets and nosepin, 1778. Drawing by John Webber.

The Aleut also practiced forms of medicine akin to acupuncture and moxabustion. In this sense, it is probable that they had some conception of Chinese yin/yang cosmology and attempted to regulate "good" and "bad" energies through the plugging of orifices.[217] To this end, it would seem to follow that the Aleut had a similar concept in regards to body piercing. Grant Keddie stated that "the labret may demonstrate one's spiritual mastery over bodily entrances from which spirits enter and exit and therefore by analogy one's power over the forces of nature."[218]

Transgendered piercings and tattoos

Aside from men's and women's personal ornaments, it should be noted that particular forms of depilation and tattooing were practiced by transgendered individuals. Langsdorff observed that on Kodiak Island, "Boys, if they happen to be very handsome, are often brought up entirely in the manner of girls, and instructed in all the arts women use to please man: their beards are carefully plucked out as soon as they begin to appear, and their chins are tattooed like those of the women."[219] Other Europeans writing in the early 19th century suggested that the existence of transgendered individuals was influenced in some way by parental guidance, for it seemed that mothers who were "very fond of their offspring; dreading the effects of war, and the dangers of the chase; some of them bring up their males in a very effeminate manner, and are happy to see them taken by chiefs, to gratify their unnatural desires."[220] Similarly in 1790 the Russian naval captain Sarychev saw among the arriving Kodiaks a "40 year-old, ugly fellow, clad in woman's garb; his face was tattooed and there were beads in his nose. This man played the role of a wife for a young islander and did all the woman's work."[221] Davydov agreed, stating: "There are among these people men with tattooed chins, carrying on solely female work, living always with women, and similarly to these having one and sometimes even two 'husbands'. They call these Achnućeks [*kássaq*]. These individuals are not only not looked down upon, but instead they are obeyed in a settlement and are not seldom wizards [shamans]."[222]

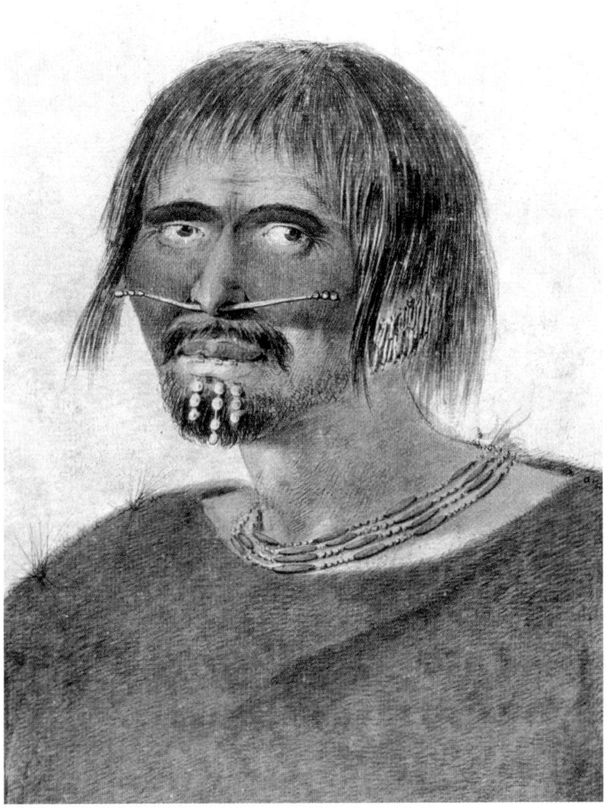

Man of Turnagain River, Alaska, 1778. Drawing by John Webber.

Throughout the circumpolar region, shamans served as intermediaries between the living and the dead, between humans and animals, between the genders, and between the spirits and deities.[223] They were considered "wisemen" able to forecast the future, the weather, and had the ability to purify or cure ailing individuals through physical and ritual diagnoses.[224] Among the Inuit of Canada, mythology reveals that a transgendered shaman created all women and this was directly associated with his ability to straddle the procreative nature of the sexes:

> They say that the world collapsed, the earth was destroyed, that great showers of rain flooded the land. All animals died, and there were only two men left. They lived together. They married, as there was nobody else, and at least one of them became with child. They were great shamans, and when the one was going to bear a child they made his penis over again so that he became a woman, and she had a child. They say it is from that shaman that woman came.[225]

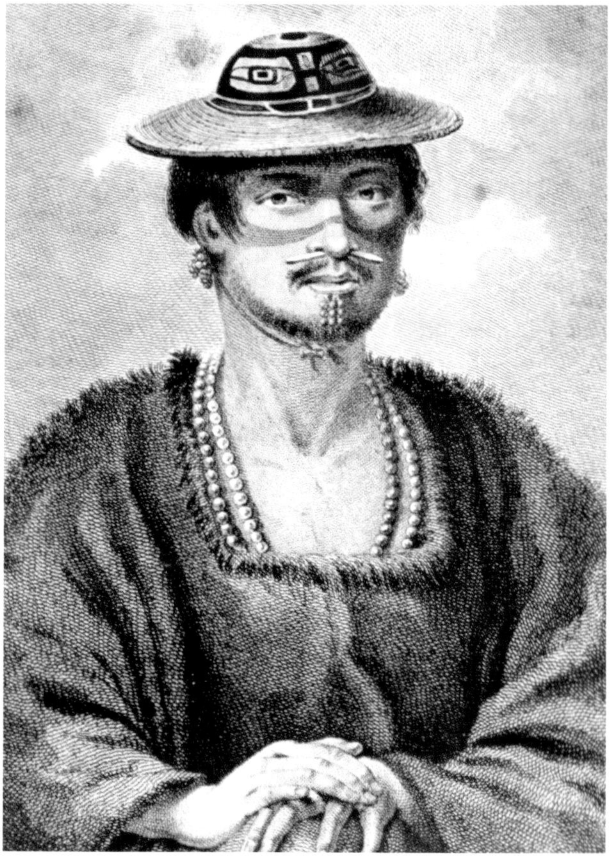

Tattooed Kodiak Island man, possibly a *kássaq*, 1791. After Sauer (1802: pl. 6).

Among the Aleut, however, shamanic powers not only came to Aleut individuals through apprenticeship,[226] but more readily through dreaming. And from the time an Aleut *kássaq* reached adolescence he was greeted by "apparitions in the shape of animals or marvelous beings until they were bewildered and willing to submit to their inevitable masters."[227] A similar pattern held for Siberian shamans, especially among the Chukchi where "soft man being" or "transformed" shamans were commanded by the *ke'let* (spirits), who sometimes were female, usually at the critical age of early youth when shamanistic inspiration first manifested itself.[228] Although there were varying degrees of transformation, the role reversal was completed once the boy left "off all pursuits and manners of his sex . . . He throws away the rifle and the lance, the lasso of the reindeer herdsman, the harpoon of the seal-hunter, and takes to the needle and the skin-scraper. He learns the use of these quickly, because the 'spirits' are helping him all the time."[229]

Aleut adornment

Aleut adornment not only satisfied the need for display, celebration, and accomplishment, it also embodied religious beliefs about the relationships between humans, animals, and the deities who controlled human destiny and the surrounding world. For the inhabitants of these windswept islands, body art was created not only to lure, please, and honor the spirits of animals; it increased the social status, spiritual power, and beauty of the adorned by inscribing male, female, and transgendered personhood.

But Aleut tattoos and piercings also cloaked or camouflaged the physical body from supernatural forces that inhabited the maritime environment. This view, widely held for many indigenous societies around the world,[230] falls into the long-standing tradition of prophylactic "magic" aimed at warding off penetration or possession by evil forces that targeted vulnerable body passageways: namely the natural openings of the body (eyes, ears, mouth, etc.). Because the fear inspired by spirits in the landscape was great, Aleut peoples were compelled to develop a complex of personal adornment to neutralize the advances of supernatural entities. And in this way, they attempted to project themselves beyond their everyday limits of space and time, and on some collective level, they perhaps envisioned supernatural control and, ultimately, their own immortality in the human bodies they manipulated.

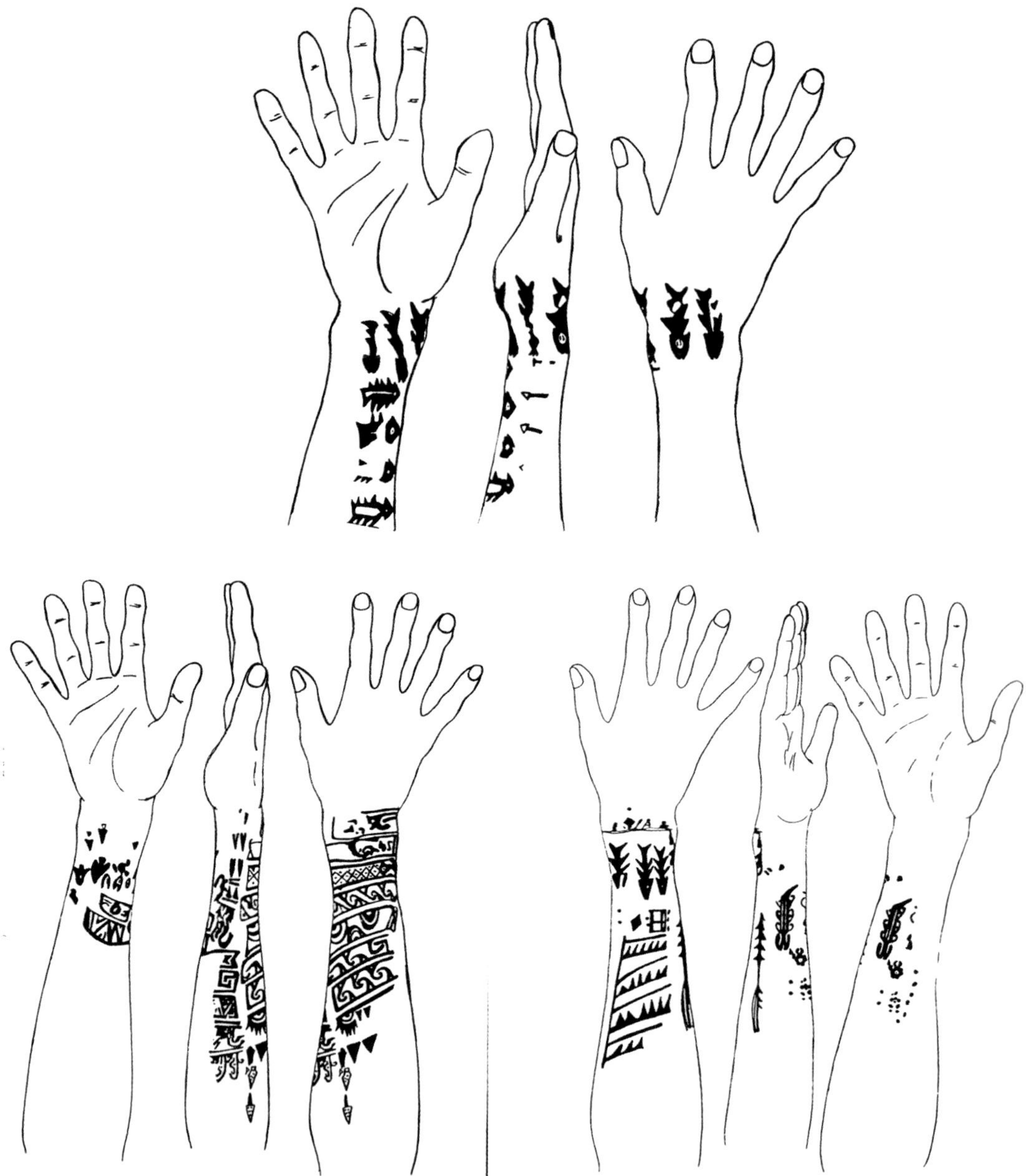

Chimú mummies with naturalistic and geometric tattooing, ca. 1200. After Allison et al. (1981: 234, fig. 11; 231, fig. 5). Reproduced courtesy of the authors. These intricately patterned tattoos adorned the skin and recorded significant events in the life history of the wearer. From top, motifs include fish and projectile points. From bottom right, motifs include fish, harpoon, and geometric designs. From bottom left, motifs include lizard, ocean wave, and projectile points.

South America, California, and the American Southwest

Coastal Peru

Hidden in shifting sands along the coastal valleys of Peru, mummies by the hundreds have been discovered—some bearing intricate tattoos on their desiccated skins. Whether depicting stylized marine and terrestrial fauna, weapons used in war or in the hunt (harpoons, projectile points), highly abstract geometric designs representing features of the surrounding landscape (ocean waves and mountains), or anthropomorphic deities, the tattoos of the sacred dead perhaps served as magical mediators between this world and the next.

Of Peru's many prehistoric cultures, the ancient Chimú (1100-1470 A.D.) were the most heavily and elaborately tattooed of all.[1] The exquisite designs tattooed on living flesh, and carved into silver, gold, and wooden burial objects, suggests that the body's integument was perceived as a kind of double-sided raiment that concealed and projected both personal power and identity across the plane of the living and the dead. Dressing oneself in a secondary skin of tattoos not only transformed the wearer visually; it established identity like a name and reconstructed personhood. And because the skin is what remained of the person after death, perhaps these markings were thought to work apotropaically in the afterlife by reinforcing the skin and its boundaries as long as the bodily envelope of mummified skin remained intact.[2]

Paleopathological studies of Chimú mummies indicate that the practice of tattooing was quite common among both males and females.[3] In some coastal settlements, it has been estimated that at least thirty percent of the population may have been tattooed.[4]

Yet until recently, little was known of the tattoo pigments used by the Chimú themselves. Although it had been conjectured that the ink was a carbon-based product,[5] no systematic study had been performed to extract,

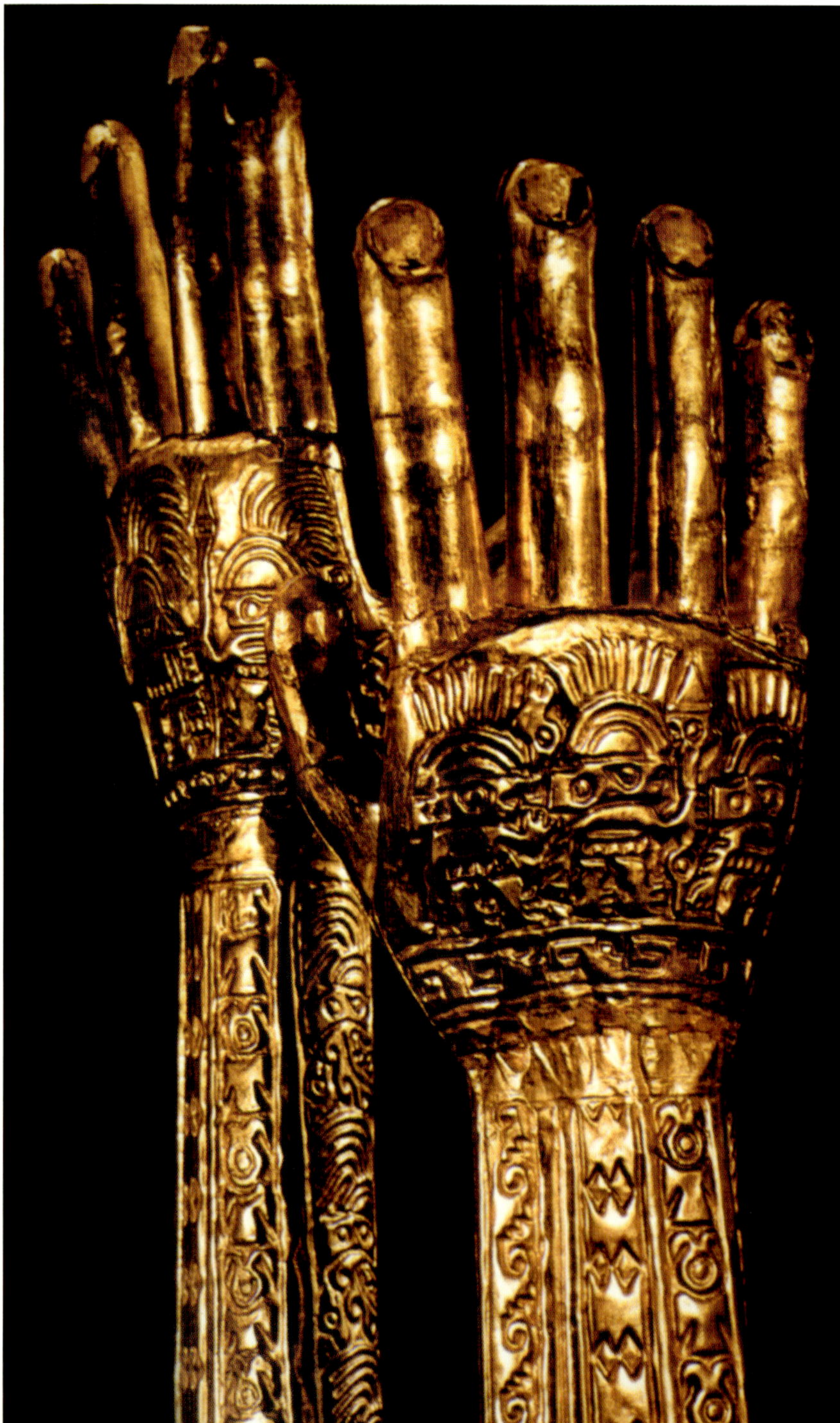

isolate, and then analyze the chemical composition of pigments. And were it not for the startling discovery made by a group of unsuspecting archaeologists, the identity of this organic material would have perhaps remained an enigma.

In the late 1980s, Peruvian archaeologists conducted a salvage operation approximately one-hundred miles north of Lima in the Huaura Valley and discovered a cache of mummies dating to the early Chimú period. This remarkable find, which has yet to be published, yielded numerous tattooed mummies dating to 1100 A.D.; each clutching the dried-up fruit of the genipap (*genipa americana* L.) in the palm of its outstretched hand.[6] Juices of the green, immature fruits of the genipap have and continue to be used as black body paint and tattoo pigment by historic and contemporary indigenes of South America.[7] Among some groups, the coloring substance was highly esteemed because it was believed to repel incorporeal spirits.[8] This was especially true of the headhunting Jívaro and Mundurucú who painted themselves and their trophy heads with genipap to protect the victor from the spirit of the deceased.[9]

Genipap is also the source of various medicinal products used to treat arthritis, venereal sores, corneal opacities, stomach ulcers, and uterine cancer in Amazonia.[10] Sometimes it is used as an abortifacient.[11] In Central America, the pulverized seeds, or a decoction of its flowers, are commonly given as a febrifuge,[12] and in Guatemala, indigenous peoples "carry the fruits in their hands in the belief that this will provide protection from disease and ill-fortune."[13] Perhaps the genipap symbolized something similar for the people of the Huaura Valley, a fundamental belief that the medicinal plant afforded a form of efficacious protection against evil influences encountered in life as well as in death.

Chimú tattooists applied their tattoo pigments with various types of fine needles (fishbone, parrot quill, spiny conch), each of which have been found in mummy burials.[14] The technical application of tattooing was a form of skin-stitching similar to the "facial embroidery" of the Inuit,[15] and it can be suggested that women were the primary tattoo artists. Their expert knowledge of working animal skins and hides would certainly have facilitated the need for precision when piercing the human epidermis with complex motifs.

Facing page: Gold burial gloves, Chimú culture. Tattoo designs reproduced in gold were meant to physically carry the tattoos into eternity. Collection of the Museo Oro del Perú.

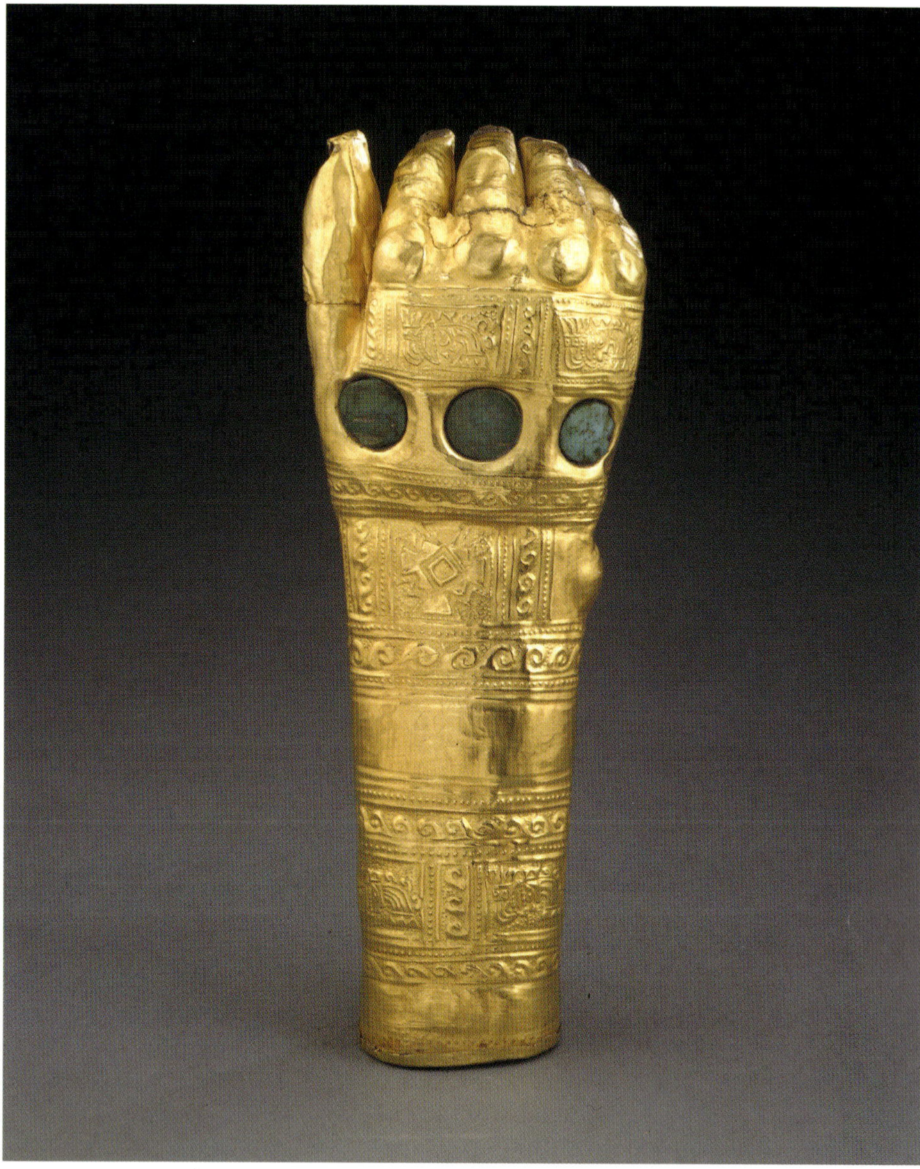

Hammered gold hand with intricate tattoo motifs. Lambayeque (Sicán) culture, 800-1370 A.D. Courtesy of Dumbarton Oaks, Pre-Columbian Collection, Washington, D.C. Through diplomacy and war, the Chimú Empire spread to the north and south of the Moche valley. As the empire grew so did its capital city Chan Chan. Here master artisans, some drawn from the conquered territories of the Lambayeque culture, crafted ornaments of finely hammered gold for the royal dead (Topic 1990: 150). Occasionally these effigy objects took the form of human appendages (arms, hands, and legs) modeled in gold with silver accents. Although the precise function of these objects is not known, many of the human appendages bear intricate tattoos that parallel those found on Chimú mummies, suggesting a symbolic function.

Although no studies have attempted to identify the work of individual Chimú tattooists from others, it is certain that skin artisans were highly skilled, probably full-time craftspeople who, working within the aesthetic canons of their art, enjoyed some degree of prestige in their communities. As in other indigenous cultures, these "dermographers" likely received high wages for their artistry, wages that perhaps only affluent or aristocratic individuals could afford. In this context, tattooists were in a good position to acquire intimate knowledge of secular, political, and religious affairs over the course of tattooing their elite clients.

From another point of view, the tattoo artist—the maker of marks on the skin—was also a repository of ritual knowledge. Her occupation encompassed not only the inscription and patterning of supernatural or other figures on human skin, but also the ritual release and manipulation of human blood. In prehistoric South American cultures, human blood, the fertilizing essence of everything animate, was a highly revered sacred substance believed to appease spiritual powers that controlled the forces of nature.[16]

Blood sacrifice in ancient Peru

Ritual blood sacrifice has a long history in the coastal valleys of ancient Peru, and almost every major culture including Cupisnique (1200-200 B.C.), Chavín (900-200 B.C.), Paracas (700 B.C.-0), Nasca (0-700 A.D.), Moche (50-800 A.D.), Wari-Tiwanaku (600-1000 A.D.), Chimú (1100-1470 A.D.), and Inca (1450-1550 A.D.) practiced it: especially the tradition of taking human heads for ritual use.[17] Among the Paracas and Nasca peoples, ritually prepared human heads were perceived as potent sources of power to be harnessed and tapped in order to promote agricultural fertility and relations with the ancestral dead and deities.[18] Analogs drawn from historical headhunting cultures of Assam, Borneo, Luzon, Taiwan, and Peru also support this model; because the ritual taking of human heads in these places was accomplished to ensure both biological and agricultural fertility.[19]

The Chimú and other prehistoric Peruvian cultures represented trophy heads in textiles, ceramics, and murals.[20] Archaeological evidence at the Chimú capital Chan Chan has shown that mass burials of a sacrificial nature were conducted, the number of dead sometimes approaching several hundred individuals.[21]

The blood cult of the Chimú, however, paled in comparison to its Moche antecedent. Indeed, many facets of Chimú culture largely grew out of older Moche traditions, including artistic iconography, architecture, and

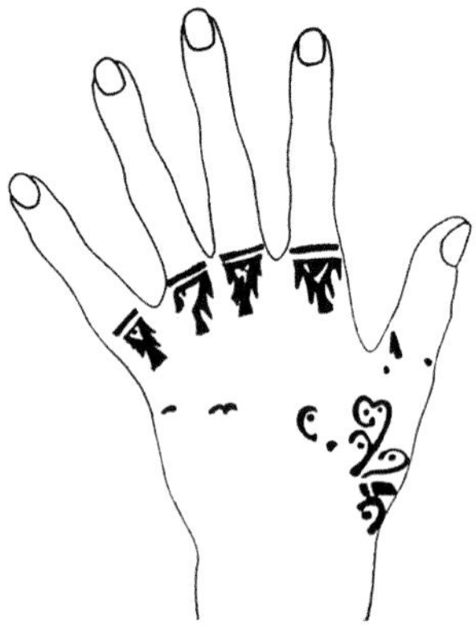

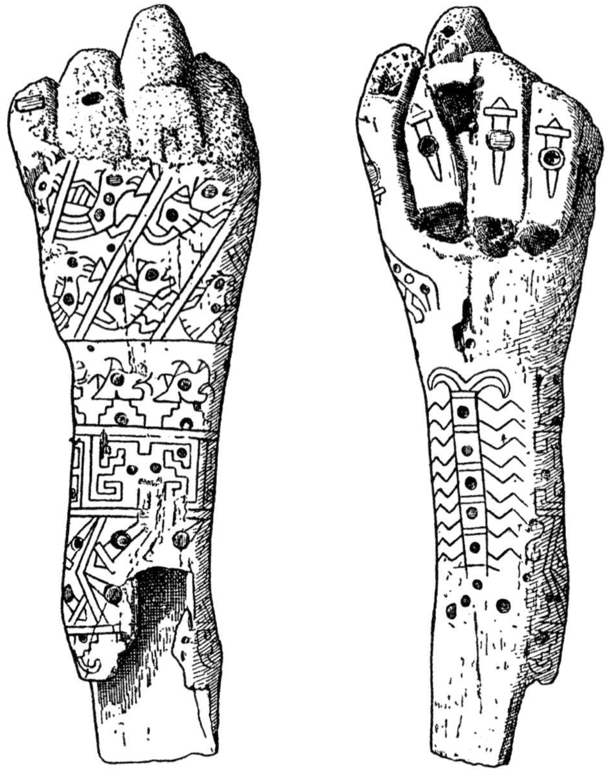

technological innovations in ceramics and casting.[22] But to the extent that we understand Chimú ritual behavior, human sacrifice appears to have been more important and widespread among the Moche. Indeed, scenes of Moche ritual sacrifice, torture, dismemberment, and decapitation are so varied and ubiquitous,[23] that we must assume that these practices were not rare or isolated occurrences; they must have formed a significant component of secular and religious life.[24] Moreover, archaeological evidence of Moche human sacrifice has been discovered at several sites, including the massive sacrificial precinct at Huaca de la Luna where the dismembered and decapitated remains of more than seventy male warriors were placed over the graves of two headless children.[25]

Above: Line drawing of Moche spatula redrawn after Kutscher (1950: fig. 40).

Above left: Chimú mummy tattoos, ca. 1200. After Allison et al. (1981: 233, fig. 8). Courtesy of the authors. Five protruding elements tattooed at the knuckles are reminiscent of earlier Moche symbols for mountains where human sacrifices were made. For contemporary Peruvian folk healers, "the highest mountain peaks . . . symbolize the soul's capacity to soar through the air. Such 'magical flight' is performed by [shamans] during the ecstatic trance state induced by the hallucinogenic San Pedro [cactus]" (Donnan 1978: 132).

References to warfare, human sacrifice, and the drinking of human blood appear on Moche ceramics, textiles, and peculiar inlaid bone objects called "spatulas." Of the eleven spatulas held in museum and private collections, each portrays similar design conventions including warriors with armaments, supernatural figures, animals, cacti, and sacrificial victims.[26] The handles of the bone spatulas resemble human fists and in Moche art it is clear that the "half-fist" with protruding knuckle symbolizes a mountain scene, precisely because nature has modeled the back of the hand like five mountain peaks.[27] The Moche, like the later Inca, held complex rituals on mountaintops often including human sacrifice. Although the function of these bone objects is not clear, they appear to have been used by shamans, priests, or priestesses to transfer liquids into the mouths of sacred individuals.[28]

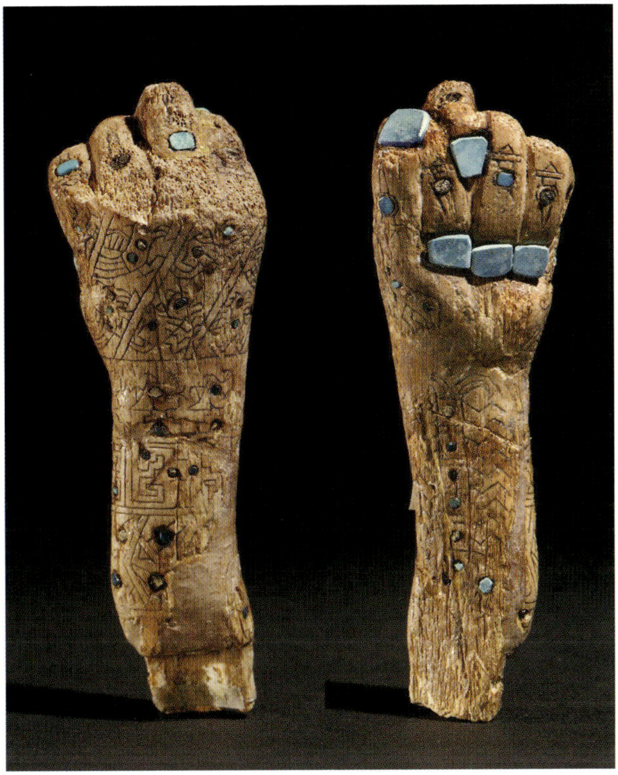

Handle of a ceremonial Moche bone spatula carved as a human fist, 100-800 A.D. Inlaid with turquoise and pyrite. Courtesy of Dumbarton Oaks, Pre-Columbian Collection, Washington, D.C. The line drawings (see page 190) depict a wide array of designs including a bird drinking from a bowl of blood, a bird warrior, and several war clubs (Donnan 1996: 139). Also shown are a mythological monster, a lizard, and a centipede. Perhaps they are shamanic or apotropaic symbols. Centipedes also appear on other Moche spatulas in museum collections.

Because it can be inferred that some of the iconography on these spatulas represents the transfer of blood between individuals, signalizing the primary dispersal and containment of a powerful sanguine substance, it could be argued that spatulas were used as the ritual vessel to accomplish these blood-transactions. To date, however, it is believed that none of the bone spatulas have been tested for blood residues.[29]

Interestingly, the deeply carved designs on bone spatulas correspond to

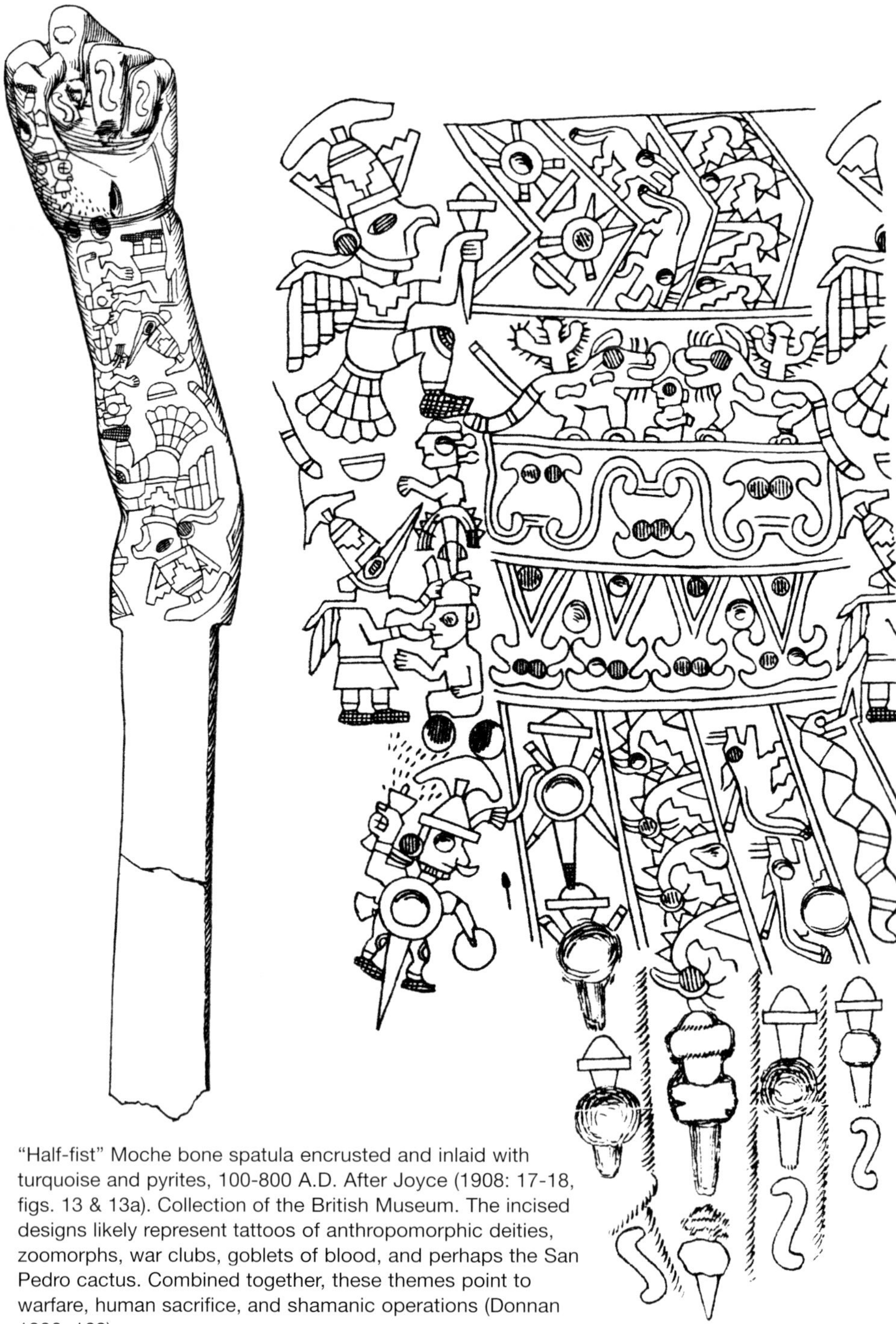

"Half-fist" Moche bone spatula encrusted and inlaid with turquoise and pyrites, 100-800 A.D. After Joyce (1908: 17-18, figs. 13 & 13a). Collection of the British Museum. The incised designs likely represent tattoos of anthropomorphic deities, zoomorphs, war clubs, goblets of blood, and perhaps the San Pedro cactus. Combined together, these themes point to warfare, human sacrifice, and shamanic operations (Donnan 1996: 162).

the actual Moche practice of tattooing the wrists, forearms, and back of the hands. One rare, remarkable example of such tattooing was discovered on the mummified skin of an eighteen year-old woman from the ancient city of Pacatnamu.[30] The figures, executed in pure Mochica style, depict some of the anthropomorphic creatures seen on the spatulas. Other examples of tattooed Moche mummies have been found in recent years at the archaeological site of El Brujo, Peru's "Temple of Doom."[31] Here an elite Moche woman dubbed "The Lady of Cao" was unearthed with intricate tattoos of supernatural creatures (e.g. spiders and birds) and geometric designs covering much of her forearms, hands, and knuckles.[32] Although similar tattoos have been found on mummies of the later Tiwanaku and Chimú cultures of Peru, scientists are perplexed by the context of this woman's burial that dates to 450 A.D. Moche

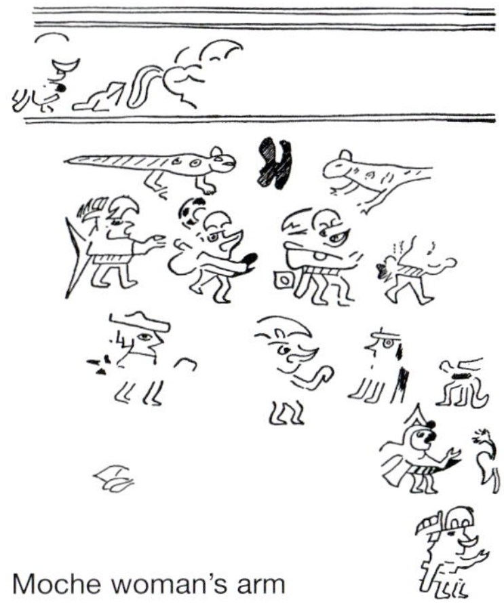

Moche woman's arm tattooing. Redrawn after Ubbelohde-Doering (1967: 30, fig. 5).

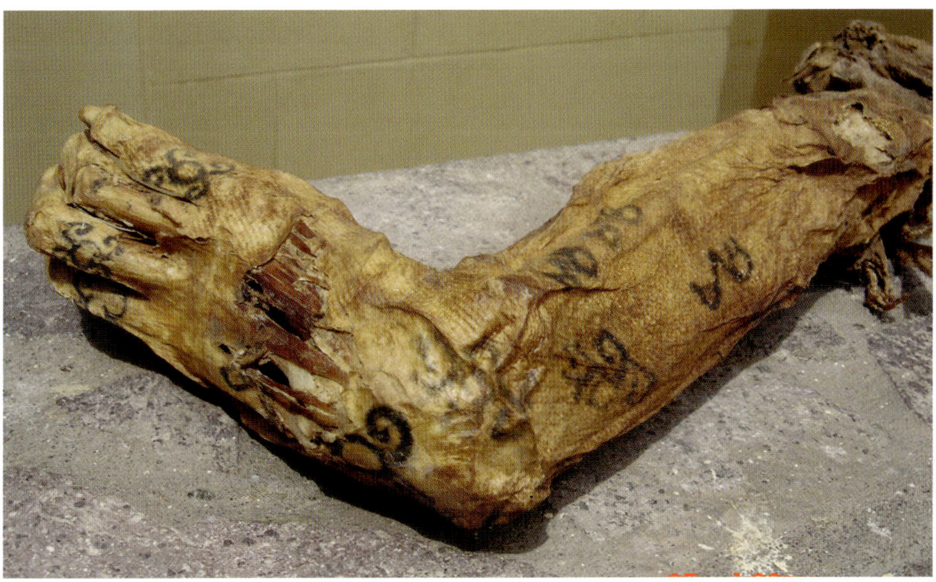

Tiwanaku culture mummy with avian tattoos on the forearm and other designs, possibly spiders, on the knuckles, 1000 A.D. Photograph courtesy of Dr. Marvin Allison, 2005. This male mummy also has tattoos on its neck and legs, and was excavated near Ilo, Peru. Interestingly, some of the mummy's tattoos resemble those worn by the Lady of Cao. Knuckle tattoos of the same form and type were also worn by peoples of the later Chiribaya culture of Peru (Reid 2001).

burials containing priestesses have been found before,[33] but never has a woman's burial been associated with weapons like war clubs and spear throwers—male symbols *par excellence*. This suggests that some Moche woman were perhaps revered for their martial abilities in combat or for their religious roles in warfare.

Of birds, lizards, serpents, and centipedes

In Moche iconography, especially in scenes of warfare, prisoners are typically shown stripped of their clothing and weapons which are hung on the victor's war clubs. They are tethered to ropes placed around their necks which are held by the victor who leads them away from the field of battle.[34] All too often, the eminent fate of the vanquished warriors is sealed; they will be processed, arraigned, and then ceremoniously sacrificed having their throats slit and their blood collected in goblets to be presented to an authority figure.[35]

In most cases, the depictions of naked and rope-bound prisoners are highly detailed, and occasionally the captives are covered with intricate, sometimes naturalistic markings on their torsos, arms, and legs that in all probability represent tattooing.[36] An example from a Moche ceramic vessel depicts two male captives both wearing a series of "V-shaped" chest markings comprised of serpentine elements. One individual is smattered with lizard-like motifs adorning his legs and shins. Although body paint could account for these designs, it seems doubtful that captives would have ornamented their bodies in such a fashion, especially since

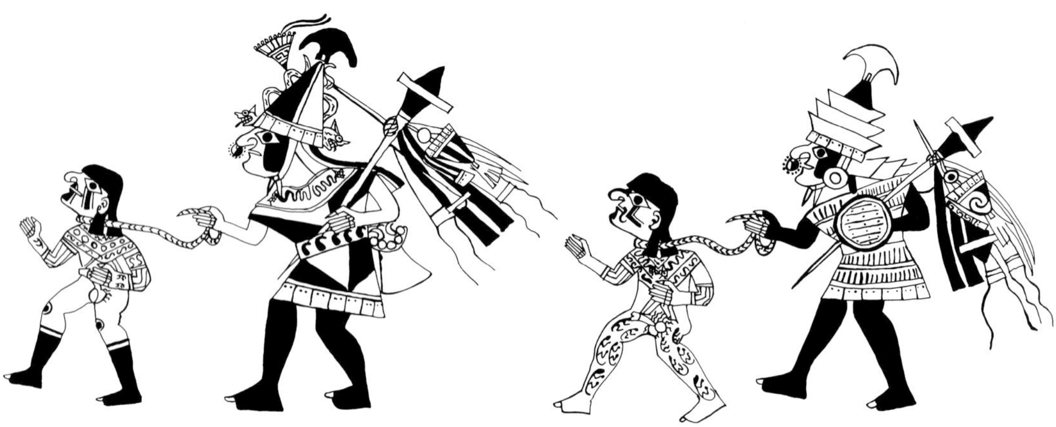

Nude prisoners with V-shaped chest markings in procession. From Moche pottery vessel in private collection. Drawing by Donna McClelland.

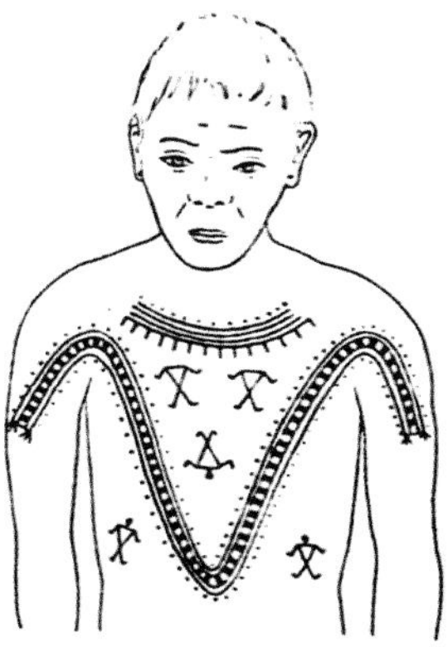

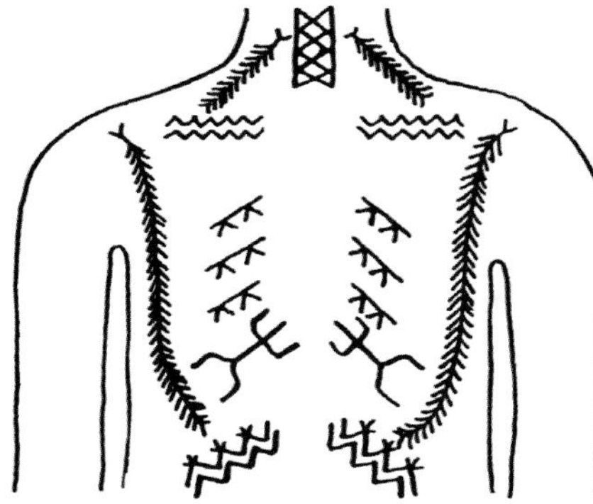

Above left: Naga headhunter's tattoo. Assam Region, India. Redrawn after Schuster (1952: 106, pl. 1).

Above right: Ifugao headhunter's tattoo with little men and centipede motifs, Cordillera Region, Philippines. Redrawn after Vanoverbergh (1929: 203, fig. 10).

Right: Ifugao headhunter's tattoo with little men and centipede motifs, Cordillera Region, Philippines. After Vanoverbergh (1929: 203, fig. 9).

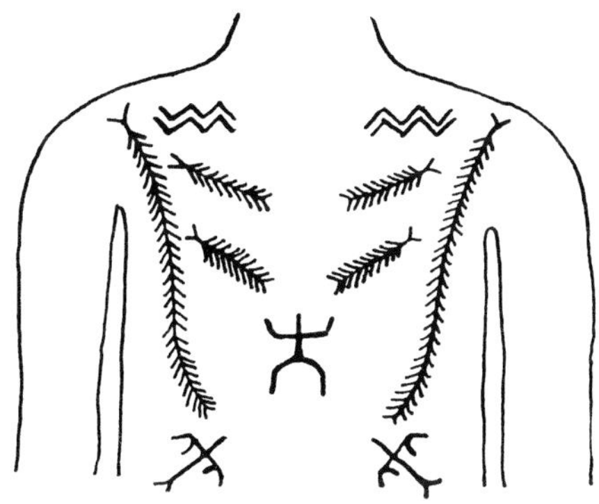

these markings would have lain underneath one or more layers of cloth armor.

Some of the most popular tattoo emblems of historic headhunting cultures of Southeast Asia and the Western Pacific were comprised of V-shaped chest markings.[37] Though puzzling in some respects, linguistic evidence supports an avian origin of this kind of body-marking, because many of the designs were called "hawks," "frigate birds," or "tropical birds."[38] We know from previous chapters that prowess in warfare or headhunting among the Iban, Kenyah, Kayan, and Lahanan of Borneo, Atayal and Paiwan of Taiwan, Mailu and Hula of Papua, and the Easter Islanders was associated with tattooing, and that many warriors in these cultures attempted to transform themselves into predatory birds via vestment and ritual adornment to ensure martial success. Of course, the headhunting Bontoc, Ifugao, and Kalinga of Luzon, Nagas of Assam, and Mentawei of Indonesia also tattooed V-shaped chest-markings.[39] But in these cultures, as well as those of Taiwan,[40] we find varying tattooed figures of sometimes headless "little men" (the victims) associated with the V-shaped markings.

Occasionally, these "little men" are replaced by lizards or other tattooed creatures that represent the prey of the predatory "birdman."[41] Lizards are frequently represented in Moche art, and one deity has been identified as a zoomorphic "Iguana God" usually on the basis of its vulture headdress.[42] Vultures, subsisting on rotting fleshy remains, are naturally connected to the world of the dead and have been found buried with sacrificial victims at the Moche site of Pacatnamu.[43] In this association, "we must remember that since the headhunter is himself identified with a bird of prey, it is only natural that his human victims should be represented alternatively as the animals [e.g. lizards] habitually preyed upon by the bird which he embodies."[44]

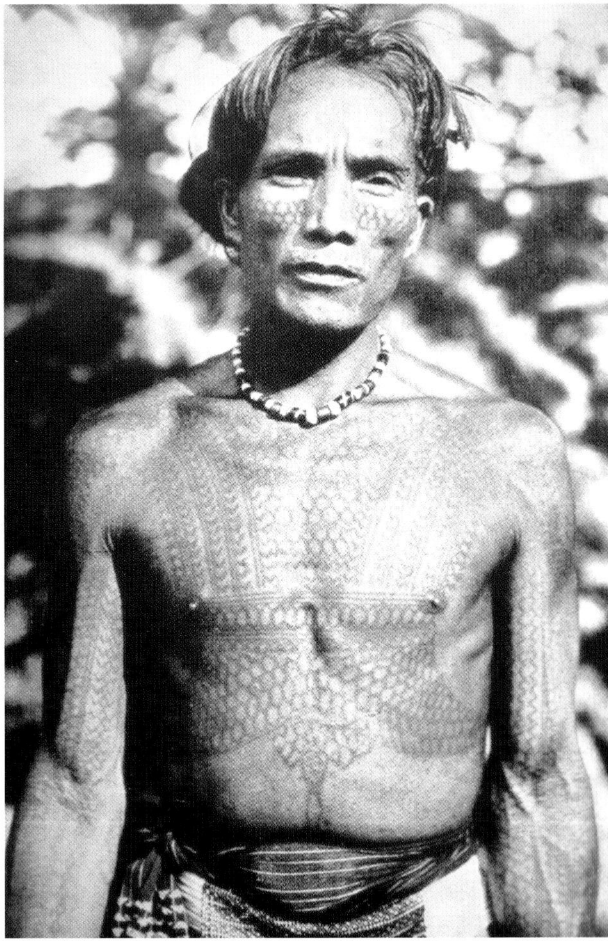

Kalinga headhunter's tattoo with little man (bottom center), centipede scales (*ufug*) and centipede (*gayaman*) motifs across chest and arms, Cordillera Region, Philippines. After Worchester (1912: 859).

Whether this form of tattoo symbolism conveyed inherent power to the Moche warriors who wore the V-shaped emblem can only be the source of conjecture. However, raptorial birds are oftentimes depicted in Moche combat scenes and are frequently shown accompanying warriors to the battlefield.[45] Although this avian imagery has yet to be thoroughly analyzed, perhaps it seems logical that many of the birds depicted symbolize omens of victory for the conquerors and ones of death for the losers. Among the headhunters of Assam, Borneo, Luzon, Taiwan, and Peru (Jívaro), omen birds were consulted to signal success in the human hunt, as they were considered messengers of the deities who ruled the cosmos.[46] On the other hand, of those birds shown hovering above the enemy troops in Moche art, perhaps they portend the coming of death; since in many headhunting cultures it was believed that the souls of victims transmigrated into various species of large birds after having met their fate on the field of battle.[47]

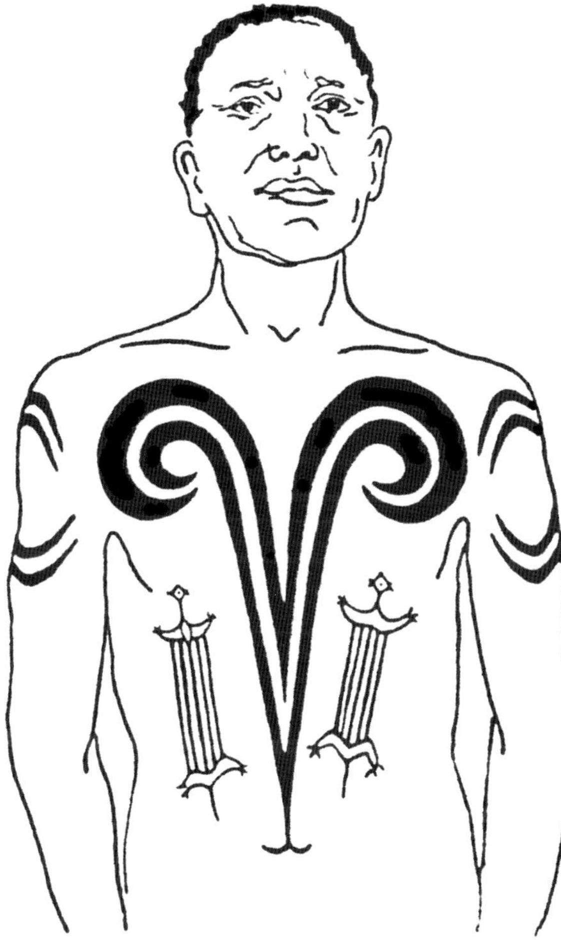

Naga headhunter's tattoo with lizard motif. Assam Region, India. Redrawn after Schuster (1952: 103, fig. 1a).

Of course, it would be fallacious to suggest that the ritual motifs just identified were the end-all of Moche V-shaped chest markings; the thesis being constructed here is not designed to place different indigenous manifestations of tattooing into "watertight compartments," but only to indicate variations of symbolic emphasis within a comparative framework.[48] In other words, our goal is to observe the beginnings of the conversion of the tattoo from an abstract sign into a living artifact worn upon the human skin.

But what can be said of serpents and centipedes? One of the least studied of iconographic elements in Moche art (and antecedent cultures) is the centipede.[49] It occurs on ceramics, textiles, spatulas, and perhaps as a tattoo motif

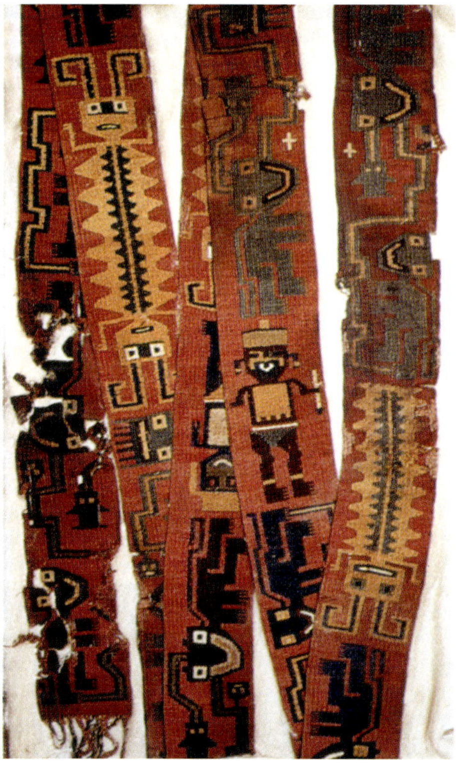

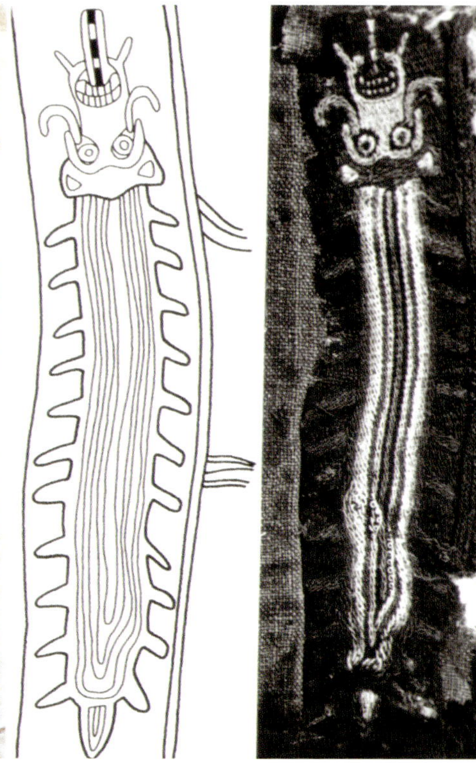

Left: Paracas burial headband with centipede motifs, Peru, 1-100 A.D. After Paul (1990: pl. 5). Copyright University of Oklahoma Press.

Center and right: Paracas burial textile with centipede motif, Peru. After Paul (1990: 142). Copyright University of Oklahoma Press.

inked on human skin. More often than not, I think, the centipede is mistakenly glossed in the Moche literature as a "worm" or "snakelike" and "serpentine" creature having "scalloped" or "serrated" edges around its undulating body.[50] Of course, the precise reference of a given design may vary according to the context of its use, so that a wavy line may indicate a snake in one context, a centipede in another.[51] Yet in many instances, and especially in prehistoric Peruvian textiles preserved in burials, I see both serpents and centipedes combining to form independent and sometimes composite images.

Centipedes are widely distributed as tattoo motifs among headhunting cultures (see pages 195 & 196).[52] And their resemblance to ramiforms of the stacked chevron variety—like a tree with many branches—is important because ramiforms are "by far the most common [genealogical] motif in

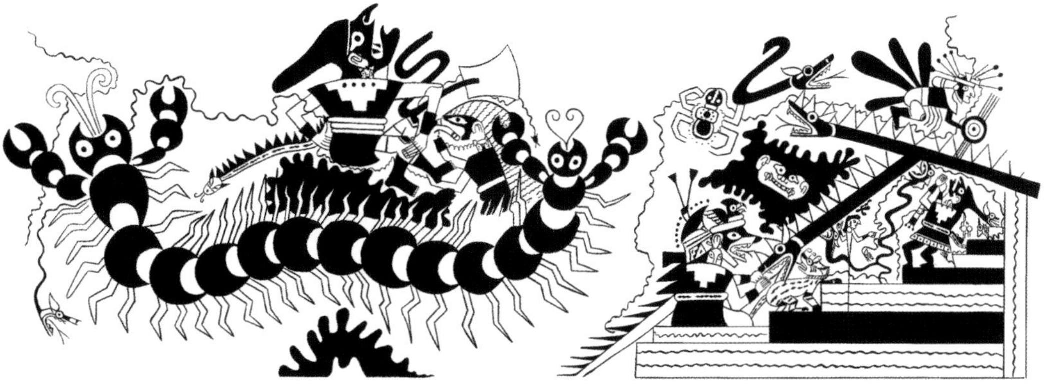

Fineline painting on Moche ceramic vessel that portrays Ai Apaec, the Creator God, being stung by a bicephalus centipede, Peru. Redrawn after Kutscher (1950: fig. 56). The lizard-like creature to the immediate right of Ai Apaec is administering a cure and symbolizes *"la curandera divina"* – a female "Divine Curer." In earlier Paracas as well as Moche art, centipedes often emanate from the heads and joints of important deities who sometimes hold human trophy heads. They also adorn Moche bone spatulas that were used in shamanic ceremonies, perhaps ones that included blood sacrifice. Such representation seems to confirm that centipedes were believed by the Moche to be liminal creatures that symbolically straddled the worlds of both life and death.

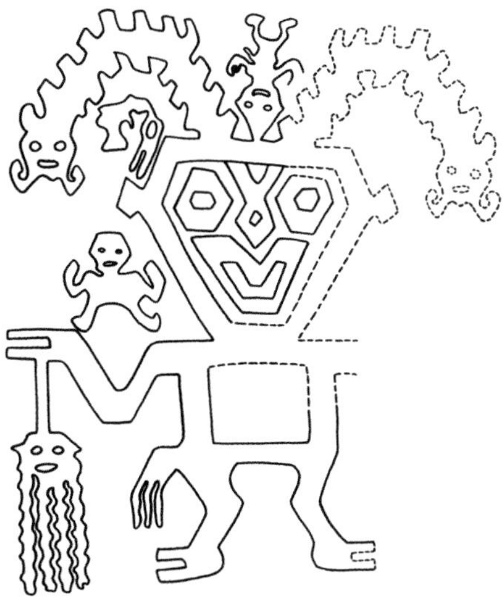

Paracas burial textile design with trophy head and centipede theme, 1-100 A.D. After Paul (1990: 73). Copyright University of Oklahoma Press.

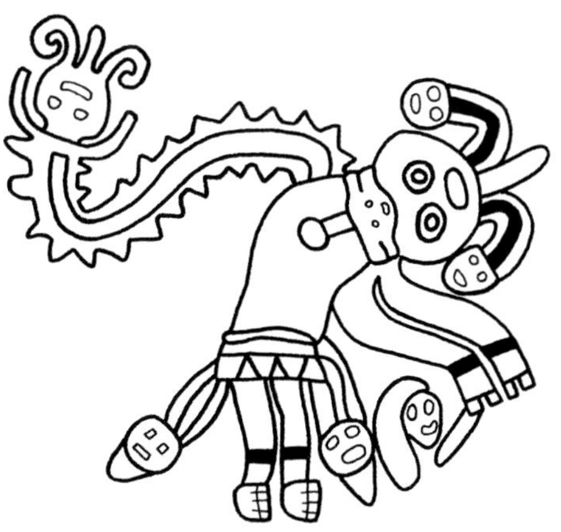

Paracas burial textile design with trophy head and centipede theme, 1-100 A.D. After Paul (1990: 133). Copyright University of Oklahoma Press.

tribal art, worldwide" especially in rock art;[53] each branch representing successive generations of genealogical relationships with the original ancestor being comprised of not one body but many, like an assemblage of homunculi.[54] No doubt, this symbolism is evident in the tattooed chest markings (*bikking*) of Filipino Kalinga headhunters, where the body of the centipede and its spine converges with its many individual legs to represent a cosmic ladder by which the ancestor spirits reach the heavens.[55] But the centipede is also *bulun*, a helper and protective spirit that is tattooed on the skins of Kalinga men and women.[56]

Amongst Peru's ancient cultures, however, there is particularly strong evidence supporting the choice of the centipede as a favored symbolic motif, since Peru is home to the world's largest centipede; the red *Scolopendra gigantea* that reaches lengths of over 30cm and possess fangs that may exceed 20mm. Centipedes are aggressive and poisonous creatures and are most frequently depicted in ancient Peruvian textiles with two heads (see previous pages). From an aesthetic standpoint, centipedes were represented in this manner for a reason; lacking a true front and back, a left and a right, the bicephalic centipede can only have a center—the fused spine from which it, and perhaps the ancestors, emerged. The combined gaze of its two sets of eyes encompasses the whole of space, and no part of its surroundings is inaccessible from the many scalloped and serrated sets of spiraling limbs. Under these circumstances, the centipede

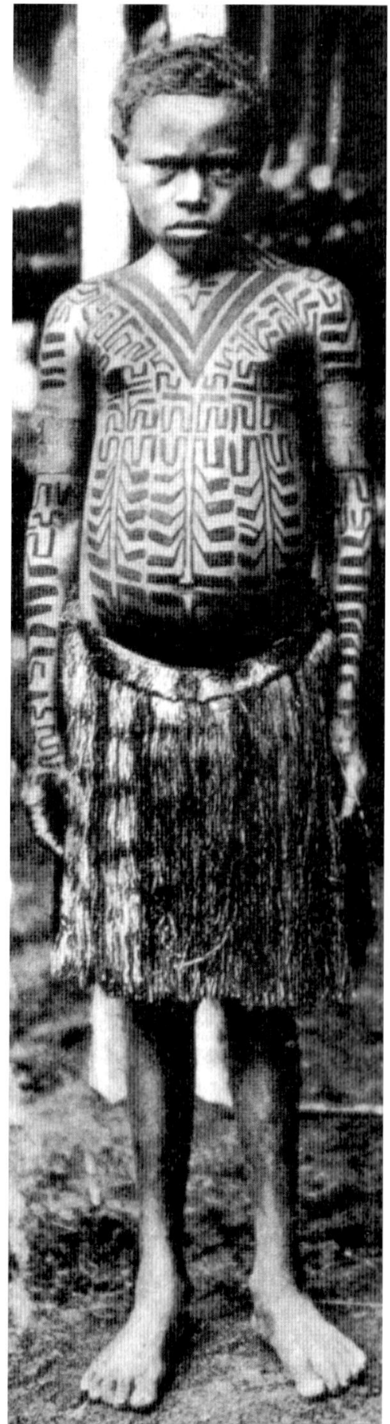

Waima girl with centipede tattoos on abdomen, Papua New Guinea. After Barton (1918: pl. III). Courtesy of Blackwell Publishing.

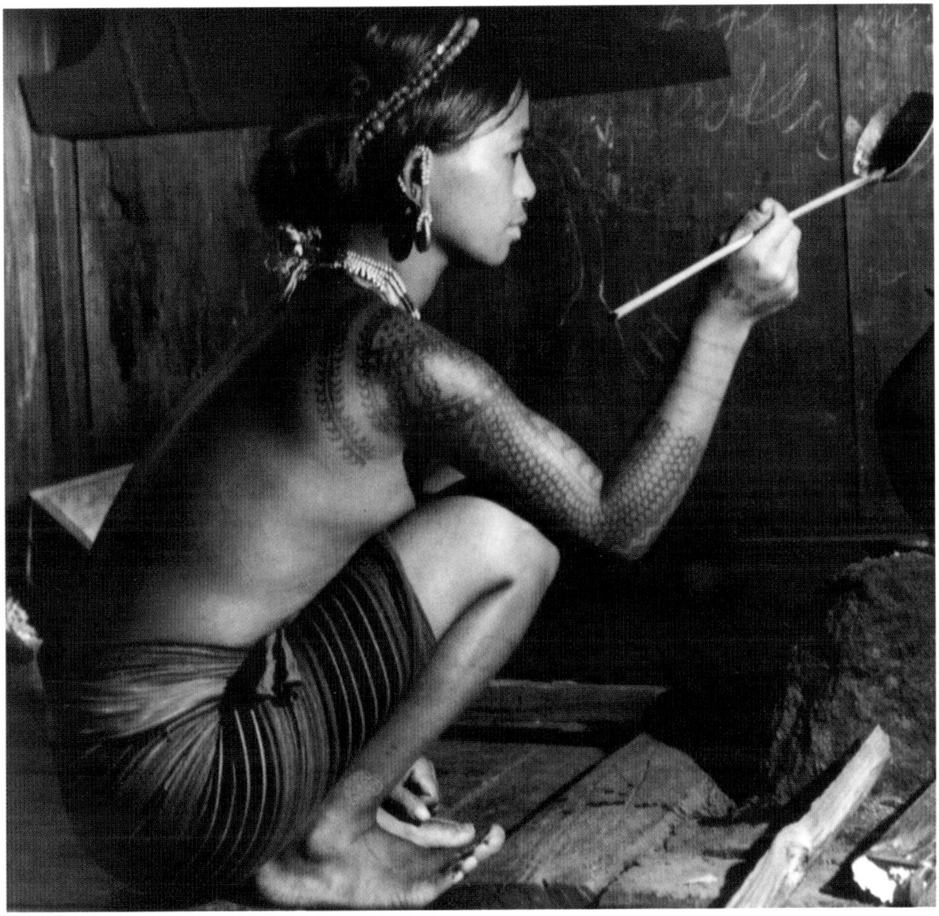

Kalinga woman with *gayaman* (centipede) tattoos on back and *ufug* (centipede scales) on shoulder and arm, Philippines, ca. 1950. Photographer Eduardo Masferre. Copyright National Anthropological Archives (N91-16835).

evokes power, multiplicity, and multiplication of the self, and when bound within the pattern of a burial textile, perhaps it reinforced the body of the deceased by preserving the integrity of the ego.

But on yet another metaphysical level, the centipede was perhaps considered a liminal creature for its ability to travel into the earth as well as on its surfaces. Furthermore centipedes, like snakes, slough off old skins and regenerate new ones, similar to the analogy between the shedding of the scabs caused by tattooing, revealing a new skin beneath the old one. In this sense, the cyclical regeneration that occurs in the centipede's world is transferred to human beings in their attempt at a magical ritual of transforming their identity; because the shedding of skin in tattooing is a metamorphosis that is both growth and death. Thus, centipedes would have been potent sources of power for the ancient Peruvians, symbolizing the transition from the world of the living to the world of the dead.

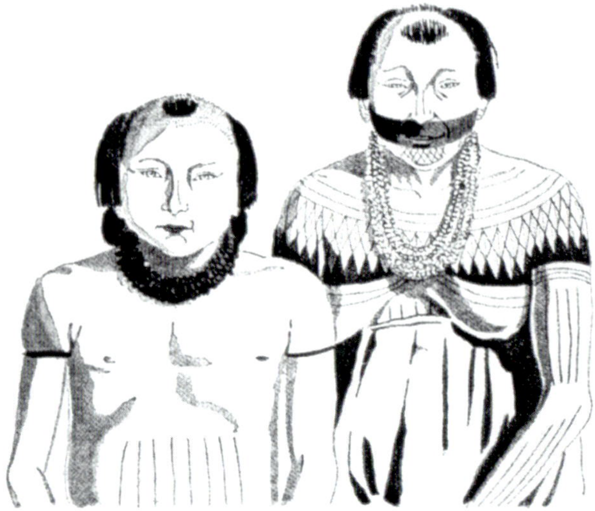

Portrait of Mundurucú man and woman, ca. 1820. Drawing by Hercules Florence. After Steinen (1899: 35, fig. 11).

Notwithstanding, it lies beyond the scope of the present work to trace further the subject of artistic parallels between the ancient Peruvians and other indigenous peoples who utilized the centipede as a tattooing motif. Instead, what we are concerned with now is not just the meaning of particular tattoo iconography, but how tattooing enmeshed its practitioners in particular types of social relations with other humans as well as mythological heroes and animals.

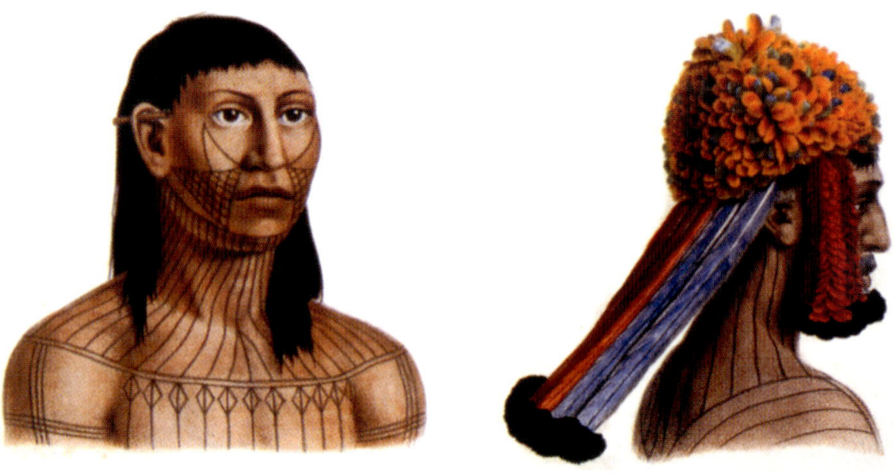

Mundurucú headhunters with elaborate tattooing, ca. 1820. Color lithographs by Spix and Martius (1823-1831).

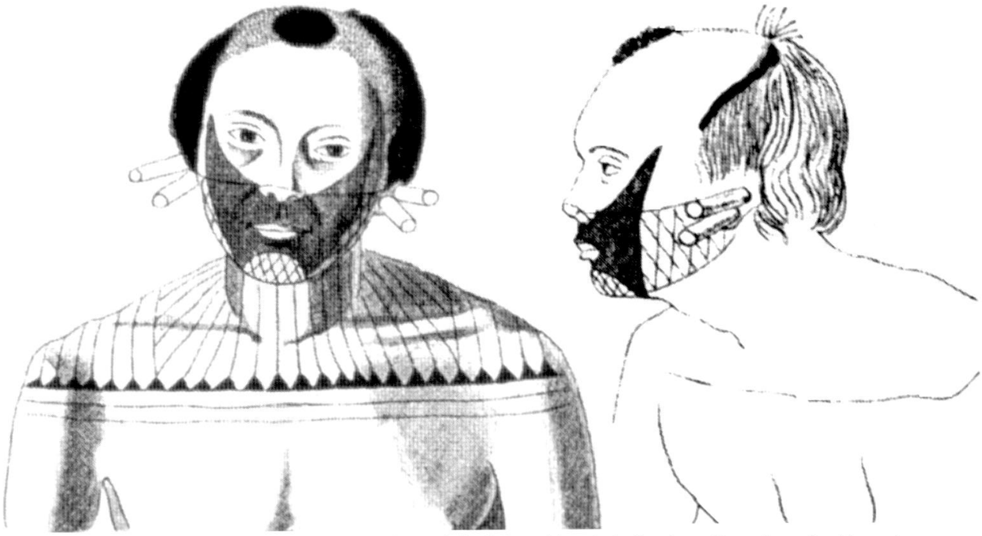

Mundurucú facial and body tattooing. Drawings by Hercules Florence, ca. 1820. After Steinen (1899: 34, fig. 10).

The Mundurucú of Amazonia

As noted in previous sections, bird iconography in tattooing was widespread and often associated with headhunting. Among the Mundurucú of Brazil, the focalization of tattooing practice followed the same general pattern and without exception it was associated with the taking of human heads.

The Mundurucú, once the mightiest headhunters in all of Amazonia,[57] were perhaps the most heavily tattooed of all indigenous groups living in South America. Although no longer practiced, tattooing commenced at the age of six or seven and terminated some ten years later, after which time the completed tattooing signified full manhood for the boys and womanhood for the girls.[58] Tattooing for both men and women consisted of fine, widely spaced parallel lines applied vertically on limbs and torso, each motif reminiscent of an abstract series of long bird plumes enveloping the body. Bands of lozenges crossed the upper part of the chest and parallel horizontal lines descended the torso towards the waist. Cross-hatchings were tattooed on other parts of the body and around each eye was tattooed a single-line ellipse; curved lines were drawn around the mouth. Lines converging towards the ears across the cheeks gave the appearance of "bird wings" spread across the face.[59]

Mundurucú tattooists were male or female,[60] and the tattooist almost always used tattooing combs made of palm thorns to insert the desired pigment.[61] After the skin was punctured, genipap juice was rubbed into the wounds to make them indelible.[62] Genipap was also used as body paint to color and emphasize those areas enclosed by the tattoo lines.

Of myths and birds

One of the distinguishing features of Mundurucú culture is its "male-centeredness" and the particular emphasis placed on the separation of the sexes. For the most part, males shunned contact with women and lived apart from their wives, sisters, and mothers in the traditional men's house (*eksa*). This structure was not just a residence and gathering place for men; it was where men ate, slept, and manufactured their hunting equipment.[63] In addition, the structure housed three sacred flutes that were exclusively owned and played by men. These flutes (*karökö*) were thought to embody ancestral and other spirits who protected, or exerted a benevolent influence over, the village.[64]

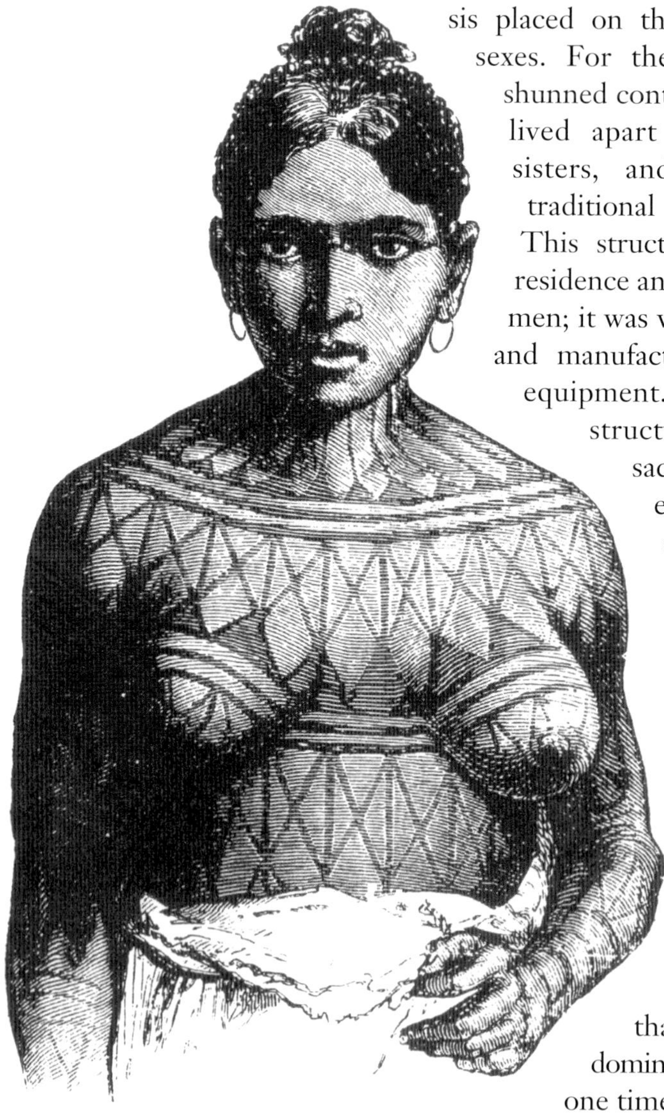
Tattooed Mundurucú woman, ca. 1870.

In the mythological past, however, it was believed that women were once dominant over males, and at one time they controlled the men's house, the flutes, and the division of labor.[65] This fact alone bespeaks of the latent fear among Mundurucú men that women can become dominant again, and today males continue to deny women access to any of the structures of power, especially the men's house.[66]

In the recent past, the men's house was the repository for all trophy heads collected in war and was the site where tattooing was conducted for men. As such, the men's house was the key symbol in which the creation of a male-centered Mundurucú universe was made possible.

The Mundurucú attribute the origins of the men's house and tattooing to their creator god and culture hero Karusakaibo. Karusakaibo was a bearer of extraordinary supernatural power who was responsible for creating people and much of the animal world. He also endowed the Mundurucú with agricultural skills and other important manifestations of culture including headhunting.[67]

Like other male culture heroes, Karusakaibo pursued many of the same worldly objectives as his male descendents. He was a great hunter, self-sufficient, and independent. He lived by himself in the forest shunning contact with women and, in this way, he set a mythic ideal for all men to follow.

But Karusakaibo also employed a physical act of transformation when he set out to model his living representatives; he tattooed all Mundurucú in his likeness after they emerged from the underworld to inhabit the earth.[68] Just as children are born from their mother, the Mundurucú emerged from the womb of the earth. But in this case emergence was only made possible after Karusakaibo had pierced the womb with his foot allowing his progeny to spring forth from the darkness.[69]

In many of his other acts of creation, Karusakaibo employed fragments of birds (feathers, bones) to work his magic. At other times he transformed himself or other mythical heroes into various bird species to facilitate and accomplish particular tasks.[70] Thus, we find in Mundurucú mythological thought a notion of spiritual beings whose form and behavior inextricably mix with prototypical human and avian attributes in what Brazilian anthropologist Viveiros de Castro terms "a common context of intercommunicability" where humans are both ex-animals and animals are ex-humans.[71] In this way, particular avian species can be associated "with the idea that the manifest bodily form of each species is an envelope (a "clothing") that conceals an internal humanoid form [that] speaks of a state of being where self and [avian] other interpenetrate."[72]

In Mundurucú ideology, for example, birds embody the same

mythic ideals as the culture hero Karusakaibo. They live in a state of self-sufficiency through hunting and many species lead a solitary existence in the jungle. Birds lay eggs and this type of "external" reproductive cycle symbolizes the ability to procreate without the act of sex.[73] This perceived form of asexual reproduction is a powerful trait, because it is mythically linked to the origin myth where Karusakaibo creates (or gives rise to) the Mundurucú without any apparent sexual act of his own. These features, combined with the fact that birds are bipedal and the Mundurucú notion that a man's penis is symbolic of a bird with a short beak, suggests that "maleness" is in fact symbolized by birds.[74] Therefore, it was the prerogative of all men to live (and look) *like a bird*, since this was considered to be nothing less than a pure and mythically potent male pursuit.

Of birds and men

It should come as no surprise, then, that many authorities have argued that the Mundurucú were perhaps the most expert featherworkers in South America within the historic period.[75] Obviously, the Mundurucú's reverence and intimate knowledge of many avian species facilitated their craftsmanship in this art form.

At feasts, the Mundurucú used scepters, hats, caps, and several varieties of garlands made of feathers, as well as feather mantles which they drew over their shoulders, and aprons of rhea feathers which they tied around their waist.[76] Feathers, as outcroppings of the body and especially the head, were thought to possess divine potency. They conveyed their inherent power to the warrior who wore them particularly because the Mundurucú associated several species of birds with the eponymous spirits of their clans.[77]

Similarly, among the headhunting Paracas and Chimú of Peru, various species of birds were also utilized for their feathers to make garments and headdresses.[78] Feathers were the "power centers" of the bird and were especially charged with supernatural energy. They were analogous to human hairs which, with their capacity for constant growth and renewal, were universally believed to be a point of concentration of the human spirit or soul.[79] For the Paracas people, unbound hair symbolized a state of susceptibility to malevolent spiritual forces, since we know from archaeological evidence that they attempted to protect these delicate parts of the body by braiding

Facing page: Tattooed Mundurucú warrior in ceremonial attire, ca. 1828. Illustration by Hercules Florence.

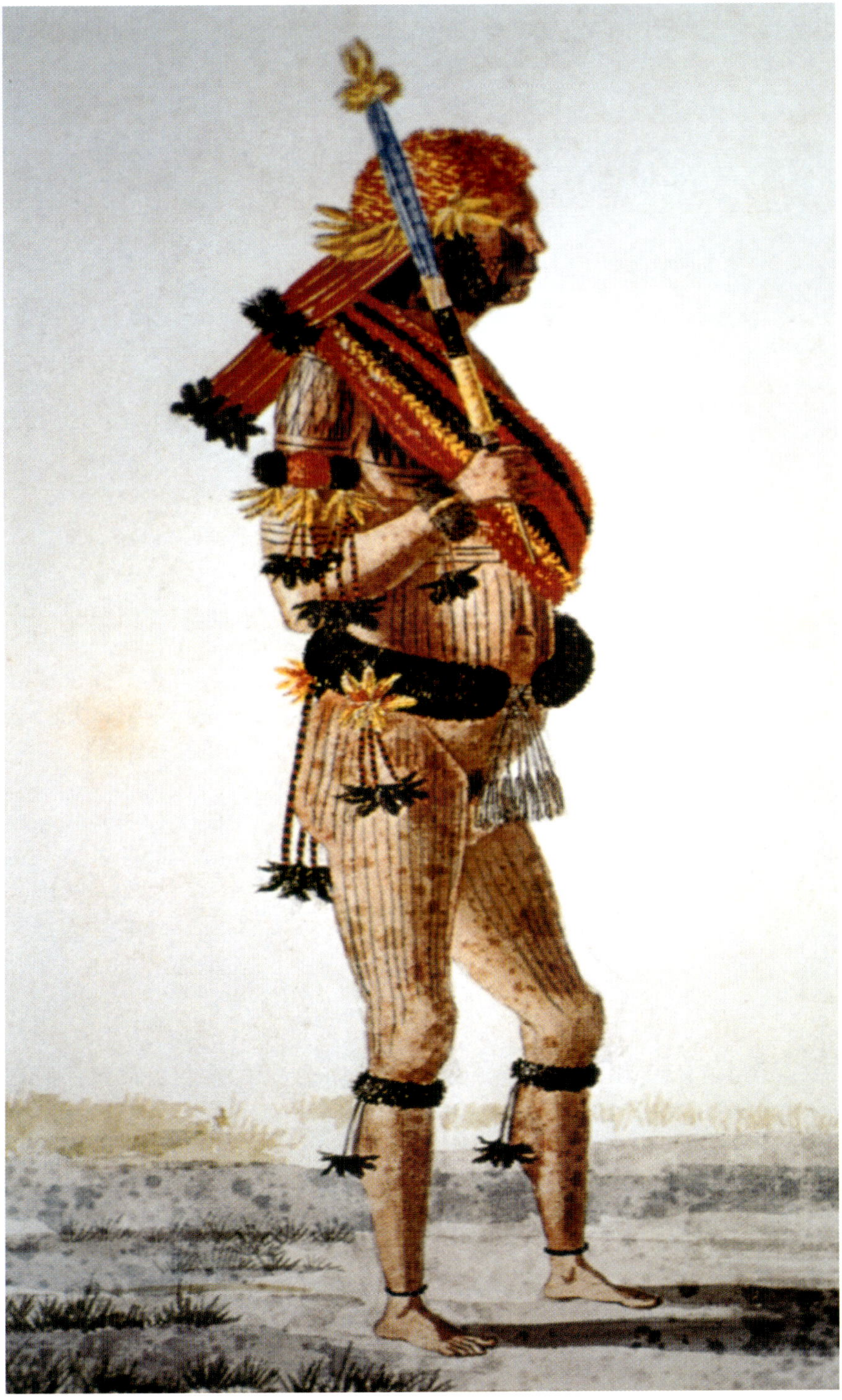

or covering their head hairs with turbans or elaborate headpieces.[80] Interestingly only trophy heads and shamans were depicted in Paracas art with unbound hair "perhaps signifying a state of immunity from spirit attack or a oneness with the spirits."[81]

In his review of feather ornaments and their use among several historic headhunting and scalping societies of South America, the ethnographer Rafael Karsten provides this perspective:

> Feathers and plumes, according to the Indian idea, not only afford an efficacious protection against evil spirits, but are powerful means whereby men can conjure and exorcise them. For this reason feather ornaments are, above all, used on occasions when the Indians enter into relation with the spiritual world, and these occasions . . . are numerous enough. Again, the magical power ascribed to feathers depends on a very natural consideration: *the feathers are the hair of the bird, and they have the same magical power as the human hair.*
>
> [T]he Indian belief endows even animals with a spirit or soul, which seems to be essentially the same kind as the human spirit. This theory is applied to birds also . . . but whatever the spirit may be which animates the bird, the efficacy ascribed to the feathers is a fact beyond dispute. Since the spirit of the bird is collected in its feathers, as the human spirit is concentrated in the hair of the head, it follows that feathers and plumes are particularly charged with supernatural power.[82]

For the Mundurucú, however, the efficacy of feathers was most clearly brought out in relation to their role in consecrating the trophy head captured in war. Feathers were considered to be the "crowning glory of a trophy head" and without them, the skull would not release its magical powers.[83]

The Mundurucú headhunt and trophy heads

Military expeditions were launched in the dry season and usually ended with the coming of the rainy season.[84] Each warrior was accompanied by his wife or sister who assisted him in carrying the necessary equipment including food, hammock, and weapons. Women also tended to the wounded and according to some reports were distinguished by their ability to "cleverly

Facing page: Tattooed Mundurucú headhunter with trophy head, ca. 1810. Illustration by Spix and Martius (1823-1831)

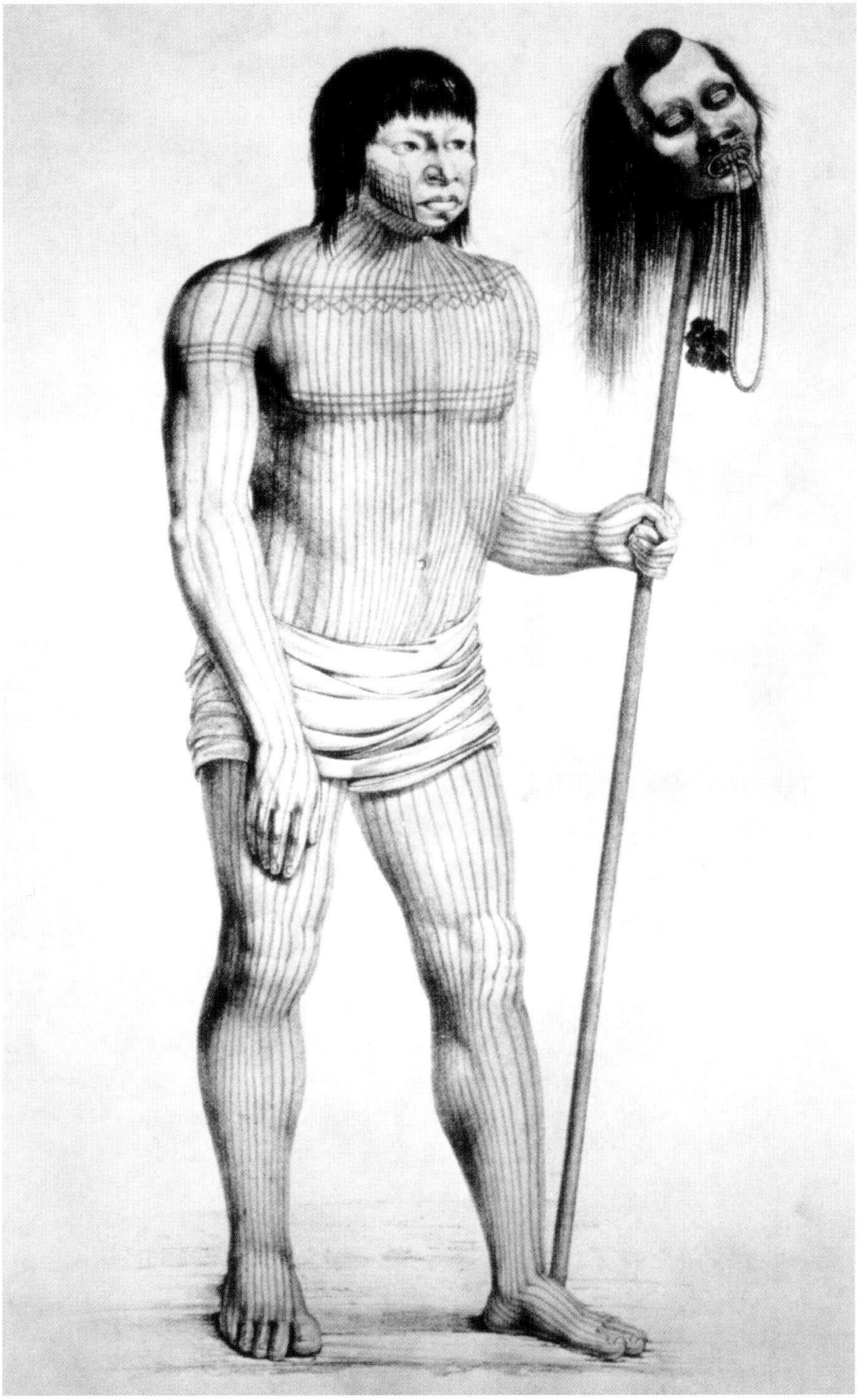

catch the arrows of the enemy in flight."[85] Attacks were waged at dawn and flaming arrows were sent aloft to set fire to the enemy's huts. The incendiary panic that ensued, combined with the visage of waves of fully tattooed warriors brandishing their headhunting gear, no doubt played a major role in the psychological dimension of Mundurucú warfare.

Enemy warriors who fell on the field of battle were decapitated if time permitted. Occasionally, the head of an enemy woman was taken, but usually they were taken prisoner instead. Children captured in war were adopted and fully incorporated into Mundurucú society.[86] A clan name was bestowed upon the child and he or she received the elaborate facial and body tattooing that distinguished the Mundurucú from other tribes living in central Brazil.

Trophy heads seized by Mundurucú warriors were not shrunken like those of the Jívaro of Ecuador, rather they were desiccated, dressed (brain removed), and colored with genipap or *urucú* (red) dye.[87] The wife or sister of the successful warrior sometimes assisted in the preliminary preparation of the heads, but not always.

Karsten describes the specifics of Mundurucú trophy preparation as follows:

> The head of the slain was severed from the trunk with a knife made of broad bamboo; the brain, the muscles, the eyes, and the tongue were taken out; the skull was repeatedly soaked in vegetable oil mixed with *urucú* [or genipap], and exposed for several days over the smoke of the fire or in the sun until it was quite dry. An artificial brain of dyed cotton was subsequently put in, the orbits of the eyes were filled with rosin, and the whole head was covered with a hood of feathers. Adorned in this manner the horrid trophy became the permanent companion of the victor, who carried it by a string at his cincture wherever he went.[88]

Unlike the Iban of Borneo and ancient Peruvians who prized trophy heads for their power to fertilize the agricultural fields, the Mundurucú believed that the efficacy of the trophy head lay in its ability to please the "spirit mothers" of the game animals, thereby promoting the fertility of animals, increasing the yield of the hunt, and making game more tractable to the male hunter.[89] According to the anthropologist Robert Murphy, "[e]ach species of game is said to have a spirit "mother" who exercises protection over the animals and insures their increase. There is also a spirit mother of the game and a principal intermediary between man and nature."[90] Therefore, it was customary for the head-taker to trek out into the forest with the hunting parties to insure a successful kill. Although the owner of the trophy would not hunt himself, his companions would feed off the charm of the head and in a short period of time dispatch all the game needed by the village.[91]

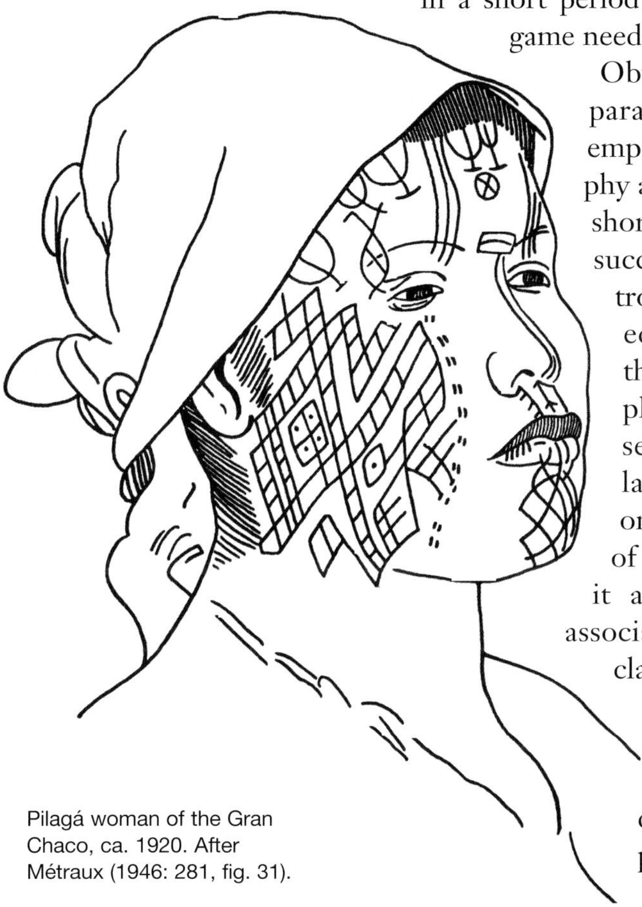

Pilagá woman of the Gran Chaco, ca. 1920. After Métraux (1946: 281, fig. 31).

Obviously, it was of paramount importance to empower the talismanic trophy as soon as possible. Thus, shortly after the return of a successful war party, the trophy head was inaugurated into ceremonial use through a series of complex rituals that involved several Mundurucú villages. This process not only validated the prowess of the head-hunter publicly, it also solidified bonds of association among scattered clansmen and women.[92]

The taker of the trophy head was given an honored title and during an extended ritual period of nearly three years, he was considered to be in a sacralized state and could not engage in ordinary discourse. He was only approachable through considerable protocol.[93]

The hallmark ceremony that consecrated the trophy was called "Decorating the Ears."[94] At its climax, feather pendants were prepared from five species of birds and were suspended from the ears of the trophy head. Each type of feather could only be attached by the clan who could claim that species of bird as an eponymous clan spirit.[95] As a rule, the feather pendants could not be longer than the human hair that remained on the trophy head. And for this reason long-haired victims were especially prized.[96]

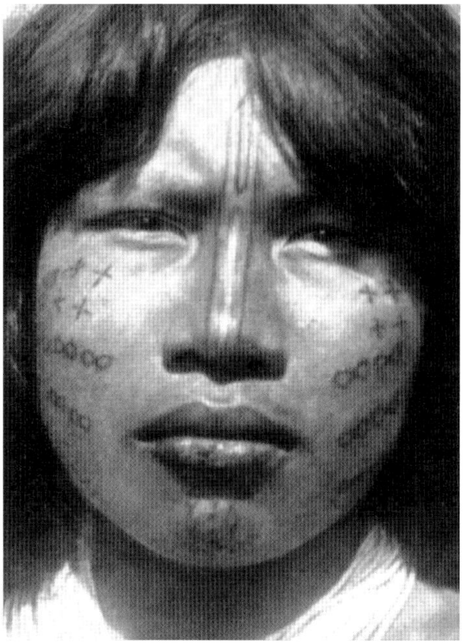

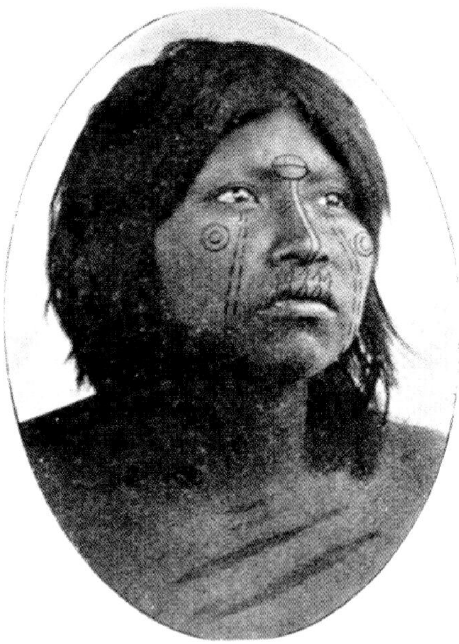

Above: Lengua woman of the Gran Chaco with facial tattoos. After Krieg (1934: fig. 84).

Below: Toba woman of the Gran Chaco with facial tattooing. After Outes and Bruch (1910: 76, fig. 33).

The Gran Chaco

Lying some 1,200 miles immediately to the south of Mundurucú territory, the Gran Chaco, which possibly derives its name from an indigenous Quechua word meaning "hunting ground," is a vast arid plain located at the center of the South American continent.[97] This very hot and semi-desertic lowland region covers portions of Argentina, Bolivia, and Paraguay, and is drained by several rivers. On the whole, the entire region is barely suitable for human settlement, yet several groups of indigenous people continue to live here despite the harsh climate and topography.

Although tattooing in the Chaco has been supplanted by less painful and infective forms of body painting in the modern era, it had "magical" implications in the past and nearly all indigenous groups practiced it. Women generally displayed more abundant tattooing than men, and it was truly exceptional to find males as profusely tattooed as women.

Girls were first marked on their foreheads when five to seven years old, and with the passing of the years they received additional tattoos consisting of small circles, crosses, half-moons, and lines on their faces.[98] By the time a girl reached maturity, her facial tattoos were finally completed, at which time she was eligible for marriage.[99]

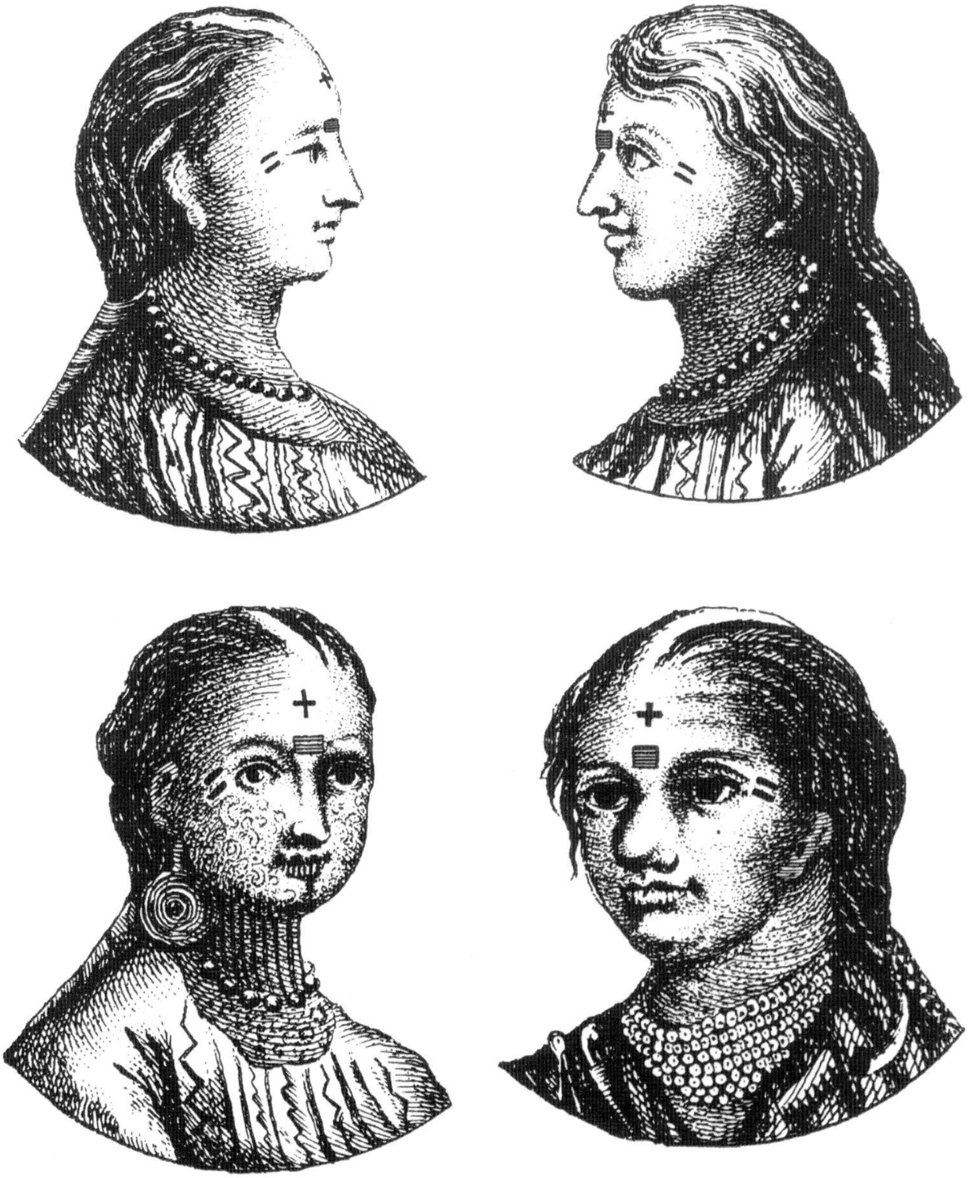

Tattooed Abipón women of the Gran Chaco, ca. 1750.
Woodblock print after Martin Dobrizhoffer.

Tattoo artists were almost always old women. They first traced the outline of the design on the client's face (or other body part) with charcoal. Then the tattooist punctured the facial skin with a small bundle of cactus thorns or a single bone awl dipped in a mixture of saliva and soot.[100]

In 1750, the Jesuit missionary Martin Dobrizhoffer provided a rare account of the actual ritual among the now-extinct Abipón. His observations are said to have been typical of all Chaco groups[101] that practiced tattooing in the past:

> Over the course of the days spent in tattooing, the girl is confined to her father's dwelling and wrapped in a hide . . . She must abstain from eating meat, fish, and other sorts of food, and is only allowed to feed upon a small amount of fruit which grows on brambles and conduces much towards cooling the blood.
>
> Tattooing among the Abipón took place over four to five days with a sharp cactus spine. The client returned everyday until the face, arms, and breasts were full of tattoos. The Abipón paid for this with an amount of blood, sweat, tears and moaning. When the girl became of age, she laid her head upon the tattoo artist's lap, generally a woman of many years, to become adorned and beautiful.
>
> If the poor little girl complained, or escaped from the tattooist's lap, she would be pinned down and told by the irritated old lady, "Enough of this cowardice, you are a disgrace to our Nation, just because I am tickling you with a few spines. Don't you know that you are the descendant of those who had their pleasures and glory in being wounded? You should be ashamed of yourself for being a timid little creature!
>
> "Be quiet and let me work, I will promise that you will become a young woman."[102]

From Dobrizhoffer's report, it does not appear that Abipón tattooing served merely as a form of "ornament" used to beautify the body. Rather, all Chaco women were tattooed in much the same way and with many of the same motifs, the only variation being in their positioning. In this way no particular woman could have hoped to gain aesthetic advantage over her "competitors" through tattooing. Furthermore, women fasted, were secluded and carefully covered during the tattoo ritual, which seems to indicate that tattooing had a religious significance. These facts, combined with the belief that tattoo pigment and the tattooist's saliva were in themselves purificatory substances utilized to repel malevolent spirits,[103] suggests that Chaco tattooing practice was not simply a form of facial adornment. It was something altogether different.

Carbon-based substances used as tattoo pigment were considered in

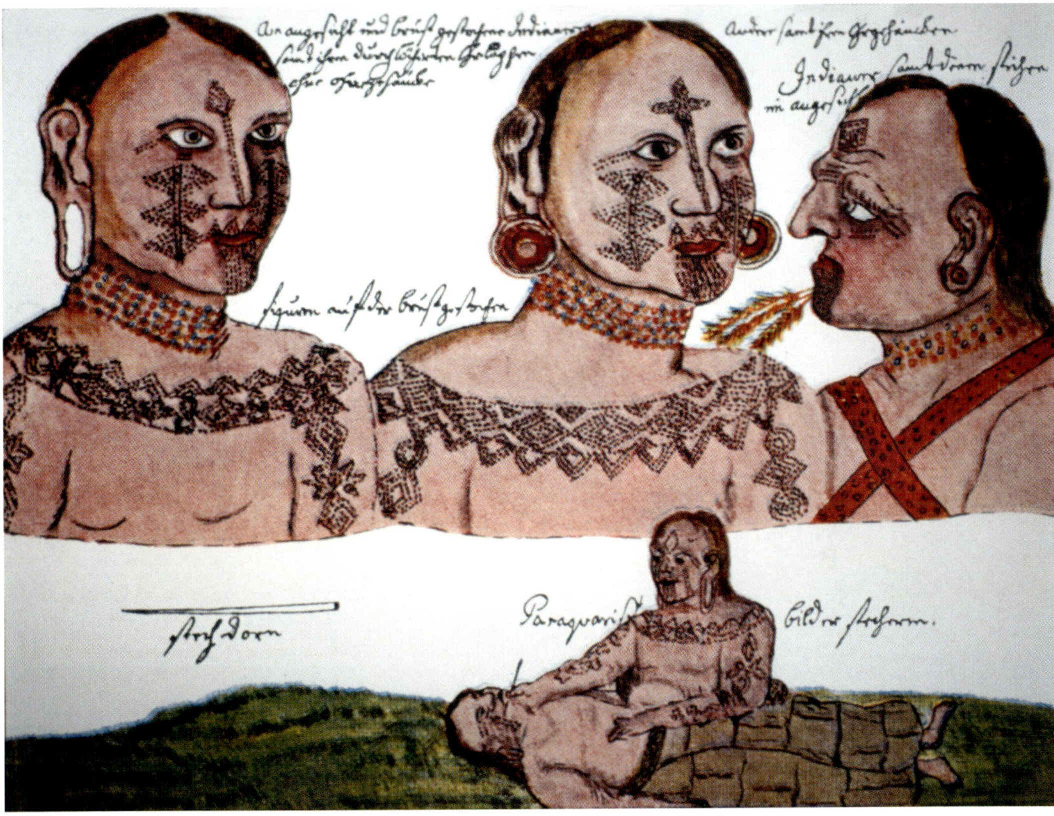

Mocoví tattoos from the Argentinean Chaco (top). Mocoví woman tattooing a man (bottom), ca. 1750. Illustrations by Florián Paucke.

nature to be prophylactic. The inherent power of the pigment lay specifically in its connection to fire, and among many indigenous peoples of the Chaco, Brazil, and Patagonia, ash or charcoal procured from fire was utilized ritually as a radical means of purification. For example, the Abipónes threw ashes in the path of whirlwinds (thought to be passing spirits) to repel them;[104] the ancient Tupis, at the ceremonial killing of enemy prisoners taken in war, painted their bodies with ashes to protect themselves from the vengeful spirits of the soon to be deceased;[105] and Fuegian shamans heaped ashes upon themselves to enter the realm of the spirits.[106]

Saliva procured from the venerated tattoo artist had magical attributes ascribed to it as well. It was a kind of sanctifying substance, perhaps in some ways similar to the African Berber concept of *baraka*, that enhanced the efficacy of the tattoo's overall magical power.[107]

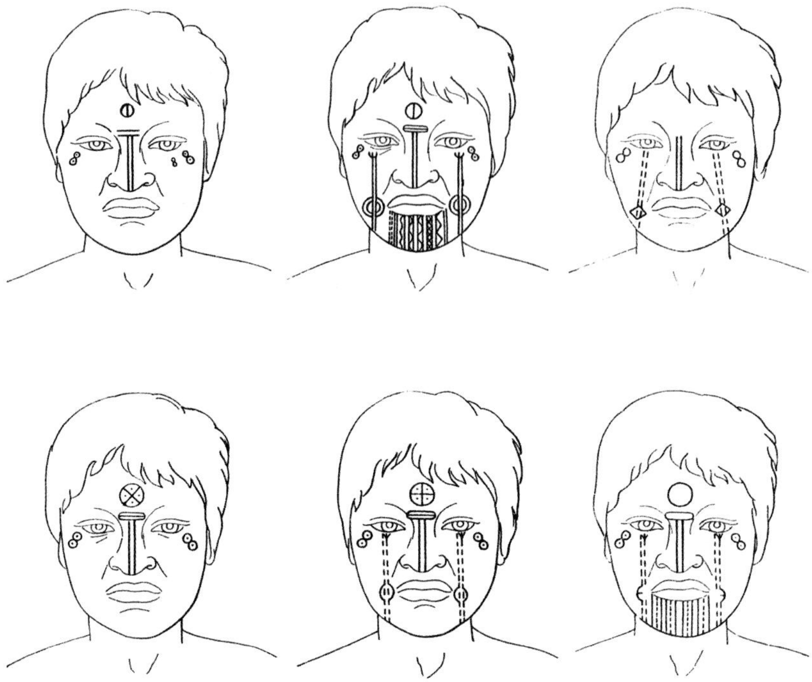

Choroti women's facial tattoos. After Lehmann-Nitsche (1908). Argentinean Chaco.

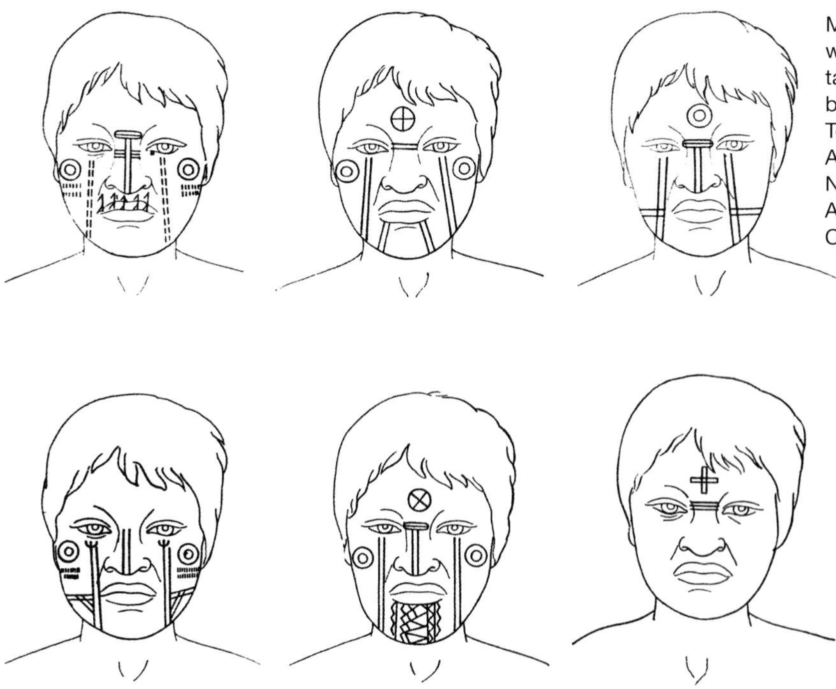

Mataco women's facial tattoos (note: bottom right Toba woman). After Lehmann-Nitsche (1908). Argentinean Chaco.

Thwarting spirits and the implications of flowing blood

In the Gran Chaco, spirits helped or harmed individuals depending on how humans behaved with respect to them. In most cases, spiritual confrontations were believed to be the result of human transgressions that in essence "activated" them. When a village was threatened by an epidemic, bad weather, or some other critical disturbance, Chaco peoples performed ceremonies aimed at curbing the influence of the supernatural entity or entities believed responsible.[108] The accompanying ceremonials that followed were characterized by collective acts of dancing, drumming, chanting, and body painting which in their inherent efficacy and agency coerced, influenced, or repelled the supernatural intruders from the community.[109]

The delicate condition of life into which an individual of the Chaco was thrust obviously served as a constant source of concern—spirits (good or bad) could be encountered anywhere and in anything. For a woman, however, the most immediate source of personal danger lay in her menstrual blood and when it flowed, she and her community became seriously exposed to evil spirits.[110]

It seems to be a common idea that among all Chaco peoples menstruation was influenced by the new moon.[111] The flowing blood of the girl "awakened" her sexual desire and was particularly enticing to evil spirits who were "angry with her."[112] Although the attainment of puberty made the woman eligible for marriage, it also marked the beginning of her journey towards a series of critical life stages (e.g. childbirth, additional menses) that would not only come to shape her physical and emotional development, but would again expose her to supernatural dangers. Therefore, the tattooing initiation ceremonies at puberty had for their object, in part, to protect women against spiritual manifestations for the time being, and more importantly "to purify her once and for all from the evils associated with her sexual functions during the years to come."[113]

As argued in previous chapters, there was a unifying thread of belief among tattooing cultures that the body's orifices worked as passageways by which malevolent spirits traveled to enter the human body to harm it. Natural openings such as the mouth, the nostrils, the eyes, and ears were especially sensitive to the actions of spiritual entities, and individuals who left their heads, bodies, or faces uncovered (and hence unprotected) were especially at risk.

Among the Toba, Choroti, and Mataco a girl arriving at puberty was kept secluded in her house for a period of four to five days and her face and entire body was carefully covered (or painted) because "evil demons" were

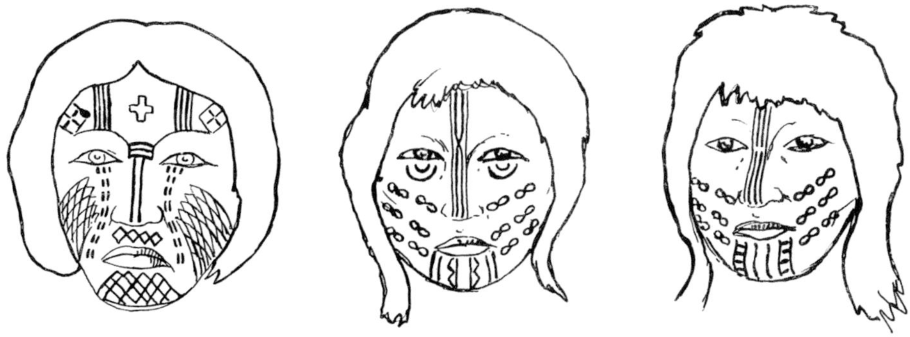

Left: Facial tattooing of a Toba woman. Redrawn after Krieg (1934: fig. 39).

Center & right: Facial tattooing of Macá women. Redrawn after Krieg (1934: fig. 85).

constantly "attacking her."[114] She was also obliged to fast strictly, ingesting only vegetable products. Sometimes she was permitted to uncover herself and exit the dwelling, but only if she moved to the center of a dance circle where a group of men (Toba) or women (Choroti) wielding deer hoof rattles attempted to shield her from the incorrigible spirits by whom she was exposed to for the moment.[115]

There is one detail, however, about which a few words of explanation may be added in regards to this complex of ritual belief. As noted, initiates were frequently subjected to periods of ceremonial fasting or restrictions in diet prior to or after the tattooing operation. According to Dobrizhoffer, the 18th century Jesuit missionary, Abipón tattoo initiates were restricted to a diet of a little fruit which grows upon brambles because it "cooled" the woman's blood.[116] In most cases, particular foodstuffs, especially those that were associated with blood in their raw state (like meat and fish), were prohibited from being ingested due to the fear of evil spirits entering into the body with the food itself causing madness.[117]

Such food restrictions also stemmed from the idea that particular prey animals (armadillo, peccary, rhea, etc.) were associated with spirit Masters who, if not properly propitiated, would either bring illness to the community or cause the game animals to disappear.[118] The meat of predatory animals was forsaken especially if that species performed a key symbolic role in mythology (e.g. jaguar, puma, hunting dogs, particular birds, etc.) or if the predatory or prey animal was one believed to "share immortality with men [and women]."[119] Thus, the result of these extended sets of food restrictions encountered in Chacoan puberty and tattooing rites was not only to enhance the power of resistance by frustrating the efficacy of the evil spirit's possessive power, but also to declare that particular animals were equivalent to humans (via reincarnation) and should not be eaten during the tabooed period. For Chacoan peoples, as for the Mundurucú, it appears that there exists a commonly shared condition of humanity between both humans and particular animals. If this is true, perhaps Viveiros de Castro is correct when he says that there is a "universal Amerindian notion" that:

> [some] animals (predators) and spirits see humans as animals (as game or prey) to the same extent that game animals see humans as spirits or as predator animals . . . Animals see their food as human food (jaguars see blood as manioc beer, vultures see the maggots in rotting meat as grilled fish); they see their bodily attributes (fur, feathers, claws, beaks) as body decorations or cultural instruments; they see their social system as organized in the same way as human institutions are (with chiefs, shamans, ceremonies, exogamous moieties, and whatnot) . . . [and they believe] that any animal can be human [since] there is more "being" to an animal than meets the eye.[120]

California and the American Southwest

Although much more could be said about such "universal Amerindian notions," similar patterns in tattooing practice surprisingly emerge when comparisons are made between the indigenous peoples of the Chaco and those of California and the American Southwest. However, before these interesting points are drawn out in detail, a few general comments should be made regarding tattooing practice in these two regions of the United States.

Throughout California, where until recently traditional tattooing was extinct, women's tattoos usually consisted of various types of chin markings among several indigenous groups (North ➛ South: Shasta, Karok, Yurok, Hupa, Wintu, Lassik, Wailaki, Sinkyone, Yuki, Huchnom, Pomo, Patwin, Konkow, Maidu, Nisenan, Eastern Miwok, Coast Miwok, Costanoan, Yokut, Wukchumni, Chukchansi, among others), although some tribes tattooed their cheeks (e.g. Yuki, Wailaki, Huchnom, Mono). Others practiced more complete forms of body tattooing (North ➛ South: Pomo, Patwin, Nisenan, Eastern Miwok, Costanoan, Yokut, Wukchumni, Chukchansi, among others) that covered breasts, abdomens, arms, and

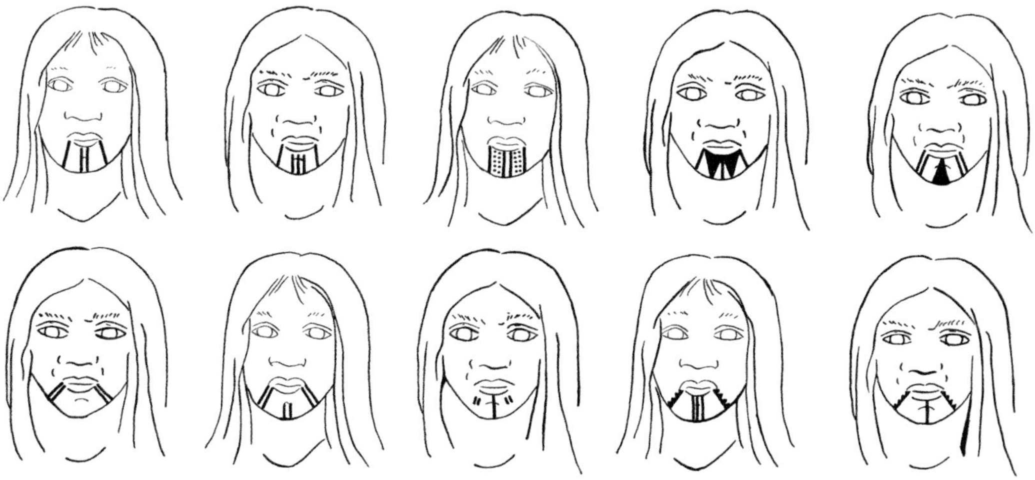

Mohave women's chin tattooing, ca. 1930. Redrawn after Taylor and Wallace (1947: 2, fig. 1).

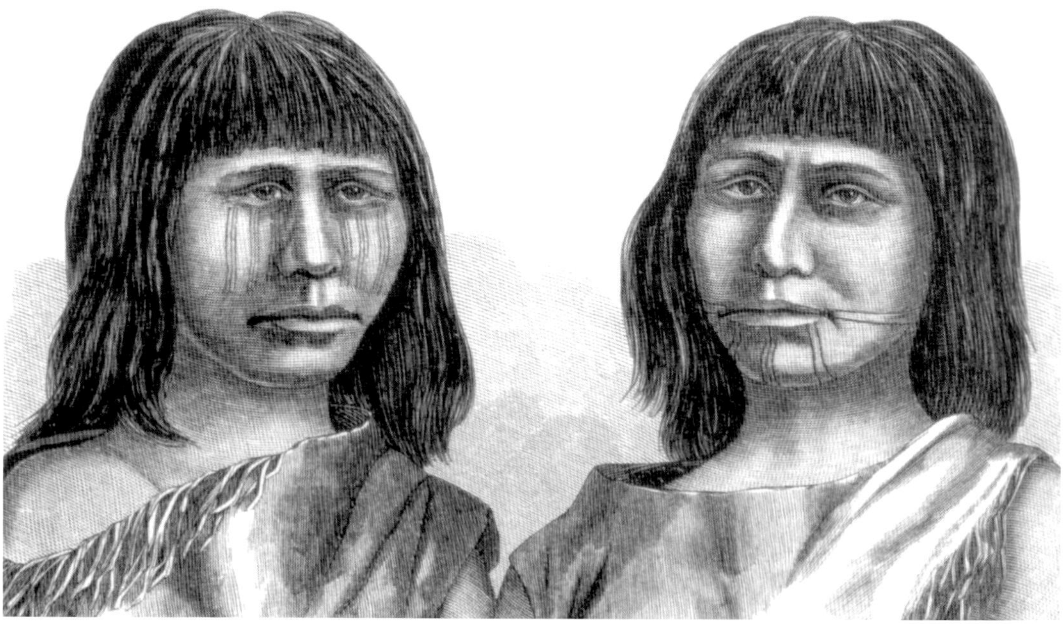

Huchnom women with facial tattooing, ca. 1870. After Powers (1877: fig. 13).

sometimes legs and thighs.[121]

In the American Southwest (especially Arizona), tattooing was almost entirely confined to the lower Colorado River tribes and their neighbors: Mohave, Yuma, Southern Diegueño, Tipai-Ipai, Cocopa, Maricopa, Pima, and Yavapai. And for the most part, women living here restricted their tattoos to the chin.[122]

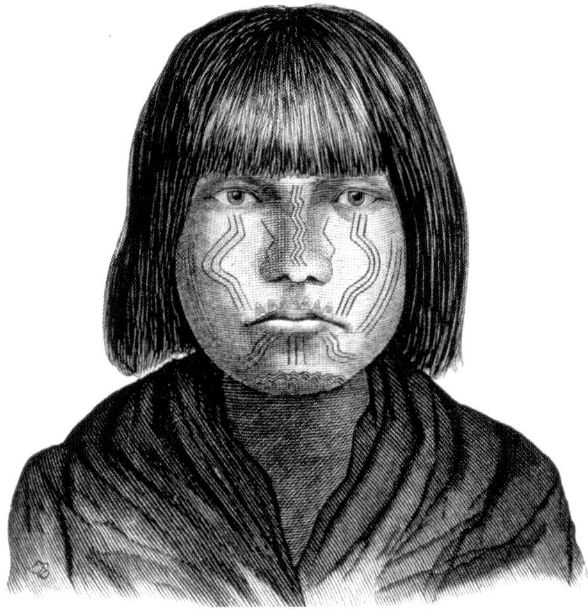

Yuki facial tattooing, ca. 1870. After Powers (1877: fig. 11).

In both California and the Southwest, elderly women specialists were almost always the tattoo artists. Tattoo pigments were usually composed of carboniferous substances which were rubbed into the skin after it had been plied with thorns, obsidian lancets or other tools.

Among the Maricopa, Tipai-Ipai (Kamia-Diegueño), Luiseño, Southern Valley Yokuts, Maidu, Konkow, Wintu, Lassik, Sinkyone and many other groups, girls who reached puberty (first menses) were secluded from the other members of the community before they were to be tattooed in a public ceremony.[123] Just like menstruants living in the Gran Chaco, girls observed a strict vegetarian diet and were prohibited from eating meat and fish products. Oftentimes, the heads of the girls were covered with animal skins or plastered over with mud and their faces were painted. Menstruants were forbidden from scratching any part of their bodies with their fingers and especially their hair. Instead, a scratching stick was employed to presumably prevent malevolent spirits from attaching themselves to vulnerable parts of the body. Among the Shasta, Achumawi, Atsugewi, Klamath, Maidu, Wintu, Karok, and Tolowa, deer hoof dance rattles were given to girls,[124] as they were in the Gran Chaco, to frighten away evil spirits.[125]

Around Maricopa, Diegueño, Kamia, and other tribal campfires in California and Oregon,[126] various songs and dances were performed by community members to purify the menstruant, to secure "spirit power," and to fortify and prepare her for womanhood.[127]

Although little is known about the experiences of women in menstrual seclusion outside of indigenous society, the various assortment of menstrual taboos recorded in ethnographies of indigenous peoples almost universally characterize menstruation as a "definitive form of pollution."[128] However, menstrual taboos, rather than protecting society from the universally ascribed feminine evil of pollution and disruption of the social order by evil spirits, can perhaps be better understood as something more positive and different.

Among the Yurok of California, for example, it has been made explicit that menstrual taboos and seclusion protected the creative spirituality of menstruous women from the influence of others in a more neutral state as well as protecting the latter in turn from the potent, positive spiritual force ascribed to such women.[129] Yurok women viewed seclusion not only as a means towards spiritual and economic ascendancy, but also as a way to enjoy a break from their normal labors around the household and agricultural fields. While in seclusion, they wove and enjoyed the camaraderie and gossip of other women. And as Buckley illustrates in his work on menstrual "Blood Magic," menstruating Yurok women isolated themselves:

> . . . because this is a time when [they are] at the height of [their] powers. Thus the time should not be wasted in mundane tasks and social distractions, nor should one's concentration be broken by concerns with the opposite sex. Rather, all of one's energies should be applied [for ten days] in concentrated meditation "to find out the purpose of your life," and toward the "accumulation" of spiritual energy. The menstrual shelter, or room, is "like the men's sweathouse," a place where you "go into yourself and make yourself stronger." As in traditional male sweathouse practice [ten days], or "training" (*hohkep-*), there are physical as well as mental aspects of "accumulation." The blood that flows serves to "purify" the woman, preparing her for spiritual accomplishment. Again, a woman must use a scratching implement, instead of scratching absentmindedly with her fingers, as an aid in focusing her full attention on her body by making even the most natural and spontaneous of actions fully conscious and intentional: "You should feel all of your body exactly as it is, and pay attention."

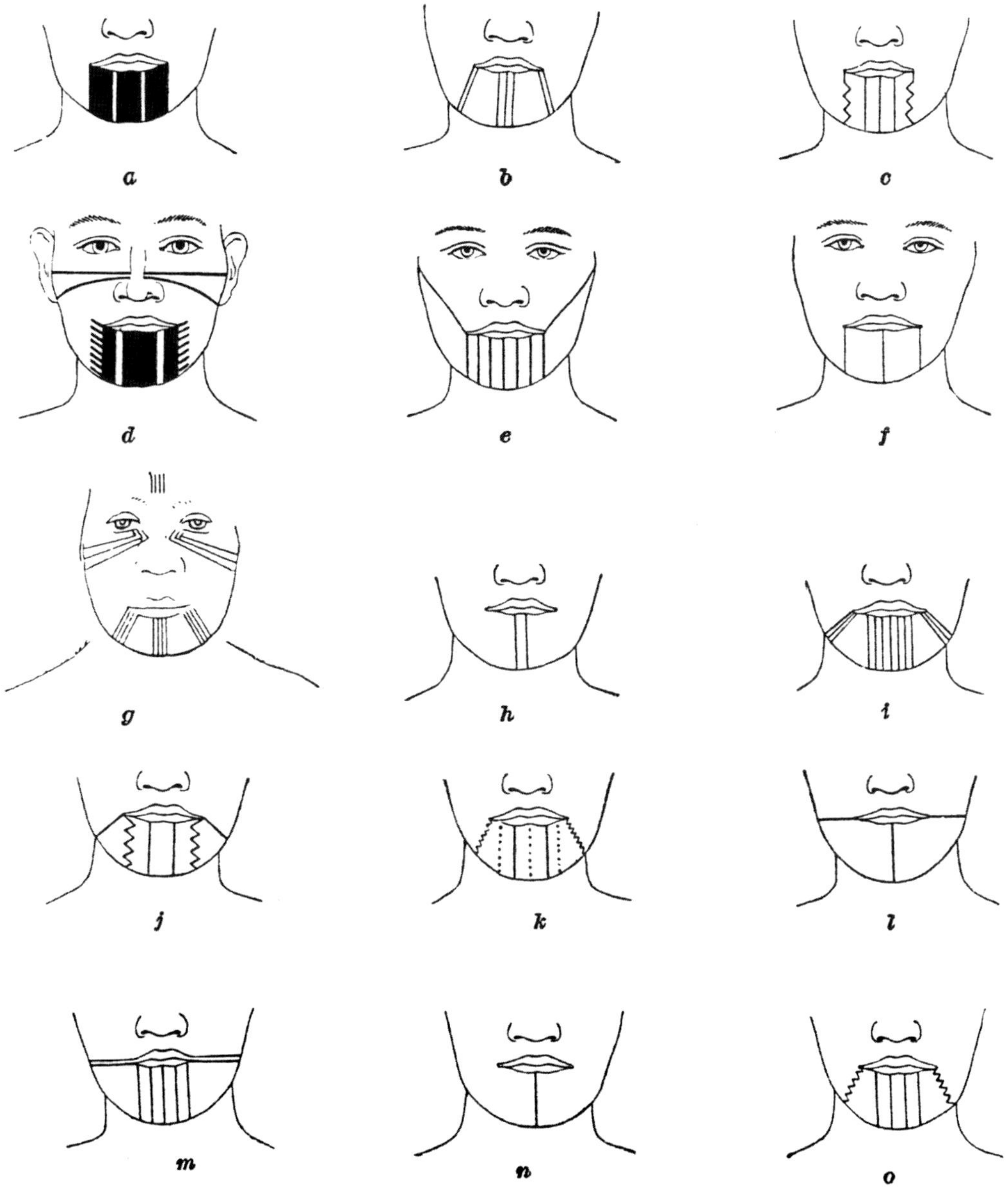

Women's facial tattooing, California: a) Yurok, b-c) Costanoan, d) Sinkyone, e-f) Maidu, g) Yuki, h-o) Chukchansi and Yokut, ca. 1920. Redrawn after Kroeber (1925: 520-521, figs. 45-46).

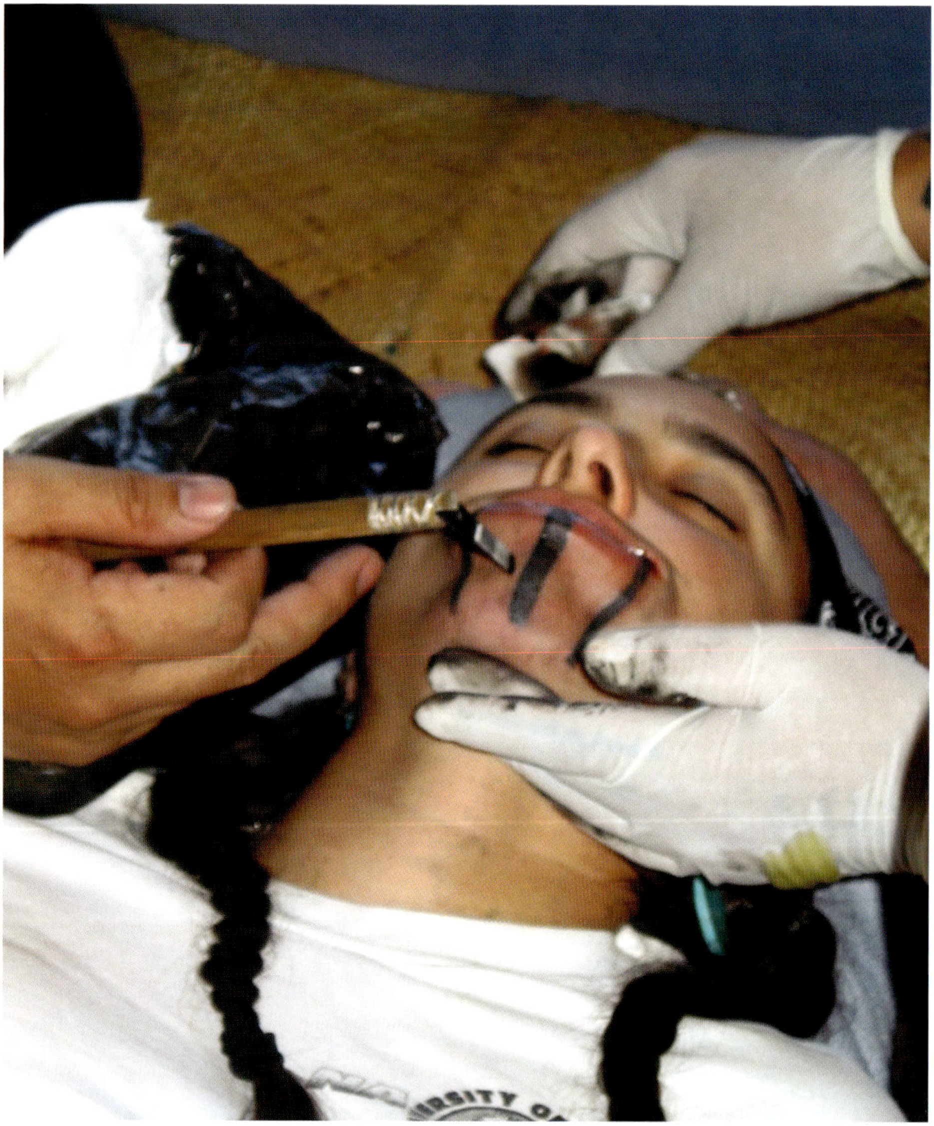

Keone Nunes tattooing a Yurok woman, 2002. Photograph courtesy of Keone Nunes. Today, traditional tattooing is making a comeback with some Northern California people like the Yurok. And about two dozen women from different indigenous groups reportedly bear the "111" tattoo on their chins. Lyn Risling, who is of Hupa, Yurok and Karok heritage said, "It's like wearing your culture on your face every day." Keone Nunes, a Native Hawaiian tattooist who is widely considered to be one of the foremost traditional hand-tapping tattooists working today, has helped spearhead this tattoo resurgence. One writer who observed a recent tattoo session stated, "As the tattoo slowly spread across [her] chin, we all felt the exact moment when the transformation occurred. It was a startling and beautiful moment that brought tears to our eyes. The shared pain and joy reminded us all of a birth. The painful bloody time had passed, and now there was a new person in our midst" (Hostler 2006).

There is, in the mountains above the old Yurok village of Meri·p, a "sacred moontime pond" where in the old days menstruating women went to bathe and to perform rituals that brought spiritual benefits. Practitioners brought special firewood back from this place for use in the menstrual shelter. Many girls performed these rites only at the time of their first menstruation, but aristocratic women went to the pond every month until menopause. Through such practice women came to "see that the earth has her moontime," a recognition that made one both "stronger" and "proud" of one's menstrual cycle.

[I]n old-time village life all of a household's fertile women who were not pregnant menstruated at the same time, a time dictated by the moon; that these women practiced the bathing rituals together at this time; and that men associated with the household used this time to "train hard" in the household's sweathouse. If a woman got out of synchronization with the moon and with the other women of the household, she could "get back in by sitting in the moonlight and talking to the moon, asking it to balance [her]."[130]

On the other hand, first-time menstruants among the Pomo, Miwok, Tubatulabal, Cahuilla, Maricopa, Tipai-Ipai, Luiseño, Havasupai, and to a lesser degree the Konkow of northern California, observed private "roasting" rites.[131] Maricopa girls lay in a hollow of sand just outside of their menstrual hut (for seclusion) and were then covered with sand. Previously a fire had been kindled in the hollow and the coals were carefully discarded. Here the girl lay in heated sand for several hours over the course of four days.[132] After a purifying tobacco beverage, a Tipai-Ipai girl laid face down, her face painted black, with a garland on her head. A warmed stone was placed between her legs to promote her future welfare and self-confidence, and to facilitate motherhood.[133] On the first day of a Luiseño girl's puberty ceremony, the menstruant was placed in a heated rock pit. On top of the stones was a layer of brush which the girl reclined upon for a period of three days and nights. Except for brief feeding periods of vegetable products (meat and fish were tabooed), the girl lay covered in the pit which was continuously surrounded by a procession of dancers and singers.[134] Then, the menstruant received counsel from an elder who, among other things, said: "And you will roast yourself at the fire (after childbirth), and then your son or daughter will grow up quickly, and sickness will not approach you."[135]

After all such private ceremonies had reached their climax (e.g. fasting, singing, dancing, and "roasting" rites) menstruants participated in a

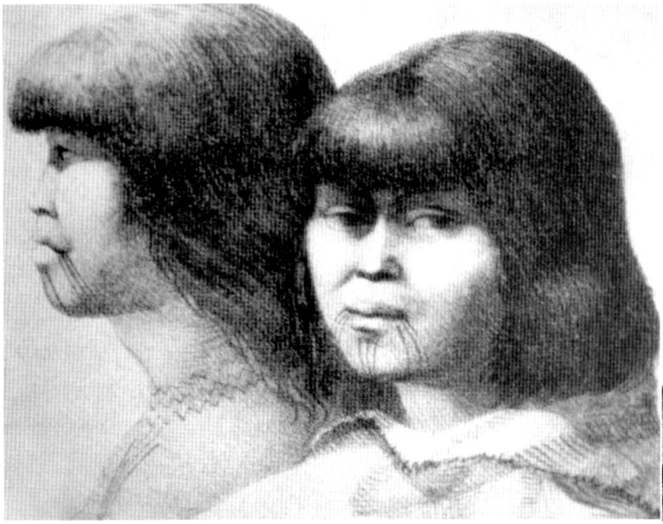

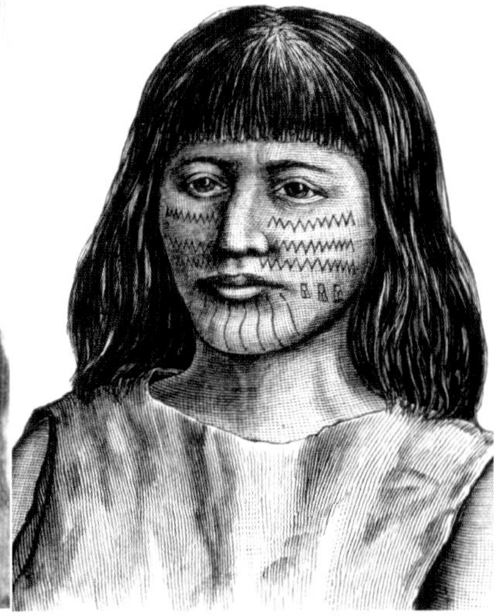

Right: Wailaki woman with facial tattooing, ca. 1870. After Powers (1877: fig. 10).

Left: Eastern Miwok women with chin and neck tattooing, 1816. Lithograph by Louis Choris (1822).

public ceremony of tattooing. Here elder women worked as the tattooist decorating the chin of the initiate and then rubbing the wounds with carbon-based pigments which had perceived purificatory properties. In turn, the menstruant—as initiate—became permanently incorporated into maternal society by her chin markings; and these tattoos symbolically solidified her physical transformation into a reproductive entity.

Tattooed skin

Tattooing performed at the time of puberty was perhaps the most important rite of passage for indigenous women among the peoples of the Gran Chaco, California, and the Native American southwest. Tattooing reconstructed personhood not only through the intervention of an exterior and environmental agent (spirits), but also through the creation of a "skin ego" which was fundamentally derived from successive stages of bodily sensations (and the memory of them) experienced at the moment of tattoo application. Tattooed skin, as the concrete boundary between the self and society, projected the psychological and biological state of the body to the external world. While at the same time, this leathery veneer worked as a boundary between the self and the world concealing a complex texture of personal power and magic illustrating an individual's desires and fears.

Tattoo patients were participants in shared pain, seclusion, transformation, and recuperation, and the skin was the location where individual and collective identity, experience, and historical memory met. Tattoo pigments and "roasting" rites, through their connection to fire, transformed female initiates into women through a symbolic process of ritual "cooking," making concrete several complicated and abstract ideas concerning the metonymic representation of the lineage through bodies, persons, and disseminations. Furthermore, tattooing enabled women to exercise control over their bodies and boundaries during the course of life and onwards into death. Because the power of the tattoos' magic not only transcended time, it provided the skin with a secondary covering that was fundamental in protecting it against the raw and spiritual elements of its environment.

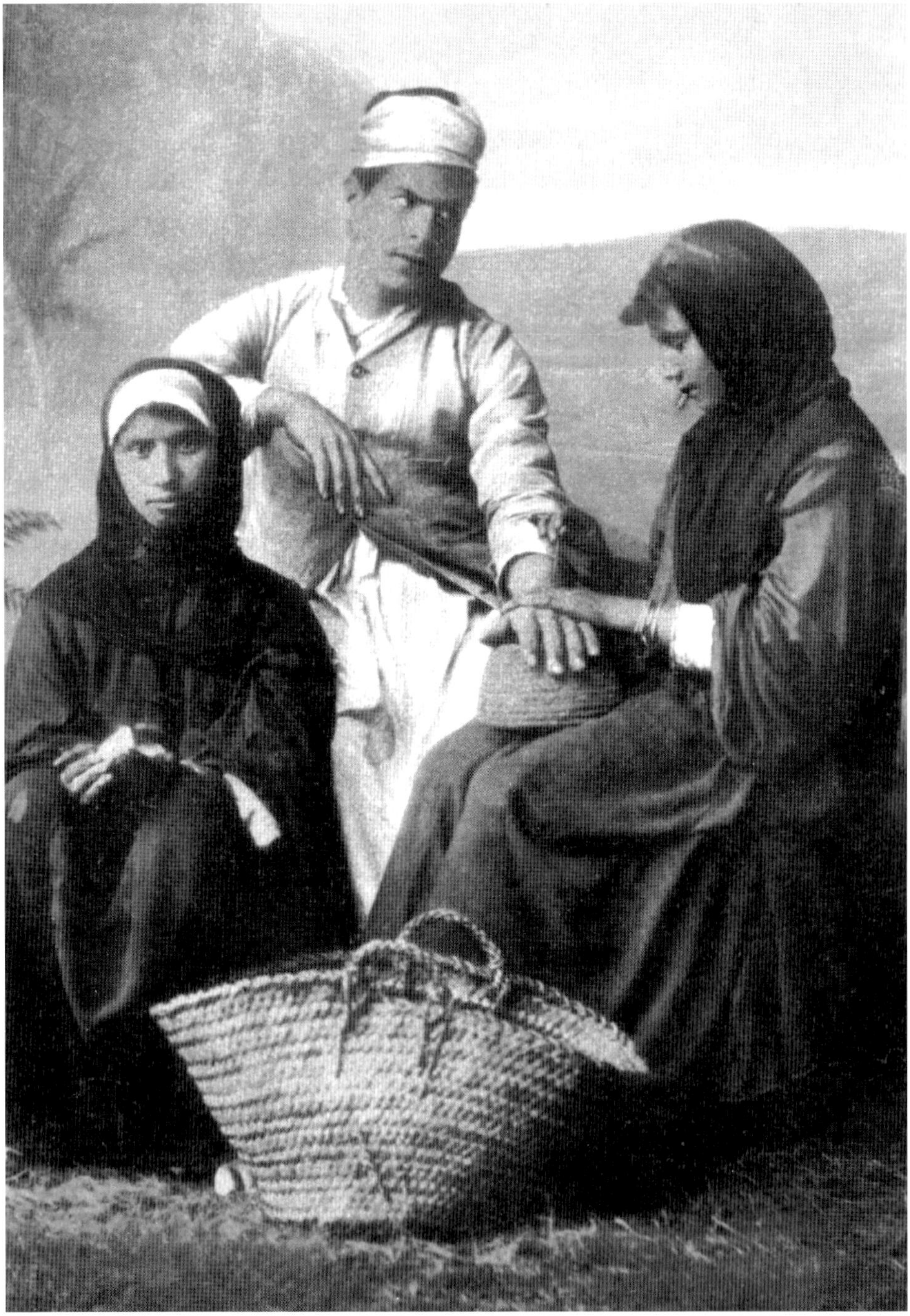

Arabs tattooing in Egypt, ca. 1920.
Postcard from the collection of the author.

Conclusion: Marks of Transformation

The indigenous need to adorn the skin with tattoos was not simply, as many early ethnographers have put it, "to make a person more beautiful." Indeed, indigenous tattoos hold an iconic allure; they adorn the body and intensify its splendor and spirituality by dramatically illuminating the human skin. However, tattoos have agency, magical power, and purpose. Some were believed to induce fertility, while others attracted prey animals, or protected women from unseen enemies or illnesses borne from spiritual contagions. Some were used to invoke the supernatural and protect ancestral lineage ensuring that tattoos were not only objects of beauty and desire, but also magical mediators between this world and the next. In this sense, the power combined in tattoo and tattooist was perhaps stronger, under certain circumstances, than that of the shaman—unless she was a tattooist herself.

Tattoo firmly anchored indigenous values on the skin by creating a visual mosaic rooted in traditional practice. Tattooing, as ritual, reenacted myth; it imitated the actions of gods and ancestors who sacrificed their own skins to make them more sacred and lasting. Although few of us today believe that our own rituals can change anything, indigenous tattoo artists certainly believed in the power of their craft, and they affected major changes in their clients. In many cases, female tattooists transformed themselves and their initiates through physical, symbolic, and metonymic processes. Sometimes these changes were due to the animism infused into what we call "pigments" and "tattoo instruments."

Moreover, tattooing functioned to communicate shared values within the group and to reduce internal dissension; and what tattoo tells us on this view is how social stability is constituted by showing us what a culture's ethos is and what sensibilities were shaped by that ethos—especially when spelled out externally on the skin and articulated via social symbolism.[1] As a symbolic collective text, tattooing thus worked to assert and inscribe affiliation, maturity and womanhood, as well as cultural pride and artistic ability.

But as a system of knowledge transmission, tattooing accounted for the ways of "being-in-the-world" by providing a visual definition of what that world was and how it was constituted through bodily experience.[2] Female bodies were not static objects or artifacts as portrayed by some photographers, rather they were subjects embodied by cumulative and ongoing processes of consciousness, memory, pain, and bodily rhythms linked to particular cultural environments. These environments surrounded the subjective body and interactively shaped it in relation to others by gradually gathering personal and collective experiences, histories, languages, and thoughts throughout lifetimes. Indigenous women got to know their worlds by moving around and through them, and by watching, listening, feeling, and actively seeking out the signs by which those worlds were revealed.[3]

From this perspective, the progressive development of indigenous knowledge and identity was constituted not only by the ways women were culturally integrated into their worlds of being through ritual (e.g. initiation, tattooing, etc.), but also by the ways they lived ordinary life within the daily routine of work and leisure. This type of life experience and the formation of the female self is the formation of an environment for that self that emerges out of a common process of maturation, and personal and collective experience.[4] In this sense, we can say that women met the world with their bodies, so that they were open to the world and not closed in by it.

For millennia the tattooed female body has served as a mediator between ancestral, human, and environmental elements, thus transcending the Cartesian absolute of a division between mind and body.[5] Inscribed bodies extended in space and place, in material culture, and to the tattooed bodies of other women—both living and dead. However, tattoos also participated in a didactic system that enculturated, instilled, and reinforced the notion that women have responsibility and are directly involved in the workings of the universe.[6] Therefore, as part of the system of tools and techniques by which indigenous women used to relate and learn about their environment, family, and culture, tattoos firmly established their identity because they were intrinsically part of daily life, experience, and society.

But over time tattooing gradually lost its importance in the cultural repertoire of many indigenous people. Disease, missionization, colonial administration, and modernity paved the way for a relinquishing of ancient customs and soon enough the rejection of traditional tattoo customs was nearly complete. By the late 19th century anthropologists and ethnographers speak of tattooing on elderly individuals, though occasionally it continued sporadically in remote areas beyond the reach of Euro-Western influences.

Today, piecing together the indelible history of indigenous tattooing practices is a painstaking process. So much does not survive the passage of time: tattoos fade to dust with the body after death, or pass into oblivion with the demise of the cultures that carried them. Yet enduring fragments worn on living bodies do remain, allowing us to partially glimpse an indigenous past that now is largely inaccessible to direct observation, but one that connects tattoo, ritual, myth, and nature from which indigenous tattoo culture ultimately sprang.

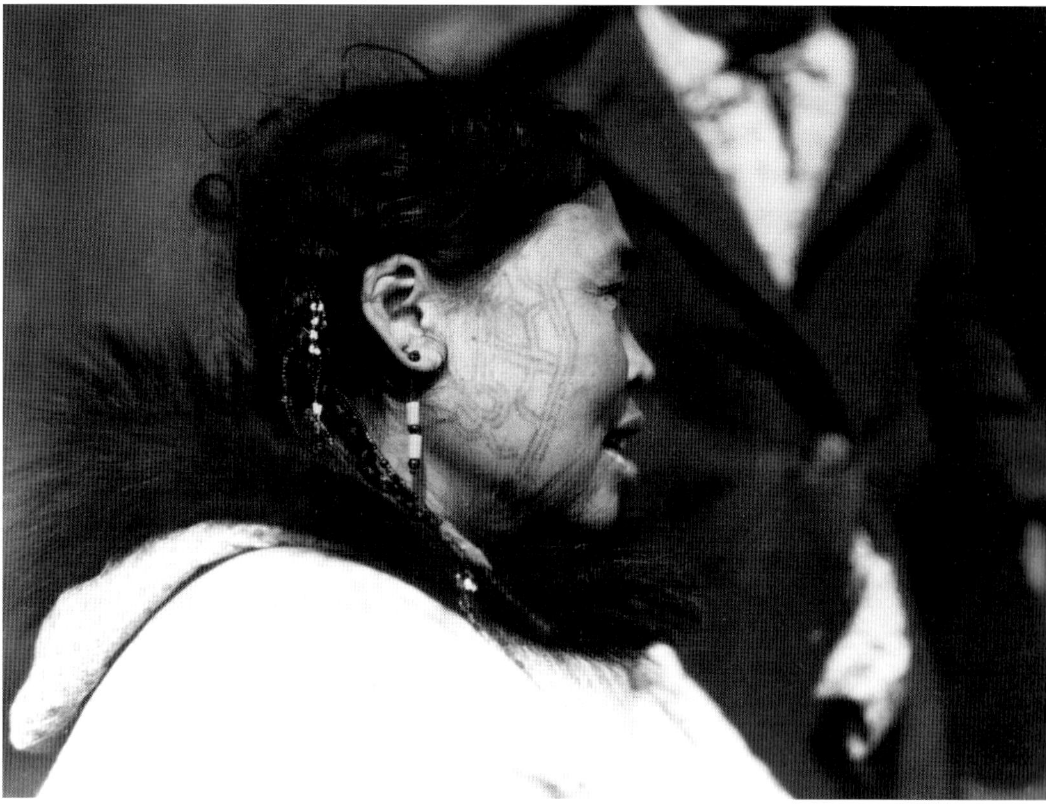

St. Lawrence Island (Alaska) Yupik tattoo.
Photograph by Dr. Leuman Waugh. Copyright
National Anthropological Archives (N-95-9742).

Notes

Introduction

1. Schuster and Carpenter (1986), 9.
2. Vogelsanger (1980).
3. McGovern (1922), 142-143.
4. Rousseau (1993).
5. J. Ting-Jui Ho (1960); Krutak (1999), (2000b).
6. Anderson and Eells (1935); Jenks (1905); Seligmann (1902).
7. Nieuwenhuis (1904), 453; Richards (1977), 265.
8. Hose and Shelford (1906), 70.
9. Karsten (1926), 111, 167.
10. Smeaton (1937), 54-44.
11. Hoppál (1993), 156.
12. cf. Casey (1997); Vitebsky (1992), 223.
13. Birket-Smith (1936), 225.
14. Spencer and Jennings (1965), 6.
15. Damas (1984), 7.
16. Fitzhugh (1999), 9.
17. Richards (1997), 11.
18. Schildkrout (2004), 237.
19. Krutak (2003a), (2004b).
20. DeMello (2000), 177.
21. Hardy (1982).
22. DeMello (2000), 88.
23. Hardy (2000), 200.
24. Hardy (1982), 6.
25. Edwards (1992), 7.
26. Rubin (1989), 12.
27. Ibid.
28. Wright (2003), 149.
29. Frič and Fričova (1997), 30.
30. Whitman (1998), 34.
31. Mason (2001), 17.
32. cf. Keesing (1997), 55.
33. Gell (1998), 6; Thomas (2001), 5.
34. Barbieri (1998); Blackburn (2000); Gell (1992); Robley (1896); Steinen (1925).

North Africa, Iraq, and the Balkans

1. Herber (1921), 69-72.
2. Field (1958), 70.
3. Ibid., 71.
4. Searight (1984, II), 177.
5. Cola Alberich (1949).
6. Kapchan (1993), 6-8; Searight (1984, II), 190-193.
7. Gobert (1956); Herber (1946); Legey (1926).
8. Searight (1984, II), 195, 235.
9. Ibid., 173.
10. Ibid., 312.
11. Coon (1931), 86.
12. Ibid.
13. Bourdieu (1990), 246-247.
14. In Kabyle riddles, the broad bean

was symbolic of death: "I put a broad bean in the ground, it didn't come up [thus] a dead man . . . I saw the dead nibbling broad beans[,] I almost died." See Genevois (1963), 10.

15. Ibid., 248.
16. cf. Kapchan (1993), 19-20.
17. Ibid., 31.
18. Bourdieu (1990), 218.
19. Ibid., 231.
20. Al-Bukhari (1903-14), cited in Searight (1984, II), 190.
21. Legey (1926), cited in Searight (1984, II), 191.
22. Michaux-Bellaire and Salmon (1905).
23. Herber (1946).
24. Westermarck (1926, I), 451.
25. Blackman (1927), 53.
26. Searight (1984, II), 192.
27. Searight (1984, I), 145.
28. Westermarck (1926).
29. Bourdieu (1990), 226-227, 250.
30. Ibid., 226.
31. Searight (1984, II), 229.
32. Westermarck (1926, I), 451.
33. Ibid., 451-452.
34. Ibid., 452.
35. Krutak (1999), 245-248; Spindler (1994), 168, 173.
36. Jereb (1996), 21.
37. Searight (1984, II), 228.
38. Gobert (1924), 75.
39. Searight (1984, II), 142-144.
40. Searight (1984, I), 67-68.
41. Touchette (1931), 18.
42. Westermarck (1926, II), 465-466.
43. Touchette (1931), 18.
44. Chantréaux (1941-42), 219.
45. Bourdieu (1990), 277.
46. Chantréaux (1941-42), 93; Genevois (1968, II), 56; Rahmani (1936), cited in Bourdieu (1990), 266.
47. Gobert (1924), 63; Roth (1905), 130; Smeaton (1937).
48. Field (1958), 68.
49. Smeaton (1937), 54-55, 59-60.
50. El Guindi (1999), 59; Fernea (1965).
51. El Guindi (1999), 86.
52. Ibid., 78.
53. Field (1958).
54. Izady (1993), 3.
55. Field (1958), 19; Izady (1993), 4.
56. Izady (1992), 153.
57. Vermaseren (1963).
58. Durham (1929); Krutak (2003a), 64.
59. Izady (1992), 249.
60. Field (1958), 19.
61. Westermark (1926), fig. 24i.
62. Cola Alberich (1949), fig. 24z.
63. Izady (1992), 249.
64. Field (1958), 19.
65. Oberling (1962).
66. cf. Davis-Kimball and Martynov (1993), 208.
67. Durham (1929), 129.
68. Ibid., 129.
69. Ibid., 121.
70. Ibid., 120.
71. Ibid., 121-122.
72. Laukien (2000), (2001a).
73. Laukien (2001a), 26.
74. Durham (1929), 104.

75. Laukien (2001a), 26; Truhelka (1896).
76. Truhelka (1896), cited in Durham (1929), 104; Laukien (2001a), 26.
77. Durham (1929), 104.
78. Ibid., 106.
79. Krutak (2003a), 64.
80. Durham (1929), 110.
81. Ibid., 110.
82. Ibid., 111.
83. Ibid., 116.
84. Krutak (2003a), 64.
85. Durham (1929), 117-118.
86. Winnifreth (1992).
87. Ibid., 74.
88. Wace and Thompson (1914), 2.
89. Krutak (2006a).
90. Ibid.; Wace and Thompson (1914), 102.
91. Wace and Thompson (1914), 102.

Taiwan and Borneo

1. Hsü (1991), 12.
2. Ho (1960), 44.
3. Hsü (1991), 12-13.
4. Ibid., 19.
5. Franck (1924), 216; Hsieh (1964), 155.
6. Formosa Bureau of Aboriginal Affairs (1911), 10, 13, 21.
7. Franck (1924), 216-217, 222.
8. Formosa Bureau of Aboriginal Affairs (1911), 21.
9. Franck (1924), 222-223.
10. McGovern (1922).
11. Norbeck (1950), 41-42.
12. Chi-Lu (1968), 247.
13. McGovern (1922), 115.
14. Ibid.
15. Chi-Lu (1968), 247.
16. McGovern (1922), 180.
17. Ibid., 147; Norbeck (1950), 28-29.
18. Campbell (1967), 23.
19. Kruijt (1906), 359-361.
20. Best (1905), 232; Taylor (1870), 231.
21. Hose and McDougall (1912), 41, 44; Tillema (1989), 163.
22. Rutter (1929), 119.
23. For Iban beliefs, see Ngadi (1998), 95, 105; and Richards (1997), 393.
24. Chi-Lu (1968), 247.
25. Ibid.
26. Norbeck (1950), 41.
27. Chi-Lu (1968), 247.
28. Ibid., 249.
29. McGovern (1922), 189.
30. Chi-Lu (1968), 249-250; Ho (1960), 46.
31. Hsü (1991), 30.
32. Chi-Lu (1968), 251.
33. Ibid.
34. Ibid.
35. Ibid.
36. Chi-Lu (1968).
37. Ho (1960).
38. Ibid., 45.
39. Sinorama (2001).
40. Ibid.; McGovern (1922), 113.
41. Norbeck (1950), 24.
42. McGovern (1922), 145-146.
43. Ibid., 124.
44. Campbell (1967), 24-25. Unfortunately, the major socio-cultural

institutions of the Atayal, including headhunting, the *gaya*, and the priestesshood, were not to last. Between 1920 and 1935, the Japanese initiated an island-wide program of forced relocation to control the Taiwanese aborigines and remove them from their ancestral lands: lands which were the basis of many inherited traditions that shaped social and life experience. This development effectively disrupted the efficacy of ancestor worship because the collective structure of the *gaya*, marked by the sharing of good luck, disaster, labor, hunting, prayer, and group responsibility for individual trespasses, soon collapsed as family members became dispersed across the country. The gradual demise of other Atayal traditions soon followed, such as weaving, headhunting, tattooing, and the communal ownership of land (see Hsü [1991], 25, 27, 35).

45. Krutak (2001a), 93.
46. Sumnik-Dekovich (1985), 101.
47. Richards (1997), 70.
48. Taylor and Aragon (1991), 147.
49. Krutak (2000c).
50. Reports (1855), 110.
51. Hose and Shelford (1906); Hose and McDougal (1912); Nieuwenhuis (1900), (1904); Tillema (1930), (1938).
52. Graham (1987), 36.
53. Krutak (2000c), (2001a), 95.
54. Graham (1987), 105; Jensen (1974), 151; Krutak (2004a).
55. Krutak (2006b); cf. Nieuwenhuis (1904), 452.
56. Howell (1909), 14: Jensen (1974), 284.
57. Graham (1987), 52, 104; Ngadi (1998), 105; Sandin (1980), 133-134.
58. Freeman (1979), 237; Graham (1987), 112-115; King (1985), 146; Taylor and Aragon (1991), 159.
59. Vayda (1975), 115.
60. Richards (1997), 375; Hose and Shelford (1906), 66-67.
61. Hose and Shelford (1906), 67, fn. 1.
62. Ibid.; Richards (1997), 84.
63. Haddon (1901), 360.
64. Lumholtz (1921).
65. Ibid.
66. Graham (1987), 82; Perham (1887), 101.
67. Gomes (1911), 211-213.
68. Zainie (1969), 26-27.
69. Haddon (1901), 395.
70. Graham (1987), 82; Lumholtz (1921); Richards (1997), 210.
71. Komanyi (1972), 102; Krutak (2004a); NHNZ (2004).
72. Vogelsanger (1980), 119.
73. Ong (1999), 9; Taylor and Aragon (1991), 168.
74. Haddon (1936), 146.
75. King (1985), 140, 146; Taylor and Aragon (1991), 159.
76. Ong (1999), 107. For example, if a weaver overstepped her com-

petency, she risked invoking the wrath of spirits who could render her *layu* or "wilted."

77. Ibid., 15.
78. Haddon (1936), 146.
79. Krutak (2004a), (2006b); Ong (1999), 106; NHNZ (2004); Vogelsanger (1980), 116.
80. Howell (1912), cited in Ong (1999), 23.
81. Graham (1987), 114.
82. Vogelsanger (1980), 118.
83. Graham (1987), 104-105; Howell (1912), cited in Ong (1999), 23.
84. Richards (1963), cited in Andaya (2004), 36-37.
85. Davidson and Sutlive (1991), cited in Andaya (2004), 37.
86. Hose and Shelford (1906), 84.
87. Haddon (1901), 373.
88. Ibid. For similar concepts regarding tattooed beads on the wrist which served to tie in the soul to the body, see Hose and McDougall (1912), 248.
89. Krutak (2006b).
90. Barton (1918), 27, 28; Ikin Salvador (2003), personal communication; Laukien (2001b), 30.
91. Hose and Shelford (1906), 68; Krutak (2003b).
92. Hose and Shelford (1906), 67.
93. Ibid., 70.
94. Ibid., 67-68.
95. Ibid., 67.
96. Ibid., 67.
97. Ibid., 68.
98. Ibid., 68.
99. Southwell (1990), 27.
100. Hose and Shelford (1906), 67.
101. Krutak (2003b).
102. Hose and Shelford (1906), 68.
103. Ibid., 67.
104. Ibid., 68.
105. Nieuwenhuis (1904).
106. Hose and Shelford (1906), 69.
107. Ibid., 69. Please note that in 1950, ten Sarawak dollars = £1, 3s, 4d (British pounds), see Geddes (1972), ix.
108. Furness (1902a), 151-152.
109. Krutak (2003b).
110. Rousseau (1998), 285.
111. Ibid., 125.
112. Ibid., 122.
113. Furness (1902a), 50-51.
114. Krutak (2003b), 73.
115. Ibid., 74.
116. Ibid., 73.
117. Ibid., 74.
118. Ibid., 74.
119. Ibid., 74.

Papua New Guinea and Easter Island

1. Krutak (2002a), 107-108; Oldham (1934), 271.
2. Ison (1974), 41, 47.
3. Barker and Tietjen (1990); NGS (2004).
4. Oldham (1934), 271; Saville (1926), 59-64.
5. Ison (1974), 43.
6. Seligmann (1902), 303.
7. Haddon (1894), 175.

8. Barton (1918), pl. X.
9. Guise (1899), 207, 215; Ison (1974), 41; Saville (1926), 59-60; Seligmann (1902), 303; Wright (2003), 153.
10. Barton (1918), 26.
11. Oldham (1934), 271.
12. Krutak (2003c,d).
13. Duke (1989), 12.
14. Seligmann (1902), 298.
15. Ibid.
16. Ibid., 299.
17. Lawes (1879), 374; Saville (1926), 285-296.
18. Guise (1899), 216.
19. Barton (1918), 24; Oldham (1934), 270; Saville (1926), 60; Seligmann (1910), 265; Turner (1878), 481.
20. Saville (1926), 60.
21. Guise (1899), 215.
22. Haddon (1901), 218; cf. Guise (1899), 216.
23. Barton (1918), 42; Chatterton (1932), 91.
24. Barton (1918), 42.
25. Ibid.
26. Dieffenback (1843), 35.
27. Best (1904), 169.
28. Jackson (1972), 50, 70-71.
29. Hau'ofa (1981), 77-83; Mosko (2002), 98; Seligmann (1910), 303-309.
30. Mosko (2002), 98.
31. Ibid., 98, 102-103.
32. Ibid., 98.
33. cf. Battaglia (1983), 292.
34. Barton (1918), 42.
35. Tregear (1891), 427.
36. Barker and Tietjen (1990), 224.
37. Guise (1899), 216.
38. Haddon (1901), 217.
39. Ison (1974), 47.
40. Seligmann (1910), 21.
41. Marquardt (1899), 12.
42. Counts (1985).
43. Barton (1918).
44. Stephen (1979), 15.
45. Seligmann (1910), 11, 322-323; Stephen (1979), 16.
46. Barker and Tietjen (1990), 228; Ison (1974), 47; Mosko (2002), 94; Seligmann (1910), 9.
47. Saville (1926), 61; Seligmann (1910), 12, 320.
48. Barton (1918), 33, 35, pl. IV.
49. Ibid., 35.
50. King (1985), 131, 132; Krutak (2001a); Thomas (1968), 215.
51. Hose and Shelford (1906); Krutak (2003b).
52. Mosko (2002), 95.
53. Guise (1899), 213.
54. Saville (1926), 57.
55. Barton (1918).
56. Ibid.
57. Schuster (1939), (1952).
58. Kjellgren (2001a), 12.
59. Ibid.
60. Schuster (1939), 232-234, (1952), 102.
61. Kjellgren (2001a), 13.
62. Métraux (1940), 55-69.
63. Kaeppler (2001), 34-35.
64. Ibid., 35.
65. Kjellgren (2001b), 58.

66. Kaeppler (2001), 37.
67. Gell (1993), 200, 203, 231, 244; Kaeppler (2001), 37; Métraux (1940), 240.
68. Métraux (1940), 237, 241.
69. Knoche (1912), 13.
70. Labiste (1998-2003).
71. Kaeppler (2001), 37.
72. Stolpe (1899), 5-6.
73. Knoche (1912), 7-8.
74. Métraux (1940), 238.
75. Ibid., 239.
76. Ibid., 237.
77. Lee (1992), 11-12.
78. Thomson (1899), 498, 533.
79. Métraux (1940), 248.
80. Ibid., 241.
81. Englert (1978), 21.
82. Métraux (1940), 242.
83. Knoche (1912), 10.
84. Englert (1978), 137.
85. Thomson (1899), 467.
86. Métraux (1940), 242.
87. Knoche (1912).
88. Ibid., 12.
89. Kjellgren (2001b), 72.
90. Métraux (1940), 244.
91. Routledge (1919).
92. Métraux (1940), 244.
93. Fuentes (1960), 816.
94. Englert (1978), 222.
95. Best (1904), cited in Gell (1993), 250.
96. Métraux (1940), 16.
97. Van Tilburg (2003), personal communication.
98. Métraux (1940), 169, 264.
99. Jackson (1972), 41, 45.
100. Ibid., 51.
101. Best (1904).
102. Wingert (1962), 325.
103. Jackson (1972), 48, 52.
104. Gell (1993), 266.
105. Fuentes (1960)
106. Jackson (1972), 50.
107. Williams (1971), cited in Gell (1993), 266.
108. Métraux (1940), 242.
109. Gell (1993), 266.
110. Métraux (1940), 248.
111. Ibid., 245.
112. Knoche (1912), figs. 5 & 6.
113. Wingert (1962), 322.
114. Best (1925), 1014.
115. Métraux (1940), 241.
116. Ibid.
117. Stolpe (1899).
118. Métraux (1940), 243.
119. Schuster (1939); (1952).
120. Lee (1992), 12, 14, 20.
121. Métraux (1940), 245.
122. Stolpe (1899).
123. Van Tilburg (2001), 31.
124. Kjellgren (2001a), 17.
125. Lee (1992), 14.
126. Kjellgren (2001a), 17.
127. Lee (1992), 14.
128. Jackson (1972), 55.
129. Kaeppler (2001), 35.
130. Jackson (1972), 56.
131. Fuentes (1960), 785; Tregear (1891), 222.

Japan, Northwest Coast, and Arctic

1. Fitzhugh (1999), 9.
2. Dubreuil (2003), 70.
3. Ibid., 70; Yamaura and Ushiro (1999), 40.
4. Dubreuil (2003), 72; Yamaura and Ushiro (1999), 40.
5. Yamaura and Ushiro (1999), 43.
6. McCallum (1988).
7. Krutak (1998); Okladnikov (1981).
8. Batchelor (1882), 213.
9. Van Gulik (1982), 194.
10. Honda (2000).
11. Dubreuil (1999), 325.
12. Hilger (1971), 150.
13. Van Gulik (1982), 238.
14. Bird (1881), 80.
15. Hilger (1971), 150.
16. Keira and Keira (1999), 235; Van Gulik (1982), 234-236.
17. Hilger (1977), 152.
18. Van Gulik (1982), 189.
19. Honda (2000), 138.
20. Munro (1963), 119.
21. Watanabe (1999), 199.
22. Ibid.
23. Van Gulik (1982), 220.
24. Hitchcock (1891), 442.
25. Honda (2000).
26. Dubreuil (1999), 292; Munro (1963), 117.
27. Hilger (1971), 151.
28. Ibid.
29. Bird (1881).
30. Dubreuil (1999), 294.
31. Kodama (1970), 121.
32. Van Gulik (1982), 215.
33. Munro (1963).
34. Van Gulik (1982), 215.
35. Tosabayashi (1948).
36. Van Gulik (1982), 216-217.
37. Philippi (1979), 50.
38. Munro (1963), 149.
39. Ibid., 143.
40. Ibid., 118.
41. Van Gulik (1982), 221.
42. Ibid.
43. Dubreuil (1999), 294.
44. Schurtz (1896), 246; Montandon (1937), 159
45. Akino (1999), 252, 255.
46. Yamaura and Ushiro (1999), 42.
47. Van Deusen (1997), 153.
48. Ibid.
49. Dubreuil (1999), 292, 296-297.
50. Ibid., 296-297.
51. Dubreuil (2003), 82-86.
52. Krutak (2002b), 12.
53. Blackman (1990), 249-251; Dauenhauer and Dauenhauer (1995), 21.
54. Krutak (2000a), 23.
55. De Laguna (1990), 213.
56. Oberg (1973), 44.
57. De Laguna (1990), 213; Krutak (2002b), 12; Swanton (1908), 415-420.
58. Oberg (1973).
59. Ibid., 51.
60. De Laguna (1972), 455.
61. Dauenhauer and Dauenhauer (1994), 15.
62. Ibid.
63. De Laguna (1972), 274.
64. Ibid., 459.

65. Krutak (2000a), 28.
66. Swanton (1908), 415.
67. Krutak (2000a), 26; (2002b), 12.
68. Krutak (2000a), 26.
69. Blackman (1990), 249-50; De Laguna (1990), 213, 215; Krutak (2000a), 28; (2002b).
70. De Laguna (1972), 457.
71. Krutak (2002b).
72. De Laguna (1990), 220.
73. Ibid.
74. Krutak (2000a), 21.
75. Olson (1967), 68-69.
76. De Laguna (1990), 221.
77. Ibid.; Emmons (1991), 253.
78. Olson (1967), 68-69.
79. Emmons (1991), 253.
80. Swanton (1905), 169.
81. Dawson (1880), 182b.
82. Krutak (2002b); Niblack (1888), 257: Swan (1874).
83. Krutak (2002b), 12.
84. Ibid., 12-13.
85. Emmons (1991), 253.
86. Ibid., 254.
87. Krutak (1998), (2000b).
88. Krutak (1999).
89. Turner (1887), n.p.; see also Turner (1894), 102.
90. Krutak (1998), (2000b).
91. Frobisher (1867[1578]), 621, 628.
92. Gilder (1881), 250.
93. Geist (1927-34), n.p.
94. Krutak (1998), 22-27.
95. Bogoras (1904-9), 298.
96. Hughes (1959), 90.
97. Silook (1940), 105-108.
98. Krutak (2003e), 14.
99. Geist (1927-34), n.p.
100. Krutak (1998), 23.
101. Ibid.
102. Ibid.
103. Oosten (1997), 88.
104. Bogoras (1904-9), 298.
105. Krutak (2003e), 15.
106. Schuster (1951).
107. Krutak (1998), 28.
108. Petersen (1996), 67.
109. Weyer (1932), 321.
110. Holm (1914), 112.
111. Krutak (1998), 32.
112. Silook (1940), 105.
113. Nelson (1899), 422.
114. Krutak (1998), 34.
115. Krutak (1999), 231.
116. Buijs and Oosten (1997), 7; Nelson (1899), 423; Oosten (1976), 72-74; Rasmussen (1929), 191, (1931), 181.
117. Krutak (1998), 34.
118. Ibid., 35.
119. Spencer (1959), 340.
120. Gordon (1906).
121. Hawkes (n.d.), 22.
122. Gordon (1906); Stevenson (1967), 39.
123. Mousalimas (1997), 8; Oosten (1997), 98.
124. Fienup-Riordan (1986), 263.
125. Hultkrantz (1965), 308.
126. Nuttall (2000), 42.
127. Ibid., 37.
128. Krutak (1998), 37.
129. Bogoras (1904-9), 457-460; Campbell (1988, 1989); Eliade (1964), 165-168; Lissner (1961),

272-274; Lommel (1967), 19; Segy (1976).
130. Krutak (1998), 38.
131. Bogoras (1904-9), 343; Collins (1930a), 79; Krutak (1998), 38, (2003e), 18-19; Moore (1923), 345.
132. Bogoras (1904-9).
133. Chamisso (1986[1836]), 172.
134. Nelson (1899), 52.
135. Bogoras (1904-9), 256.
136. Anderson and Eells (1935), 175.
137. Gordon (1906); Weyer (1932), 316-317.
138. Collins (1930b), n.p.
139. Collins (1930a), 90.
140. Coe (1976), 111.
141. Fitzhugh and Kaplan (1982), 186.
142. Silook (1940), 68.
143. Leighton (1982[1940]), 16-17.
144. Krutak (1998), 45.
145. Anderson and Eells (1935), 175.
146. Bogojavlensky (1969), 158.
147. Hughes (1959), 72.
148. Bogoras (1904-9), 359.
149. Bodenhorn (1990), 65.
150. Doty (1900), 218.
151. Bogoras (1904-9), 254.
152. Krutak (1998), 49.
153. Neuman (1917), 5.
154. Bogoras (1904-9), 254.
155. Driscoll (1987), 198.
156. Krutak (1998), 52.
157. Neuman (1917), 5.
158. Krutak (1998), 52.
159. Krutak (2003e), 25.
160. Hughes (1960), 90.
161. Krutak (1999), 230; Rudenko (1949).
162. Anderson and Eells (1935), 175.
163. Gordon (1906), 81.
164. Nelson (1899), 309-310.
165. Lantis (1984), 173.
166. Krutak (1999), 231.
167. Fortuine (1985), 35.
168. Krutak (1999), 231.
169. Weyer (1932), 324.
170. Krutak (1999), 231-232.
171. Compilation (1981).
172. Krutak (1998), 58; (1999), 231.
173. Chu (1979), 7.
174. Scheper-Hughes and Lock (1987), 12.
175. Krutak (1999), 232-244.
176. Chu (1979), 32.
177. Ibid., 2.
178. Marsh and Laughlin (1956).
179. Lantis (1984), 174.
180. Krutak (1999).
181. Kapel et al. (1991).
182. Holm (1914), 29.
183. Krutak (1999), 244.
184. Smith and Zimmerman (1975), 433.
185. Holm (1914).
186. Steller (1741), cited in Golder (1925, II), 103.
187. Clark (1984), 136.
188. Pullar and Knecht (1995), 15.
189. Clark (1984), 187.
190. Langsdorff (1813-14), 40.
191. Merck (1980[1790-1791]), 103, 170.
192. Veniaminov (1840, II), 113.
193. Hrdlička (1945), 83; Lisiansky (1812, II), 73, 81.
194. Krutak (2001b).
195. Lisiansky (1814), 195.

196. Cook and King (1784, II), 357; Rickman (1782, II), 243.
197. Davydov (1977[1802-7]), 149.
198. Ibid.
199. Coxe (1803), 195; Davydov (1977[1802-7]), 104.
200. Langsdorff (1813-14), 38-39.
201. Black (1991).
202. Jochelson (1933), 10.
203. Hrdlička (1945), 89, 109, 183.
204. Lisiansky (1812, II), 58.
205. Black (1991), 65.
206. Ibid., 40.
207. Fitzhugh (1993), 7.
208. Krutak (2001b).
209. Cook and King (1784, III), 1427.
210. Bushnell (1928), 8.
211. Merck (1980[1790]), 102.
212. Davydov (1977[1802-7]), 48.
213. Laughlin (1983), 41.
214. Laughlin (1980), 104.
215. Marsh and Laughlin (1956), 40.
216. Laughlin (1980), 103.
217. Ibid., 114-115.
218. Keddie (1989), 8.
219. Langsdorff (1813-14), 47-48.
220. Sauer (1802), 176.
221. Sarychev (1806-7).
222. Davydov (1810-1812), cited in Hrdlička (1944), 79.
223. Saladin D'Anglure (1994), 83.
224. Clark (1984), 194; Lantis (1984), 178; Merck (1980), 107.
225. Rasmussen (1931), 209.
226. Black (1977), 99.
227. Veniaminov (1840, II), 122, 125-126.
228. Bogoras (1904-9), 450.
229. Ibid., 450-451.
230. Eicher and Roach-Higgins (1992), 26; Frazier (1960); Gell (1993); Karsten (1926); Keddie (1981); Krutak (1999).

South America, California, and the American Southwest

1. Allison (1996), 127; Allison et al. (1981), 220. Archaeological evidence indicates that the earliest form of tattooing was cosmetic. And around 8,000 years ago, at least one man of the Chinchorro culture of Chile was tattooed with what looks like a small mustache on his upper lip.
2. cf. Anzieu (1989), 50.
3. Allison et al. (1981).
4. Allison (1996), 127.
5. Allison et al. (1981), 221.
6. Knol (1990). Genipap is also known as *jagua* or *huito* in Spanish-speaking areas.
7. Karsten (1926), 13, 39, 192; Levi-Strauss (1970), 166; Steward (1946), (1948); von den Steinen (1899), 32-33.
8. Karsten (1926), 13, 39, 63, 232.
9. Horton (1948), 278; Karsten (1923a), 18, 25, 38-39, 43-48; Rivet (1907-8), 248.
10. Castner et al. (1998), 55; Morton (1987), 443.
11. Duke and Vasquez (1994), 79.
12. Castner et al. (1998), 55; Morton (1987), 443.
13. Morton (1987), 443.

14. Allison et al. (1981), 221.
15. Ibid.
16. Alva and Donnan (1994); Cordry-Collins (2001); Proulx (1996); Silverman and Proulx (2002).
17. Proulx (2001), 121.
18. Proulx (1996), 110-112; Silverman and Proulx (2002), 229.
19. Franck (1924), 227; Freeman (197); Jacobs (1990), 121; Jenks (1905), 174; Karsten (1923a), 89, (1926), 66.
20. Alva and Donnan (1994), 127-141; Kolata (1993); Paul (1990), (1996), 429-430; Proulx (1996), 111-115; Verano (2001), 115-116.
21. Benson (2001), 9; Rowe (1995), 30.
22. Cordry-Collins (1996), 190.
23. Alva and Donnan (1994); Bourget (2001a,b); Verano (2001).
24. Bourget (2001a), 106.
25. Bourget (2001b), 100-102; Verano (2001), 116.
26. Donnan (1996), 137-139; Joyce (1908), 17-18.
27. Donnan (1996), 137.
28. Ibid., 139.
29. Donnan (2004), personal communication.
30. Ubbelohde-Doering (1967).
31. Gwin (2004).
32. Williams (2006).
33. Alva and Donnan (1994).
34. Verano (2001), 114.
35. Alva and Donnan (1994), 127-141; Verano (2001), 114.
36. Donnan and McClelland (1999).
37. Schuster (1952).
38. Barton (1918); Schuster (1939), (1952), 102-103.
39. Barton (1949), 238; Furness (1902b), 455; Godden (1898), 21; Jenks (1905), 188; Loeb (1935), 186; Salvador (2004); Vanoverbergh (1929), 203; Volz (1905); Worchester (1912), 879-893.
40. Ho (1960), 23, pl. 10.
41. Schuster (1952), 103-104.
42. Benson (1997), 104; Berezkin (1980), 3.
43. Rea (1986), cited in Benson (1997), 88.
44. Schuster (1952), 104.
45. Bourget (2001a), 93.
46. Jenks (1905), 214-215; Karsten (1923a), 24; McGovern (1922), 145-146; Richards (1972), 74; Smith (1925), 95.
47. cf. Barton (1918), 74; Gomes (1911), 140; Hutton (1921), 208; Karsten (1923a), 45; Smith (1925), 95.
48. cf. Gell (1993), 307.
49. Bourget (2004), personal communication.
50. Paul (1982), (1990), (1996), 356; Proulx (2004), personal communication; Schindler (2000), 35, 41; Seler (1923), 206-210; Wolfe (1981).
51. cf. Allen (1981), 45.
52. Barton (1918), 28, 77; Schuster and Carpenter (1986), 469; Vanoverbergh (1929), 204.
53. cf. Gell (1998), 139-141.
54. Schuster and Carpenter (1996), 59.

55. Salvador (2003), personal communication.
56. Salvador (2005), personal communication.
57. Herndon (1853), 314.
58. Murphy (1958), 53.
59. Horton (1948), 275.
60. Herndon (1853), 314.
61. Ibid.
62. Horton (1948), 276; Murphy and Murphy (1974), 52.
63. Nadelson (1996), 242.
64. Murphy (1958), 22.
65. Kruse (1934), 57; Murphy (1956), 427.
66. Murphy and Murphy (1974), 90.
67. Horton (1948), 281; Murphy (1958), 12.
68. Horton (1948), 281; Tocantins (1877).
69. Horton (1948), 280.
70. Nadelson (1996).
71. Viveiros de Castro (2004), 464.
72. Ibid., 464-465.
73. Nadelson (1996), 260.
74. Ibid., 250, 253, 260.
75. Horton (1948), 275.
76. Karsten (1926), 83.
77. Murphy (1958), 55.
78. Benson (1997), 73; Paul (1990), 80-83.
79. Paul (1996), 359.
80. Ibid., 359; Paul and Turpin (1986), 24.
81. Paul and Turpin (1986), 24.
82. Karsten (1926), 77.
83. Murphy (1958), 54.
84. Murphy (1974), 80.
85. Horton (1948), 278.
86. Murphy (1960), 127.
87. Horton (1948), 278; Murphy (1974), 80.
88. Karsten (1926), 67.
89. Murphy (1958), 55, 58.
90. Murphy (1974), 81-82.
91. Ibid., 81.
92. Murphy (1958), 58.
93. Murphy (1974), 80-81.
94. Murphy (1958), 54.
95. Ibid., 55.
96. Ibid.
97. Métraux (1946), 197.
98. Nordenskiold (1910), (1912).
99. Rosen (1924), 75.
100. Karsten (1926), 190; Rosen (1924), 75-76.
101. Karsten (1926), 190.
102. Furlong (1938), 24-25.
103. Karsten (1926), 189.
104. Ibid., 191.
105. Ibid.
106. Bove (1883), 134 cited in Karsten (1926), 191.
107. Karsten (1926), 191.
108. Métraux (1946), 354.
109. Karsten (1923b), (1926); Métraux (1946), 353; Nordenskiöld (1999), 101.
110. Karsten (1926), 10.
111. Karsten (1923b), 26.
112. Ibid., 28.
113. Ibid., 26-27.
114. Karsten (1926), 12-13.
115. Karsten (1923b), 27, 65, (1926), 11; Métraux (1946), 323.

116. Karsten (1932), 91.
117. Karsten (1926), 114.
118. cf. Métraux (1946), 323, 352.
119. Grubb (1911), 125; Karsten (1926), 272-273.
120. Viveiros de Castro (2004), 466, 468.
121. Elasser (1978), 196; Foster (1944), 181; Gayton (1948), 69-70; Kroeber (1925), 519; Levy (1978a), 407, (1978b), 495; Merriam (1966), 85-95; Powers (1877); Sapir (1936), 273.
122. Gifford (1933), 277; Luomala (1978), 603; Spier (1933), 207.
123. Bean and Shipek (1978), 556; Dixon (1905), 233-237; Du Bois (1935), 52-54; Elsasser (1978), 196; Essene (1942); Harrington (1955), 23; Lapena (1978), 328, 336; Luomala (1978), 598, 603; Riddell (1978), 381; Rose (1979), 11-12; Spier (1930), 314-325, (1933), 102, 324-327; Wallace (1978), 451, 455.
124. Riddell (1978), 381; Spier (1930), 323.
125. Lapena (1978), 328.
126. Spier (1930), 318.
127. Rose (1979), 19-20; Spier (1923), (1930), 325; (1933), 268.
128. Buckley (1988), 192.
129. Buckley and Gottlieb (1988), 7.
130. Buckley (1988), 190-191, 194-195.
131. Riddell (1978), 381; Spier (1930), 318.
132. Spier (1933), 325.
133. Luomala (1978), 603.
134. Sparkman (1908), 224-225.
135. Ibid., 225.

Conclusion

1. cf. Connerton (1994), 49-50.
2. cf. Clammer et al. (2004).
3. cf. Ingold (2004), 39.
4. Ibid., 40.
5. Poirier (2004), 60.
6. Rubin (1989), 16.

Literature

Akino, Shigeki. (1999). "Spirit-Sending Ceremonies." Pp. 248-255 in *Ainu: Spirit of a Northern People* (W.W. Fitzhugh and C. O. Dubreuil, eds.). Washington: Smithsonian Institution.

Allen, Catherine J. (1981). "The Nasca Creatures: Some Problems of Iconography." *Anthropology* V(1): 43-70.

Allison, J. Marvin. (1996). "Early Mummies from Coastal Peru and Chile." Pp. 125-130 in *The Man in Ice*, vol. 3, *Human Mummies, A Global Survey of Their Status and the Techniques of Conservation* (K. Spindler, H. Wilfring, E. Rastbichler-Zissernig, D. zur Nedden, H. Nothdurfter, eds.). Vienna: Springer.

Allison, J. Marvin, Lawrence Lindberg, Calogero Santoro, and Guillermo Foracci. (1981). "Tatuajes y Pintura Corporal de Los Indígenas Precolumbinos de Perú y Chile." *Chungara* 7: 218-225.

Alva, Walter and Christopher B. Donnan. (1994). *Royal Tombs of Sipán*. Los Angeles: UCLA Fowler Museum of Cultural History.

Andaya, Barbara Watson. (2004). "History, Headhunting and Gender in Monsoon Asia: Comparative and Longitudinal Views." *South East Asia Research* 12(1): 13-52.

Anderson, H. Dewey and Walter C. Eells. (1935). *Alaska Natives: A Survey of Their Sociological and Educational Status*. Stanford: University of Stanford Press.

Anzieu, Didier. (1989). *The Skin Ego*. New Haven, Conn.: Yale University Press.

Barbieri, Gian Paolo. (1998). *Tahiti Tattoos*. Köln: Taschen.

Barker, John and Anne Marie Tietjen. (1990). "Women's Facial Tattooing Among the Maisin of Oro Province, Papua New Guinea: The Changing Significance of an Ancient Custom." *Oceania* 60(3): 217-234.

Barton, Francis R. (1918). "Tattooing in South Eastern New Guinea." *Journal of the Royal Anthropological Institute of Great Britain and Ireland* 48: 22-79.

Barton, Roy F. (1949). *The Kalingas: Their Institutions and Custom Law*. Chicago: University of Chicago Press.

Batchelor, John. (1882). "Notes on the Ainu." Transactions of the Asiatic Society of Japan X (II): 206-219.

—— (1901). *The Ainu and Their Folk-Lore*. London: The Religious Tract Society.

—— (1927). *Ainu Life and Lore: Echoes of a Departing Race*. Tokyo: Kyobunkan.

Battaglia, Debbora. (1983). "Projecting Personhood in Melanesia: The Dialectics of Artefact Symbolism on Sabarl Island." *Man* (n.s.) 18: 289-304.

Bean, Lowell John and Florence C. Shipek. (1978). "Luiseño." Pp. 550-563 in *California*, vol. 8, *Handbook of North American Indians* (R. F. Heizer, ed.). Washington: Smithsonian Institution Press.

Benson, Elizabeth P. (1997). *Birds and Beasts of Ancient Latin America*. Gainesville: University of Florida Press.

—— (2001). "Why Sacrifice?" Pp. 1-20 in *Ritual Sacrifice in Ancient Peru* (E.P. Benson and A.G. Cook, eds.). Austin: University of Texas Press.

Berezkin, Yuri E. (1980). "An Identification of Anthropomorphic Mythological Personages in Moche Representations." *Ñawpa Pacha* 18: 1-26.

Bertholon, L. J. and E. Chantre. (1913). *Récherches anthropologiques dans la Bérberie Orientale/Tripolitaine, Tunisie, Algerie*. Lyon: A. Rey. 2 vols.

Best, Elsdon. (1904). "The Uhi-Maori or Native Tattooing Implements." *Journal of the Polynesian Society* 13: 166-172.

—— (1905). "Maori Eschatology." *Transactions of the New Zealand Institute* (38): 147-239.

—— (1925). *Tuhoe*, vol. 1. Memoirs of the Polynesian Society 6. New Plymouth: Thomas Avery and Sons Ltd.

—— (1952). *The Maori as He Was: A Brief Account of Maori Life as it Was in Pre-European Days.* Wellington: R.E. Owen.

Bird, Isabella L. (1881). *Unbeaten Tracks in Japan: An Account of Travels on Horseback in the Interior Including Visits to the Aborigines of Yezo and the Shrines of Nikkô and Isé*, vol. II. New York: G.P. Putnam's Sons.

Birket-Smith, Kaj. (1936). *The Eskimos* (W.E. Calvert, trans.). London: Methuen.

Black, Lydia T. (1977). "The Konyag (the Inhabitants of the Island of Kodiak) by Iosaf [Bolotov] (1784-1799) and by Gideon (1804-1807)." *Arctic Anthropology* 14(2): 79-108.

—— (1991). "The Hunter's Dress as Metaphor of Power." Pp. 63-67 in *Proceedings of the 5th International Abashiri Symposium: Hunting Rituals of Northern Peoples.* Abashiri: Abashiri Museum of Northern Peoples.

Blackburn, Mark. (2000). *Tattoos from Paradise: Traditional Polynesian Patterns.* Atglen, PA: Schiffer Publishing, Ltd.

Blackman, Margaret. (1990). "Haida: Traditional Culture." Pp. 240-260 in *Northwest Coast*, vol. 7, *Handbook of North American Indians* (W. Suttles, ed.). Washington: Smithsonian Institution Press.

Blackman, Winifred S. (1927). *The Fellāhīn of Upper Egypt*. London: George G. Harrap & Co., Ltd.

Boas, Franz. (1901-1907). The Eskimo of Baffin Land and Hudson Bay. *Bulletin of the American Museum of Natural History* 15. New York.

Bodenhorn, Barbara. (1990). "'I'm Not the Great Hunter, My Wife Is': Iñupiat and Anthropological Models of Gender." *Études/Inuit/Studies* 14(1-2): 55-74.

Bogojavlensky, Sergei. (1969). *Imaangmiut Eskimo Careers: Skinboats in Bering Strait*. (Unpublished Ph.D. Dissertation in Social Relations, Harvard University, Cambridge, Mass.)

Bogoras, Waldemar. (also Bogoraz, V.G.). (1904-9). The Chukchee. *The Jesup North Pacific Expedition* 7, *Memoirs of the American Museum of Natural History*. New York.

Bourdieu, Pierre. (1990). *The Logic of Practice*. Stanford: Stanford University Press.

Bourget, Steve. (2001a). "Rituals of Sacrifice: Its Practices at Huaca de la Luna and Its Representation in Moche Iconography." Pp. 89-109 in *Moche Art and Archaeology in Ancient Peru* (J. Pillsbury, ed.). Washington: National Gallery of Art.

—— (2001b). "Children and Ancestors: Ritual Practices at the Moche Site of Huaca de la Luna, North Coast of Peru." Pp. 93-118 in *Ritual Sacrifice in Ancient Peru* (E.P. Benson and A. Cook, eds.). Austin: University of Texas Press.

Bove, Giacomo. (1883). *Expedición Austral Argentina*. Buenos Aires: Imp. del Departamento Nacional de Agricultura.

Buckley, Thomas. (1988). "Menstruation and the Power of Yurok Women." Pp. 187-209 in *Blood Magic: The Anthropology of Menstruation* (T. Buckley and A. Gottlieb, eds.). Berkeley: University of California Press.

Buckley, Thomas and Alma Gottlieb. (1988). "A Critical Appraisal of Theories of Menstrual Symbolism." Pp. 3-50 in *Blood Magic: The Anthropology of Menstruation* (T. Buckley and A. Gottlieb, eds.). Berkeley: University of California Press.

Buijs, Cunera and Jarich Oosten. (1997). "Continuity and Change in Arctic Clothing: An Introduction." Pp. 1-10 in *Braving the Cold: Continuity and Change in Arctic Clothing* (C. Buijs and J. Oosten, eds.). Leiden: CNWS.

Bushnell, David I., Jr. (1928). Drawings by John Webber of Natives of the Northwest Coast of America, 1778. *Smithsonian Miscellaneous Collections* 80(10). Washington.

Campbell, Joseph. (1988). *Historical Atlas of World Mythology*. Vol. I: *The Way of the Animal Powers* (2 Parts). New York: Harper & Row.

—— (1989). *Historical Atlas of World Mythology*. Vol. II: *The Way of the Seeded Earth* (3 Parts). New York: Harper & Row.

Campbell, Rev. William. (1967). *Formosa Under the Dutch: Described from Contemporary Records with Explanatory Notes and a Bibliography of the Island.* Taipei: Ch'eng-wen Publishing Company.

Cantwell, John C. (1902). *Report of the U.S. Steamer Nunivak on the Yukon River Station, Alaska, 1899-1901.* Washington: U.S. Government Printing Office.

Carton, L. (1909). "Ornementation et stigmates tégumentaires chez les indigenes de l'Afrique du nord." *Mémoires de la Société d'Anthropologie de Bruxelles* 28: 1-128.

Casey, Edward S. (1997). "How to Get from Space to Place in a Fairly Short Stretch of Time: Phenomenological Prolegomenon." Pp. 13-52 in *Senses of Place* (S. Feld and K. Basso, eds.). Santa Fe: School of American Research Press.

Castner, James L., Stephen L. Timme and James A. Duke. (1998). *A Field Guide to Medicinal and Useful Plants of the Upper Amazon*. Gainesville, Fl: Feline Press.

Chamisso, Adelbert von. (1986[1836]). *A Voyage Around the World with the Romanzov Exploring Expedition in the Years 1815-1818 in the Brig Rurik*. (H. Kratz, trans. and ed., reprinted 1986. Honolulu: University of Hawaii Press.)

Chantréaux, G. (1941-1942). "Le tissage sur métier de haute-lisse à Aït Hichem et dans le Haut-Sebaou." *Revue Africaine* 85: 78-116, 212-229; 86: 261-313.

Chatterton, Percy (ed.). (1932). *A Dictionary of the Motu Language of Papua* (R. Lister-Turner and J.B. Clark, comps). 2nd ed. Sydney: A.H. Pettifer.

Chi-Lu, Chen. (1968). *Material Culture of the Formosan Aborigines*. Taipei: The Taiwan Museum.

Choris, Ludovik (Louis). (1822). *Voyage pittoresque autour du monde, avec des portraits de sauvages d'Amérique, d'Asie, d'Afrique, et des îles du Grand Océan* . . . Paris: Firmin Didot.

Chu, L.S.W., S.D.J. Yeh, and D.D. Wood. (1979). *Acupuncture Manual: A Western Approach*. New York: Marcel Dekker, Inc.

Clammer, John, Sylvie Poirier, and Eric Schwimmer. (2004). "Introduction: The Relevance of Ontologies in Anthropology—Reflections on a New Anthropological Field." Pp. 3-22 in *Figured Worlds: Ontological Obstacles in Intercultural Relations* (J. Clammer, S. Poirier, and E. Schwimmer, eds.). Toronto: University of Toronto Press.

Clark, Donald W. (1984). "Pacific Eskimo: Historical Ethnography." Pp. 185-197 in *Arctic*, vol. 5, *Handbook of the North American Indians* (D. Damas, ed.). Washington: Smithsonian Institution Press.

Codrington, Rev. R.H. (1891). *The Melanesians: Studies in Their Anthropology and Folk-lore*. Oxford: Clarendon Press.

Coe, Ralph T. (1976). *Sacred Circles: Two Thousand Years of North American Indian Art*. Arts Council of Great Britain. London: Lund Humphries.

Cola Alberich, Julio. (1949). *Amuletos y tatuajes marroquíes*. Madrid: Instituto de Estudios Africanos.
Collins, Henry B., Jr. (1929). "Prehistoric Art of the Alaskan Eskimo." *Smithsonian Miscellaneous Collections* 81(14): 1-52.
—— (1930a). "Notebook A." Unpublished Fieldnotes from the H.B. Collins Collection, Box 45, St. Lawrence Island. National Anthropological Archives, National Museum of Natural History, Smithsonian Institution. Washington.
—— (1930b). "Ethnographic Information: St. Lawrence Island 1/15/30." Unpublished Fieldnotes from the H.B. Collins Collection, Box 54. National Anthropological Archives, National Museum of Natural History, Smithsonian Institution, Washington.
[Compilation.] (1981). *Essentials of Chinese Acupuncture*. Oxford: Pergamon Press.
Connerton, Paul. (1994). *How Societies Remember*. Cambridge: Cambridge University Press.
Cook, J. and J. King. (1784). *A Voyage to the Pacific Ocean Undertaken, by the Command of His Majesty, for Making Discoveries in the Northern Hemisphere. Performed Under the Direction of Captains Cook, Clarke, and Gore, in His Majesty's Ships the Resolutions and Discovery; in the Years 1776, 1777, 1778, 1779, and 1780*. 3 vols. London: G. Nicol and T. Cadell.
Coon, Carleton S. (1931). *Tribes of the Rif*. Cambridge, MA: Peabody Museum of Harvard University.
Cordry-Collins, Alana. (1996). "Lambayeque." Pp. 189-222 in *Andean Art at Dumbarton Oaks*, vol. 1 (E.H. Boone, ed.). Washington: Dumbarton Oaks.
—— (2001). "Blood and the Moon Priestesses: Spondylus Shells in Moche Ceremony." Pp. 35-54 in *Ritual Sacrifice in Ancient Peru* (E.P. Benson and A. Cook, eds.). Austin: University of Texas Press.
Counts, Dorothy A. (1985). Infant Care and Feeding in West New Britain." Pp. 155-170 in *Infant Care and Feeding in the South Pacific* (L. B. Marshall, ed.). New York: Gordon and Breach.
Coxe, William. (1803). *Account of the Russian Discoveries Between Asia and America to Which Are Added, the Conquest of Siberia and the History of the Transactions and Commerce Between Russia and China*. 4th enl. ed. London: Cadell and Davies.

Damas, David. (1984). "Introduction." Pp. 1-7 in *Arctic*, vol. 5, *Handbook of the North American Indians* (D. Damas, ed.). Washington: Smithsonian Institution Press.
Dauenhauer, Nora M. and Richard Dauenhauer (eds.). (1994). *Haa Kusteeyí, Our Culture: Tlingit Life Stories*. Classics of Tlingit Oral Literature, vol. 3. Seattle: University of Washington Press.

—— (1995). “Tlingit.” Pp. 20-21 in *Crossroads Alaska: Native Cultures of Alaska and Siberia* (V. Chaussonnet, ed.). Washington: Smithsonian Institution Press.

Davidson, J. and V.H. Sutlive, Jr. (1991). “The Children of Nising: Images of Headhunting and Male Sexuality in Iban Ritual and Oral Literature.” Pp. 153-220 in *Female and Male in Borneo: Contributions and Challenges to Gender Studies* (V.H. Sutlive, ed.). Williamsburg, VA: Borneo Research Council.

Davis-Kimball, Jeannine and Anatoly I. Martynov. (1993). “Solar Rock Art and Cultures of Central Asia.” Pp. 207-222 in *The Sun: Symbol of Power and Life* (M. Singh, comp.). New York: Harry N. Abrams.

Davydov, Gavrila Ivanovich. (1810-1812). *Dvukratnoe puteshestvie v Ameriku morskikh ofitserov Khvostova I Davydova, pisannoe sim posliednim* [A Double Voyage to America by the Naval Officers Khvostov and Davydov, Written by the Latter]. St. Petersburg: Morskaia Tipografiia.

—— (1977). Two Voyages to Russian America, 1802-1807 (R.A. Pierce, ed.). *Materials for the Study of Alaska History* 10. Kingston, Ont.: Limestone Press.

Dawson, George M. (1880). “Report on the Queen Charlotte Islands, 1878.” Pp. 1B-239B in *Geological Survey of Canada. Report of Progress for 1878-1879.* Montreal.

De Laguna, Frederica. (1972). Under Mount Saint Elias: The History and Culture of the Yakutat Tlingit. 3 pts. *Smithsonian Contributions to Anthropology* 7. Washington.

—— (1990). “Tlingit.” Pp. 203-228 in *Northwest Coast*, vol. 7, *Handbook of North American Indians* (W. Suttles, ed.). Washington: Smithsonian Institution Press.

DeMello, Margo. (2000). *Bodies of Inscription: A Cultural History of the Modern Tattoo Community*. Durham: Duke University Press.

Dieffenbach, E. (1843). *Travels in New Zealand*, vol. 2. London: John Murray.

Dixon, Roland B. (1905). “The Northern Maidu.” *Bulletin of the American Museum of Natural History* 17(3): 119-346. New York.

Donnan, Christopher B. (1978). *Moche Art of Peru*. Los Angeles: UCLA Fowler Museum of Cultural History.

—— (1996). “Moche.” Pp. 123-162 in *Andean Art at Dumbarton Oaks*, vol. 1 (E.H. Boone, ed.). Washington: Dumbarton Oaks.

Donnan, Christopher B. and Donna McClelland. (1999). *Moche Fineline Painting: Its Evolution and Its Artists*. Los Angeles: UCLA Fowler Museum of Cultural History.

Doty, William F. (1900). “The Eskimo on St. Lawrence Island, Alaska.” Pp. 186-223 in *9th Annual Report on Introduction of Domestic Reindeer into Alaska* (S. Jackson, comp.). Washington: U.S. Government Printing Office.

Driscoll, Bernadette. (1987). “The Inuit Parka as an Artistic Tradition.” Pp. 170-

200 in *The Spirit Sings: Artistic Traditions of Canada's First Peoples* (D.F. Cameron, ed.). Toronto: McClelland and Stewart.
Du Bois, Cora A. (1935). "Wintu Ethnography." *University of California Publications in American Archaeology and Ethnology* 36(1): 1-148. Berkeley.
Dubreuil, Chisato O. (1999). "Ainu Art: The Beginnings of Tradition." Pp. 287-300 in *Ainu: Spirit of a Northern People* (W.W. Fitzhugh and C. O. Dubreuil, eds.). Washington: Smithsonian Institution.
—— (2003). "The Enduring Art of the Ainu." *Tribal* 8(1): 70-91.
Duke, James A. (1989). *Handbook of Nuts*. Boca Raton, Fl: CRC Press.
Duke, James A. and Rodolfo Vasquez. (1994). *Amazonian Ethnobotanical Dictionary*. CRC Press.
Durham, Mary E. (1929). *Some Tribal Origins Laws and Customs of the Balkans*. New York: Macmillan Co.

Edwards, Elizabeth. (1992). "Introduction." Pp 3-17 in *Anthropology and Photography 1860-1920* (E. Edwards, ed.). New Haven: Yale University Press.
Eicher, Joanne B. and Mary E. Roach-Higgins. (1992). "Definition and Classification of Dress: Implications for Analysis of Gender Roles." Pp. 8-28 in *Dress and Gender: Making and Meaning* (R. Barnes and J.B. Eicher, eds.). Oxford: Berg.
El Bokhari. (1903-14). *Les traditions d'Islam* (O. Houdas, trans.). Paris.
El Guindi, Fadwa. (1999). *Veil: Modesty, Privacy, and Resistance*. Oxford: Berg.
Eliade, Mircea. (1964). *Shamanism: Archaic Techniques of Ecstasy* (W.T. Trask, trans.). Bollinger Series 76. Princeton: Princeton University Press.
Elsasser, Albert B. (1978). "Mattole, Nongatl, Sinkyone, Lassik, and Wailaki." Pp. 190-204 in *California*, vol. 8, *Handbook of North American Indians* (R. F. Heizer, ed.). Washington: Smithsonian Institution Press.
Emmons, George T. (1991). *The Tlingit Indians* (F. de Laguna, ed.). Anthropological Papers of the American Museum of Natural History 70. Seattle: University of Washington Press.
Englert, Sebastián. (1978). *Idioma rapanui: gramática y diccionario del antiguo idioma de la Isla de Pascua*. Santiago: Universidad de Chile.
Esaka, Teruya. (1967). *Dogū*. Tokyo.
Essene, Frank. (1942). "Culture Element Distributions: XXI—Round Valley." *Anthropological Records* 8(1): 1-97.

Fernea, Elizabeth W. (1965). *Guests of the Sheik: An Ethnography of an Iraqi Village*. Garden City, NY: Doubleday, Anchor Books.

Field, Henry. (1958). "Body-Marking in Southwestern Asia." *Papers of the Peabody Museum of Archaeology and Ethnology, Harvard University* XLV, no. 1.

Fienup-Riordan, Ann. (1986). "The Real People: The Concept of Personhood Among the Yup'ik of Western Alaska." *Études/Inuit/Studies* 10(1-2): 261-270.

Finsch, Otto. (1885). "Ueber Bekleidung, Schmuck und Tätowirung der Papuas der Südostküste von Neu-Guinea." *Mitteilungen der Anthropologischen Gesellschaft in Wien* XV.

Fitzhugh, William W. (1993). "Art and Iconography in the Hunting Ritual of North Pacific Peoples." Pp. 1-13 in *Proceedings of the 7th International Abashiri Symposium*. Abashiri: Abashiri Museum of Northern Peoples.

—— (1999). "Ainu Ethnicity: A History." Pp. 9-27 in *Ainu: Spirit of a Northern People* (W.W. Fitzhugh and C. O. Dubreuil, eds.). Washington: Smithsonian Institution.

Fitzhugh, William W. and Susan Kaplan. (1982). *Inua: Spirit World of the Bering Sea Eskimo*. Washington: Smithsonian Institution Press.

Formosa Bureau of Aboriginal Affairs. (1911). *Report on the Control of the Aborigines in Formosa*. Taihoku: Bureau of Aboriginal Affairs.

Fortuine, Robert. (1985). "Lancets of Stone: Traditional Methods of Surgery among the Alaska Natives." *Arctic Anthropology* 22(1): 23-45.

Foster, George M. (1944). "A Summary of Yuki Culture." *University of California Anthropological Records* 5(3): 155-244. Berkeley.

Franck, Harry A. (1924). *Glimpses of Japan and Formosa*. New York: Century.

Fraser, John F. (1909). *Quant Subjects of the King*. London: Cassell and Co.

Frazier, Sir James G. (1960). *The Golden Bough*. New York: Macmillan.

Freeman, John D. (1979). "Severed Heads that Germinate." Pp. 233-246 in *Fantasy and Symbol* (R.H. Hook, ed.). London: Academic Press.

Frič, Pavel and Yvonna Fričová. (1997). *Guido Boggiani: Photographer*. Praha: Titanic.

Fritze, Adolph. (1893). "Ein Besusch bei den Ainu." *Globus* LXIV (3): 41-47.

Frobisher, Sir Martin. (1867[1578]). *A True Discourse of the Late Voyages of Discovery for Finding of a Passage to Cathaya and India by the North West*. London: no publisher. (Reprinted: The Three Voyages of Martin Frobisher . . . Works Issued by the Hakluyt Society, 1st ser. Vol. 38, London, 1867.)

Fuentes, Jordi. (1960). *Diccionario y Gramática de la Lengua de la Isla de Pascua: Pascuense-Castellano; Castellano-Pascuense*. Santiago: Editorial Andrés Bello.

Furlong, Guillermo. (1938). *Entre Los Abipones del Chaco: Según Noticias de los Misioneros Jesuitas Martin Dobrizhoffer, Domingo Muriel, José Brigniel, Joaquín Camaño, José Jolis, Pedro Juan Andreu, José Cardiel y Vicente Olcina*. Buenos Aires.

Furness, W.H. (1902a). *The Home-Life of Borneo Head-Hunters: Its Festivals and Folklore*. Philadelphia: J.B. Lippincott Company.
—— (1902b). "The Ethnography of the Nagas of Eastern Assam." *Journal of the Royal Anthropological Institute* 32: 445-466.

Ganjing, Augustine A. (2001). *Basic Iban Design: An Introduction* (G. Ngadi, trans.). Kuala Lumpur: Dewan Bahasa dan Pustaka.
Gayton, Anna H. (1948). "Yokuts and Western Mono Ethnography." *University of California Anthropological Records* 10(1-2): 1-302. Berkeley.
Geddes, W.R. (1972). *Nine Dayak Nights*. London: Oxford University Press.
Geist, Otto W. (1927-1934). Field Notes. On file, Alaska and Polar Regions Archives, University of Alaska, Fairbanks.
Gell, Alfred. (1993). *Wrapping in Images: Tattooing in Polynesia*. Oxford: Clarendon Press.
—— (1998). *Art and Agency: An Anthropological Theory*. Oxford: Clarendon Press.
Genevois, H. (1963). *Trois cent cinquante enigmas kabyles*. Fort-National: Fichier de documentation berbére.
—— (1968). *Superstition, recours des femmes kabyles*. Fort-National: Fichier de documentation berbére, nos. 97; 100.
Gifford, Edward W. (1933). "The Cocopa." *University of California Publications in American Archaeology and Ethnology* 31(5): 257-334. Berkeley.
Gilder, William H. (1881). *Schwatka's Search: Sledging in the Arctic in Quest of the Franklin Records*. New York: Charles Scribner's Sons.
Glück, Leopold. (1894). "Die Tätowirung der Haut bei den Katholiken Bosniens und der Hercegovina." *Wissenschaftliche Mitteilungen aus Bosniens und der Herzegowina*, sv. 2. str. 455-462.
Gobert, E. (1924). "Notes sur les tatouages des indigénes tunisiens." *L'Anthropologie* 34: 57-90.
—— (1956). "Remarques sur les tatouages nord-africains." *Revue Africaine* 100: 446-449.
Godden, Gertrude, M. (1898). "Naga and Other Frontier Tribes of North-East India." *Journal of the Royal Anthropological Institute* 27: 2-51.
Golder, Frank A. (1922-25). Bering's Voyages: An Account of the Efforts of the Russians to Determine the Relation of Asia and America. 2 vols. *American Geographical Society Research Series 1-2*. New York.
Gomes, Edwin H. (1911). *Seventeen Years Among the Sea Dyaks of Borneo*. London: Seeley.
Gordon, George B. (1906). "Notes on the Western Eskimo." *Transactions of the*

Department of Archaeology, Free Museum of Science and Art 2(1): 69-101. Philadelphia.
Graham, Penelope. (1987). *Iban Shamanism: An Analysis of the Ethnographic Literature*. Canberra: Australian National University Press.
Grubb, Wilfrid B. (1911). *An Unknown People in an Unknown Land; An Account of the Life and Customs of the Lengua Indians of the Paraguayan Chaco, with Adventures and Experiences Met with During Twenty Years Pioneering and Exploration amongst Them*. Philadelphia: J.B. Lippincott Company.
Guise, R.E. (1899). "On the Tribes Inhabiting the Mouth of the Wanigela River, New Guinea." *Journal of the Anthropological Institute of Britain and Ireland* 28(3-4): 205-219.
Gwin, Peter. (2004). "Temple of Doom." *National Geographic Magazine* 206(1): 102-117.

Haddon, Alfred C. (1894). *The Decorative Art of British New Guinea: A Study in Papuan Ethnography*. Dublin: Academy House.
—— (1901). *Head-hunters; Black, White, and Brown*. London: Methuen & Co.
—— (1936). *Iban or Sea Dayak Fabrics and Their Patterns: A Descriptive Catalogue of the Iban in the Museum of Archaeology and Ethnology Cambridge*. Cambridge: Cambridge University Press.
Hardy, Don Ed. (1982). "New Tribalism." Pp. 4-9 in *TattooTime: New Tribalism*, no. 1 (D.E. Hardy, ed.). Honolulu: Hardy Marks Publications.
—— (2000). "Current Events." Pp. 196-207 in *Tattoo History: A Source Book* (S. Gilbert, ed.). New York: Juno Books.
Harrington, M. R. (1955). "Ancient Life Among the Southern California Indians." *Southwest Museum Leaflets* 26: 1-38.
Hau'ofa, Epeli. (1981). *Mekeo: Inequality and Ambivalence in a Village Society*. Canberra: Australian National University Press.
Hawkes, Edward W. (n.d). "Notes on the Asiatic Eskimo." Unpublished notes from the Bogoras Papers, Box 131-F-4, fldr. E 1.1. New York City Public Library.
Herber, J. (1921). "Tatouages marocains: tatouage et religion." *Revue de l'Histoire des Religions* 83: 69-83.
—— (1923). "Les tatouages du pied au Maroc." *L'Anthropologie* 33: 87-102.
—— (1946). Les tatouages de la face chez la Marocaine." *Hespéris* 33(3-4): 323-351.
—— (1949). "Les tatouages du cou, de la poitrine et du genou chez la Marocaine." *Hespéris* 36(3-4): 333-346.
Herndon, William L. (1853). *Exploration of the Valley of the Amazon*. Washington: Robert Armstrong.

Hilger, M. Inez. (1971). *Together with the Ainu: A Vanishing People*. Norman: University of Oklahoma Press.

Hitchcock, Romyn. (1891). "The Ainos of Yezo, Japan." Pp. 428-502 in *Report of the U.S. National Museum for 1889-1890*. Washington: U.S. Government Printing Office.

Ho, J. Ting-Jui. (1960). "A Study on Tattooing Customs among the Formosan Aborigines." *Bulletin of the Department of Archaeology and Anthropology* 15: 1-48.

Holm, Gustav F. (1914). Ethnological Sketch of the Angmagsalik Eskimo. *Meddelelser om Grønland* 39. Copenhagen.

Honda, Katsuichi. (2000). *Harukor: An Ainu Woman's Tale* (K. Selden, trans.). Berkeley: University of California Press.

Hoppál, Mihaly. (1993). "Pain in Shamanic Initiation." Pp. 151-157 in *Northern Religions and Shamanism* (M. Hoppál and J. Pentikainen, eds.). Budapest: Akadémiai Kiadó.

Horton, Donald. (1948). "The Mundurucú." Pp. 271-282 in *Handbook of South American Indians* (J.H. Steward, ed.), vol. 3, *The Tropical Forest Tribes*. Washington: U.S. Government Printing Office.

Hose, Charles and W. McDougall. (1912). *The Pagan Tribes of Borneo*. London: Macmillan and Co., Ltd.

Hose, Charles and R. Shelford. (1906). "Materials for a Study of Tatu in Borneo." *The Journal of the Anthropological Institute of Great Britain and Ireland* 36: 60-91.

Hostler, Allie. (2006). "Taking It on the Chin." http://www.reznetnews.org/culture/051121_tattoo/

Howell, William. (1909). "The Sea Dyak Religion." Pp. 14-17 in *The Sea Dyaks and other Races of Sarawak: Contributions to the Sarawak Gazette between 1888 and 1930*. Kuching: Borneo Literature Bureau.

—— (1912). "The Sea-Dyak Method of Making and Dyeing Thread from Their Home-grown Cotton." *Sarawak Museum Journal* 1: 61-64.

Hrdlička, Aleš. (1944). *The Anthropology of Kodiak Island*. Philadelphia: The Wistar Institute of Anatomy and Biology.

—— (1945). *The Aleutian and Commander Islands and Their Inhabitants*. Philadelphia: The Wistar Institute of Anatomy and Biology.

Hsieh, Chiao-min. (1964). *Taiwan—Ilha Formosa: A Geography in Perspective*. Washington: Butterworths.

Hsü, Mu-Chu. (1991). *Culture, Self, and Adaptation: The Psychological Anthropology of Two Malayo-Polynesian Groups in Taiwan*. Taipei: Institute of Ethnology, Academia Sinica.

Hughes, Charles C. (1959). "Translation of I.K. Voblov's 'Eskimo Ceremonies.'" *Anthropological Papers of the University of Alaska* 7(2): 71-90.

—— (1960). *An Eskimo Village in the Modern World*. Ithaca, N.Y.: Cornell University Press.

Hultkrantz, Åke. (1965). "Type of Religion in the Arctic Hunting Cultures: A Religio-Ecological Approach." Pp. 265-318 in *Hunting and Fishing* (H. Hvarfner, ed.). Luleå: Norrbottens Museum.

Hutton, J.H. (1921). *The Angami Nagas: With Some Notes on Neighboring Tribes*. London: Macmillan and Co., Ltd.

Ingold, Tim. (2004). "A Circumpolar Night's Dream." Pp. 25-57 in *Figured Worlds: Ontological Obstacles in Intercultural Relations* (J. Clammer, S. Poirier, and E. Schwimmer, eds.). Toronto: University of Toronto Press.

Inō, Y. (1910). "The Marks of the Chiefs among the Tsarisen [Rukai] in Formosa." *Journal of the Anthropological Society of Tokyo*. 25: 131-140.

Ison, Barry. (1974). "Motu Tattoos from Pari and Hanuabada." *Gigibori* 1(1): 41-57.

Izady, Mehrdad R. (1992). *The Kurds: A Concise Handbook*. London: Crane Russak.

—— (1993). "Exploring Kurdish Origins." *Kurdish Life* 7: 2-6.

Jackson, Michael. (1972). "Aspects of Symbolism and Composition in Maori Art." *Bijgragen tot de Taal-, Land-en Volkenkunde* 128: 33-80.

Jackson, Sheldon. (1902). *Eleventh Annual Report on the Introduction of Domesticated Reindeer into Alaska*. Washington: U.S. Government Printing Office.

Jacobs, Julian. (1990). *The Nagas, Hill Peoples of Northeast India: Society, Culture and the Colonial Encounter*. London: Thames and Hudson.

Jenks, Albert E. (1905). *The Bontoc Igorot*. Manila: Bureau of Public Printing.

Jensen, Erik. (1974). *The Iban and Their Religion*. Oxford: Clarendon Press.

Jereb, James F. (1996). *Arts and Crafts of Morocco*. San Francisco: Chronicle Books.

Jochelson, Waldemar. (1933). History, Ethnology and Anthropology of the Aleut. *Carnegie Institution of Washington Publication* 432. Washington.

Joyce, Thomas. (1908). "The Southern Limit of Inlaid and Incrusted Work in Ancient Peru." *American Anthropologist* 19: 16-23.

Kaeppler, Adrienne L. (2001). "Rapa Nui Art and Aesthetics." Pp. 32-41 in *Splendid Isolation: Art of Easter Island* (E. Kjellgren, ed.). New York: The Metropolitan Museum of Art.

Kapchan, Deborah. (1993). "Moroccan Women's Body Signs." Pp. 3-35 in *Bodylore* (K. Young, ed.). Knoxville: University of Tennessee Press.

Kapel, H., N. Kronmann, F. Mikkelsen, and E.L. Rosenlov. (1991). "Tattooing." Pp. 102-115 in *The Greenland Mummies* (J.P.H. Hansen, J. Meldgaard, J. Nordqvist, eds.). London: British Museum Publications.

Karsten, Rafael. (1923a). *Blood Revenge, War, and Victory Feasts Among the Jibaro Indians of Eastern Ecuador.* Wash, D.C.: United States Government Printing Office. BAE Bulletin 79.

—— (1923b). "The Toba Indians of the Bolivian Gran Chaco." *Acta Akademi Aboensis* 4: 1-126.

—— (1926). *Civilization of the South American Indians: With Special Reference to Magic and Religion.* London: Kegan Paul.

—— (1932). *Indian Tribes of the Argentine and Bolivian Chaco.* Helsingfors: Ethnological Studies, Societas Scientiarum Fennica, vol. 4(1).

Keddie, Grant. (1981). "The Use and Distribution of Labrets on the North Pacific Rim." *Syesis* 14: 59-80.

—— (1989). "Symbolism and Context: The World History of the Labret and Cultural Diffusion on the Pacific Rim." (Unpublished paper presented at the Circum-Pacific Prehistory Conference, Seattle. Pp. 1-27.)

Keesing, Roger. (1997). "Experienced Bodies as Contested Sites." *Visual Anthropology* 13(1): 52-58.

Keira, Mitsunori and Tomoko Keira. (1999). "Village Work: Gender Roles and Seasonal Work." Pp. 234-239 in *Ainu: Spirit of a Northern People* (W.W. Fitzhugh and C. O. Dubreuil, eds.). Washington: Smithsonian Institution.

King, Michael. (1972). *Moko: Maori Tattooing in the 20th Century.* Wellington: Alister Taylor.

King, Victor T. (1985). "Symbols of Social Differentiation: A Comparative Investigation of Signs, the Signified and Symbolic Meanings in Borneo." *Anthropos* 80: 125-152.

Kjellgren, Eric. (2001a). "Introduction: Remote Possibilities." Pp. 11-23 in *Splendid Isolation: Art of Easter Island* (E. Kjellgren, ed.). New York: Metropolitan Museum of Art.

—— (2001b). "Catalogue." Pp. 42-78 in *Splendid Isolation: Art of Easter Island* (E. Kjellgren, ed.). New York: Metropolitan Museum of Art.

Knoche, Walter. (1912). *Tres notas sobre la isla de Pascua: I. Observaciones de algunas pinturas, en sus reproducciones. II. Los últimos tatuajes en la isla de Pascua. III. Un cuento y dos canciones.* Santiago, Chile: Imprenta universitaria.

Knol, Ann S. (1990). "SIUC Botanist Cooks up an Old Recipe." http://

www.science.siu.edu/plantbiology/emeritus/ugent/news/ugent15.htm
Kodama, Sakuzaemon. (1970). *Ainu: Historical and Anthropological Studies*. Sapporo: Hokkaido University School of Medicine.
Kolata, Alan. (1993). *The Tiwanaku: Portrait of an Andean Civilization*. Cambridge, MA: Blackwell.
Komanyi, Gitta I. (1972). *The Real and Ideal Participation in Decision-making of Iban Women: A Study of a Longhouse Community in Sarawak, East Malaysia*. (Unpublished Ph.D. dissertation, New York University, New York City, NY.)
Krieg, Hans. (1934). *Chaco-Indianer: Wissenschaftliche Ergebnisse der Deutschen Gran Chaco-Expedition*. Stuttgart: Verlag von Strecker und Schröder.
Kroeber, Alfred L. (1925). Handbook of the Indians of California. *Bureau of American Ethnology Bulletin* 78. Washington: U.S. Government Printing Office.
Kruijt, Albertus C. (1906). *Het Animisme in der Indischen Archipel*. 's-Gravenhage: Martinus Nijhoff.
Kruse, Rev. Albert. (1934). "Mundurucú Moieties." *Primitive Man* 7(4): 51-57.
Krutak, Lars. (1998). *One Stitch at a Time: Ivalu and Sivuqaq Tattoo*. (Unpublished Master's Thesis, University of Alaska Fairbanks, Fairbanks, AK.)
—— (1999). "St. Lawrence Island Joint-Tattooing: Spiritual/Medicinal Functions and Inter-Continental Possibilities." *Études/Inuit/Studies* 23(1-2): 229-252.
—— (2000a). "Harriman-Cape Fox Village Collection." Technical Report, *National Museum of the American Indian* (NMAI). (On file NMAI Office of Repatriation, Suitland, MD. 90 pp.)
—— (2000b). "The Arctic." Pp. 172-185 in *Tattoo History: A Source Book* (S. Gilbert, ed.). New York: Juno Books.
—— (2000c). "In the Realm of Spirits: Traditional Dayak Tattoo in Borneo." http://www.vanishingtattoo.com/borneo_tattoos_1.htm
—— (2001a). "Der Passierschenin Ins Totenreich: Traditionelle Tätowierungen der Dayak auf Borneo" [In the Realm of Spirits: Traditional Dayak Tattoo in Borneo]. *Tätowier Magazin*. February. Pp. 92-98.
—— (2001b). "Piercing Praktiken auf den Aleuten" [Piercing Practices of the Aleut]. *TätowierMagazin*. July. Pp. 112-118.
—— (2002a). "Der Vergessene Code: Stammestätowierungen in Papua NeuGuinea" [The Forgotten Code: Tribal Tattoo in Papua New Guinea]. *TätowierMagazin*. July. Pp. 106-111.
—— (2002b). "Rediscovered! An Early Haida Tattoo Kit from the Queen Charlotte Islands." *Skin and Ink*. November. Pp. 11-13.
—— (2003a). "Landmines and Tough Times: Tattoo Art in Kosovo." *Skin and Ink*. July. Pp. 61-67.

—— (2003b). “Fackel ins Jenseits: Tätowierungen der Orang Ulu auf Borneo” [Torches for the Afterlife: Tattooing of the Orang Ulu of Borneo]. *TätowierMagazin*. April. Pp. 70-74.
—— (2003c). “Rapa Nui Skin: Easter Island Ink.” *Skin and Ink*. November. Pp. 14-16.
—— (2003d). “Die Vergessenen Tätowierungen der Osterinsulaner: Rapa Nui” [The Forgotten Tattooing of the Easter Islanders: Rapa Nui]. *TätowierMagazin*. March. Pp. 56-59.
—— (2003e). *Uglalghii Keluk Unguvalleghmun: Many Stitches for Life, History of St. Lawrence Island Tattoo*. (Unpublished Manuscript. 101 pp.)
—— (2004a). “Der Krieg der Frauen: Die Webarbeiten der Skrang-Iban” [The War of Women: Weavers of the Skrang Iban]. *TätowierMagazin*. January. Pp. 62-65.
—— (2004b). “Four Tattoo Artists in Havana.” *Skin and Ink*. January. Pp. 68-77.
—— (2006a). “Greece’s Oldest—Jimmy’s Tattoo Studio.” *Skin and Ink*. February. Pp. 14-16.
—— (2006b). “Tattoos of the Iban Weaver’s Art.” *Skin and Ink*. August. Pp. 11-13.
Kutscher, Gerdt. (1950). *Chimu: Eine altindianische Hochkultur*. Berlin: Verlag Gebr. Mann.

Labiste, Dino. (1998-2003). “The Ti Plant Called Ki.” http://www.primitiveways.com/ki.html
Langsdorff, Georg H. von. (1813-14). *Voyages and Travels in Various Parts of the World During the Years 1803, 1804, 1805, 1806, and 1807*. 2 vols. London: H. Colburn.
Lantis, Margaret. (1984). “Aleut.” Pp. 161-184 in *Arctic*, vol. 5, *Handbook of the North American Indians* (D. Damas, ed.). Washington: Smithsonian Institution Press.
Lapena, Frank R. (1978). “Wintu.” Pp. 324-340 in *California*, vol. 8, *Handbook of North American Indians* (R. F. Heizer, ed.). Washington: Smithsonian Institution Press.
Laughlin, William S. (1980). *Aleuts: Survivors of the Bering Land Bridge*. New York: Holt, Rinehart and Winston.
—— (1983). “Aleut Mummies: Their Significance for Longevity and Culture.” Pp. 41-61 in *Cultures of the Bering Sea Region: Papers from an International Symposium* (H.N. Michael and J.W. VanStone, eds.) New York: IREX.
Laukien, Michael. (2000). “Die traditionellen tätowierungen der Katholiken Bosnien” [The Traditional Tattooing of the Bosnian Catholics]. *TätowierMagazin*. December. Pp. 92-97.
—— (2001a). “Catholic Tattoos in Bosnia.” *Skin and Ink*. March. Pp. 24-28.
—— (2001b). “In the Philippines.” *Skin and Ink*. July. Pp. 29-30.

Lawes, W.G. (1879). "Ethnological Notes of the Motu, Koitapu and Koiari Tribes of New Guinea." *Journal of the Anthropological Institute of Great Britain and Ireland* 8: 369-377.

Lee, Georgia. (1992). *The Rock Art of Easter Island: Symbols of Power, Prayers to the Gods*. Monumenta Archaeologica 17. Los Angeles: Institute of Archaeology UCLA.

Legey, Doctoreses (Françoise). (1926). *Contes et légendes populaires du Maroc: recueil-lis à Marrakech*. Publications de l'Institut des hautes études marocaines v. 16. Paris: E. Leroux.

Lehmann-Nitsche, Robert. (1908). "Estudios antropológicos sobre los Chiriguanos, Chorotes, Matacos y Tobas (Chaco occidental)." *Anales del Museo de la Plata*, vol. 1, entrega 2ª (ser. 2).

Leighton, Dorothea. (1982). Field Notes (1940) of Dorothea Leighton and Alexander Leighton. (On file, Alaska and Polar Regions Archives, University of Alaska, Fairbanks.)

Lévi-Strauss, Claude. (1970). *Tristes Tropiques: An Anthropological Study of Primitive Societies in Brazil* (J. Russell, trans.). New York: Atheneum.

Levy, Richard. (1978a). "Eastern Miwok." Pp. 398-413 in *California*, vol. 8, *Handbook of North American Indians* (R. F. Heizer, ed.). Washington: Smithsonian Institution Press.

—— (1978b). "Costanoan." Pp. 485-495 in *California*, vol. 8, *Handbook of North American Indians* (R. F. Heizer, ed.). Washington: Smithsonian Institution Press.

Lisiansky, Urey. (1812). *Putĕšestvie vokrug svieta v 1803-6 godakh . . . na korablie Nievie pod načaljstvom Iuriia Lisianskago* [Voyage around the world, 1803-6, in the ship Neva under command of I. Lisianski]. 2 vols. St. Petersburg.

—— (1814). *A Voyage Round the World in the Years 1803, 4, 5, & 6: Performed by Order of His Imperial Majesty Alexander the First, Emperor of Russia, in the Ship Neva*. London: Printed for J. Booth.

Lissner, Ivar. (1961). *Man, God, and Magic*. New York: G.P. Putnam's Sons.

Loeb, Edwin M. (1935). *Sumatra, Its History and People*. Vienna: Institut für Völkerkunde der Universität.

Lommel, Andreas. (1967). *Shamanism: The Beginnings of Art* (M. Bullock, trans.). New York: McGraw-Hill.

Lowenstein, Tom. (1993). *Ancient Land: Sacred Whale, The Inuit Hunt and Its Rituals*. New York: North Point Press.

Lumholtz, Carl. (1921). *Through Central Borneo; an Account of Two Years' Travel in the Land of the Head-hunters Between the Years 1913 and 1917*. New York: C. Scribner's Sons.

Luomala, Katharine. (1978). "Tipai-Ipai." Pp. 592-609 in *California*, vol. 8, *Handbook of North American Indians* (R. F. Heizer, ed.). Washington: Smithsonian Institution Press.

McGovern, Janet M. (1922). *Among the Head-hunters of Formosa*. London: T. Fisher Unwin, Ltd.

Marquardt, Carl. (1899). *Die Tätowierung beider Geschlechter in Samoa*. Berlin: Verlag von Dietrich Reimer.

Marsh, Gordon H. and William S. Laughlin. (1956). "Human Anatomical Knowledge among the Aleutian Islanders." *Southwestern Journal of Anthropology* 12(1): 38-78.

Mashman, Valerie. (1989). "Ethnic Arts and Society—An Orang Ulu Study." *The Sarawak Museum Journal* XL(61): 215-230.

Mason, Peter. (2001). *The Lives of Images*. London: Reaktion Books Ltd.

Merck, Carl H. (1980). Siberia and Northwestern America, 1788-1792: The Journal of Carl Heinrich Merck, Naturalist with the Russian Scientific Expedition Led by Captains Joseph Billings and Gavril Sarychev (F. Jaensch, trans., R. Pierce, ed.). (*Materials for the Study of Alaska History* 17) Kingston, Ont.: Limestone Press.

Merriam, C. Hart. (1966). Ethnographic Notes on California Indians (R.F. Heizer, ed.), part 1. *University of California Archaeological Survey Reports* 68. Berkeley.

Métraux, Alfred. (1940). *Ethnology of Easter Island*. Bernice P. Bishop Museum Bulletin 160. Honolulu.

—— (1946). "Indians of the Gran Chaco: Ethnography of the Chaco." Pp. 197-370 in *Handbook of South American Indians* (J.H. Steward, ed.), vol. 1, *The Marginal Tribes*. Washington: U.S. Government Printing Office.

Michaux-Bellaire, E. and G. Salmon. (1905). "Les tribus arabes de la vallée de Lekkous." *Archives Marocaines*, t. IV. Paris.

Montandon, George. (1937). *La Civilisation Aïnou: et les Cultures Arctiques*. Paris: Payot.

Moore, Riley D. (1923). "Social Life of the Eskimos of St. Lawrence Island." *American Anthropologist* 25(3): 339-375.

Morton, Julia F. (1987). "Genipap." Pp. 441-443 in *Fruits of Warm Climates* (C.F. Dowling, Jr., ed.). Miami: J.F. Morton.

Mosko, Mark S. (2002). "Totem and Transaction: The Objectification of 'Tradition' Among North Mekeo." *Oceania* 73(2): 89-109.

Mousalimas, S.A. (1997). "Editor's Introduction." Pp. 1-30 in *Arctic Ecology and Identity* (S.A. Mousalimas, ed). Budapest: Akadémiai Kiadó.

Munro, Neil Gordon. (1963). *Ainu Creed and Cult*. New York: Columbia University Press.

Murphy, Robert F. (1956). "Matrilocality and Patrilineality in Mundurucú Society." *American Anthropologist* 50: 414-434.

—— (1958). *Mundurucú Religion*. Berkeley: University of California Press.

—— (1960). *Headhunter's Heritage: Social and Economic Change Among the Mundurucú Indians*. Berkeley: University of California Press.

Murphy, Yolanda and Robert F. Murphy. (1974). *Women of the Forest*. New York: Columbia University Press.

Nadelson, Leslee. (1996). "Pigs, Women, and the Men's House in Amazonia: An Analysis of Six Mundurucú Myths." Pp. 240-272 in *Sexual Meanings: The Cultural Construction of Gender and Sexuality* (S.B. Ortner and H. Whitehead, eds.). Cambridge: Cambridge University Press.

Nelson, Edward W. (1899). "The Eskimo About Bering Strait." Pp. 3-518 in *18th Annual Report of the Bureau of American Ethnology for the Years 1896-1897*. Washington.

Neuman, Daniel S. (1917). "Tattooing on St. Lawrence Island." *The Eskimo* 1(11): 5. Nome.

Ngadi, Henry G. (1998). *Iban Rites of Passage and Some Related Ritual Acts: A Description of Forms and Functions*. Kuala Lumpur: Dewan Bahasa dan Pustaka, Kementerian Pendidikan.

NGS (National Geographic Society). (2004). "Taboo: Body Art." National Geographic Channel US. Lars Krutak, Anthropological Consultant.

NHNZ (Natural History New Zealand). (2004). "The Vanishing Tattoo: A Search for the Last Tribal Tattoo." 49 min., distributed by Natural History New Zealand (NHNZ), Dunedin, New Zealand. Lars Krutak, Anthropological Consultant and Technical Advisor.

Niblack, Albert P. (1890). "The Coast Indians of Southern Alaska and Northern British Columbia." Pp. 225-386 in *Annual Report of the U.S. National Museum for 1888*. Washington: U.S. National Museum.

Nieuwenhuis, A.W. (1900). *In Centraal Borneo*. Leiden: E.J. Brill.

—— (1904). *Quer durch Borneo*. Leiden: E.J. Brill.

Norbeck, Edward. (1950). Folklore of the Atayal of Formosa and the Mountain Tribes of Luzon. *Anthropological Papers, Museum of Anthropology, University of Michigan*, no. 5. Ann Arbor: University of Michigan Press.

Nordenskiöld, Erland. (1910). *Indianlif i El Gran Chaco (Südamerika)*. Stockholm.

—— (1912). *Indianerleben, El Gran Chaco (Südamerika)*. Leipzig: A. Bonnier.

—— (1999). *The Cultural History of the South American Indians* (C. Lindberg, ed.). New York: AMS Press.

Nuttall, Mark. (2000). "Becoming a Hunter in Greenland." *Études/Inuit/Studies* 24(2): 33-45.

Oberg, Kalervo. (1973). The Social Economy of the Tlingit Indians. *American Ethnological Society Monograph*. Seattle: University of Washington Press.

Oberling, Pierre. (1962). "A Note on Tattooing and Branding among the Aghāch Eris of Southwestern Iran." *Ethnos* 27: 126-128.

Okladnikov, Alexei P. (1971). *Petroglify nizhnego Amura*. Leningrad.

—— (1981). *Ancient Art of the Amur Region: Rock Drawings, Sculpture, Pottery*. Leningrad: Aurora Art Publishers.

Oldham, Roland V. (1934). "Tattooing of the Motu Tribe, Papua." *The Australian Museum Magazine* 5: 269-272.

Olson, Ronald L. (1967). "Social Structure and Social Life of the Tlingit in Alaska." *University of California Anthropological Records* 26. Berkeley.

Ong, Edric. (1999). *Pua: Iban Weavings of Sarawak*. Society Atelier Sarawak.

Oosten, Jarich. (1976). *The Theoretical Structure of the Religion of the Netsilik and Iglulik*. Meppel: Krips Repro.

—— (1997). "Cosmological Cycles and the Constituents of the Person." Pp. 85-102 in *Arctic Ecology and Identity* (S.A. Mousalimas, ed.). Budapest: Akadémiai Kiadó.

Outes, Félix F. and Carlos Bruch. (1910). *Los Aborígenes de la República Argentina*. Buenos Aires: Ángel Estrada y Cía.

Paul, Anne. (1982). "The Symbolism of Paracas Turbans: A Consideration of Style, Serpents, and Hair." *Ñawpa Pacha* 20: 41-60.

—— (1990). *Paracas Ritual Attire: Symbols of Authority in Ancient Peru*. Norman: University of Oklahoma Press.

—— (1996). "Paracas Textiles." Pp. 347-363 in *Andean Art at Dumbarton Oaks*, vol. 2 (E.H. Boone, ed.). Washington: Dumbarton Oaks.

Paul, Anne and Solveig A. Turpin. (1986). "The Ecstatic Shaman Theme of Paracas Textiles." *Archaeology* 39(5): 20-27.

Perham, John. (1887). "Manangism in Borneo." *Journal of the Royal Asiatic Society, Straits Branch* 19: 87-103.

Petersen, Robert. (1996). "Body and Soul in Ancient Greenlandic Religion." Pp. 67-78 in *Shamanism and Northern Ecology*, (J. Pentikainen, ed.). Berlin: Mouton de Gruyter.

Phillippi, Donald L. (1979). *Songs of Gods, Songs of Humans: The Epic Tradition of the Ainu*. Tokyo: University of Tokyo Press.

Poirier, Sylvie. (2004). "Ontology, Ancestral Order, and Agencies among the Kukatja of the Australian Western Desert." Pp 58-82 in *Figured Worlds: Ontological Obstacles in Intercultural Relations* (J. Clammer, S. Poirier, and E. Schwimmer, eds.). Toronto: University of Toronto Press.

Powers, Stephen. (1877). Tribes of California. *Contributions to North American Ethnology* 3. Washington: U.S. Geographical and Geological Survey of the Rocky Mountain Region.

Proulx, Donald A. (1996). "Nasca." Pp. 107-122 in *Andean Art at Dumbarton Oaks*, vol 1. (E.H. Boone, ed.). Washington: Dumbarton Oaks.

—— (2001). "Ritual Uses of Trophy Heads in Ancient Nasca Society." Pp. 119-136 in *Ritual Sacrifice in Ancient Peru* (E.P. Benson and A. Cook, eds.). Austin: University of Texas Press.

Pullar, Gordon L. and Richard A. Knecht. (1995). "Alutiiq." Pp. 14-15 in *Crossroads Alaska: Native Cultures of Alaska and Siberia* (V. Chaussonnet, ed.). Washington: Arctic Studies Center, National Museum of Natural History, Smithsonian Institution.

Rahmani, S. (1936). "Rites relatifs à la vache et au lait." Pp. 791-809 in *2e Congrès de la Fédération des sociétés savants de l'Afrique du Nord*. Algiers: Tlemcen.

Rasmussen, Knud. (1931). *The Netsilik Eskimos: Social Life and Spiritual Culture*. Report of the Fifth Thule Expedition 1921-1924. Vol. VIII (1-2). Copenhagen: Glydendalske Boghandel, Nordisk Forlag.

Rea, Amadeo M. (1986). "Black Vultures and Human Victims: Archaeological Evidence from Pacatnamu." Pp. 139-144 in *The Pacatnamu Papers*, vol. 1 (C.B. Donnan and G.A. Cock, eds.). Los Angeles: UCLA Museum of Cultural History.

Reid, Howard. (2001). *In Search of the Immortals: Mummies, Death, and the Afterlife*. New York: St. Martin's Press.

Reports. (1855). *Reports of the Commissioners Appointed to Inquire into Certain Matters Connected with the Position of Sir James Brooke* (Parliamentary Command Paper 1976). London: Harrison and Sons.

Richards, Anthony. (1963). *The Sea Dayaks and Other Races of Sarawak*. Kuching: Borneo Literature Bureau.

—— (1972). "Iban Augury." *Sarawak Museum Journal* 20 (40-41): 63-81.

—— (1997). *An Iban-English Dictionary*. Oxford University Press.

Rickman, John. (1782). *An Authentic Narrative of a Voyage Performed by Captain Cook and Captain Clarke in His Majesty's Ships Resolution and Discovery During the Years*

1776, 1777, 1778, 1779, and 1780, in Search of a North-west Passage Between the Continents of Asia and America—by W. Ellis, Assistant Surgeon. 2 vols. London: Printed for G. Robinson, J. Sewell, and J. Debrett.

Riddell, Francis A. (1978). "Maidu and Konkow." Pp. 370-386 in *California*, vol. 8, *Handbook of North American Indians* (R. F. Heizer, ed.). Washington: Smithsonian Institution Press.

Rivet, Paul. (1907-8). "Les Indiens Jívaros." *L'Anthropologie* 18: 333-368, 583-618; 19: 69-87, 235-259.

Robley, Horatio. (1896). *Moko or Maori Tatooing*. London: Chapman and Hall.

Rose, Wendy. (1979). *Aboriginal Tattooing in California*. Berkeley: Archaeological Research Facility.

Rosen, Eric von. (1924). *Popular Account of Archaeological Research during the Swedish Chaco-Cordillera-Expedition, 1901-1902*. Stockholm: C.E. Fritze.

Roth, Henry L. (1905). "Tatu in Tunis." *Man* 72-73: 129-131.

Rousseau, Jérôme. (1993). "From Shamans to Priests: Religious Specialists Among the Kayan." Pp. 131-140 in *The Seen and the Unseen: Shamanism, Mediumship and Possession in Borneo* (R. Winzeler, ed.). Borneo Research Council Monograph Series, vol. 2.

—— (1998). *Kayan Religion: Ritual Life and Religious Reform in Central Borneo*. Leiden: KITLV Press.

Routledge, Katherine P. (1919). *The Mystery of Easter Island: The Story of an Expedition*. London: Hazell, Watson and Viney.

Rowe, John P. (1995). "Behavior and Belief in Ancient Peruvian Mortuary Practice." Pp. 27-41 in *Tombs of the Living: Andean Mortuary Practices* (T. Dillehay, ed.). Washington: Dumbarton Oaks.

Rubin, Arnold. (1989). *Art as Technology: The Arts of Africa, Oceania, Native America, Southern California* (A. Rubin and Z. Pearlstone, eds.). Beverly Hills: Hillcrest Press.

Rudenko, Sergei I. (1949). "Tatuirovka aziatskikh eskimosov." *Sovetskaia Etnografiia* 14: 149-54.

Rutter, Owen. (1929). *The Pagans of North Borneo*. London: Hutchison & Co.

Ryuzo, Torii. (1990). *The Torii Ryuzo Photographic Record of East Asian Ethnography*, vol. III. Tokyo: University Museum.

Saladin D'Anglure, Bernard. (1993). "Mythology of the Inuit of the Central Arctic." Pp. 25-32 in *American, African, and Old European Mythologies* (Y. Bonnefoy, comp.). Chicago: University of Chicago Press.

—— (1994). "From Foetus to Shaman: The Construction of an Inuit Third Sex." Pp.

83-106 in *Amerindian Rebirth: Reincarnation Belief Among North American Indians and Inuit* (A. Mills and R. Slobodin, eds.). Toronto: University of Toronto Press.
Salvador, Ikin. (2004). *Signs on Skin, Beauty and Being: Traditional Tattoos and Tooth Blackening Among the Philippine Cordillera*. Baguio: Baguio Allied Printers.
Sandin, Benedict. (1975). "The Traditional Folklores of the Kayan of Upper Rejang." *Sarawak Museum Journal* 23(44): 53-80.
—— (1980). *Iban Adat and Augury*. Pulau Pinang: Universiti Sains Malaysia.
Sapir, Edward. (1936). "Hupa Tattooing." Pp. 273-277 in *Essays in Anthropology Presented to A.L. Kroeber* (R. Lowie, ed). Berkeley: University of California Press.
Sarychev, Gavriil A. (1806-7). *Account of a Voyage of Discovery to the North-east of Siberia, the Frozen Ocean, and the North-east Sea*. 2 vols. London: Printed for R. Phillips by J.G. Barnard.
Sauer, Martin. (1802). *An Account of a Geographical and Astronomical Expedition to the Northern Parts of Russia*. London: A. Strahan.
Saville, W.J.V. (1926). *In Unknown New Guinea*. London: Seeley Service & Co., Ltd.
Scheper-Hughes, Nancy and Margaret Lock. (1987). "The Mindful Body: A Prolegomenon to Future Work in Medical Anthropology." *Medical Anthropological Quarterly* 1: 6-41.
Scheube, Botho. (1882). "Die Ainos." *Mittteilungen der Deutschen Gessellschaft für Natur- und Völkerkunde Ostasiens* 3(26): 220-250, 255-256.
Schildkraut, Enid. (2004). "Inscribing the Body." *Annual Review of Anthropology* 33: 319-344.
Schindler, Helmut. (2000). *The Norbert Mayrock Art Collection from Ancient Peru*. Munich: Staatliches Museum für Völkerkunde.
Schurtz, H. (1896). "Zur Ornamentik der Ainu." *Internationales Archiv für Ethnographie* IX: 233-251.
Schuster, Carl. (1939). "Bird-Designs in the Western Pacific: Indonesia, Melanesia, Polynesia." *Cultureel Indië* 1: 232-235.
—— (1951). "Joint-Marks: A Possible Index of Cultural Contact Between America, Oceania and the Far East." *Koninklijk voor Tropen, Medeleling* 44, *Afdeling Culturale en Physiche Anthropologie* 39: 3-51.
—— (1952). "V-Shaped Chest-Markings: Distribution of a Design-Motive in and Around the Pacific." *Anthropos* 47: 99-118.
Schuster, Carl and Edmund S. Carpenter. (1986). *Materials for the Study of Social Symbolism in Ancient & Tribal Art: A Record of Tradition & Continuity*. 3 vols. New York: Rock Foundation.
—— (1996). *Patterns that Connect: Social Symbolism in Ancient & Tribal Art*. New York: Harry N. Abrams.

Searight, Susan. (1984). *The Use and Function of Tattooing on Moroccan Women*. 3 vols. New Haven, Conn.: Human Relations Area Files.

Segy, Ladislas. (1976). *Masks of Black Africa*. New York: Dover.

Seler, Eduard. (1923). "Die buntbemalten Gefässe von Nazca im sudlichen Peru und die Hauptelemente irher Verzierung." Pp. 169-338 in *Gesammelte Abhandlungen zur Amerikanischen Sprachund Altertumskunde*. Berlin: Verlag Behrend.

Seligmann, Charles G. (1902). "The Medicine, Surgery, and Midwifery of the Sinaugolo." *Journal of the Anthropological Institute of Great Britain and Ireland* 32: 297-304.

—— (1910). *The Melanesians of British New Guinea*. Cambridge: University Press.

Shibatani, Masayoshi. (1990). *The Languages of Japan*. Cambridge: Cambridge University Press.

Siebold, Heinrich von. (1881). *Ethnologische Studien Über die Aino auf der Insel Yesso*. Berlin: Verlag von Paul Parey.

Silook, Paul. (1940). "Life Story" and "Tattooe of Man." Unpublished Notes from the Dorothea C. Leighton Collection, Box 3, Folder 67 and 68, pp. 103-14, and p. 1-2. Alaska and Polar Regions Archives, University of Alaska, Fairbanks.

Silverman, Helaine and Donald A. Proulx. (2002). *The Nasca*. Malden, Mass.: Blackwell.

Sinorama. (2001). "King of Taiwan's Snakes." http://www.taiwanheadlines.gov.tw/features/20010306f2.html

Smeaton, Winifred. (1937). "Tattooing Among the Arabs of Iraq." *American Anthropologist* 39: 53-61.

Smith, George S. and Robert Zimmerman. (1975)."Tattooing Found on a 1600 Year Old Frozen, Mummified Body from St. Lawrence Island, Alaska." *American Antiquity* 40(4): 433-437.

Smith, William C. (1925). *The Ao Naga Tribe of Assam: A Study in Ethnology and Sociology*. London: Macmillan and Co., Ltd.

Southwell, C. Hudson (comp.). (1990). *Kayan-English Dictionary*. Selangor, Malaysia: Sarawak Literary Society.

Sparkman, Philip Stedman. (1908). "The Culture of the Luiseño Indians." *University of California Publications in American Archaeology and Ethnology* 8(4): 187-234.

Spencer, Robert F. (1959). The North Alaskan Eskimo: A Study in Ecology and Society. *Bureau of American Ethnology Bulletin* 171. Washington.

Spencer, Robert F. and Jesse D. Jennings. (1965). *The Native Americans*. New York: Harper and Row.

Spier, Leslie. (1923). "Southern Diegueño Customs." *University of California*

Publications in American Archaeology and Ethnology 20(16): 297-358.
—— (1930). "Klamath Ethnography." Pp. 1-338 in *University of California Publications in American Archaeology and Ethnology* 30. Berkeley: University of California Press.
—— (1933). *Yuman Tribes of the Gila River*. Chicago: University of Chicago Press.
Spindler, Konrad. (1994). *The Man in the Ice: The Discovery of a 5,000-Year-Old Body Reveals the Secrets of the Stone Age* (E. Osers, trans.). New York: Harmony Books.
Spix, Johann B. von and Karl F. Phil. von Martius. (1823-1831). *Reise in Brasilien . . . 1817 bis 1820*. 3 vols. München: Gedruckt M. Lindauer.
Starr, Frederick. (1904). *The Ainu Group at the Saint Louis Exposition*. Chicago: Open Court Publishing Company.
Steinen, Karl von den. (1899). "Indianerskizzen von Hercules Florence." *Globus* 75: 5-9, 30-35.
—— (1925). *Die Marquesaner und ihre Kunst.* Tatauierung. Berlin: D. Reimer.
Stephen, Michele. (1979). "Dreams of Change: The Innovative Role of Altered States of Consciousness in Traditional Melanesians Religion." *Oceania* 50(1): 3-22.
Stevenson, A. (1967). "Telltale Tattoos." *North* 14(6): 37-43.
Steward, Julian H. (ed.). (1946). *Handbook of South American Indians*, vol. 1, *The Marginal Tribes*. Washington: U.S. Government Printing Office.
—— (1948). *Handbook of South American Indians*, vol. 3, *The Tropical Forest Tribes*. Washington: U.S. Government Printing Office.
Stolpe, Hjalmar. (1899). "Über die Tätowirung der Oster-Insulaner." *Abhandlungen und Berichte des Königlischen, Zoologischen und Antropologisch-Ethnographischen Museums zu Dresden* 8 (6): 1-13.
Stübel, Hans. (1937). *Die Li Stämme der Insel Hainan: Ein Betrag zur Volkskunde Südchinas*. Berlin: Klinkhardt & Biermann.
Sumnik-Dekovich, Eugenia. (1985). "The Significance of Ancestors in the Arts of the Dayak of Borneo." Pp. 101-128 in *The Eloquent Dead: Ancestral Sculpture of Indonesia and Southwest Asia*. Los Angeles: UCLA Fowler Museum of Cultural History.
Swan, James G. (1874). "The Haidah Indians of Queen Charlotte's Islands, British Columbia: With a Brief Description of Their Carvings, Tattoo Designs, Etc." Pp. 1-15 in *Smithsonian Contributions to Knowledge*. Washington.
—— (1886). "Tattoo Marks of the Haida Indians of Queen Charlotte Islands, B.C., and the Prince of Wales Archipelago, Alaska." Pp. 66-73 in *Fourth Annual Report of the Bureau of American Ethnology for the Years 1882-1883*. Washington: U.S. Government Printing Office.
Swanton, John R. (1905). "Contributions to the Ethnology of the Haida." Pp. 1-300

in *Publications of the Jesup North Pacific Expedition* 5; *Memoirs of the American Museum of Natural History* 8(1). New York.
—— (1908). "Social Condition, Beliefs, and Linguistic Relationship of the Tlingit Indians." Pp. 391-485 in *26th Annual Report of the Bureau of American Ethnology to the Secretary of the Smithsonian Institution for the Years 1904-1905*. Washington: U.S. Government Printing Office.

Taylor, Edith and William J. Wallace. (1947). "Mohave Tattooing and Face-Painting." *Southwest Museum Leaflets* 20: 1-13.
Taylor, John G. (1984). "Historical Ethnography of the Labrador Coast." Pp. 508-521 in Arctic, vol. 5, *Handbook of the North American Indians* (D. Damas, ed.). Washington: Smithsonian Institution Press.
Taylor, Paul M. and Lorraine V. Aragon. (1991).*The Java Sea: Art of Indonesia's Outer Islands*. Washington: National Museum of Natural History, Smithsonian Institution.
Taylor, Rev. Richard. (1870). *Te Ika a Maui*: *or*, *New Zealand and Its Inhabitants. Illustrating the Origin*, *Manners*, *Customs*, *Mythology*, *Religion . . . of the Maori and Polynesian Races in General; Together with the Geology*, *Natural History*, *Productions*, *and Climate of the Country*. London: W. Macintosh; H.I. Jones.
Thomas, Nicholas. (2001). "Introduction." Pp. 1-12 in *Beyond Aesthetics: Art and the Technologies of Enchantment* (C. Pinney and N. Thomas, eds.). Oxford: Berg.
Thomas, Sharon. (1968). "Women's Tattoo of the Upper Rejang." *Sarawak Museum Journal* 16: 209-234.
Thomson, William J. (1899). "Te Pito te Henua, or Easter Island." Pp. 447-552 in *United States National Museum*, *Annual Report for the Year Ending 30 June*, *1889*. Washington: Smithsonian Institution.
Tillema, Hendrik F. (1930). "Tatoeëeren op Borneo." *Nederlandsch-Indië Oud en Nieuw* 15(7) : 193-208.
—— (1938). *Apo-Kajan*, *een filmreis naar en door Centraal-Borneo*. Amsterdam, Van Munster.
—— (1989). *A Journey among the Peoples of Central Borneo in Word and Picture* (V.T. King, ed.). Singapore: Oxford University Press.
Tocantins, Antonio Manoel G. (1877). "Estudos sobre a tribu Mundurukú." *Revista Trimensal do Instituto Histórico Geográphico e Ethnográphico do Brasil* 40(2): 73-161.
Topic, John R. (1990). "Craft Production in the Kingdom of Chimor." Pp. 145-176 in *The Northern Dynasties: Kinship and Statecraft in Chimor* (M.E. Moseley and A. Cordy-Collins, eds.). Washington, D.C: Dumbarton Oaks Research Library and Collection.

Tosabayashi, Yoshio. (1948). "Ainu irezumi moyō no kōsei." *Minzokugaku kenkyū* 13(4): 72-78.

Touchette, Joseph I. (1931). "The Manners, Customs, and Economic Activity of the Chaouian Berbers of Algeria." (Unpublished manuscript. On file in the John Wesley Powell Library of Anthropology, Smithsonian Institution, Washington, D.C.)

Tregear, Edward. (1891). *The Maori-Polynesian Comparative Dictionary*. Wellington: Lyon and Blair.

Truhelka, Ćiro. (1896). "Die Tätowirung bei den Katholiken Bosniens und der Hercegovina." *Wissenschaftliche Mitteilungen aus Bosniens und der Herzegowina*, sv. 4. str. 493-508.

Turner, Lucien M. (1887). *Ethnological Catalogue of Ethnological Collections made by Lucien M. Turner in Ungava and Labrador, Hudson Bay Territory, June 24, 1882 to October 1, 1884*. Prepared for the U.S. National Museum, May 1887. Smithsonian Institution Archives. Washington. (Reprinted: "Ethnology of the Ungava District, Hudson Bay Territory." Pp. 159-350 in *11th Annual Report of the Bureau of American Ethnology for the Years 1889-1890* [J. Murdoch, ed.]. Washington, 1894.)

Turner, William Y. (1878). "The Ethnology of the Motu." *Journal of the Anthropological Institute of Great Britain and Ireland* 7: 470-497.

Ubbelohde-Doering, Heinrich. (1967). *On the Royal Highways of the Inca*. New York: Frederick A. Praeger.

Van Deusen, Kira. (1997). "Protection and Empowerment: Clothing Symbolism in the Amur River Region of the Russian Far East." Pp. 149-168 in *Braving the Cold: Continuity and Change in Arctic Clothing* (C. Buijs and J. Oosten, eds.). Leiden: CNWS.

Van Gulik, W.R. (1982). *Irezumi: The Pattern of Dermatography in Japan*. Leiden: E.J. Brill.

Van Tilburg, Jo Anne. (2001). "Changing Faces: Rapa Nui Statues in the Social Landscape." Pp. 24-31 in *Splendid Isolation: Art of Easter Island* (E. Kjellgren, ed.). New York: The Metropolitan Museum of Art.

Vanoverbergh, Morice. (1929). "Dress and Adornment in the Mountain Province of Luzon, Philippine Islands." *Publications of the Catholic Anthropological Conference* 1(5): 181-242.

Vayda, Andrew P. (1975). "Headhunting Near and Far: Antecedents and Effects of Coastal Raiding by Iban in the Nineteenth Century." *The Sarawak Museum Journal* 23(44): 111-138.

Veniaminov, Ivan E.P. (comp.). (1840). *Zapiski ob ostrovakh Unalashkinskago otdiela* [Notes on the Islands of the Unalaska District]. 3 vols. in 2. St. Petersburg: Russian-American Company.

Verano, John W. (2001). "War and Death in the Moche World: Osteological Evidence and Visual Discourse." Pp. 111-125 in *Moche Art and Archaeology in Ancient Peru* (J. Pillsbury, ed.). Washington: National Gallery of Art.

Vermaseren, M.J. (1963). *Mithras, The Secret God*. New York: Barnes & Noble.

Vitebsky, Piers. (1992). "Landscape and Self-determination among the Eveny: The Political Environment of Siberian Reindeer Herders Today." Pp. 223-246 in *Bush Base: Forest Farm: Culture, Environment and Development* (E. J. Croll and D. Parkin, eds.). London: Routledge.

Viveiros de Castro, Eduardo. (2004). "Exchanging Perspectives: The Transformation of Objects into Subjects in Amerindian Ontologies." *Common Knowledge* 10(3): 463-484.

Vogelsanger, Cornelia. (1980). "A Sight for the Gods: Notes on the Social and Religious Meaning of Iban Ritual Fabrics." Pp. 115-126 in *Indonesian Textiles* (M. Gittinger, ed.). Washington: The Textile Museum.

Volz, Wilhelm. (1905). "Beiträge zur Anthropologie und Ethnographie von Indonesien, II: Zur Kenntnis der Mentawei-Inseln." *Archiv für Anthropologie* 32: 93-109.

Wace, A.J.B. and M.S. Thompsen. (1914). *The Nomads of the Balkans: An Account of Daily Life and Customs among the Vlachs of the Northern Pindus*. London: Methuen.

Wallace, William J. (1978). "Southern Valley Yokuts." Pp. 448-461 in *California*, vol. 8, *Handbook of North American Indians* (R. F. Heizer, ed.). Washington: Smithsonian Institution Press.

Watanabe, Hitoshi. (1999). "The Ainu Ecosystem." Pp. 198-201 in *Ainu: Spirit of a Northern People* (W.W. Fitzhugh and C. O. Dubreuil, eds.). Washington: Smithsonian Institution.

Westermarck, Edward. (1926). *Ritual and Belief in Morocco*. 2 vols. London: Macmillan and Company, Ltd.

Weyer, Edward M., Jr. (1932). *The Eskimos: Their Environment and Folkways*. New Haven: Yale University Press.

Whitman, Nicholas. (1998). "Technology and Vision: Factors Shaping Nineteenth-Century Arctic Photography." Pp. 29-35 in *Imaging the Arctic* (J.C.H. King and H. Lidchi, eds.). Seattle: University of Washington Press.

Williams, A.R. (2006). "Mystery of the Tattooed Mummy." *National Geographic Magazine* 209(6): 70-83.

Williams, Herbert W. (1971). *Maori Dictionary* (7th ed.). Wellington: Government Printer.

Wingert, Paul S. (1962). *Primitive Art*. New York: Oxford University Press.

Winnifrith, Tom. (1992). *The Vlachs*. London: Duckworth Press.

Wolfe, Elizabeth F. (1981). "The Spotted Cat and the Horrible Bird: Stylistic Change in Nasca 1-5 Ceramic Decoration." *Ñawpa Pacha* 19: 1-62.

Worchester, Dean C. (1912). "Head-Hunters of Northern Luzon." *National Geographic Magazine* 23(9): 833-930.

Wright, Christopher. (2003). "Supple Bodies: The Papua New Guinea Photographs of Captain Francis R. Barton, 1899-1907." Pp. 146-275 in *Photography's Other Histories* (C. Pinney and N. Peterson, eds.). Durham: Duke University Press.

Yamaura, Kiyoshi and Hiroshi Ushiro. (1999). "Prehistoric Hokkaido and Ainu Origins." Pp. 39-46 in *Ainu: Spirit of a Northern People* (W.W. Fitzhugh and C. O. Dubreuil, eds.). Washington: Smithsonian Institution.

Yang, Mu. (1995-96). "Music Loss among Ethnic Minorities in China: A Comparison of the Li and Hui Peoples." *Asian Music* 27(1): 103-131.

—— (1997). "On Musical Instruments of the Li People of Hainan (China)." *The World of Music* 39(3): 91-112.

Zainie, Carla. (1969). *Handcraft in Sarawak*. Kuching: Borneo.

Index

S

T

Z

THE ARMENIANS

People, Culture and History

edited by
Nicholas Awde

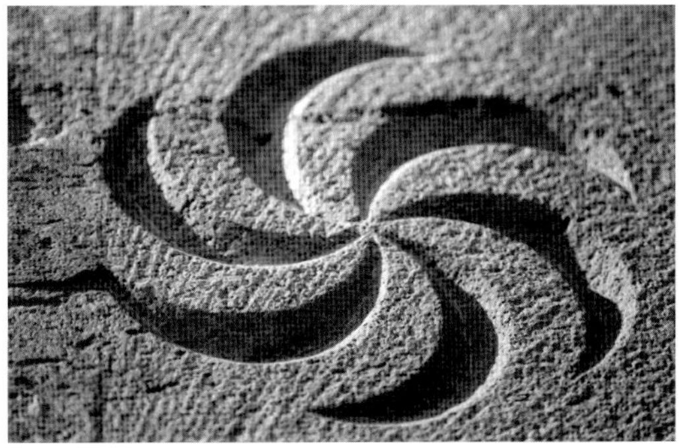

A sourcebook on the history, people, traditions, arts, language, literature, and media of the Armenians that looks at the past, present and future of the pople of both the Armenian Diaspora and the Republic of Armenia. In addition to the regular chapters, special boxes focus on subjects such as folklore and major festivals, the medieval kingdom of Cilicia, artist Arshile Gorky, the bard Sayat Nova and film-maker Atom Egoyan. Rounding off this wealth of detailed information are more than 100 b/w photographs, illustrations and maps, a list of proverbs, suggestions for further reading, a chronology of historical events, and a discography.

Paperback • 978-1-898948-53-7 • £16.99
Hardback • 978-1-898948-33-9 • £45.00
224 pp. 100 illustrations & maps.

Published by Bennett & Bloom

THE AZERBAIJANIS

People, Culture and History

edited by
Nicholas Awde
& Fred James Hill

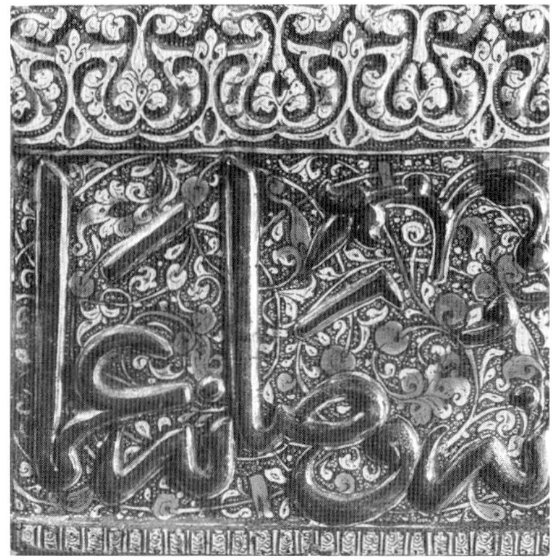

This sourcebook on the history, people, diaspora, traditions, arts, language, literature, and media of the Azerbaijanis looks at the past, present and future of both the Republic of Azerbaijan as well as the millions of Azerbaijanis who live in northern Iran. In addition to the regular chapters, special boxes focus on subjects such as folklore and major festivals, the origins of Zoroastrianism, the great poets Fizuli and Nizami (writer of the epics Khosrow and Shirin, Leyla and Majnun and the Iskandar-nameh), and the growth of the oil city of Baku. Rounding off this wealth of detailed information are 90 b/w photographs, illustrations and maps, a list of proverbs, suggestions for further reading, a chronology of historical events, and a discography.

Paperback • 978-1-898948-54-4 • £16.99
Hardback • 978-1-898948-346- • £45.00
272 pp. 90 illustrations & maps

Published by Bennett & Bloom

WOMEN IN ISLAM

An Anthology from the Qur'an and Hadiths

translated & edited by
Nicholas Awde

NEW EDITION OF
THE DEFINITIVE
REFENCE WORK

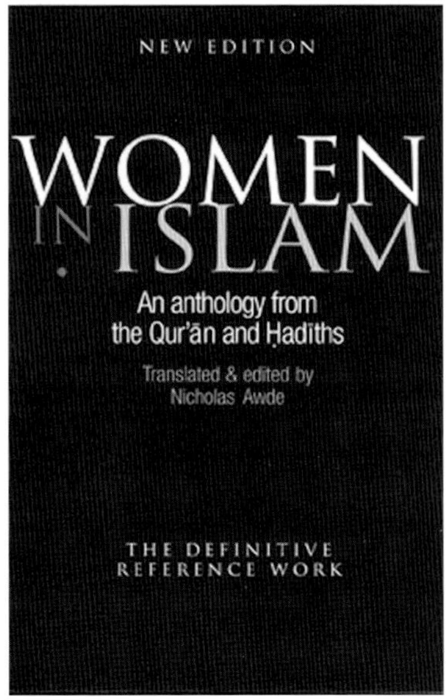

What does Islam really say about women?

Much of the answer may be found in this collection of major references to women in the Qur'an and the Hadiths — the two holy writings on which Islamic legislation and social practice are based. The role of women in Islam is a growing area of study and this collection, drawing on the Sahih of al-Bukhari, fulfils the need for a definitive resource which gathers together all the significant source material on the subject and presents it in an accessible way.

Comprehensively indexed, the topics covered include hygiene, divorce, marriage, sex and chastity, inheritance, and status and rights. Extensive notes help to explain the cultural background of the first Muslims, including short biographies of the women of the Prophet Muhammad's household. All this draws a vivid picture of the era in which they lived — at the same time revealing an intimate portrait of the Prophet himself — and reinforces the central position of women in the Revelation of Islam and its subsequent development up to the present.

Paperback • 978-1-898948-84-1 • £16.99
Hardback • 978-1-898948-83-4 • £45.00
256pp.

Published by Bennett & Bloom

DESERT♥HEARTS • BENNETT & BLOOM
www.deserthearts.com • www.bennettandbloom.com
PO Box 2131, London W1A 5SU, UK
info@bennettandbloom.com

Music from Desert♥Hearts

MELLOTRON

The Machine and the Musicians that Revolutionised Rock

by Nick Awde

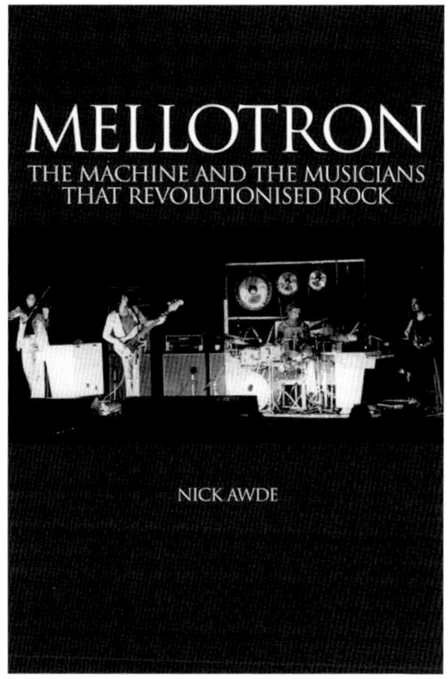

Some of Britain and Europe's most influential musicians, songwriters and producers chart their careers with the Mellotron, the world's first sampler keyboard. The result is a unique insight into the history of British rock and pop and its lasting influence worldwide. Over 20 interviews feature classic acts that include the Moody Blues, Strawbs, King Crimson, Yes, Genesis, and Orchestral Manoeuvres In The Dark (O.M.D.), plus later groups such as I.Q. and the Flower Kings.

Hardback • 978-1-898948-02-5 • £19.95
352pp. 40 b&w images.

THE VIBRATORS

21 Years Of Punk Mania

by Ian M. Carnochan (a.k.a. "Knox")

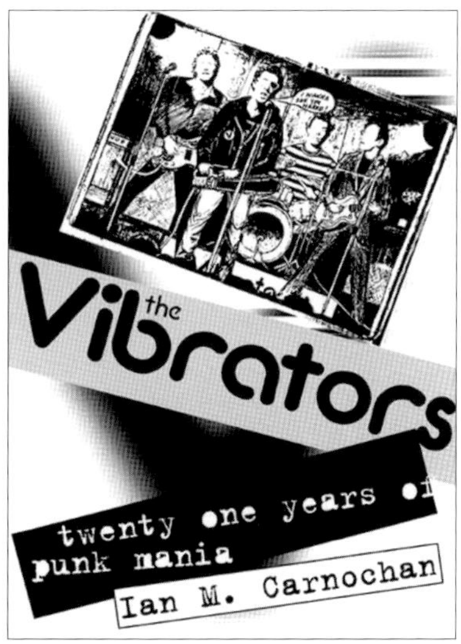

Riveting account of a life on the road from one of the godfathers of punk: Knox, singer and guitarist with the Vibrators. Gigs, tours, singles, albums and more...

Ringbound • 978-1-898948-10-0 • £8.99
92pp. Illustrated throughout.

DESERT♥HEARTS • BENNETT & BLOOM
www.deserthearts.com • www.bennettandbloom.com
PO Box 2131, London W1A 5SU, UK
info@bennettandbloom.com